Investors' Environmental Guidelines:
Bulgaria, Czech Republic and Slovak Republic, Estonia, Hungary, Latvia, Lithuania, Poland, Romania

Investors' Environmental Guidelines:
Bulgaria, Czech Republic and Slovak Republic, Estonia, Hungary, Latvia, Lithuania, Poland, Romania

Developed by the
European Bank for Reconstruction and
Development
and the
European Community's PHARE Programme

European Bank
for Reconstruction and Development

Graham & Trotman/Martinus Nijhoff
Members of the Kluwer Academic Publishers Group
LONDON/DORDRECHT/BOSTON

PHARE

Graham & Trotman Limited
Sterling House
66 Wilton Road
London SW1V 1DE
UK

Kluwer Academic Publishers Group
101 Philip Drive
Assinippi Park
Norwell, MA 02061
USA

ISBN 1-85333-961-X
Series ISSN 1351-8267

© European Bank for Reconstruction and Development, 1994
First Published 1994

British Library Cataloguing in Publication Data is available

Library of Congress Cataloging-in-Publication Data

Investors' environmental guidelines: Bulgaria, Czech and Slovak
    Republics, Estonia, Hungary, Latvia, Lithuania, Poland, Romania/
    edited by the European Bank for Reconstruction & Development.
        p.   cm.
    Includes index
    ISBN 1–85333–961–X.
    1. Environmental law—Europe, Eastern. 2. Environmental permits—
— Europe, Eastern. 3. Investments, Foreign—Law and legislation—
— Europe, Eastern. I. European Bank for Reconstruction and
Development.
KJC6242. I58   1993
344. 47′ 043—dc20
[344. 70443]   93–34906
                                                                                              CIP

Typeset in Times and Palatino by EXPO Holdings, Malaysia
Printed and bound in Great Britain by Hartnolls Ltd, Bodmin, Cornwall

Contents

Contents

CZECH REPUBLIC AND SLOVAK REPUBLIC   77

Contents

ESTONIA   **171**

Contents

HUNGARY   **223**

Contents

LATVIA 289

Contents

Contents

POLAND 399

Contents

Contents

Foreword

Uncertainty about environmental requirements is a major deterrent to those considering investing in central and eastern Europe. As a consequence, the European Bank for Reconstruction and Development, together with the European Community's PHARE programme, has prepared these 'Investors' Environmental Guidelines' for nine European countries which are in the process of transition from central planning to the market economy. This work has formed part of a wider programme of research on the implications of the harmonisation of environmental legislation and regulations between western and eastern Europe undertaken by the European Bank for Reconstruction and Development and the European Community. The programme also includes a guidebook to Western environmental product standards, a comparison between regulatory trends in various countries, and examinations of the economic and institutional implications of harmonisation.

The magnitude and type of private sector investment will have a major influence on the way countries of central and eastern Europe will achieve their goal of moving to a market-based economy. Anything that institutions can do to encourage investment through improving transparency of operations, while at the same time respecting the need for environmental protection and clean-up should be welcomed. I think this publication is a helpful contribution to this objective, as well as to the objective of fuller integration of central and eastern Europe with western Europe.

I should like to thank the members of the PHARE programme both for ensuring that funding was made available for this important project and for the guidance they have provided as joint executors of the project. Thanks are also due to the members of the projects's Advisory Board, drawn from Ministries of Environment in central and eastern Europe and in the West and from international organisations including the World Bank, the European Investment Bank and the OECD. The substantive work on the project was the responsibility of two consultancy firms, Environmental Resources Management and White & Case, to whom thanks are also due.

I would finally like to thank my colleagues from the Bank's Environmental Appraisal Group who have steered the overall harmonisation study.

Jacques de Larosière
President
European Bank for Reconstruction and Development

Bulgaria

Prepared for the European Bank for Reconstruction and Development and the
Commission of the European Communities by
White & Case*

1. Overview

1.1 The Guidelines

1.1.1 Background

Investments in Bulgaria are subject to many legal and economic requirements. This document focuses specifically on those compliance, operational and liability issues which arise from environmental protection measures and affect investments.

The Guidelines are intended to enable investors to familiarise themselves with the basic environmental regulatory regime relating to commercial and industrial greenfield site developments, joint venture operations or company acquisitions in Bulgaria.

The Guidelines review institutional arrangements for environmental control, legislative requirements and procedures, time implications for permitting, public access to information, liability and sanctions. Because environmental policy, legislation and infrastructure in Bulgaria are currently undergoing radical changes the review covers both current and proposed future arrangements.

Guidelines for the following CEE countries have been prepared on behalf of the European Bank for Reconstruction and Development and the Commission of the European Communities by Environmental Resources Limited and White & Case:

- Bulgaria;[1]
- Czech Republic and Slovak Republic;[1]

---

[1]   Guidelines prepared by White & Case.

*   White & Case acknowledges the valuable contribution in the preparation of the *Investors' Environmental Guidelines: Bulgaria* of Richard A. Horsch, Esq., Sophia Drewnowski, Esq. and Kalinka Moudrova, Esq. of White & Case.

White & Case would like to thank Dr. Georgi Penchev of the Institute for Legal Studies at the Bulgarian Academy of Sciences, and the Center for the Study of Democracy, in particular, Assen Rizov, Milena Rizova and Katya Gyulemetova, who acted as consultants to White & Case in its preparation of these Guidelines.

- Estonia;[2]
- Hungary;[1]
- Latvia;[2]
- Lithuania;[2]
- Poland;[1]
- Romania;[2]

These Guidelines present a description of the environmental regulatory framework as of February 1993. They provide a first step for investors in understanding environmental requirements but do not substitute for specific legal advice relating to particular sites.

Administrative and legal arrangements for environmental regulation are in a transition phase in the countries covered by these Guidelines. Requirements and implementation systems are subject to change. Investors are advised to discuss details of requirements with the authorities and check for any changes which may have taken place since February 1993.

1.1.2 Using the Guidelines

The Guidelines provide general guidance on environmental regulatory requirements applicable to foreign investment in commercial and industrial sectors of the economy. Some sections of the Guidelines, such as *Section 4* on Land Use Planning and *Section 5* on EIA are also applicable to other sectors of the economy such as agriculture, mining, forestry and fisheries. In relation to such types of activities however, it is advisable to review other applicable requirements which are outside the scope of the Guidelines.

Section 1 provides a quick reference to environmental regulatory requirements in two case studies, and in *Figure 1.1.2(a) and Figure 1.1.2(b). Figure 1.1.2(b)* indicates how the Guidelines should be used by reference to the type of investment decision that has to be made.

The remainder of this section provides background information on the country and the following:

- Administrative structure;
- Legislative process and key items of legislation;
- Quick reference to the permitting process;
- Enforcement;
- Public participation.

Section 2 highlights the potential liabilities of investors. Liabilities potentially arising from past pollution to be taken into account at the time an investment is made and liabilities arising in the course of operating commercial and industrial facilities are presented separately. Additional details relating to specific sectors of control are provided in subsequent sections.

Section 3 identifies environmental auditing requirements and comments on the role of voluntary audits in achieving compliance.

---

[1]   Guidelines prepared by White & Case.
[2]   Guidelines prepared by Environmental Resources Limited.

Figure 1.1.2(a) Using the Guidelines: report structure

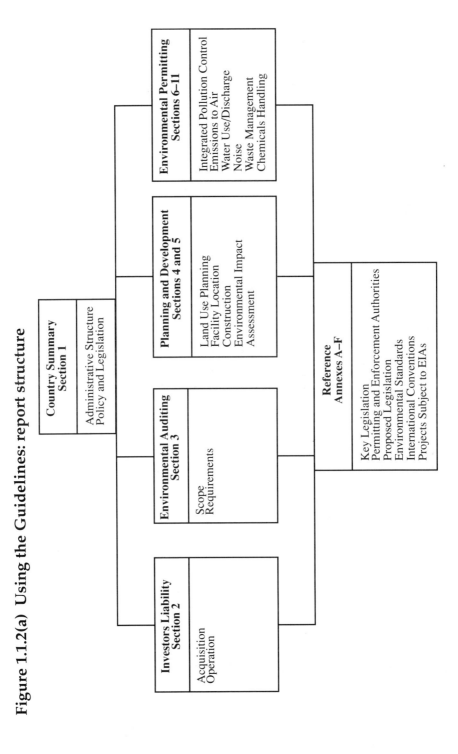

Figure 1.1.2(b) Using the Guidelines: summary by type of investment decision

Investment Decisions	*Environmental Concerns*	*Sections in Guidelines*
Choice of investment sector (e.g. commercial, services, manufacturing, energy)	Government and environmental bodies	1.4, 1.7, Annex B
	Existing and proposed legislation	1.5, Annex A & C
	Available forms of investment	1.2, 2.3.2
	Purchase of land	4.3
	Investments subject to EIA	5, Annex F
	Activities subject to permitting	6–11
	Permitting overview and examples	1.6
Development of a "greenfield site"	Government and environmental bodies	1.4, 1.7, Annex B
	Existing and proposed legislation	1.5, Annex A & C
	Purchase of land	4.3
	EIA requirements	5, Annex F
	Public participation	1.8
	Environmental standards	7, 8, 9, Annex D
Acquisition of existing facility and privatisation	Government and environmental bodies	1.4, 1.7
	Privatisation	1.2, 2.3.2
	Environmental liability	2
	Cleanup of contaminated sites	2.3
	Indemnification by government	2.3
	Environmental audits	3
	Environmental standards	7, 8, 9, Annex D
	EIA requirements (especially where modifications are made to existing facilities)	5, Annex F

Investment Decisions	Environmental Concerns	Sections in Guidelines
Redevelopment and expansion of commercial and industrial facilities	Government and environmental bodies	1.4, 1.7, Annex B
	Change of land use	4
	Construction permits	4
	EIA requirements	5, Annex F
	Permitting requirements	6–11
	Public participation	1.8
Operation of industrial and commercial facilities	Government and environmental bodies	1.4, 1.7, Annex B
	Environmental liability	2
	EIA requirements	5, Annex F
	Public participation	1.8
	Integrated permitting	6
	Air requirements	7, Annex D
	Water requirements	8, Annex D
	Noise requirements	9, Annex D
	Waste management	10
	Chemical storage and handling	11
	Permitting overview and examples	1.6
	Compliance with international law	Annex E

Sections 4–11 provide guidance on permitting and related regulatory requirements for setting up and operating a commercial or industrial enterprise. Key aspects are presented at the beginning of each section for quick reference. Each section identifies the following:

- Key legislation;
- Activities covered;
- Requirements and Procedures;
- Timing;
- Public participation;
- Enforcement and sanctions.

Sections 4 and 5 outline requirements and procedures relating to land use planning, facility location and construction, and environmental impact assessment ("EIA"). *Section 6* indicates the extent to which environmental permitting is integrated. Permitting and other regulatory requirements relating to air, water, noise, waste and chemicals are set out in *Sections 7–11*.

Annexes provide quick reference to existing and proposed legislation, contact points for the regulatory agencies, environmental standards, ratification of multilateral international conventions and investment projects subject to EIAs which are specifically identified in legislation.

1.2 The country

The Republic of Bulgaria has a population of 8.75 million and covers a territory of 110,000 sq. km. In 1990, following the first free elections after World War II, the former communist regime was replaced by a parliamentary democracy. Bulgaria has embarked on a programme of privatisation and reforms to restructure its economy. Central to this programme was the enactment of the *Law on Transformation and Privatisation of State-owned and Municipal-owned Enterprises* in 1992 ("Privatisation Law") and the creation of the Privatisation Agency in the same year. The following economic priorities have been set in Bulgaria as part of the reform process:

- Privatisation of viable industries with the help of foreign investment;
- Introduction of tax concessions to the private sector;
- Return of agricultural land to private ownership;
- Expansion of selected industries.

Environmental issues became a serious public concern in Bulgaria beginning in 1989–1990. One of the first examples of the growing influence of environmental activism on Bulgarian public policy were the public protests, and labour strikes in 1990 against the construction of the Belene Nuclear Power Station. After eight months of opposition the Bulgarian Council of Ministers suspended the project. A plan to divert the flow of the Rila River to Sofia as part of the Rila-Mesta Hydro project and the Cherni Osam Dam were also suspended after protests. Uranium mines in Bulgaria were closed in the summer of 1992 after organised public action.

Bulgaria enacted the *Environmental Protection Law* in 1991 which was amended in 1992. This new statute sets out a broad framework for environmental regulation and provides the legal basis for EIAs, citizens' suits and the indemnification of investors for the liabilities of former state enterprises arising from past pollution. Bulgaria's new environmental policy includes the implementation of a decentralised, integrated environmental management system providing a balance between "command and control" regulatory methods and market mechanisms. Economic instruments, such as tax breaks, will be relied on to promote a cleaner environment.

On 8 March 1993 Bulgaria signed an Association Agreement with the European Community ("EC"). The Agreement will enter into force upon ratification by the Bulgarian National Assembly and the parliaments of the 12 EC countries. Bulgaria's goal is political and economic integration with Western Europe. The government's intention is to introduce new environmental standards which are consistent with EC standards.

1.3 Administrative structure

The Republic of Bulgaria is a centralised country consisting of eight Districts and 251 Municipalities. The Greater Sofia Municipality has the status of a District.

Most legislative and executive powers are concentrated at the central government level and lie with the National Assembly — Bulgaria's Parliament and with the Council of Ministers.

The administrative structure at the local government level is currently being reorganised. It is expected that within the next two years Counties will be created. These will be intermediate units of government between Districts and Municipalities.

Municipalities are empowered to develop their own environmental protection programmes in co-ordination with the Environment Ministry ("Environment Ministry") and, where applicable, the Ministry of Health and the Ministry of Agriculture. The environmental functions of the Municipalities include:

- Disposal of waste and toxic substances within their territory;
- Collection and disposal of solid household waste;
- Management of Municipal Environmental Protection Funds;
- Development, maintenance and operation of facilities for the treatment of potable and effluent waters;
- Protection of air, water and soil from pollution;
- Noise control.

1.4 Government and environmental bodies

1.4.1 Ministries

Environmental decision-making is carried out principally by the central government. With respect to environmental protection, the most significant central government institution is the Environment Ministry.

The Environment Ministry acts through 16 Regional Environmental Inspectorates.

The functions of the Environment Ministry are to:

- Draft environmental legislation;
- Co-ordinate environmental protection activities and pollution control;

- Monitor the state of the environment and compliance with environmental legislation;
- Manage the National Environmental Protection Fund and control the use of Municipal Environmental Protection Funds;
- Supervise the EIA process;
- Issue permits for waste water discharges.

Acting jointly with the Ministry of Health, the Ministry of Agriculture and the Ministry of Regional Development and Construction, the Environment Ministry:

- Develops air, water and soil ambient standards, standards for the emission or discharge of hazardous substances into air and water and rules and regulations governing the use of natural resources;
- Sets environmental charges;
- Issues regulations and procedures for regions with an endangered environment;
- Determines the procedure for EIAs;
- Issues instructions for the transportation, storage, use and disposal of hazardous substances.

The Ministry of Health exercises government control over the state of air, water, soil and its impact on the human body. It acts through 28 Sanitary Epidemiological Institutes.

The Ministry of Interior issues permits for manufacture, sale, storage, transportation and use of highly active toxic substances.

The functions of the Ministry of Agriculture in the environmental area are to:

- Protect agricultural land and crops from damage and pollution by pesticides, nitrates and heavy metals;
- Develop programmes to remediate polluted land;
- Introduce environmental principles into agriculture.

The Ministry of Regional Development and Construction is responsible for:

- Central and regional land use planning;
- Development of land;
- Construction.

1.4.2 Environmental bodies

The Environment Ministry acts in the territory of Bulgaria through 16 Regional Environmental Inspectorates. The Regional Environmental Inspectorates assist the Environment Ministry on the regional level in the following areas:

- Enforcing of environmental laws;
- Preparing of programmes for the improvement of the environment;
- Informing the public on the state of the environment.

The Laboratory Information Complex at the Environment Ministry collects information about the state of the environment and issues a publication every three months on air and water quality in Bulgaria.

The 28 Sanitary Epidemiological Institutes assist the Ministry of Health by supervising the operation of pollution monitoring equipment and collecting data regarding the quality of air, water and soil. They are empowered to halt polluting activities when ambient standards are violated and there is a danger to human health.

The National Water Council at the Council of Ministers controls water resource use and is assisted by six Regional Departments.

A number of other specialised central government committees and councils assist the Council of Ministers in the environmental area and have executive powers. These include the following:

- The Committee on Geology and Mineral Resources controls the mining of mineral resources;
- The Commission on Land controls the use of arable land and issues permits for the transfer of land to non-agricultural use;
- The Committee of Forests manages forests and most protected nature areas;
- The Committee on the Use of Nuclear Energy for Peaceful Purposes controls nuclear safety;
- The Permanent Governmental Commission on Natural Disasters and Large Industrial Accidents, together with various bodies under its supervision, enforces legislation on emergency response. The Commission can conduct inspections of facilities at its discretion and its recommendations are mandatory for persons dealing with hazardous chemicals;
- The Chief Inspectorate on Governmental Technical Control at the Ministry of Regional Development and Construction appoints and supervises the Governmental Approval Commissions which inspect and approve the construction projects, once they are completed.

1.4.3 Environmental Funds

The *Environmental Protection Law* of 1991, as amended, provides for the creation of a National Environmental Protection Fund and Municipal Environmental Protection Funds. These Funds will derive their income from the collection of environmental charges for the use of natural resources and from the imposition of monetary sanctions for exceeding permissible environmental standards. The Funds' income is intended to finance the clean-up of environmental pollution.

The income from charges is to be distributed in the following way:

- 40% to the Municipal Environmental Protection Funds
- 60% to the National Environmental Protection Fund.

The income from monetary sanctions is to be distributed in the following way:

- 30% to the Municipal Environmental Protection Funds
- 70% to the National Environmental Protection Fund.

The *Regulation on the Collection, Spending and Control of the Environmental Protection Funds* of 1993 states that the National and Municipal Environmental Funds will be used for the following purposes:

- Funding environmental protection research projects;
- Participation in joint environmental activities with Municipalities;
- Payment for scientific and technical services, evaluations, assessments of designs and facilities, assessment of environmental risks and other services ordered by the Environment Ministry or by Municipalities;
- Maintenance and improvement of the system of environmental monitoring and control;
- Payment of debts;
- Grants to non-government environmental protection organisations;
- Financing of environmental protection conferences, symposia, exhibitions and publications.

The National Environmental Protection Fund will also be used to:

- Finance environmental protection activities involving more than one Municipality;
- Make loans for construction, purchase of equipment and other environmental purposes;
- Provide interest-free or low-interest loans for environmental activities of companies in polluted areas of the country;
- Make grants to Municipalities for environmental activities.

Municipal Environmental Protection Funds will also be used to:

- Finance environmental protection activities involving more than one Municipality;
- Finance environmental protection activities of local companies;
- Pay damages assessed against a Municipality by a court decision for environmental damage.

1.5 Environmental legislation

1.5.1 Legislative process

The supreme legislative body in Bulgaria is the National Assembly. All basic social, economic and political questions are regulated by Laws. Other sources of legislation can be found in Ordinances, Regulations and Instructions.

The process of passing a Law is commenced at the initiative of one of the following:

- Members of the National Assembly;
- The Council of Ministers.

Under the new *Constitution of 1991* the President does not have a right to initiate legislation.

When the Council of Ministers initiates the process of enacting a Law, the draft Law is prepared within the relevant Ministry.

Draft environmental Laws must first be presented to the Parliamentary Environmental Commission which issues an opinion recommending enactment. If a draft environmental Law does not conflict with Bulgaria's *Constitution* and the body of Bulgarian law, the National Assembly's Legislative Commission will present it to the National Assembly. A simple majority of the Members of the National Assembly is required for the passage of a Law. Two readings are required before a Law is enacted. The National Assembly can decide to submit a draft Law for public approval through a referendum.

A draft Law is enacted once it is published by a Decree of the President. The President has a power of veto over legislation. His veto power may be overridden by an absolute majority of the National Assembly.

The Council of Ministers can adopt Ordinances and Regulations for the implementation of Laws. In addition, individual Ministers can also adopt Ordinances and Regulations and issue Instructions.

Regulations can be enacted at the local government level on issues of local importance which fall within the competence of Districts and Municipalities.

All legislation is published in *Darjaven Vestnik*, the official legal journal of the National Assembly.

1.5.2 Legislation

The new *Constitution* of Bulgaria, adopted in July 1991, provides for the right of all citizens to a healthy environment. The *Constitution* of 1991 is the supreme law and other laws cannot be inconsistent with it.

The *Environmental Protection Law*, passed by the National Assembly on 2 October 1991 provides the foundation for Bulgaria's environmental policy. It establishes a system for the implementation of environmental policy and establishes environmental objectives including the following:

- Development of an EIA programme;
- Adherence to the "polluter pays" principle;
- Introduction of charges for use of natural resources;
- Establishment of a National Environmental Protection Fund and Municipal Environmental Protection Funds;
- Provision for citizens' suits;
- Harmonisation of existing environmental standards with EC standards;
- Provision for right of access to information on the state of the environment.

Amendments to the *Environmental Protection Law* of 1991 were drafted by the Environment Ministry and passed on 4 December 1992. They provide for:

- Revised EIA provisions;
- Supplementing the income of Environmental Protection Funds by monetary sanctions;
- Increases in the level of fines;
- Indemnification of investors from liability for past pollution.

A number of old environmental laws are still in force and will be replaced by new legislation. These old laws include:

- *Law on Mines and Quarries* of 1957;
- *Law on Protection of Air, Water and Soil from Pollution* of 1963;
- *Law on Protection of Nature* of 1967;
- *Law on Waters* of 1969;

- *Law on Regional Development and Town Planning* of 1973;
- *Law on Protection of Arable Land and Pastures* of 1973;
- *Law on Public Health* of 1973;
- *Law on Marine Environment* of 1987.

New laws are currently being drafted on the following:

- Protected areas;
- Waste;
- Protection of biological diversity;
- Land protection;
- Marine environment;
- Water;
- Air

All new environmental ambient and emission standards will be drafted after joint consultation among the Environment Ministry, the Ministry of Health, the Ministry of Agriculture and the Ministry of Regional Development and Construction.

Every piece of legislation may be interpreted by the body issuing it. The decisions of courts are generally binding only on the case under decision; the only exception being a decision of the Supreme Court sitting in General Assembly, which may settle controversial issues for consistency of judicial interpretation.

1.6 Overview of permitting process and other regulatory requirements

The principal permits and approvals required by an investor intending to build and operate a commercial or industrial facility in Bulgaria fall into three categories: land use and construction permits, EIAs and operational requirements.

Land use and construction permits are discussed in detail in *Section 4* below. EIAs, which must be performed for certain projects including those identified in Appendices I and II to the *Environmental Protection Law* of 1991, as amended, are discussed in detail in *Section 5*. Operational requirements as regards air, water, noise, waste and chemical storage are discussed in detail in *Sections 6–10* below.

As regards operational requirements, permits are needed only for water use and for the discharge of waste water. There is no integrated permitting system in Bulgaria. Special permits are not required either for air, noise emissions, the generation of waste or for the operation of waste treatment facilities.

The role of permits is performed by the EIA. If the proposed project is likely to violate any ambient or emission standards the EIA will not be approved and the project will not be allowed to proceed. The EIA is mandatory for projects listed in the Appendices to the *Environmental Protection Law* of 1991, as amended. It can also be requested upon the discretion of the Municipalities or the Environment Ministry.

The principal steps of the permitting and approval process are summarised in *Figure 1.6.1*. The practical application of the permitting and approval process is illustrated in the two case studies discussed below.

Figure 1.6.1 Environmental permitting procedure

Main Steps	*Authority*	*Timing*
Step 1. Permit for Change of Use of Land		
Application through the Municipality	Commission on Land	No time set
Step 2. Approval of the Environmental Impact Assessment		
Application to	National Water Council	1 month
Step 3. Permit for Water Use		
Application to	Environment Ministry	1 month
Step 4. Permit for Water Discharge		
Application to	Environment Ministry	1 month
Step 5. Construction Permit		
Application for approval of the proposed investment	State Expert Council Municipal Expert Council	
Application for a construction permit	Municipality	1 month
Step 6. Construction of Facilities		
Step 7. Post-Completion Construction Approval and Permits		
Application to	Chief Inspectorate on Governmental Technical Control Regional Inspectorate on Governmental Technical Control	

Steps of the permitting process:

- If the construction is to take place on a "greenfield site" an approval from the Commission on Land for change of use of arable land is required.
- Where mandatory EIAs are required, EIA approval must be obtained from the Environment Ministry or the Regional Environmental Inspectorate.
- A permit for water use must be obtained from the Water Council.
- A permit for water discharge must be obtained from the Environment Ministry.
- A construction permit must be obtained from the Municipality after approval of the investment proposal by the state or Municipal Expert Council.
- Construction of the facility must be completed within three years.
- Once construction of the facility is completed, it must be approved and a permit to set it into operation must be obtained from a specially appointed Governmental Approval Commission.

At present the law does not require that permits be obtained in any special sequence. It does require that a mandatory EIA be performed before a construction permit is issued. The draft Law on Proposed Investments and Construction requires that permits for water use and waste water discharge be submitted with the application for a construction permit.

1.6.1 Case study 1

Foreign investor forming a joint venture with an existing company, with the joint venture acquiring two industrial plants and wishing to close one and refurbish the other to produce tyres.

Land use

Bulgarian joint ventures with foreign participation may own non-arable land. As regards the first industrial plant which is to be closed down, no special land use procedures are mandatory. A special permit from the local government will be necessary for the destruction of any building. As regards the second plant no permit is required for change of use of land in connection with its refurbishment.

Consequently, the acquisition of the two industrial plants can take place in compliance with the usual commercial requirements under Bulgarian law.

Environmental Impact Assessments (EIAs)

EIA approval must be obtained before a construction permit can be issued.

Mandatory EIAs are required for the installation of any pollution control equipment, as well as for any facilities for the treatment, neutralisation and storage of waste.

While the production of tyres does not require a mandatory EIA, approval of the development project to refurbish the company to produce tyres might be required under the EIA procedure at the discretion of the Municipality or the Regional Environmental Inspectorate.

The EIA approval may be subject to conditions such as emissions limits and waste treatment and disposal requirements.

Operating permits

Operating permits are required before the construction permit will be issued.
Operating permits are needed for:

- Use of water, to be obtained from the National Water Council;
- Discharge of waste water, to be obtained from the Environment Ministry.

No permits are needed for air or noise emissions or for the treatment and disposal of waste. A similar effect is achieved by the requirement for EIA approval, which will be refused by the authorities if ambient or emission standards are likely to be violated.

Construction permits

If the refurbishment of the second plant entails modifications to the buildings, a construction permit will be required. The investor must apply for a construction permit to the Municipality.

When the draft Law on Proposed Investments and Construction becomes effective, before a construction permit is granted, an approval of the proposed investment by the Municipal or State Expert Council will be required.

Once the construction is completed a construction approval and a permit for the new use must be obtained from a specially appointed Governmental Approval Commission.

1.6.2 Case study 2

Foreign company wishing to acquire a greenfield site and build a new paper mill.

Land use

Neither arable nor non-arable land may be owned by a foreign person, but foreign persons have been granted limited rights over land. Consequently, a foreign company can acquire the right to construct a building on a greenfield site from the owner of that site in accordance with the usual commercial requirements under Bulgarian law.

The foreign company must apply to the Municipality, which in turn applies to the Commission on Land, for permission to convert the arable land to industrial use.

Environmental Impact Assessments (EIAs)

EIA approval must be obtained before a construction permit can be obtained.

Since projects for manufacture of pulp, paper and cardboard are subject to mandatory EIAs, the construction of a paper mill will require prior approval under the EIA procedure. An application is made to the Regional Environmental Inspectorate which sets a date for the proceedings.

The Regional Environmental Inspectorate jointly with the Municipality review and approve the EIA. In case the EIA is not approved or if no EIA was carried out as required, the Municipality can ban or enjoin the activities or the realisation of the project. EIA approval may be subject to conditions such as emissions limits and waste treatment and disposal requirements.

Operating permits

Operating permits are required before a construction permit can be issued.
Operating permits will be needed for:

- Use of water, to be obtained from the National Water Council;
- Discharge of waste water, to be obtained from the Environment Ministry.

No permits are needed for air or noise emissions or for the treatment and disposal of waste. A similar effect is achieved by the requirement for an EIA approval, which will be refused if the ambient or emission standards are likely to be violated.

Construction permits

After obtaining the permission for change of use of land, EIA approval and permits for water use and waste water discharge, the company must obtain a construction permit from the Municipality.

When the draft Law on Proposed Investments and Construction becomes effective, before a permit is granted, an approval of the proposed investment by the Municipal or State Expert Council will be required.

After the paper mill is completed, a permit for its use must be obtained from a specially appointed Governmental Approval Commission.

1.7 Enforcement of environmental legislation

The Environment Ministry, the Regional Environmental Inspectorates and the Municipalities are responsible for the enforcement of environmental legislation. The *Environmental Protection Law* of 1991 does not give any enforcement role to the Districts. It allocates enforcement responsibility among these three bodies as follows:

- The Environment Ministry is the enforcement authority if the result of a person's polluting activity occurs or may occur within the territory under the authority of more than one Inspectorate.
- The Regional Environmental Inspectorate is the enforcement authority if the result of a person's polluting activity occurs or may occur within the territory of one, or more than one Municipality.
- The Municipality is the enforcement authority if the result of a person's polluting activity occurs or may occur wholly within its territorial area.

Companies are not required to submit periodic reports of their air emission and water discharge levels. However, periodic checks of compliance with permissible environmental standards are conducted by the Regional Environmental Inspectorates. Each Inspectorate has its own laboratory and a staff of technical specialists working on a territorial basis. The Municipalities rely on the Regional Environmental Inspectorates for monitoring functions because they lack the necessary equipment. If violations of standards are noted by the Inspectorates, monetary sanctions may be imposed on companies and fines may be imposed on individuals by an order of the Environment Minister.

Regional Environmental Inspectorates and the Municipalities have the power to halt the activities of specific enterprises or organisations if environmental protection requirements are being violated. They may also impose measures to remedy the consequences of environmental damage.

Sanitary Epidemiological Institutes may prohibit any activity which violates the relevant health standards.

Any person or citizens' group or Municipality may apply to a court to require a person who is in violation of the provisions of the *Environmental Protection Law* of 1991, as amended, to stop the violation and to repair the damage caused.

Enforcement actions are subject to administrative and judicial review. Regional Environmental Inspectorates review decisions of the Municipalities. Decisions of the Inspectorates are in turn reviewed by the Environment Ministry. The administrative decisions of the Municipalities, Regional Environmental Inspectorates and the Environment Ministry may be appealed to the Courts.

1.8 Public participation

1.8.1 Public access to information

The new *Constitution* of 1991 sets forth general principles regarding the environment and provides a general guarantee of access to information by the public. Under Article 41 of the *Constitution* of 1991, each citizen has a right to seek, receive and distribute information and to receive information from the government on issues of his/her legitimate interest. This right however, may not be exercised to the detriment of national security, public order, health or morality.

Under the *Environmental Protection Law* of 1991, as amended, every person, citizens' group and state or local government body has a right of access to information on the state of the environment. Anyone whose request for information has not been satisfied, who has been provided with false information, or whose right of access to information has been restricted, may seek a remedy through the administrative or judicial procedure.

A draft Freedom of Information Law is in existence. The current draft contains general statements concerning the right of free access to information which is the subject of a person's legitimate interest. The law would place an obligation on the government to disseminate any information that is of public interest.

1.8.2 Provision of information

Information about the state of the environment is gathered by the specialised bodies of the Environment Ministry, Ministry of Health, Ministry of Agriculture and the National Statistics Institute, by persons authorised by them and by the Municipalities.

They are required on a continuing basis, "to supply and publicise the information on the state of the environment by means of the mass media, or by any other means accessible to citizens". Information must be made available to the public on a continuing basis if it contains data about the alteration of the state of the environment.

Natural and legal persons and the producers of goods and services are obliged to provide information to the authorities regarding the results of their actions which cause or could cause pollution or damage to the environment.

The Laboratory Information Complex at the Environment Ministry issues a publication every three months on air and water quality in Bulgaria.

The Council of Ministers is required annually to publish a report on the state of the environment and to present it to the National Assembly.

In addition, the *Environmental Protection Law* of 1991 states that, in the event of environmental pollution or damage, including natural disasters, industrial accidents and fires, the public must immediately be informed by the Environment Ministry, the Regional Environmental Inspectorates, the Municipalities and the producers of goods and services about the environmental impact of the event, the measures taken to restrict and eliminate it and any action citizens must take for their own safety. The *Environmental Protection Law* of 1991, as amended, extends this obligation to provide information to cases of immediate danger of pollution or damage to the environment. The relevant persons must take urgent measures to prevent potential harm to human health and the environment.

1.8.3 Public consultation

Public consultation on environmental issues is required in a number of instances.

The *Law on Local Self-government and Local Administration* of 1991 provides for direct participation of citizens in matters of local importance through the attendance of public meetings, referenda or otherwise, as well as through their elected representatives. The local authorities must notify the public about their decisions. Meetings of the Municipal Councils are advertised and open to the public. Members of Municipal Councils have a duty to liaise with their constituency and to provide information about the activities and decisions of the Municipal Councils.

The *Environmental Protection Law* of 1991, as amended on 4 December 1992, specifically requires the participation of Municipalities, social organisations and the public in the EIA process.

2. Environmental liability

2.1 Summary

Environmental Liabilities of Investors:	The *Environmental Protection Law,* as amended, provides that at the time of restitution, privatisation and of investment in new constructions, new owners are not liable for past pollution.
Successor Liability:	The purchaser of an enterprise is jointly and severally liable with the seller for past liabilities.
Clean-up Standards:	No standards exist which specifically trigger a clean-up obligation. For ambient standards for soil and water; *see Annex D.*
Civil Liability:	The law provides for fault-based and strict liability. Liability to compensate injured parties can arise even in cases where the activity is administratively permitted.

Administrative Liability:	Violations of environmental laws can result in fines and monetary sanctions.
	Administrative orders can be issued to halt the polluting activity and to shut down the facility, and to remedy the consequences of the environmental damage.
Criminal Liability:	Only natural persons are liable for crimes. Penalties for environmental crimes include imprisonment up to five years, fines of up to 250,000 leva or corrective labour of up to one year.

2.2 Sources of legislation relating to environmental liability

- Article 45 and Article 50 of the *Law on Obligations and Contracts* of 1950, (d.v.275/50, as amended);
- *Law on Ownership* of 1951 (d.v.19/51, as amended);
- *Law on the Protection of Air, Water and Soil from Pollution* of 1963 (d.v.84/63, as amended);
- *Criminal Code* of 1968 (d.v.26/68, as amended);
- *Law on Waters* of 1969 (d.v.29/69, as amended);
- *Law on Administrative Offences and Penalties* of 1969 (d.v.92/69, as amended);
- *Law on Protection of Agricultural Property* of 1974 (d.v.54/74, as amended);
- *Law on the Protection of Arable Land and Pastures* of 1973 (d.v.27/73, as amended);
- *Law on Regional Development and Town Planning* of 1973 (d.v.29/73, as amended) ;
- *Administrative Procedure Law* of 1979 (d.v.90/79, as amended);
- *Law on Ownership and Use of Arable Lands* of 1991, Article 10(10) (d.v.17/91, as amended);
- *Commercial Law* of 1991, Article 15 (d.v.48/91);
- *Environmental Protection Law* of 1991 (d.v.86/91 and 100/92);
- *Law on Economic Activity of Foreign Persons and on Protection of Foreign Investments* of 1992 (d.v.8/92);
- *Law on Transformation and Privatisation of State-Owned and Municipal-Owned Enterprises* of 1992 (d.v.38/92);
- *Ordinance on Manufacture, Sale, Storage, Transportation and Use of Highly Active Toxic Substances* (d.v.34/73);
- *Regulation of the Council of Ministers on the Procedure of Assessing and Imposing Sanctions for Environmental Damage or Pollution beyond Permissible Levels* of 1993 (d.v.15/93);
- *Regulation No. 3 of Environment Ministry on the Standards for Permissible Concentrations of Hazardous Substances in the Soil* of 1979 (d.v.36/79);
- *Regulation No. 7 of the Environment Ministry on Determining the Quality of Running Surface Waters* of 1986 (d.v.96/86);
- *Regulation No. 2 on Protection from Accidents from Activities Connected with Hazardous Chemicals* of 1990 (d.v.100/90).

2.3 Environmental liabilities for past pollution

2.3.1 Environmental liabilities and investment

An investor has to be aware of two types of potential environmental liabilities when making an investment in Bulgaria:

- Liabilities arising from past environmental pollution caused by the former operation of Bulgarian state enterprises. These liabilities can encompass pollution at the site of the enterprise, contamination migrating from off-site landfills used by the enterprise and damage claims of employees and nearby residents.
- Liabilities associated with the current operations of a facility by the investor. These liabilities can encompass violations of law relating to permitting and other issues and liability for environmental damage under civil and criminal statutes.

An investor's exposure to environmental liabilities arising from past pollution is discussed in this section. Liabilities associated with the current operations of a facility are discussed below in *Section 2.4*.

The exact extent of an investor's liability for the past pollution will depend on a variety of factors including the form of the investment transaction and the commercial laws governing that transaction, various environmental liability provisions and any indemnification provided to investors by the government. Should the investor become responsible for the remediation of past pollution, the applicable environmental clean-up standards will have a bearing on the cost of such remediation.

2.3.2 Types of environmental liabilities

Investments in Bulgaria may take a variety of forms. Recent legislation permits the acquisition of companies owned by the Bulgarian state which have undergone privatisation, as well as the purchase of stock or assets of such companies, the creation of joint ventures and the establishment of new corporations wholly or partially owned by foreign investors. Whether an investor runs the risk of liability for past pollution will depend on the specific form of the investment transaction and the applicable commercial laws.

Under the *Privatisation Law* of 1992 the privatisation of state-owned and municipal-owned enterprises may take one of two forms: (i) the sale of interest or shares by companies owned by the Bulgarian government or (ii) the sale of entire companies, separate parts thereof or the assets of former enterprises which have been liquidated. The *Privatisation Law* does not contain any provisions governing the environmental liabilities of successor corporations or of the purchasers of company stock or assets.

The *Law on Economic Activity of Foreign Persons and on the Protection of Foreign Investment* of 1992 ("*Foreign Investment Law*") provides for the creation of Bulgarian joint ventures and the establishment of companies wholly-owned or partially-owned by foreign investors. The *Foreign Investment Law* contains no environmental liability provisions.

Pursuant to the *Foreign Investment Law*, a foreign person may not acquire ownership over land but can have limited rights, such as the right to construct a building on the land, in accordance with the terms of the law. The law does not mention the ownership of land by firms with foreign participation, except to say that Bulgarian companies with foreign participation in excess of 50% may not own arable land. It is thus possible to interpret the

Foreign Investment Law as permitting Bulgarian firms with foreign participation to own non-arable land. The question of environmental liabilities associated with the transfer of non-arable land to private ownership is not regulated by legislation. Under Article 10(10) of the *Law on the Ownership and Use of Arable Land* of 1991 the Bulgarian government must clean up arable land before its restitution to private ownership. Consequently, such land should be free of environmental liabilities.

The *Commercial Law* of 1991 specifically addresses the liabilities of new owners of enterprises. Article 15 provides that the seller of an enterprise is jointly and severally liable with the purchaser for past liabilities of the enterprise. Creditors must first seek redress from the new owner. It is presumed that this provision might be applicable to most of the sale transactions contemplated by the privatisation process. It is probable that the purchasers of assets of liquidated companies can acquire those assets free of liabilities. It is unclear, however, who remains responsible for the past environmental liabilities of those enterprises.

2.3.3 Government indemnification of environmental liabilities

No practice has been developed in Bulgaria regarding the indemnification by the government of individual investors for specific environmental liabilities. In principle environmental indemnifications could be obtained by investors to the extent that under Bulgarian law contracting parties are free to agree on the specific terms of their agreement.

In a recently enacted provision (Paragraph 9(1) of the *Transitional and Concluding Provisions of the Environmental Protection Law* of 1991), the Bulgarian government has made a statement of intent regarding the handling of environmental liability for past pollution. This provision states that: "at the time of restitution, privatisation and investment in projects of new construction by foreign and Bulgarian natural and legal persons, these persons are not liable for environmental damage caused by past action or inaction." The *Environmental Protection Law* of 1991, as amended, provides no further details how this provision is to be implemented and who retains the environmental liabilities associated with the former operation of enterprises in Bulgaria.

In view of the fact that environmental indemnification of investors may be a possibility in the future, it is advisable for investors to conduct environmental audits to obtain an environmental baseline of any property which is likely to be used in an investor's future operations in Bulgaria.

Environmental audits are already required by law to evaluate the environmental liabilities of enterprises slated for privatisation as well as in the case of investment in new construction projects to determine past liability (*see Section 3* below).

2.3.4 Investor clean-up of contaminated sites

Environmental clean-up standards

No environmental standards that specifically trigger an obligation to clean up contaminated sites are in existence. Nevertheless, there are ambient standards for soil and water which should be used as a reference as to the permissible concentrations of pollutants pending the enactment of clean-up standards.

These standards are covered in two regulations. *Regulation No. 3 of the Environment Ministry on the Standards for Permissible Concentrations of Hazardous Substances in the Soil* of 1979 sets standards for the permissible concentrations in soil of heavy metals and herbicides. *Regulation No. 7 of the Environment Ministry for Determining the Quality of Running Surface Waters* of 1986 sets ambient surface water quality standards. In practice, the same standards are used for groundwater.

Escrow accounts

Some Central and East European governments have adopted escrow accounts as a financial mechanism in privatisation sales to help finance the cost of site remediation. To date, the Bulgarian government has not adopted this approach. The Environment Ministry is currently considering whether this concept should be adopted in draft legislation. In order to expedite the clean-up of contaminated sites in Bulgaria, a portion of the purchase price of a privatised company might be paid by an investor into a special escrow account. The funds could be made available to the investor if an acceptable site remediation plan is presented to the government and is carried out by the investor.

Environmental Funds

Environmental Funds to be created under the *Environmental Protection Law* of 1991, as amended, at national and municipal level, are intended to finance the clean-up of the environment. It is unclear whether investors will have access to income from these Funds to finance clean-up of sites which formerly belonged to the state.

2.3.5 Case examples

No privatisations of state enterprises have taken place to date. No examples of investor clean-up of contaminated sites are available.

2.4 Environmental liabilities arising from facility operation

2.4.1 Civil liability

Fault-based liability

Article 45(1) of the *Law on Obligations and Contracts* of 1950 provides that any person who through his own fault causes damage to another person has an obligation to redress the damage. Fault is presumed until proven otherwise. A person is liable for all damages which are the direct and immediate consequence of the injury. Damages for pain and suffering are allowed.

Article 29 of the *Environmental Protection Law* of 1991 creates a new cause of action for environmental torts. Any person who intentionally or negligently harms another through environmental pollution or damage must pay compensation. Injured persons can obtain an injunction to halt the polluting activity and an order for the restoration of the environment.

Strict liability

Strict liability in civil law is imposed under Article 50 of the *Law on Obligations and Contracts* of 1950. The owner of a property which causes loss is strictly liable for the loss it causes.

22

The liability of polluters to clean up the pollution they cause and to conduct remedial actions in accordance with the instructions of specialised bodies or local government authorities may be interpreted as strict liability.

Liability to compensate injured parties can arise even in cases where the activity is administratively permitted.

Nuisance

Under Article 50 of the *Law on Ownership* of 1951, the owner of an immovable property may not act in such a way as to interfere unreasonably with the use of his neighbour's property. Action or inaction which constitutes unreasonable interference with the neighbour's use and enjoyment of his property may be enjoined. The interference may take the form of smoke, dust, vapour, odour or causing excessive noise.

Trespass

Under Article 109 of the *Law on Ownership* of 1951 the owner of land may seek to enjoin every unreasonable act which interferes with the exercise of his rights of ownership, such an act which causes unlawful invasion on his property or which interferes with the possession of his property.

Statutes of limitation

The general limitation period for every type of claim is five years. No special rules apply in environmental cases. The statutory period for tort actions starts to run when the liable person has been identified.

Remedies

The law provides for monetary damages or remedies such as specific performance and injunction. A polluter is liable to compensate those on whom damage is intentionally or negligently inflicted. Additionally such person can be compelled to halt the polluting activity and to clean up the environment.

Case examples

- In an interpretative decision (133/1988), the Supreme Court has stated that the activity of a craftsman creating noise in excess of permissible sanitary-hygienic norms may constitute unreasonable activity which interferes with the rights of a property owner to enjoy his property. The decision further stated that all activity preventing an owner from enjoying his property rights, which is not based on a law limiting this right, is considered unreasonable.
- In another interpretative decision (216/1985), the Supreme Court has stated that an owner of real property may be obliged to terminate or limit his actions in such a way as not to create obstacles greater than the norm for the use of neighbouring property.
- This case concerned a sheep barn which had polluted the air and the ground and made it impossible for a neighbour to use his yard and dwelling, thus creating an extraordinary obstacle to the use of the neighbouring property. In the opinion of the Supreme Court, the defendant was not required to remove his sheep but to terminate the actions

or perform the necessary actions to remove the obstacles to the use of neighbouring property. The same principle holds true when a business emits gases and chemicals, hazardous for the health and the environment. The business should be ordered to eliminate them or reduce them to the permissible levels but the whole activity of the business should not be banned.

• There are no cases known under the new provision of Article 29 of the *Environmental Protection Law* of 1991.

2.4.2 Administrative liability

Types of administrative liability

Administrative liability arises in the event of violations of environmental permits or statutes, regulations and other legal requirements.

There are three types of administrative remedies: (i) fines, which are imposed upon proof of fault; (ii) monetary sanctions, which are imposed in the event of strict liability for violation of standards; and (iii) administrative orders to halt the polluting activity.

Fines

Fines are imposed on natural persons in the event of violations of the *Environmental Protection Law* of 1991, as amended, including:

• Failure to supply information;
• Failure to obtain an EIA;
• Failure to use required pollution control equipment;
• Failure by an independent expert preparing an EIA to base his/her conclusion on the principle of reducing the risk to human health and the environment as well as on the effective norms and standards.

Under the *Environmental Protection Law* of 1991, as amended, fines range from 1,000 leva to 150,000 leva or in the event of repeated violations or those committed by government officials, from 3,000 to 300,000 leva.

The *Environmental Protection Law* of 1991, as amended, provides for fines for legal persons as well. Firms and enterprises are liable for administrative fines from 5,000 to 350,000 leva (or from 20,000 to 2,000,000 leva for repeated violations, irreparable damage or violation of a court order) for:

• Importing hazardous substances, waste or environmentally unsound technologies;
• Constructing and operating enterprises without requisite pollution control technologies;
• Failing to provide information about the hazardous ingredients of goods and services provided or the possible harmful impact of services;
• Failing to comply with a prohibition order of a competent body.

Monetary sanctions

Monetary sanctions can only be imposed on legal persons or sole proprietors.

The *Law on the Protection of Air, Waters and Soil from Pollution* of 1963 and the *Regulation of the Council of Ministers on the Procedure of Assessing and Imposing Sanctions for Environmental Damage or Pollution beyond Permissible Levels* of 1993 provide for monetary sanctions up to 30,000,000 leva per month for enterprises that emit hazardous and polluting substances in excess of permissible levels.

Monetary sanctions are imposed by the Environment Minister or by an official authorised by him. The sanctions are determined according to the nature, quantity and duration of the pollution. They can be reviewed by the Supreme Court within seven days.

Violations of environmental laws are monitored by the Regional Environmental Inspectorate or the Municipality. Samples of air, soil and groundwater pollution must be taken in the presence of a representative of the enterprise. If the enterprise refuses to send a representative or the representative refuses to sign the document certifying that samples have been taken, two witnesses must sign the document.

The imposition of monetary sanctions does not relieve the violator from civil liability for damages or criminal and administrative liability.

Administrative orders

Under the *Environmental Protection Law* of 1991, as amended, the Environment Ministry, the Regional Environmental Inspectorates and the Municipalities may halt or prohibit the operations of an enterprise if environmental damage is likely to be caused. Activity may also be halted if required approval under the EIA procedure was not obtained or the necessary pollution control equipment is not used.

Orders to cease operation may be issued under the *Law on Regional Development and Town Planning* of 1973 if a building permit was not obtained, under the *Law on the Protection of Arable Land and Pastures* of 1973 if approval was not obtained to alter the use of the land from agriculture to industry and if arable land is being damaged and the instructions of the Commission on Land are not being complied with.

The Environment Ministry, the Regional Environmental Inspectorates and the Municipalities may issue orders for remedying the consequences of the environmental damage.

Permits may be revoked in the following circumstances:

- A permit for water use can be withdrawn for violation of its terms;
- A permit for the discharge of waste water can be withdrawn if the conditions upon which it was issued have changed;
- A construction permit may be withdrawn if the local land use plan, the procedure for issue of the permit or provisions governing the carrying out of the project are violated.

Case examples
- Fines:
    - (i)   A fine of 1,000 leva was imposed on a manager of a company for failure to obtain an EIA for the mining of quartz (April 1992).
    - (ii)   A fine of 1,000 leva was imposed on a manager of a slaughter house for allowing it to operate without pollution control equipment in violation of Article 7(3) of the *Environmental Protection Law* of 1991 (September 1992).

(iii) A company was fined 10,000 leva for discharging waste water polluted with copper sulphate without pre-treatment (April 1992).

- Monetary sanctions:
  (i) An alcohol manufacturing plant discharged over 800 cubic metres of alcohol into surface waters without pre-treatment. The deadline for installing control equipment was 1978. A monetary sanction of 12,000 leva per month was imposed. In 1981, after the installation of new equipment, the monetary sanctions were reduced to 5,000 leva per month. The factory did not stop the pollution and the sanctions were increased to 100,000 leva per month in 1986. The imposition of monetary sanctions did not act as a deterrent although they exceeded the company profit because the company was state owned.
  (ii) The largest petrochemical plant in Bulgaria has regularly paid up to 200,000 leva per month in monetary sanctions. In 1988 the sanctions were reduced to 100,000 leva per month.
  (iii) 50,000 leva per year in monetary sanctions were imposed on a cattle-breeding farm for polluting with manure (in 1988).

2.4.3 Criminal liability

Types of criminal liability

Under Bulgarian law only natural persons may be liable for crimes.

The *Criminal Code* of 1968 provides for a number of different crimes in the environmental area:

- Ordering the use of arable land or pastures for other purposes without obtaining the necessary exemptions;
- Damaging or destroying forests, game or fish either through action or inaction;
- Destroying or damaging protected nature sites, exceptionally valuable, unique and irreparable land formations or protected wildlife or plants;
- Polluting or allowing acts causing pollution of the environment if such pollution constitutes a threat to humans, animals or plants;
- Wilfully causing damage to radioactive material, a radioactive facility or other source which has caused significant damage to the environment;
- Failing to take measures necessary to prevent dangerous pollution of protected water zones or an increase in the level of underground water in inhabited or recreational areas by officials while designing, constructing or operating sewage or irrigation systems;
- Setting or ordering by government officials an enterprise or a power plant into operation without the installation of pollution control systems;
- Failure to fulfill obligations for the construction of pollution control systems or for the correct operation of such systems by government officials;
- Misrepresentation or concealment of information about the state of the environment by a government official when such acts result in significant damage to the environment, life or human health.

Penalties

- Imprisonment from three months to five years.
- Fines up to a maximum of 250,000 leva depending on the type of crime.
- For insignificant breaches of the *Criminal Code* of 1968, including polluting air, water or soil or allowing them to be polluted, an administrative fine may be imposed which varies from 500 to 2,000 leva.
- Corrective labour from three months to one year. The corrective labour penalty is carried out at the place of current employment of the convicted person (for unemployed — at another suitable job in their place of residence). This penalty consists of withholding of 10–15% of the salary as determined by the sentence. The period of the penalty is not considered as employment for pension plans, etc.

  In negligence cases the sanction is corrective labour or fine up to 1,000 leva.

- Deprivation of the right to practice a profession.

Case example

- A person was sentenced to three months of corrective labour and 10% deductions from his monthly salary for a period of three months by failing to take certain spill prevention measures which resulted in the pollution of a river rendering it unfit for industrial use (1987).

3. Environmental audits

3.1 Summary

Scope of Activities:	Privatisation, restitution and investment in new construction projects.
Approved Consultants:	The Privatisation Agency licenses general.consultants to evaluate enterprises in the privatisation process. No individual licensing procedure exists for environmental consultants.
Applicable Clean-up Standards:	No specific standards exist which trigger an. obligation to clean up contaminated sites. Ambient standards exist for soil and water. *See Annex D.*

3.2 Sources of legislation relating to environmental audits

- Paragraph 9(2) of the *Transitional and Concluding Provisions of the Environmental Protection Law* of 1991 (d.v.86/91 and 100/92);
- *Regulation No. 3 of the Environment Ministry on the Standards for Permissible Concentrations of Hazardous Substances in the Soil* of 1979 (d.v.36/79);

- *Regulation No. 7 of the Environment Ministry for Determining the Quality of Running Surface Waters* of 1986 (d.v.96/86);
- Article 6(3) of the *Regulation of the Council of Ministers on the Appraisal of Units of Property Slated for Privatisation* of 1992 (d.v.50/92);
- *Regulation No.1 on Environmental Impact Assessments* of 1992 (d.v.10/93);
- Article 2(1) of the *Regulation of the Council of Ministers on Mandatory Information Which Must Be Provided to Potential Buyers of Interests and Shares in Transformed State-Owned and Municipal-Owned Enterprises* of 1993 (d.v.9/93).

3.3 Scope of activities subject to environmental audits and audit process

Paragraph 9(2) of the *Transitional and Concluding Provisions to the Environmental Protection Law* of 1991 introduces a legal requirement for environmental audits of state enterprises. This provision requires the evaluation of environmental liabilities of state-owned enterprises during the privatisation process, during restitution of property to former owners and at the time of investment in new construction projects.

The *Regulation of the Council of Ministers on the Appraisal of Units of Property Slated for Privatisation* of 1992 regulates the procedure and criteria for the appraisal of state-owned and municipal-owned enterprises that will be wholly sold and of any assets of such enterprises which are in liquidation. Article 6(3) of this *Regulation* states that: "where an appraisal is made, the environmental impact of production shall be mandatorily taken into consideration."

Pursuant to Article 2(1) of the *Regulation of the Council of Ministers on Mandatory Information which Must Be Provided to Potential Buyers of Interests and Shares in Trans-formed State-Owned and Municipal-Owned Enterprises* of 1993, the government has undertaken to provide information to investors prior to purchase about the legal, financial, economic, technological, organisational and environmental condition of enterprises which are being privatised. The environmental information shall be in the form of a memoran-dum regarding air emissions and water and soil pollution, which shall be compiled or certified by a body of the Ministry of the Environment.

No formal guidelines regarding the scope and methodology of environmental audits have been prepared to date.

3.4 Requirements relevant to environmental audits

Approved consultants
Pursuant to Article 7 of the *Regulation of the Council of Ministers on the Appraisal of Units of Property Slated for Privatisation* of 1992, comprehensive evaluations of all aspects of enterprises slated for privatisation shall be performed by Bulgarian or foreign persons licensed by the Privatisation Agency. Applicants for a licence shall file an application to the Privatisa-tion Agency. There are no special licensing procedures for environmental consultants.

Applicable clean-up standards
No clean-up standards have been drafted specifically for contaminated sites nor have any clean-ups of environmental pollution taken place since the enactment of

Bulgaria's new investment, privatisation and environmental legislation. Legislation in force since the 1970s sets ambient standards for soil and water which might be applicable in the context of clean-up of past pollution, pending the enactment of new standards.

Regulation No. 3 of the Environment Ministry on the Standards for Permissible Concentrations of Hazardous Substances in the Soil of 1979 sets ambient standards for the permissible concentrations of heavy metals and herbicides in soil.

Regulation No. 7 of the Environment Ministry for Determining the Quality of Running Surface Waters of 1986 sets the ambient surface water quality standards which, in practice are also applied to groundwater.

Preparation and approval of remediation plans

At present no procedures have been developed by the Environment Ministry or the Privatisation Agency regarding the preparation and approval of remediation plans relating to sites contaminated by the operations of former state enterprises.

3.5 National experience with environmental audits

At present no environmental audits have been carried out pursuant to the new legislation.

4. Land use planning

4.1 Summary

Permits Required:	Approval for the conversion of arable land to commercial or industrial use must be obtained from the Commission on Land.
	Investment projects must be approved either by the State Expert Council at the Ministry of Territorial Development, Housing and Construction or by the Expert Technical Councils at Municipalities, at the investor's discretion.
	Construction permits for new buildings or expansions must be obtained from the Municipalities.
Timing:	One month.
Public Participation:	The Municipality informs affected parties about each application for a construction permit.
Enforcement:	If no permit is obtained or its conditions, or other legal provisions regarding construction are violated, the construction may be prohibited, or an order to destroy the building may be issued.

4.2 Sources of legislation relating to land use

- *Law on Regional Development and Town Planning* of 1973 (d.v.29/73, as amended) as supplemented by the *Ordinance on the Implementation of the Law on Regional Development and Town Planning* of 1973 (d.v.62/73, as amended);
- *Law on Protection of Arable Land and Pastures* of 1973 (d.v.27/73, as amended) as supplemented by the *Ordinance on the Implementation of the Law on Protection of Arable Land and Pastures* of 1973 (d.v.65/73, as amended);
- *Tariff on Local Fees of the Council of Ministers Enacted in Furtherance of the Law on Local Taxes and Fees* of 1951 (d.v.45/75, as amended);
- *Tariff on the Amount of Deposits according to Article 15 and 17 of the Law on Protection of Arable Land and Pastures* of 1986 (d.v.33/86, as amended);
- *Regulation No. 6 on Governmental Approval of Completed Construction Work* of 1989 (d.v.5/89, as amended) adopted by the Ministry of Economics and Planning and the Committee on Regional Development and Town Planning;
- *Regulation No. 7 on the Sanitary Requirements for Health Protection of Residential Areas* of 1992 (d.v.46/92);
- Draft Law on Protection of Land;
- Draft Law on Land Use and Development;
- Draft Law on Proposed Investments and Construction which will replace the Law on Regional Development and Town Planning.

4.3 Scope of activities subject to land use regulation

Investors planning to build new facilities on greenfield sites or to expand existing facilities will have to comply with Bulgarian land use and building regulations.

Land use is governed by the *Law on Regional Development and Town Planning* of 1973 as implemented by detailed provisions in the *Ordinance on the Implementation of the Law on Regional Development and Town Planning* of 1973.

Land use plans delineate the basic principles for use and development of Bulgaria's territory and set out construction regulations. Plans are prepared at national, regional and local level.

Land is classified by the land use plans into three categories:

- Arable land;
- Forest land;
- Development land.

Although the ownership rights of foreign natural and legal persons over real property in Bulgaria are restricted, companies with foreign participation may own non-arable land.

Arable land cannot be owned by foreign persons or Bulgarian firms in which there is more than 50% foreign participation.

Investors wishing to build facilities on "greenfield" sites should be aware that an exemption of the site from arable land classification must first be obtained to meet the requirements of the *Law on Protection of Arable Land and Pastures* of 1973.

4.4 Permitting process

4.4.1 Authorities

Amending municipal plans

The use of land proposed by an investor must conform to the municipal land use plans before the Municipality will issue a construction permit to develop the land. Otherwise an investor must apply to the Chief Architect at the Municipality for the municipal plan to be amended.

Change of use of arable land

The Commission on Land, a central government body, grants exemption from arable land classification allowing it to be developed as a commercial or industrial site.

Construction permits

Construction permits, which are issued by Municipalities, are required for the construction of new buildings and for the expansion or renovation of existing ones.

Before a construction permit can be issued, the investment proposal must be approved. Since the *Regulation on Relations in the Investment Process* and the *Ordinance on Capital Investment* were repealed in 1991, currently there is no law governing this approval process.

A draft Law on Proposed Investments and Constructions provides for the following system of approval:

- The investment proposal must be reviewed by the Ministry of Health, the Environment Ministry, the Fire Protection Agency, and the Ministry of Internal Affairs.
- The investment proposal will then be subject to an expert assessment either by the State Expert Council at the Ministry of Regional Development and Construction or by the Expert Technical Councils at Municipalities at the investor's discretion.

Once the construction is completed, construction approval must be obtained before its operations can commence. Construction approvals are the responsibility of the Governmental Approval Commissions specially appointed by the Chief Inspectorate on Governmental Technical Control at the Ministry or by the Regional Inspectorates on Governmental Technical Control. The Chief Inspectorate on Governmental and Technical Control supervises the Governmental Approval Commissions.

4.4.2 Application requirements

Change of use of arable land

Pursuant to the *Law on Protection of Arable Land and Pastures* of 1973, an investor must request the Municipality to propose a change of use of arable land to the Commission on Land which grants exemption from arable land classification.

The draft Law on Protection of Land simplifies the procedure for the change of use of arable land by allowing an investor to make a direct application either to the Commission on Land with respect to large tracts of land (more than 30,000 square metres) or to the Municipality in case of smaller lots.

Construction permits

Before a construction permit can be granted an investor must obtain approval of:

- The investment proposal;
- Any EIA which may be required (*see Section 5* below).

For the construction of buildings used for economic purposes the investor must submit a written application to the Municipality. The application must specify the construction work to be performed.

Under Article 234 of the *Ordinance on the Implementation of the Law on Regional Development and Town Planning* of 1973, the following documents must accompany the application:

- Document establishing the title to the land or the right to construct a building on the real property;
- Copy of the relevant part of the detailed municipal plan relating to the plot of land to be developed.

In addition the Municipality can require copies of the following:

- A construction plan;
- Architectural working design with the calculations on the price of the construction. It must be signed by the architect and the investor. The architectural design must be approved by the Chief Architect of the Municipality before the permit is issued.

The draft *Law on Proposed Investments and Construction* specifically requires submission of the following permits with the application for a construction permit:

- A permit and paid fees for change of use of arable land, when applicable;
- Permits for use of water for drinking and industrial purposes, for discharge of effluent, for electricity, heating, gas, communications and deviation from national rail and road work.

Under the *Tariff on Local Fees of the Council of Ministers Enacted in Furtherance of the Law on Local Taxes and Fees* of 1951 (d.v.45/75, as amended), a 0.2% fee on the value of the project is payable to the Municipality for the construction permit.

4.4.3 Timing

According to the *Administrative Procedure Law* of 1979 once all the required documents are presented, all of the above permit procedures should be completed within one month. In practice these procedures may take longer.

4.4.4 Permit conditions

Change of use of arable land

Investors must make payments to the budget when proposing to change the use of arable land in accordance with the *Tariff on the Amount of Deposits according to Article*

15 and 17 of the Law on Protection of Arable Land and Pastures of 1986, which determines prices according to the prospective use and the category of the land.

Under Article 18(1) of the *Law on Protection of Arable Land and Pastures* before starting construction on arable land from the first three most fertile categories, the investors are obliged to prepare a plan and have it approved for the collecting of the humus layer of the soil and replanting it on a land as large as the one transferred for non-agricultural use.

Construction permits

The construction permit is issued for the whole project. It contains all conditions related to the carrying out of the project.

The draft Law on Proposed Investments and Construction requires the investor to apply for a construction permit within two years after the investment proposal is approved.

If in two years the foundation of the construction is not laid the permit must be renewed. If the approved design is not changed only one third of the fee is to be paid.

The construction permit expires in three years.

4.5 Public participation

Amending municipal plans

The public has the right to be heard on any application to amend municipal plans.

Draft municipal plans are published in *Darjaven Vestnik* and the press. They are made available to the public for comment prior to their review by the Municipal Council. The public has 30 days to comment on general municipal plans and 14 days in the case of detailed municipal plans. All other draft plans which are of public importance, have a significant impact on living conditions or the environment, or concern construction projects or towns or villages of high architectural and artistic value are subject to public comment before being reviewed.

Approvals of municipal plans are published in *Darjaven Vestnik*, the official legal journal of the National Assembly.

Change of use of arable land

There are no specific public participation procedures applicable in this context.

Construction permits

The Municipality informs affected parties about each application for a construction permit. The parties concerned have seven days to submit comments.

4.6 Enforcement

Change of use of arable land

The Commission on Land can take the following action:

- Halt construction when no proper exemption was obtained for change of use of arable land;
- Impose specific requirements on plants damaging adjoining arable land and halt their operation if the requirements are not complied with.

33

Construction permits

Where no construction permit has been obtained, or its conditions or other legal provisions regulating construction have been violated, the Ministry of Regional Development and Construction and the Municipalities can halt construction, destroy buildings or order owners to tear them down.

Where no construction permit has been obtained, the Ministry of Regional Development and Construction can also issue a penal order seizing the buildings together with the land. The same governmental action can be taken with regard to individual floors of buildings.

Criminal sanctions may be imposed for:

- Violating building, sanitary or fire protection rules or managing or constructing buildings which endanger the lives of others. The maximum period of imprisonment is two years.
- Constructing a building on arable land without permission. The maximum penalty is two years, imprisonment or a fine from 500 to 1,000 leva.

5. Environmental impact assessments (EIAs)

5.1 Summary

Scope of Activities:	Potentially all activities, at the initiative of the Environment Ministry, Regional Environmental Inspectorates or the Municipalities; and projects subject to mandatory EIAs.
Procedure:	A description of the project and its expected environmental impact, and a conclusion of experts are submitted either to the Environment Ministry or to the Regional Environmental Inspectorates.
Timing:	The decision of the authorities must be rendered in three months after the hearing and reported within 14 days.
Public Participation:	All natural and legal persons concerned as well as the Municipalities, public organisations and the public have the right to participate in the EIA procedure.
Enforcement:	Any project requiring an EIA may not proceed until the EIA is approved.

5.2 Sources of legislation relating to the environmental impact of industrial and commercial developments

- Articles 19 to 23 of the *Environmental Protection Law* of 1991 (d.v.86/91 and 100/92, as amended);

- Regulation No.1 on *Environmental Impact Assessment* ("*Regulation No. 1 on EIAs*") of December 28, 1992 (d.v.10/93) adopted by the Environment Minister jointly with the Minister of Regional Development and Construction, the Minister of Health and the Minister of Agriculture.

5.3 Scope of activities subject to EIA process

Under the *Environmental Protection Law* of 1991, as amended, all activities of natural and legal persons and government bodies may be subject to EIAs at the initiative of the Environment Ministry, the Regional Environmental Inspectorate or the Municipality, or concerned natural or legal persons.

In addition, the following projects are subject to mandatory EIAs:

- National and regional development programmes, territorial and urban development plans and amendments thereto;
- Projects for reconstruction or enlargement of existing facilities which would be subject to mandatory EIA before construction or adoption;
- Major projects are subject to EIAs to be carried out periodically as determined by the Environment Ministry, but at least once every five years;
- Projects and facilities described in Appendices 1 and 2 to the *Environmental Protection Law* of 1991, as amended. *See Annex F.*

All existing programmes, plans and projects as well as the firms, companies or operations in question could be subject to EIAs, if there is an indication that their operations are polluting the environment. In case of a negative EIA, the Ministry of Health may order an evaluation of the state of health of the affected personnel and an epidemiological study of the population. The firm or company in question is given a time limit by the Environment Ministry, not to exceed five years, to comply with the standards.

5.4 EIA process

5.4.1 Authority

The Environment Ministry approves EIAs of international and national importance.

The Regional Environmental Inspectorate with the participation of the Municipality, approves projects of local importance which have an effect on the territory under their control.

Under *Regulation No. 1 on EIAs* of 1992 the Environment Ministry approves, based on decisions of its Supreme Environmental Experts Council, the following EIAs relating to :

- Listed projects of international importance;
- Projects whose impact affects the region controlled by more than one Regional Environmental Inspectorate;
- Projects which will generate wastewater over 30 litres per second, or incinerated waste over 750 kg;
- Projects where the amount of the investment exceeds 50 million leva.

The Regional Environmental Inspectorate jointly with the Municipality approves EIAs of all other projects, based on decisions of its advisory body, the Environmental Experts Council.

Representatives of the Ministry of Regional Development and Construction, the Ministry of Health and the Ministry of Agriculture participate in the meetings of the Environmental Experts Councils *ex officio*.

5.4.2 Documentation

Under the *Environmental Protection Law* of 1991, as amended, an investor must submit the following documentation to the Environment Ministry or the Regional Environmental Inspectorate in order to obtain EIA approval:

- Summary of the project;
- Description of the environment which is expected to be affected;
- Forecast of the expected impact;
- Presentation of alternatives to implementing the project, including withdrawal;
- List of the parties who could be affected by the project;
- Any other materials required by the Environment Ministry;
- Conclusion of the experts who have performed the EIA.

Regulation No. 1 on EIAs of 1992 requires the submission of a preliminary EIA report to the relevant authority which determines whether a final EIA will be necessary. The steps of the EIA procedure are described in this regulation as follows:

- Preliminary EIA report to be submitted to the relevant authorities at the same time as the approval of the investment project is being requested;
- Final EIA report to be submitted to the relevant authority at the same time as the application for a construction permit is being made;
- Hearing on the EIA as a condition for approval of the investment proposal and the issuance of a construction permit;
- Amending the final EIA report to reflect hearing discussions and public comments;
- EIA approval.

Regulation No. 1 on EIAs of 1992 states that the preliminary EIA report must contain a summary of the project, a description of the environment to be affected, a forecast of the expected impact and a conclusion.

The final EIA report in addition to the above documents must contain project alternatives and measures for reducing the harmful environmental impact, an evaluation of the damages, a plan of action in case of accidents and spills, and a plan for self-monitoring.

Where an EIA is required, the project subject to an EIA may not proceed until approval under the EIA process has been obtained. For example construction permits cannot be obtained without an EIA approval.

5.4.3 Experts and consultants

Under the *Environmental Protection Law* of 1991, as amended, EIAs are conducted by independent experts appointed and paid for by the investor.

The experts must be professionally competent and they must declare that they are not directly involved in the realisation of the project or the activity and that they have not participated in the designing of the project.

There is currently no procedure for licensing experts.

5.4.4 *Timing*

The approval authority (either the Environment Ministry or the Regional Environmental Inspectorate) sets the timetable for a hearing on the EIA of a particular development project. The authority, jointly with the investor and the Municipality, determines the place, date and hour of the hearing and makes an announcement in the national and local mass media.

The decision of the authority on the preliminary report must be rendered in one month's time. A decision regarding the final EIA report must be rendered within three months after the hearing and reported within 14 days. The authority reports its decision in writing to the investor or the promoter of the activity. It also announces its decision in the mass media or in another suitable way to satisfy the public's right to information.

The project must be started within one year of approval or a new EIA approval must be obtained.

5.4.5 *Standard of review*

The *Regulation on EIAs* provides that the EIA is a procedure to study and analyse projects, facilities and activities and to prepare and adopt a conclusion relating to the protection of the environment, stating whether the projects, facilities and activities are permissible, in light of their compliance with the existing standards as well as their environmental and socio-economic value.

The *Environmental Protection Law* of 1991, as amended, does not expressly set any standards for review of EIAs. It states that the experts should be guided by the provisions of Article 2. This Article provides that:

Reducing the risk to human health and to the environment and its correlation to the damages suffered and benefits forfeited shall constitute the basis for the setting up of environmental policy.

The experts are also to be guided by the effective levels and standards for admissible environmental pollution.

Regulation No. 1 on EIAs of 1992 sets criteria for assessing the state of the air, waters, soils, flora, fauna, noise and waste.

It provides that an EIA may be approved or denied. A request may be made to the investor to redraft the final report.

Approval of the EIA may require the investor to meet certain conditions in the implementation of the project. The fulfillment of these conditions may be checked by the approval authority.

The Environment Ministry or the Regional Environmental Inspectorate will approve the project if:

• The project complies with the existing laws and regulations and the existing technical and environmental standards;

- The report on the EIA is prepared in compliance with the requirements of *Regulation No. 1 on EIAs* of 1992;
- The necessary land use, town development and technical measures for the rational use of natural resources, protection and remediation of the environment are provided for.

If any of the existing laws, regulations and applicable standards are violated or the requirements of *Regulation No. 1 on EIAs* of 1992 are not complied with, the authority will not approve the project.

If the necessary land use, town development and technical measures for the rational use of natural resources, protection and remediation of the environment are not provided for, the investor may be required to redraft the final report.

5.5 Public participation

All natural and legal persons concerned by the development project have the right to participate in the discussion of the results of the EIA. The authority must inform them about such a discussion, at least one month in advance, through the mass media or through another appropriate channel. The approval authority must obtain the views of the parties involved. The *Environmental Protection Law* of 1991, as amended, specifically requires the participation of the Municipality, the public organisations and the public in the EIA procedure. The public participation in the discussion of the results of the EIA is further specified in *Regulation No. 1 on EIAs* of 1992.

The investor must exhibit the materials (plans, drafts, tables, models) at places determined by the Municipality and announce the time when the results of the EIA will be available to the public.

Under Article 9 of *Regulation No. 1 on EIAs* of 1992, however, the Environment Ministry and the Regional Environmental Inspectorates are obliged not to disseminate information which is a state, professional or other secret. Non-compliance with this rule will lead to criminal liability. The approval authority is obliged to comply with the provisions of the *Law on Protection of Competition* of 1991.

The investor must collect and describe all the written statements, comments and proposals of the participants in the procedure.

In case controversial issues arise during the first hearing, the authority decides whether a second hearing will be necessary. The second hearing is preceded by new consultations and statements of experts.

After the public discussion, the final EIA report must take account of any public comments. The final EIA report must then be presented by the investor to the approval authority, together with all the records and the proceedings from the discussion.

5.6 Enforcement

Article 23(iii) of the *Environmental Protection Law* of 1991, as amended, obliges the competent authority (Environment Ministry, Regional Environmental Inspectorate and Municipality) to ban or enjoin the activities or the realisation of the project if a mandatory EIA was not carried out, or the EIA was not approved.

Under the *Environmental Protection Law* of 1991, as amended, decisions on EIAs are subject to judicial review before the District Court. *Regulation No. 1 on EIAs* of 1992 specifies that the decisions of the Environment Ministry are reviewed by the Supreme Court. The period for judicial review for local projects is 14 days after the notification on the decision of the approval authority. For projects of national and international significance the period is 30 days.

5.7 National experience with EIAs

Two EIAs were carried out in Bulgaria in 1992: Cascade Gorna Arda and Cascade Sreden Iscar. Both were approved at Ministerial level. EIAs are pending on the Kalotino Highway and the Orizovo-Capitan Andreevo Highway and on a concession on the Black Sea continental shelf for the drilling of oil.

No EIAs have been carried out to date in accordance with the requirements of the newly enacted *Regulation No. 1 on EIAs* of 1992.

6. Integrated permitting requirements applicable to the operation of industrial and commercial facilities

6.1 Extent of integrated permitting

There is no integrated permitting system in Bulgaria. Permits are only needed for water use and for the discharge of waste water. Special permits are not required either for air, noise emissions, the generation of waste or for the operation of waste treatment facilities. For further information see *Sections 7–11*.

To some extent the role of integrating permitting is performed by the EIA. If the proposed project is likely to violate any ambient or emission standards the EIA will not be approved and the project will not be allowed to proceed. The EIA is mandatory for projects listed in the Appendices to the *Environmental Protection Law* of 1991, as amended. It can also be requested upon the discretion of the Municipalities or the Environment Ministry. For further information on EIAs, see *Section 5* above.

7. Air emission requirements applicable to the operation of industrial and commercial facilities

7.1 Summary

Air Requirements:	No permits have to be obtained by individual facilities for sources of air emissions, nor are charges payable for air emissions. Approval of an EIA will be refused if air standards are violated.

Public Participation:	The public has a right of access to information on the state of the environment, providing a legitimate interest can be demonstrated. The public has a right to participate in the EIA procedure.
Enforcement:	The Environment Ministry can impose fines for violations of air protection laws and monetary sanctions for violation of air emission standards. The Environment Ministry, the Regional Environmental Inspectorates and the Municipalities can issue orders to halt or terminate activities which cause pollution. Criminal sanctions can be imposed if a violation constitutes a crime.

7.2 Sources of legislation relating to air emissions

- Articles 5–7 of the *Law on Protection of Air, Water and Soil from Pollution* of 1963 (d.v.84/63, as amended) as supplemented by Articles 1–22 of the *Ordinance on the Implementation of the Law on Protection of Air, Water and Soil from Pollution* of 1964 (d.v.80/64, as amended);
- *Environmental Protection Law* of 1991 (d.v.86/91, as amended);
- *Regulation of the Council of Ministers on the Procedure of Assessing and Imposing Sanctions for Environmental Damage or Pollution beyond Permissible Levels* of 1993 (d.v.15/93);
- *Regulation No. 2 on the Maximum Permissible Concentrations of Hazardous Substances in the Air of Residential Areas* of 1984 (d.v.16/84, as amended);
- *Norms on Maximum Permissible Level of Emissions into Air* of 1991 (d.v.81/91);
- *Regulation No. 7 on the Sanitary Requirements for Health Protection of Residential Areas* of 1992 (d.v.46/92);
- Draft Law on Air;
- Draft Regulation on Ambient Air Quality.

7.3 Air protection zones

Air quality in certain protected areas such as reserves, national parks and historic places is protected to the extent that construction and development projects in such areas are subject to special permits from the Environment Minister.

Regulation No. 7 on the Sanitary Requirements for Health Protection of Residential Areas of 1992 provides for sanitary protective zones around industrial enterprises. The factories should be built at a distance of at least 100 m to 3,000 m from the nearest residential areas depending on the nature of the industrial activity.

The *Environmental Protection Law* of 1991, as amended, provides that the Environment Minister jointly with the Minister of Health and the Minister of Agriculture and with other competent bodies will develop special regimes for areas with an endangered environment in order to restore their environmental quality. Steps taken will include limits on air emissions.

7.4 Scope of activities subject to air emission regulations

Bulgarian regulations govern the level of pollutants in ambient air.

Bulgarian law distinguishes two types of air pollution sources — stationary sources and mobile sources generated by combustion engines. Emissions from stationary sources are regulated by reference to standards applicable to the industry in question.

7.5 Standards

7.5.1 Ambient quality standards

Regulation No. 2 on the Maximum Permissible Concentrations of Hazardous Substances in the Air of Residential Areas of 1984 sets the ambient air quality standards. It lists 170 hazardous substances and determines their maximum permissible concentrations in the air. These standards are so strict as to be virtually unenforceable. They are to be amended to conform to EC standards.

7.5.2 Emission limit values

Norms on Maximum Permissible Levels of Emissions into Air adopted by the Environment Ministry in September 1991, establish new standards for both existing and new sources of air emissions. They set emission standards for particulates, organic and inorganic pollutants applicable to all industries. They also provide specific emission standards for approximately 20 different industries including power generation, cement and steel industries. The emission standards for old sources are valid until the end of 1995. Old sources of air emissions are expected to phase in new standards by that date.

7.5.3 Technology based standards

New air pollution sources and modifications of existing sources must be constructed using the best available technology and there must be an attempt to reduce emissions to levels even below maximum permissible levels.

7.6 Permitting process

7.6.1 Authorities

Currently there are no requirements for air emission permits. Nevertheless, EIA approval will be refused if a facility violates or is likely to violate ambient air standards or air emission standards.

7.6.2 Application requirements
No air emission permits are currently required.

7.6.3 Timing
No air emission permits are currently required.

7.6.4 Permit conditions
No air emission permits are currently required.

7.6.5 Charges for emissions
At present there are no charges for air emissions which are within the air emission standards, but the *Environmental Protection Law* of 1991, as amended, requires their introduction. The proposal is to impose charges on the emission of six or seven principal air pollutants including sulphur dioxide, particulates, nitrous oxides and carbon dioxide.

7.6.6 Public participation
The public has a right of access to information on the state of the environment and a right to participate in the EIA procedure.

7.7 Enforcement

7.7.1 Compliance checking and monitoring
Laboratories at industrial enterprises and power stations are periodically required to perform studies at the request of the authorities. This provision is not usually enforced because few enterprises or authorities have monitoring devices. The Environment Ministry has stated that there is no requirement for enterprises to report their emission level of pollutants to the authorities.

The proposed Law on Air will require the reporting of air emissions.

Enforcement of air regulations is performed by the Municipalities, the Regional Environmental Inspectorates or the Environment Ministry as follows:

- The Municipality is the enforcement authority if the affected area falls wholly within its jurisdiction;
- The Regional Environmental Inspectorate is the enforcement authority if one or more than one municipality within its region is affected. The Regional Environmental Inspectorate is the investigation body for all breaches of air emission standards;
- The Environment Ministry is the enforcement authority if more than one region is affected. The Ministry can impose fines and monetary sanctions.

7.7.2 Penalties and sanctions
Municipalities, Regional Environmental Inspectorates and the Environment Ministry may require the violator to:

- Discontinue manufacture and other industrial or commercial activities until the violation is eliminated;

- Terminate manufacture and other industrial or commercial activities which cause or may cause irreversible damage to the environment and human health;
- Repair the damage caused.

In addition, under the *Environmental Protection Law* of 1991, as amended, every citizen, citizens' group and Municipality may apply to the courts for the violator to be ordered to discontinue the violation.

The Sanitary Epidemiological Institutes are empowered to halt polluting activities when ambient air standards or air emission standards are violated and there is a danger to human health.

Fines may be imposed by the Environment Ministry on natural and legal persons for breach of air protection rules under the *Environmental Protection Law* of 1991, as amended.

Monetary sanctions for air pollution may be imposed by the Environment Ministry on legal persons and sole proprietors. The level depends on the quantities of the emitted substances and the length of the period of emission.

Criminal sanctions may be imposed if the violation constitutes a crime.

8. Water requirements applicable to the operation of industrial and commercial facilities

8.1 Summary

Water Requirements:	Permits for water use can be obtained from the National Water Council. Permits for water discharge can be obtained from the Environment Ministry.
Timing:	One month for both types of permits.
Standards:	There are no water effluent standards. Water discharges must not violate ambient water standards. There are no charges for water use or water discharge at present.
Public Participation:	No public participation is provided for in the permitting process. The public has a right of access to information on the state of the environment, provided a legitimate interest can be demonstrated. The public has a right to participate in the EIA procedure.
Enforcement:	The Environment Ministry, Regional Environmental Inspectorates and the Municipalities can issue remedial orders and orders to halt or terminate activities. The Environment Ministry imposes fines and monetary sanctions. Criminal sanctions can be imposed if the violation constitutes a crime.

> The National Water Council enforces the legislation on water use. The permit for water use may be withdrawn if its terms are violated.

8.2 Sources of legislation relating to water requirements

- Articles 8–13 of the *Law on Protection of Air, Water and Soil from Pollution* of 1963 (d.v.84/63, as amended) as supplemented by Articles 23–37 of the *Ordinance on the Implementation of the Law on Protection of Air, Water and Soil from Pollution* of 1964 (d.v.80/64, as amended);
- *Law on Waters* of 1969 (d.v.29/69, as amended);
- *Environmental Protection Law* of 1991 (d.v.86/91, as amended);
- *Regulation on Water Use of the National Water Council* of 1971 (d.v.16/71);
- *Regulation on Issuing Permits for Constructions which Might Negatively Affect the Natural Flow of Water, Drainage, Navigation, the Movement of Ice or Water Quality* of 1973 (d.v.82/73);
- *Regulation No. 6 of the Ministry of Health and the Environment Ministry on the Discharge Underground of Effluent Containing Hazardous Substances* of 1981 (d.v.87/81);
- *Regulation No. 7 of the Environment Ministry for Determining the Quality of Running Surface Waters* of 1986 (d.v.96/86);
- *Regulation No. 9 of the Ministry of Regional Development and Construction on the Use of Water Supply and Sewage Systems* of 1987;
- *Regulation No. 2 on Sanitary Protective Zones around the Water Sources and the Equipment for Drinking Household Water Supply* of 1989 (d.v.68/89);
- *Regulation of the Council of Ministers on the Procedure of Assessing and Imposing Sanctions for Environmental Damage or Pollution beyond Permissible Levels* of 1993 (d.v.15/93);
- Draft Law on Waters which will regulate both water use and the protection of waters from pollution;
- Draft Regulation on Determining Standards for Industrial Waste Water Discharged Directly into Water Basins;
- Draft Regulation on the Admissible Content of Harmful Substances in Industrial Waste Water Discharged Into the Sewer Systems;
- Draft Regulation on Determining Charges for Waste Water Discharge;
- Draft Regulation on the Quality of Surface Waters;
- Draft Regulation on the Requirements for the Quality of Waters Designated for the Main Types of Water Usage.

8.3 Water management

8.3.1 Water management bodies

Administration of water resources is exercised by the National Water Council. It is assisted by six Regional Departments on Waters which:

- Control compliance with permits and conditions for water use;
- Investigate violations of water legislation;
- Render opinions on requests for water use;
- Collect information for water management;
- Collect information regarding water resources;
- Render decisions on issues of local water use;
- Interact with other state and public institutions during natural disasters;
- Control the water levels of water basins;
- Control conditions of water beds;
- Control extraction of inert materials from rivers.

The Committee on Geology and Mineral Resources at the Council of Ministers carries out research and studies of groundwater.

8.3.2 *Water quality categories*

There are currently three water quality categories as provided in the *Ordinance on the Implementation of the Law on Protection of Air, Water and Soil from Pollution* of 1964:

- Waters used for drinking, in foodstuffs, in industries requiring potable water, in swimming pools, etc;
- Waters used for animals to drink, in the fishing industry and in water sports;
- Waters used for irrigation or for industrial purposes.

A new draft Regulation on the Quality of Surface Waters places water in five categories, based on the environmental quality of the water (and not on water use).

The draft Regulation on the Requirements for the Quality of Waters Designated for the Main Types of Water Usage introduces differentiated requirements regarding the quality of waters intended for domestic drinking water supply, irrigation, recreation and fish breeding. These requirements and standards have mainly been adopted from the EC.

Under *Regulation No. 2 on Sanitary Protective Zones around the water sources and the equipment for drinking household water supply* of 1989, sanitary protective zones are created around water sources and water facilities where water is used for drinking, household or medical purposes.

8.3.3 *Activities subject to regulation*

The *Law on Waters* of 1969 regulates water use. The issuance of permits for water use is governed by the *Regulation on Water Use* of 1971.

Permits are also required to discharge waste water. The *Law on Protection of Air, Water and Soil from Pollution* of 1963 (Articles 8–13) and the *Ordinance on the Implementation of the Law on Protection of Air, Water and Soil from Pollution* of 1964 (Articles 23–37) regulate the procedure for issuing permits for waste water discharge.

Permits are required to construct anything which might impede the natural flow of water. The *Regulation on Issuing Permits for Constructions which Might Negatively Affect the Natural Flow of Water, Drainage, Navigation, the Movement of Ice or Water Quality* of 1973 governs the issue of permits for constructions affecting water flow.

8.4 Standards

8.4.1 Ambient quality standards

Regulation No. 7 of the Environment Ministry for Determining the Quality of Running Surface Waters of 1986 sets the ambient surface water quality standards. The same standards are used for groundwater. The regulation provides for several categories of indicators: inorganic, organic, inorganic from industrial origin, organic from industrial origin and biological indicators. The standards differ for the three different categories of water.

8.4.2 Discharge limit values

There are no water discharge standards. A new draft Regulation on Determining Standards for Industrial Waste Water Discharged Directly into Water Basins is being considered. The discharge standards are being developed on the basis of the best available technology for about 50 types of products in different sectors. These standards have been adopted from similar product standards in Germany and the United States. If local conditions so require, more stringent requirements can be implemented. Similar discharge standards are also being developed for waste water discharged by municipal waste treatment plants with stricter requirements applying to larger facilities.

A new Regulation on the Admissible Content of Harmful Substances in Industrial Waste Water Discharged Into the Sewer Systems has been drafted.

Water discharge permits issued to individual facilities require them to comply with ambient water quality standards.

8.4.3 Technology based standards

There are no technology based standards. The proposed discharge standards mentioned above, however, are being drafted on the basis of the best available technology.

8.5 Water use permitting process

8.5.1 Authorities

Water use

A number of different authorities issue permits relating to water use depending on the source of water and the type of water use contemplated:

• The National Water Council issues permits for the use of water for commercial and industrial purposes.
• The Committee on Geology and Mineral Resources at the Council of Ministers issues permits for the use of water from aquifers.
• The National Water Council jointly with the Ministry of Health, the Committee on Geology and Mineral Resources and the respective Municipality issue permits for the use of mineral waters.
• The Ministry of Health issues permits for use of mineral waters for medicinal purposes, for bottling and for extracting substances for public health purposes.

- The Municipality, upon the consent of the Ministry of Health, issues permits for the use of water for household needs.
- The Environment Ministry issues permits for constructions affecting the flow of rivers outside built-up areas.
- The Municipality with the consent of the Environment Ministry issues permits for constructions affecting the flow of rivers in built-up areas.

8.5.2 Application requirements

An investor seeking to obtain a permit for water use by his commercial or industrial facility should submit the following documents to the National Water Council in accordance with Article 15 of the *Regulation on Water Use*:

- A written application with the name and address of the applicant;
- Exact data about the amount of water required measured in litres per second;
- Data about the water basin;
- Data regarding the location of water use and the place of its eventual use;
- Design of the project accompanied by a scheme prepared by an architect setting forth the necessity for the quantity of water required, the capacities of the water basin and the needs of the other water users;
- Written opinions of the concerned parties;
- Proof of the fee paid.

8.5.3 Timing

The National Water Council must review applications for water use permits within one month. All permits issued, denied or repealed by other authorities may be appealed before the National Water Council within 30 days. The National Water Council may review its own decisions by which a permit is denied or repealed.

8.5.4 Permit conditions

Water use permits are issued either for a definite time, or with no time limit. They may be subject to certain conditions.

A water use permit contains the following information:

- The names and the permanent address of the water user;
- The name of the water basin, the place of extraction of water, water quantity in litres per second and the purpose for which the water will be used;
- The conditions of the water use;
- The period for which the water use is permitted.

8.5.5 Charges for water use

Water charges are paid by the user. The amount of charges is determined by the state enterprises supplying the water.

Those who use their own water sources or water from their own water facilities do not pay charges.

8.6 Water discharge permitting process

8.6.1 Authorities

The Environment Ministry, in consultation with the Ministry of Health, the Municipality and the company in charge of the water basin or sewer system, issue permits for waste water discharge.

8.6.2 Application requirements

Two kinds of water discharge permits must be obtained: preliminary and final permits.

Preliminary permits are issued prior to the approval of an investment proposal and are based on the design specifications.

To obtain a preliminary permit the following documents must be submitted to the Environment Ministry which acts through the Regional Environmental Inspectorates:

- A written application from the investor;
- Data about the nature and volume of the industrial process and the quantity and composition of the waters to be discharged.

Final permits are issued by the Environment Ministry after the compliance of the facility with the permit conditions has been tested. The tests are conducted by a commission appointed by the Environment Ministry and consisting of representatives of the Environment Ministry, Ministry of Health, Ministry of Regional Development and Construction and the Ministry of Agriculture.

Temporary permits may be issued for an interim period when the facility commences operations.

8.6.3 Timing

Applications are to be reviewed in one month according to the *Law on Administrative Procedure* of 1979.

8.6.4 Permit conditions

Waste water discharge permits may be subject to certain conditions.

Preliminary permits indicate the category of water stream affected, the quantity of waste waters, their type and the conditions for their discharge.

Final permits are issued for an indefinite period. The draft *Law on Waters* provides for the permits to be issued for a limited period based on an assessment of the technological standards of the enterprise and its waste treatment capabilities.

No permit fees are charged.

A permit may be modified or withdrawn if the conditions upon which it was issued have changed.

Under the new Law on Waters, which is being drafted, the permit will specify the exact amount of water to be discharged and the permitted concentrations. Individual emission standards will be set for each facility and will depend on the nature of its operations and the quality of the water in the water basin.

8.6.5 *Charges for water discharge*

At present there are no charges for water discharge. As required by the *Environmental Protection Law* of 1991, as amended, a draft Regulation on Determining Charges for Waste Water Discharge is ready to be adopted.

Fees are paid to the companies which run the sewage systems if water is discharged into the sewage systems.

8.6.6 *Public participation*

No public participation is provided for in the permitting process. The public has a right of access to information on the state of the environment and a right to participate in the EIA procedure.

8.7 *Enforcement*

8.7.1 *Compliance checking and monitoring*

The Environment Ministry enforces the legislation on water quality, waste water discharge and on constructions affecting water.

- The Environment Ministry is the enforcement authority if more than one region is affected. The Ministry can impose fines and monetary sanctions.
- The Regional Environmental Inspectorate is the enforcement authority if one or more than one municipality within its region is affected. The Regional Environmental Inspectorate is the investigation body for all breaches of air emission standards.
- The Municipality is the enforcement authority if the affected area falls wholly within its jurisdiction.

In addition, under the *Environmental Protection Law* of 1991, as amended, every citizen, citizens' group and Municipality may apply to the courts for the violator to be ordered to discontinue the violation.

- The National Water Council enforces the legislation on water use.
- The Ministry of Regional Development and Construction enforces legislation on management and use of drinking water, sewer systems and waste water treatment in settlements.
- The Ministry of Health enforces legislation on use of waters (including mineral waters) for sanitation-hygienic and medical treatment purposes and monitors the quality of the drinking water.
- The Ministry of Agriculture monitors the quality of waters for agricultural use.

8.7.2 *Penalties and sanctions*

The Municipality, the Regional Environmental Inspectorates and the Environment Ministry may require the violator of the *Environmental Protection Law* of 1991, as amended, to:

- Discontinue manufacture and other industrial or commercial activities until the violation is eliminated;

- Terminate manufacture and other industrial or commercial activities which cause or may cause irreversible damage to the environment and human health;
- Repair the damage caused.

The Sanitary Epidemiological Institutes are empowered to halt polluting activities when ambient standards are violated and there is a danger to human health.

Fines may be imposed by the Environment Ministry on natural and legal persons for breach of water protection rules under the *Environmental Protection Law* of 1991, as amended.

Monetary sanctions may be imposed by the Environment Ministry on legal persons and sole proprietors for violation of water standards. The level depends on the nature and quantities of the emitted substances and the length of the period of emission.

Criminal sanctions may be imposed if the violation constitutes a crime.

The permit for water use can be withdrawn if its terms are violated.

9. Noise requirements applicable to the operation of industrial and commercial facilities

9.1 Summary

Noise Requirements:	While ambient standards exist, no permits are required. Governmental control of noise is performed through the EIA process.
Public Participation:	The public has a right of access to information on the state of the environment, provided a legitimate interest can be demonstrated. The public has a right to participate in the EIA procedure.
Enforcement:	The Environment Ministry and the Regional Environmental Inspectorates can halt activities producing noise above the prescribed limits. Fines may be imposed for violating noise regulations.

9.2 Sources of legislation relating to environmental noise

- *Sanitary Norms 0–64 on the Permissible Levels of Noise in Housing and Public Buildings and Residential Areas* of 1972 (d.v.87/72, as amended);
- *Sanitary Norms on Industrial Noise 0–64* of 1973 (d.v.23/73);
- *Regulation of the Council of Ministers on the Procedure of Assessing and Imposing Sanctions for Environmental Damage or Pollution beyond Permissible Levels* of 1993 (d.v.15/93);
- A draft Law on Noise.

9.3 Noise zones

Municipal land use plans may provide for noise zones and determine the environmental status of the area according to the level of noise pollution.

9.4 Activities subject to noise regulation

Sanitary Norms 0–64 on the Permissible Levels of Noise in Housing and Public Build-ings and Residential Areas of 1972 prohibit activities which result in noise in excess of permitted levels and concentrations.

9.5 Standards

Sanitary Norms 0–64 on the Permissible Levels of Noise in Housing and Public Build-ings and Residential Areas of 1972 set the ambient noise standards.

Ambient standards are determined in decibels and depend on the area affected and on the time of day.

Zones	Day Standards	Night Standards
Inner cities	60 db	50 db
Industrial zones	70 db	70 db
Hospitals, resorts etc	45 db	35 db

Sanitary Norms on Industrial Noise 0–64 of 1973 set noise standards for industrial sources.

Standards for industrial noise depend on the type of work performed at the place of work.

Places of Work	Standards
Industrial companies	85 db
Laboratories	75–65 db
Offices	60 db
Places of intensive intellectual work	50 db

9.6 Permitting process

9.6.1 Authorities

No special permits are required. Government control of noise is performed through the EIA process. An investment project will not be allowed to proceed if it is determined that it would violate applicable noise standards.

9.6.2 Application requirements

No noise emission permits, apart from EIA approval, are required.

9.6.3 Timing

No noise emission permits, apart from EIA approval, are required.

9.6.4 Permit conditions

No noise emission permits, apart from EIA approval, are required.

9.6.5 Public participation

The public has a right of access to information on the state of the environment and a right to participate in the EIA procedure.

9.7 Enforcement

9.7.1 Compliance checking and monitoring

The Environment Ministry and its Regional Environmental Inspectorates enforce noise limits.

The Sanitary Epidemiological Institutes exercise sanitary control over the impact of noise on human health.

9.7.2 Penalties and sanctions

The activity of installations which produce noise above the prescribed limits can be halted by the Environment Ministry and the Ministry of Health.

Monetary sanctions may be imposed by the Environment Ministry on legal persons or sole proprietors for violation of noise standards. The level depends on the amount of the violation of the noise limits and the length of the violation.

Fines may be imposed for violating noise regulations.

10. Hazardous and non-hazardous waste management

10.1 Summary

Waste Handling Requirements:	Waste is categorised into industrial waste and municipal waste.
	No permitting system exists as regards the generation, treatment or disposal of waste. EIA approval is required for storage and waste disposal facilities.
	There is a prohibition against the importation of hazardous waste into Bulgaria.

Public Participation:	The public has a right of access to information on the state of the environment, provided a legitimate right to know can be demonstrated. The public has a right to participate in the EIA procedure.
Enforcement:	The Ministry of Regional Development and Construction enforces the legislation on waste. The Environment Ministry imposes monetary sanctions for pollution of the soil with heavy metals or waste.

10.2 Sources of legislation relating to waste management

- *Law on Protection of Air, Water and Soil from Pollution* of 1963 (d.v.84/63, as amended);
- *Environmental Protection Law* of 1991 (d.v.86/91, as amended);
- *Ordinance on Public Sanitation* of 1973 (d.v.79/66);
- Article 201(4) of the *Ordinance on the Implementation of the Law on Regional Development and Town Planning* of 1973 (d.v.62/73);
- *Regulation of the Council of Ministers on the Procedure of Assessing and Imposing Sanctions for Environmental Damage or Pollution beyond Permissible Levels* of 1993 (d.v.15/93);
- Draft Law On Solid Waste;
- Draft Regulation On Hazardous Waste.

10.3 Categories of waste

Under Bulgarian law waste is categorised into industrial and municipal solid waste. There is no special legislation regarding the treatment, storage and disposal of hazardous waste separate from that on non-hazardous waste.

The draft Law on Solid Waste will categorise the waste into municipal waste and special (industrial) waste. The enforcement authority for the special waste will be the Environment Ministry and the Ministry of Regional Development and Construction will enforce legislation regarding municipal waste.

The draft Regulation on Hazardous Waste creates two new categories: hazardous and non-hazardous waste. Although Bulgaria is still not a party to the *Basle Convention*, hazardous waste will be classified into four categories depending on its origin and chemical composition based on the classification system of the *Basle Convention*.

10.4 Waste storage and treatment

10.4.1 Generator requirements

Waste management plans

The *Law on Protection of Air, Water and Soil from Pollution* of 1963 provides that industrial plants are obliged to maintain facilities for waste collection and for the treatment of effluents, hazardous substances and other waste which pollutes the soil. Under Article 201(4) of the *Ordinance on the Implementation of the Law on Regional Development and Town Planning* of 1973, any plans for the treatment of industrial waste must contain measures for recycling and be pre-approved. Since laws governing recycling of waste were repealed in 1991 it is not clear what authority must approve the waste management plans.

At present there are no specific regulations and requirements for the storage and treatment of industrial waste.

Permits

Under current laws no permits are required for waste storage and treatment.

The draft Law on Solid Waste establishes a permit system for the transportation, storage, treatment and disposal of waste. Permits for industrial waste will be issued by the Environment Ministry.

Generators of waste have no record keeping requirements under current laws.

The draft Regulation on Hazardous Waste will impose record keeping requirements on generators of hazardous waste. Reporting will be required twice a year. At the beginning of the year expected levels of waste are to be estimated. At the end of the year the waste generated during the previous year must be reported.

Similar record keeping requirements are to be provided for in the Law on Waste for all solid waste.

10.4.2 Operator requirements

There are 23 joint stock corporations and eight state-owned companies which recycle metal, paper, plastic, textiles. There are no specific regulations governing their activity.

Facilities for treatment of hazardous waste must be at least 3,000 m away from residential areas.

All facilities for treatment, neutralisation and storage of waste are subject to mandatory EIA by the Regional Environmental Inspectorates.

The draft Law on Solid Waste establishes a permit system for the transportation, storage, treatment and disposal of waste. Permits for industrial waste will be issued by the Environment Ministry.

10.4.3 Public participation

The public has a right of access to information on the state of the environment, provided a legitimate interest can be demonstrated and a right to participate in the EIA procedure.

10.5 Waste Disposal

10.5.1 Generator requirements

In general enterprises must ensure that their industrial waste discharges do not violate ambient quality standards of water, air and soil.

Under current laws no permits are required for waste disposal.

The draft Law on Solid Waste will provide for a permit system for the disposal of hazardous and non-hazardous waste.

10.5.2 Operator requirements

Most waste disposal facilities in Bulgaria are run by the Municipalities which do not require permits under current legislation. Household waste as well as the waste of smaller generators is disposed there.

Most big industrial concerns operate their own landfills. Municipalities determine the location of the landfills according to specific requirements. Plans for landfills have to include measures for the protection of natural resources and for capping the landfills and replanting the land. No special permits are required for operators of landfills. But the location of a landfill and any other facility for waste disposal under ground are subject to mandatory EIA.

The sanitary protection zone around the landfills must be 3,000, 1,000 or 300 m depending on their size, the kind of waste disposed and the method of operating them.

10.5.3 Charges

No charges for waste disposal exist at present. The imposition of charges is considered in the draft Law on Solid Waste. The charges will depend on the level of toxicity and the effectiveness of the method of disposal or neutralisation of the waste.

10.5.4 Public participation

The public has a right of access to information on the state of the environment, provided a legitimate interest can be demonstrated and a right to participate in the EIA procedure.

10.6 Transport of waste

10.6.1 Labelling and containers

There are no requirements governing the transport of industrial waste.

The Environment Ministry is empowered by the *Environmental Protection Law* of 1991, as amended, to issue instructions for the transportation of hazardous waste. No such instructions have been issued to date.

10.6.2 Transboundary movement

Under Article 7(1) of the *Environmental Protection Law* of 1991, as amended, it is forbidden to import waste and hazardous substances into the country in the following circumstances:

- When the chemical composition of waste has not been determined or if there are no methods for its analysis available in Bulgaria;
- To store, dispose, destroy or recycle waste and hazardous substances;
- To use waste and hazardous substances in manufacturing if an EIA is not approved.

If provided in an international treaty to which Bulgaria is a party, and if the necessary security measures are complied with, the government of Bulgaria may allow waste and hazardous substances to be transported across its territory in transit to another final destination. In that event a permit is required from the Environment Ministry.

10.7 Recycling requirements

There are no recycling requirements at present.

Decree No. 1541 of the former State Council of 1983 governing recycling and reuse of waste was repealed in 1991. The administration of recycling in Bulgaria has been decentralised. The central Recycling Company was closed. Twenty-three joint stock corporations and eight state companies were formed. They collect waste metal, paper and plastic, among other wastes.

10.8 Enforcement

10.8.1 Compliance checking and monitoring

The Environment Ministry and the Regional Environmental Inspectorates monitor the contamination of soil by hazardous materials and waste.

The Ministry of Health monitors the risks to human health.

The Ministry of Regional Development and Construction monitors compliance with waste management and disposal regulations.

There is no comprehensive record of the hazardous waste sites in Bulgaria. Efforts are currently being made to identify existing hazardous waste sites.

10.8.2 Penalties and sanctions

The Environment Ministry imposes monetary sanctions for pollution of the soil with pesticides, heavy metals, organic waste, construction waste, inert waste, manure, fertilizers, radioactive substances and industrial waste. Sanctions depend on the nature of the pollutant and the size of the polluted area.

11. Chemicals storage, handling and emergency response

11.1 Summary

Types of Activity:	The manufacture, sale, storage, transportation and use of highly active toxic substances requires a permit from the Ministry of the Interior. The manufacture and sale of goods having an impact on human health requires a permit from the Sanitary Epidemiological Institute.

Timing:	One month.
Emergency Response:	Persons dealing with hazardous chemicals have a duty to prepare remedial plans and train staff to handle emergencies.
Public Participation:	No public participation is provided for in the permitting process. In the event of environmental pollution or damage, as well as in case of immediate danger of significant pollution or damage to the environment, the public must immediately be informed.
Enforcement:	The Ministry of Interior, the Ministry of Health, the Ministry of Agricultural Development, Land Use and Restitution of Real Property, the Committee of Forests and the Environment Ministry can halt the operations if a permit for toxic substances is violated or no permit has been obtained. The Ministry of the Interior can revoke the permit if its conditions are violated. The Permanent Governmental Commission on Natural Disasters and Large Industrial Accidents or the bodies authorised by it can conduct checks at any time and their recommendations are mandatory for persons dealing with hazardous substances.

11.2 Sources of legislation relating to chemicals storage, handling and emergency response

11.2.1 Storage

- *Environmental Protection Law* of 1991 (d.v.86/91, as amended);
- *Ordinance on the Manufacture, Sale, Storage, Transportation and Use of Highly Active Toxic Substances* of 1973 (d.v.34/73);
- *Regulation No. 7 on the Sanitary Requirements for Health Protection of Residential Areas* of May 25, 1992 (d.v.46/92).

11.2.2 Handling

- *Environmental Protection Law* of 1991 (d.v.86/91, as amended);
- Article 15 and Article 21(4) of the *Law on Public Health* of 1973, (d.v.88/73, as amended);
- *Regulation 5190 of Ministry of Health on the Procedure of Issuing Permits by the State Sanitary Inspection for the Manufacture and Sale of Goods Having Impact on Human Health* of 1966 (d.v.85/66);
- *Ordinance on Manufacture, Sale, Storage, Transportation and Use of Highly Active Toxic Substances* of 1973 (d.v.34/73);

- *Regulation No. 7 on the Sanitary Requirements for Health Protection of Residential Areas* of May 25, 1992 (d.v.46/92).

11.2.3 Emergency response

- *Regulation No. 2 on Protection from Accidents from Activities Connected with Hazardous Chemicals* of 1990 (d.v.100/90)

11.3 Regulatory Requirements

11.3.1 Storage and handling

The *Environmental Protection Law* of 1991, as amended, provides that the Environment Ministry, jointly with other Ministries, issues instructions for the transportation, storage and disposal of hazardous substances including various chemicals. No instructions have been issued yet.

At present provisions exist relating to highly active toxic substances. The *Ordinance on the Manufacture, Sale, Storage, Transportation and Use of Highly Active Toxic Substances* of 1973 sets forth the general regulations concerning the manufacture, sale and storage of highly active toxic substances classified according to their degree of toxicity.

Permits

Every activity connected with highly active toxic substances requires a permit from the Ministry of Interior.

Permits for the manufacture, sale, storage, regular use, analysis or testing of highly active toxic substances are valid for one year. Permits for transportation, one time use, import or export and destruction of highly active toxic substances are valid for 30 days.

A permit is issued to the manager of a facility who is directly responsible for health and safety matters relating to the handling of highly active toxic substances.

The Sanitary Epidemiological Institute issues permits for the manufacture and sale of goods having an impact on human health. Such a permit is required for the import and production of chemicals and synthetic materials to be used for industrial, agricultural or household purposes; additives to the foodstuffs; disinfectants, cosmetic and cleaning solvents. The Sanitary Epidemiological Institute issues a written permit within 30 days of the filing of the application.

Construction

Industrial facilities which intend to use highly active toxic substances in their production process must be built under the direct supervision of the Ministry of Health, the Environment Ministry and the Ministry of Interior. Representatives of these Ministries are members of the Governmental Approval Commissions which approve the construction of such industrial facilities.

Facilities for storage of highly active toxic substances must comply with certain requirements such as being surrounded by wire and cement poles, and having separate entrances for people and cars.

Labelling

Labelling is required for the transportation of highly active toxic substances (substances with lethal dose of 100 mg/1 kg). Permits by the Department of the Ministry of Interior, to the region of which the toxic substances are transported, are required when the toxic substances are to be transported from the region of one Department of Ministry of Interior to another.

Transportation

The vehicles used for transportation should be suitable for transport of toxic substances, covered and provided with necessary equipment in case of fire or spills.

The vehicles must have a red flag 40/40 centimetres on the left back side and labels marked "highly toxic" both on the front and back sides. Along with the driver there should be another person acquainted with the basic qualities of the transported cargo and responsible for it.

11.3.2 Emergency response

The Permanent Governmental Commission on Natural Disasters and Large Industrial Accidents determines protective zones around the enterprises manufacturing and storing hazardous chemicals which have toxic and explosive characteristics. In other cases sanitary protective zones vary from 3,000 m, to 100 m, depending on the nature of the manufacturing activity.

Regulation No. 2 on Protection from Accidents from Activities Connected with Hazardous Chemicals of 1990 determines the duties of persons dealing with hazardous chemicals: to estimate annually the danger and consequences of accidents; to develop plans of action in case of accidents; to train staff to handle emergencies and to possess the necessary equipment for use in case of accidents.

11.4 Public participation

The *Environmental Protection Law* of 1991 states that in the event of environmental pollution or damage, including the case of natural disasters, industrial accidents and fires, the public must be immediately informed by the Environment Ministry, the Regional Environmental Inspectorates, the Municipalities, the manufacturers of goods and the providers of services regarding the environmental impact of the environmental pollution or damage, the measures taken to restrict and eliminate it and any action citizens must take for their own safety.

The *Environmental Protection Law* of 1991, as amended on 4 December, 1992, extends the obligation of the above mentioned persons and entities to provide the public with information in cases of imminent threats of significant pollution or damage to the environment. The obligation requires urgent measures to prevent the potential harmful consequences of pollution.

11.5 Enforcement

11.5.1 Compliance checking and monitoring

Enforcement of legislation on the import, manufacture, use, storage and transport of highly active toxic substances is carried out by the Ministry of Health, the Ministry of

Interior Affairs, the Ministry of Agriculture, the Committee of Forests and the Environment Ministry.

Enforcement of legislation on emergency response is carried out by the Permanent Governmental Commission on Natural Disasters and Large Industrial Accidents or the bodies authorised by it. They can conduct checks at any time and their recommendations are mandatory for persons dealing with hazardous chemicals.

Municipalities also have enforcement functions. They check the state of the facilities. If the requirements of *Regulation No. 2 on Protection from Accidents from Activities Connected with Hazardous Chemicals* of 1990 are violated they inform the Permanent Governmental Commission.

11.5.2 Penalties and sanctions

Companies may be required to discontinue operations if they violate the *Ordinance on the Manufacture, Sale, Storage, Transportation and Use of Highly Active Toxic Substances* of 1973.

The permit issued allowing the activity involving highly active toxic substances may be revoked by the Ministry of Interior Affairs.

The Permanent Governmental Commission and bodies authorised by it can require companies to discontinue operations if they breach *Regulation No. 2 on Protection from Accidents from Activities Connected with Hazardous Chemicals* of 1990.

Annex A

List of Key Legislation

1. Overview

- *Constitution* (d.v.56/91), Articles 15, 18(1) & (2), 21(1) and 55;
- *Law on Mines and Quarries* (d.v.92/57, 17/58, 68/59, 104/60, 84/63, 27/73, 36/79);
- *Law on Protection of Air, Water and Soil from Pollution* (d.v.84/63, 26/68, 29/69, 95/75, 3/77, 1/78, 26/88, 86/91);
- *Law on Protection of Nature* (d.v.47/67, 3/77, 39/78, 28/82, 26/88, 86/91);
- *Law on Waters* (d.v.29/69, 3/77, 36/79, 44/84, 36/86, 24/87);
- *Law on Regional Development and Town Planning* (d.v.29/73, 32/73, 87/74, 3/77, 102/77, 36/79, 3/80, 45/84, 19/85, 36/86, 14/88, 31/90, 32/90, 15/91);
- *Law on Protection of Arable Land and Pastures* (d.v.27/73, 3/77, 102/77, 102/81);
- *Law on Public Health* (d.v.88/73, 92/73, 63/76, 28/83, 66/85, 27/86, 89/88, 87/89, 99/89, 15/91);
- *Law on Marine Environment* (1987);
- *Law on Local Self-government and Local Administration* (d.v.77/91);
- *Environmental Protection Law* (d.v.86/91 and 100/92);
- *Law on Transformation and Privatisation of State-owned and Municipal-owned Enterprises* (d.v.38/92);
- *Ordinance on Law on Protection of Air, Water and Soil from Pollution* (d.v.80/64 and 9/78);
- *Ordinance on the Implementation of the Law on Protection of Nature* (d.v.33/69 and 9/78);
- *Regulation on the Collection, Spending and Control of the Environmental Protection Funds* (d.v.5/93).

2. Environmental liability

- *Law on Obligations and Contracts*, Articles 45 and 50 (d.v.275/50, 2/50, 2/50, 69/51, 92/52, 65/63, 27/73, 16/77, 28/82, 30/90);
- *Law on Ownership* (d.v.19/51, 12/58, 90/60, 99/63, 26/73, 27/73, 54/74, 87/74, 55/78, 36/79, 19/85, 14/88, 91/88, 38/89, 31/90, 77/91);
- *Law on the Protection of Air, Water and Soil from Pollution* (d.v.84/63, 26/68, 29/69, 95/75, 3/77, 1/78, 26/88, 86/91);

- *Criminal Code* (d.v.26/68, 29/68, 92/69, 26/73, 27/73, 89/74, 95/75, 3/77, 54/78, 89/79, 28/82, 31/82, 44/84, 41/85, 79/85, 80/85, 89/86, 90/86);
- *Law on Waters* (d.v.29/69, 3/77, 36/79, 44/84, 36/86, 24/87);
- *Law on Administrative Offenses and Penalties* (d.v.92/69, 88/73, 54/78, 28/82);
- *Law on the Protection of Arable Land and Pastures* (d.v.27/73, 3/77, 102/77, 102/81);
- *Law on Regional Development and Town Planning* (d.v.29/73, 32/73, 87/74, 3/77, 102/77, 36/79, 3/80, 45/84, 19/85, 36/86, 14/88, 31/90, 32/90, 15/91);
- *Law on Protection of Agricultural Property* (d.v.54/74, 22/76, 36/79, 28/82);
- *Administrative Procedure Law* (d.v.90/79, 9/83, 26/88, 94/90, 25/91, 61/91);
- *Law on Ownership and Use of Arable Land*, Article 10(10) (d.v.17/91, 20/91, 74/91, 18/92, 28/92);
- *Commercial Law*, Article 15 (d.v.48/91);
- *Environmental Protection Law* (d.v.86/91 and 100/92);
- *Law on Economic Activity of Foreign Persons and on Protection of Foreign Investment* (d.v.8/92);
- *Law on Transformation and Privatisation of State-Owned and Municipal-Owned Enterprises Act* (d.v.38/92);
- *Ordinance on Manufacture, Sale, Storage, Transportation and Use of Highly Active Toxic Substances* (d.v.34/73);
- *Regulation of the Council of Ministers on the Procedure of Assessing and Imposing Sanctions for Environmental Damage or Pollution beyond Permissible Levels* of 1993 (d.v.15/93);
- *Regulation No. 3 of Environment Ministry on the Standards for Permissible Concentrations of Hazardous Substances in the Soil* (d.v.36/79);
- *Regulation No. 7 of the Environment Ministry on Determining the Quality of Running Surface Water* (d.v.96/86);
- *Regulation No. 2 on Protection from Accidents from Activities Connected with Hazardous Chemicals* (d.v.100/90).

3. Environmental audits

- *Environmental Protection Law*, Paragraph 9(2) of the Transitional and Concluding Provisions (d.v.86/91 and 100/92);
- *Regulation No. 3 of the Environment Ministry on Standards for Permissible Concentrations of Hazardous Substances in the Soil* (d.v.36/79);
- *Regulation No. 7 of the Environment Ministry for Determining the Quality of Running Surface Water* (d.v.96/86);
- *Regulation of the Council of Ministers on the Appraisal of Units of Property Slated for Privatisation*, Article 6(3) (d.v. 50/92);
- *Regulation No. 1 on Environmental Impact Assessments* (d.v.10/93);
- Article 2(1) of the *Regulation of the Council of Ministers on Mandatory Information Which Must Be Provided to Potential Buyers of Interests and Shares in Transformed State-Owned and Municipal-Owned Enterprises* (d.v.9/93).

4. Land use planning

- *Law on Regional Development and Town Planning* (d.v.29/73, 32/73, 87/74, 3/77, 102/77, 36/79, 3/80, 45/84, 19/85, 36/86, 14/88, 31/90, 32/90, 15/91);
- *Law on Protection of Arable Land and Pastures* (d.v.27/73, 3/77, 102/77, 102/81, 58/85, 24/87, 26/89);
- *Administrative Procedure Law* (d.v.90/79, 9/83, 26/88, 94/90, 25/91, 61/91);
- *Ordinance on the Implementation of the Law on Regional Development and Town Planning* (d.v.62/73, 24/75, 87/76, 37/78, 7/80, 44/80, 38/83, 48/85);
- *Ordinance on the Implementation of the Law on Protection of Arable Land and Pastures* (d.v.65/73, 35/75, 5/76, 9/78);
- *Tariff on Local Fees of the Council of Ministers Enacted in Furtherance of the Law on Local Taxes and Fees* (d.v.45/75, 64/76, 73/79, 78/80, 17/82, 68/82, 77/83, 78/84, 48/85, 2/86, 19/88, 62/88, 23/89, 33/90);
- *Tariff on the Amount of Deposits according to Article 15 and 17 of the Law on Protection of Arable Land and Pastures* (d.v.33/86 and 83/89);
- *Regulation No. 6 on Governmental Approval of Completed Construction Work* (d.v.5/89 and 6/89) adopted by Ministry of Economics and Planning and the Committee on Regional Development and Town Planning;
- *Regulation No. 7 on the Sanitary Requirements for Health Protection of Residential Areas* (d.v.46/92).

5. Environmental Impact Assessments (EIAs)

- *Environmental Protection Law*, Articles 19–23 (d.v.86/91 and 100/92);
- *Regulation No. 1 on Environmental Impact Assessments* (d.v.10/93).

6. Air emission requirements applicable to the operation of industrial and commercial facilities

- *Law on Protection of Air, Water and Soil from Pollution*, Articles 5–7 (d.v.84/63, 26/68, 29/69, 95/75, 3/77, 1/78, 26/88, 86/91);
- *Environmental Protection Law* (d.v.86/91 and 100/92);
- *Ordinance on the Implementation of the Law on Protection of Air, Water and Soil from Pollution*, Articles 1–22 (d.v.80/64 and 9/78);
- *Regulation No. 2 on the Maximum Permissible Concentrations of Hazardous Substances in the Air of Residential Areas* (d.v.16/84 and 17/92);
- *Norms on Maximum Permissible Level of Emissions into Air adopted by the Ministry of Environment* (d.v.81/91);

- *Regulation No. 7 on the Sanitary Requirements for Health Protection of Residential Areas* (d.v.46/92);
- *Regulation of the Council of Ministers on the Procedure of Assessing and Imposing Sanctions for Environmental Damage or Pollution beyond Permissible Levels* of 1993 (d.v.15/93).

7. Water requirements applicable to the operation of industrial and commercial facilities

- *Law on Protection of Air, Water and Soil from Pollution*, Articles 8–13 (d.v.84/63, 26/68, 29/69, 95/75, 3/77, 1/78, 26/88, 86/91);
- *Law on Waters* (d.v.29/69, 3/77, 36/79, 44/84, 36/86, 24/87);
- *Environmental Protection Law* (d.v.86/91 and 100/92);
- *Ordinance on the Implementation of the Law on Protection of Air, Water and Soil from Pollution*, Articles 23–37 (d.v.80/64 and 9/78);
- *Regulation on Water Use of National Water Council* (d.v.16/71);
- *Regulation on Issuing Permits for Constructions Which Might Negatively Affect the Natural Flow of Water, Drainage, Navigation, the Movement of Ice or Water Quality* (d.v.82/73);
- *Regulation No. 6 of the Ministry of Health and the Environment Ministry on the Discharge Underground of Effluent Containing Hazardous Substances* (d.v.87/81);
- *Regulation No. 7 of the Environment Ministry for Determining the Quality of Running Surface Water* (d.v.96/86);
- *Regulation No. 9 of the Ministry of Regional Development and Construction on the Use of Water Supply and Sewage Systems* (d.v.88/87).
- *Regulation No. 2 on Sanitary Protective Zones around the Water Sources and the Equipment for Drinking Household Water Supply* of 1989 (d.v.68/89)
- *Regulation of the Council of Ministers on the Procedure of Assessing and Imposing Sanctions for Environmental Damage or Pollution beyond Permissible Levels* (d.v.15/93)

8. Noise requirements applicable to the operation of industrial and commercial facilities

- *Sanitary Norms 0–64 on the Permissible Levels of Noise in Housing and Public Buildings and Residential Areas* (d.v.87/72 and 16/75);
- *Sanitary Norms on Industrial Noise 0–64* (d.v.23/73);
- *Regulation of the Council of Ministers on the Procedure of Assessing and Imposing Sanctions for Environmental Damage or Pollution beyond Permissible Levels* (d.v.15/93).

9. Hazardous and non-hazardous waste management

- *Law on Protection of Air, Water and Soil from Pollution* (d.v.84/63, 26/68, 29/69, 95/75, 3/77, 1/78, 26/88, 86/91);
- *Environmental Protection Law* (d.v.86/91 and 100/92);
- *Ordinance on Public Sanitation adopted with Decision No. 127 of Council of Ministers* (d.v.79/66);
- *Ordinance on the Implementation of the Law on Regional Development and Town Planning*, Article 201 (d.v.62/73);
- *Regulation of the Council of Ministers on the Procedure of Assessing and Imposing Sanctions for Environmental Damage or Pollution beyond Permissible Levels* (d.v.15/93).

10. Chemicals storage, handling and emergency response

- *Law on Public Health*, Articles 15 and 21(4) (d.v.88/73, 92/73, 63/76, 28/83, 66/85, 27/86, 89/88, 87/89, 99/89, 15/91);
- *Environmental Protection Law* (d.v.86/91 and 100/92);
- *Regulation 5190 of Ministry of Health on the Procedure of Issuing Permits by the State Sanitary Inspection for the Manufacture and Sale of Goods having Impact on Human Health* (d.v.85/66);
- *Ordinance on Manufacture, Sale, Storage, Transportation and Use of Highly Active Toxic Substances* (d.v.34/73);
- *Regulation No. 2 on Protection from Accidents from Activities Connected with Hazardous Chemicals* (d.v.100/90);
- *Regulation No. 7 on the Sanitary Requirements for Health Protection of Residential Areas* of 25 May, 1992 (d.v.46/92).

Annex B

List of Permitting and Enforcement Authorities

Environment Ministry
67 William Gladstone Street
Sofia
tel.(02) 87-61-51

Ministry of Health
5 Sveta Nedelia Square
Sofia
tel. (02) 86-31

Ministry of Agriculture
55 Hristo Botev Boulevard
Sofia
tel. (02) 85-31

Privatisation Agency
P.O.B. 1397
29 Aksakov Street
Sofia
tel.(02) 87-59-87

Ministry of Regional Development and
Construction
17 Cyril and Metodi Street
Sofia
tel.(02) 8-38-41

Committee of Forests
17 Antim I Street
Sofia
tel.(02) 86-171

Committee on Geology and Mineral
Resources
22 Kniagina Luisa Boulevard
Sofia
tel.(02) 83-851

National Water Council
12 Uzundjovska Street
Sofia
tel. (02) 83-08-87

Permanent Governmental Commission on
Natural Disasters and Large Industrial
Accidents
30 Nikola Gabrovski Street
Sofia
tel.(02) 61-10-67

Commission on Land
55 Hristo Botev Boulevard
Sofia
tel.(02) 85-31 /ext.343/

Ministry of Interior
P.O.B. 192
29 Shesti Septemvri Street
Sofia
tel.(02) 87-75-11

Chief Inspection on Governmental and
Technical Control
47 Hristo Botev Street
Sofia
tel.(02) 51-06-00

Sofia Regional Environmental
Inspectorate
26 Lavele Street
Sofia
tel.(02) 87-26-73

Blagoevgrad Regional Environmental
Inspectorate
21 Todor Alexandrov Street
tel.(073) 2-54-92
Blagoevgrad

Burgas Regional Environmental
Inspectorate
63 Perushtitsa Street
Burgas
tel.(056) 3-60-68

Haskovo Regional Environmental
Inspectorate
28 Saedinenie Street
Haskovo
tel.(038) 2-21-73

Mihailovgrad Regional Environmental
Inspectorate
4 Zitomirska Street
Mihailovgrad
tel.(096) 2-25-45

Pasardzik Regional Environmental
Inspectorate
3 Gourko Street
Pasardzik
tel.(034) 2-83-89

Pernik Regional Environmental
Inspectorate
24 Krakra Street
Pernik
tel.(076) 2-25-71

Pleven Regional Environmental
Inspectorate
1 Alexander Stamboliiski Street
Pleven
tel.(064) 2-91-36

Plovdiv Regional Environmental
Inspectorate
122 Maritsa Street
Plovdiv
tel.(032) 22-89-74

Rousse Regional Environmental
Inspectorate
3 Dobri Nemirov Street
Rousse
tel.(082) 27-80-28

Shoumen Regional Environmental
Inspectorate
77 Chervenoarmeiska Street
Shoumen
tel.(054) 5-14-97

Smolian Regional Environmental
Inspectorate
10 Bulgaria Street
Smolian
tel.(0301) 2-70-04

Stara Zagora Regional Environmental
Inspectorate
119 Stoletov Street
Stara Zagora
tel.(042) 2-38-73

Varna Regional Environmental
Inspectorate
4 D. Orlov Street
Varna
tel.(052) 23-43-81

Veliko Turnovo Regional Environmental
Inspectorate
19 Hristo Botev Street
Veliko Turnovo
tel.(062) 2-03-51

Vratsa Regional Environmental
Inspectorate
81 Eksarh Josif Street
Vratsa
tel.(092) 2-47-61

Annex C

List of Proposed Legislation

1. Overview

- Law on Marine Environment;
- Law on Protected Areas;
- Law on Protection of Biological Diversity;
- Freedom of Information Law.

2. Land use planning

- Law on Protection of Land;
- Law on Proposed Investments and Construction;
- Law on Land Use and Development.

3. Air emission requirements applicable to the operation of industrial and commercial facilities

- Law on Air;
- Regulation on Ambient Air Quality.

4. Water requirements applicable to the operation of industrial and commercial facilities

- Law on Waters;
- Regulation on Determining Standards for Industrial Waste Discharged Directly into Water Basins;
- Regulation on the Admissible Content of Harmful Substances in Industrial Waste Water Discharged Into the Sewer Systems;
- Regulation on Determining Charges for Waste Water Discharge;
- Regulation on the Quality of Surface Waters;
- Regulation on the Requirements for the Quality of Waters Designated for the Main Types of Water Usage.

5. Noise requirements applicable to the operation of industrial and commercial facilities

- Law on Noise.

6. Hazardous and nonhazardous waste management

- Law on Solid Waste;
- Regulation on Hazardous Waste.

Annex D

Environmental Standards

- *Norms on Maximum Permissible Level of Emissions into Air* (d.v.81/91);
- *Regulation No.2 on the Maximum Permissible Concentrations of Hazardous Substances in the Air of Residential Areas of the Ministry of Health jointly with the Environment Ministry* (d.v.16/84 and 17/92);
- *Regulation No.7 of the Ministry of Environment on Determining the Quality of Running Surface Waters* (d.v.96/86);
- *Regulation No.3 of the Ministry of Environment on the Standards for Permissible Concentrations of Hazardous Substances in the Soil* (d.v.36/79);
- *Sanitary Norms 0–64 on the Permissible Levels of Noise in Housing and Public Buildings and Residential Districts* (d.v.87/72 and 16/75).

Annex E

International Conventions

- Convention on the Conservation of European Wildlife and Natural Habitats, 19 September 1979, Europ. T.S. No. 104.
- Protocol of 1978 Relating to the International Convention for the Prevention of Pollution from Ships, 17 February 1978, 17 I.L.M. 546 (entered into force 2 October 1983).
- Convention for the Protection of the Ozone Layer, 22 March, 1985, 26 I.L.M. 1529 (entered into force 22 September 1988).
- Montreal Protocol on Substances that Deplete the Ozone Layer, 16 September 1987, 26 I.L.M. 1550 (entered into force 1 January 1989).
- Convention on Long-Range Transboundary Air Pollution, 13 November 1979, 18 I.L.M. 1442 (entered into force 16 March 1983).
- Convention on Early Notification of a Nuclear Accident, 26 September 1986, 25 I.L.M. 1370 (entered into force 27 October 1986).
- Convention on Assistance in the Case of a Nuclear Accident or Radiological Emergency, 26 September 1987, 25 I.L.M. 1377 (entered into force 26 February 1987).

Annex F

Investment Projects Subject to EIAs

Appendix No. 1 to the *Environmental Protection Law* of 1991 lists projects of international significance:

- Crude oil refineries (with the exception of plants producing only lubricants from crude oil) and facilities for gasifying and burning coal and bituminous shales with a daily capacity of 500 tons and more;
- Thermal power stations and other combustion facilities, with a heat output of at least 300 megawatts as well as nuclear power stations and other facilities equipped with nuclear reactors (with the exception of research facilities for the production and conversion of nuclear fuel and nuclear fuel raw materials, the maximum capacity of which does not exceed 1 KWh of constant thermal load);
- Facilities for the storage, neutralisation or reprocessing of radioactive nuclear waste;
- Complex metallurgical facilities for the primary production of cast iron and steel;
- Facilities for obtaining, processing and revising asbestos and asbestos products, for annual production of asbestos cement products exceeding 20,000 tons, and for other uses of asbestos exceeding 200 tons a year;
- Facilities for the drilling of crude-oil and gas;
- Complex chemical facilities;
- First-class roads, highways, national railways as parts of international railway traffic and airports with the main take-off and landing runways longer than 2,100 metres;
- Commercial water routes as well as inland water routes and ports for inland navigation, which enable the navigation of ships with a tonnage exceeding 1,350 tons;
- Facilities for the neutralisation of waste, underground storage sites and surface storage sites for wastes.

Appendix No. 2 to the *Environmental Protection Law* of 1991 lists projects of national and local significance:

Agriculture
- Restructuring of rural land holdings;
- Use of uncultivated land or semi-natural lands for intensive agricultural purposes, as well as projects for the utilization of agricultural lands, damaged by the operation of industrial installations;
- Water-management and land reclamation projects in agriculture;

72

- Initial deforestation where this may lead to ecologically negative after-effects, and projects for deforestation for the purposes of land use for agricultural production or of another type of land use;
- Poultry-rearing installations (for more than 20,000 heads of poultry);
- Livestock-rearing installations (for more than 50 heads of cattle, 100 heads of pigs or 200 heads of sheep);
- Fish-breeding installations;
- Reclamation of land from the sea by means of drainage and drainage of swamps.

Mining Industry
- Peat mining;
- Deep drillings (with the exception of drillings for seismological investigations) for the purposes of: geothermal energy from earth bowels; deposit of radioactive waste; water-supplies;
- Mining of inert, lining-rock and effective materials;
- Underground and open-cast coal mining;
- Petroleum exploration;
- Natural gas exploration;
- Mining and processing of ores;
- Bituminous shale mining;
- Bituminous shale, non-ore and mineral resources mining;
- Surface facilities for the mining of petroleum, natural gas and ores;
- Coke works and dry coal distillation;
- Production of cement and other building materials and products.

Energy Industry
- Industrial facilities for the generation of electricity, steam and hot water, unless included in Appendix No. 1 to the *Environmental Protection Law* of 1991;
- Gas, steam and hot water, conduits and their facilities including electric energy transmission by overhead circuits;
- Natural gas surface storage facilities;
- Underground storage facilities for explosive and inflammable gases;
- Industrial briquetting of coal;
- Surface storage of fossil fuels;
- Nuclear fuel production and enrichment facilities;
- Facilities for the reprocessing of irradiated nuclear fuels and processing and final deposit of radioactive waste, unless included in Appendix No. 1;
- Hydroelectric power generation.

Metallurgical industry, engineering industry and electronics
- Iron works and steel works, including foundries, forges and rolling mills, unless included in Appendix No. 1;
- Production, smelting, refining, drawing and rolling of non-ferrous metals, excluding precious metals;
- Production of pressed, drawn and stamped products;

- Surface inoculation and mechanical treatment of metals;
- Production of boilers, reservoirs, tanks and other sheetmetal containers;
- Works for production and assembly of motor vehicles and motor-vehicle engines;
- Construction of shipyards;
- Facilities for construction and repair of aircraft;
- Manufacture of railway equipment;
- Excavations by explosives;
- Facilities for the roasting and sintering of ores;
- Manufacture of accumulators;
- Manufacture of electric-insulation materials;
- Manufacture of glass, faience and porcelain.

Chemical Industry
- Treatment of intermediate chemical products and production of chemicals, unless included in Appendix No. 1;
- Preparation of plant-protection products and pesticides, pharmaceutical and cosmetic products, paint, dyeing-materials, elastomers and peroxides;
- Manufactures on the basis of biotechnological processes;
- Storage of petroleum, petrochemical and chemical products.

Food Industry
- Manufacture of vegetable and animal oils and fats;
- Canning industry for meat, fruits and vegetables;
- Manufacture of dairy products;
- Breweries and malt plants;
- Manufacture of confectionery, syrup and alcoholic beverages;
- Construction of facilities for the slaughter of animals;
- Starch manufacture;
- Factories for fish-meal and fish-oil;
- Sugar factories;
- Manufacture of spirit and bread-yeast;
- Processing of vegetal raw materials, manufacture of fodder mixtures, flours and tobacco products.

Textile, Leather, Wood and Paper Industries
- Wool scouring, degreasing and bleaching installations;
- Manufacture of fibre board, particle board and plywood;
- Manufacture of pulp, paper and cardboard;
- Fibre-dyeing factories;
- Manufacture and processing of cellulose;
- Tannery and leather-dressing workshops;
- Processing of raw rubber and the manufacture and treatment of elastomer-based products.

Infrastructure
- Development plans;
- Construction of roads, internal railway sections, harbours, including river ports, and airfields, including for agricultural aviation, unless included in Appendix No. 1;
- Cableways and other mountain lines;
- Canalisation and correction of river beds;
- Dams and other water reservoirs designed to collect water and store it on a long-term basis;
- Tramway routes, speedy urban underground and elevated railways, suspended lines, railways with a particular designation, and similar railways for passenger transport;
- Construction of oil and gas pipeline installations;
- Long-distance aqueduct installations;
- Yacht harbours.

Other Projects
- Development plans and projects in zones and complexes for recreation and tourism;
- Racing and test tracks for cars and motorcycles;
- Installations for the reprocessing, rendering harmless and storage of waste, unless included in Appendix No. 1;
- Treatment facilities;
- Sludge-deposition sites;
- Storage of scrap iron;
- Test sites for engines, turbines or reactors;
- Manufacture of artificial mineral fibres;
- Manufacture, packing, loading or placing (in cartridges or in relevant capsules) of gunpowder and explosives;
- Slaughterhouses;
- Radio and TV transmitters and other emitters of electromagnetic fields.

Project Modifications
- Modification of projects, included in Appendices No. 1 and 2 to the *Environmental Protection Law* of 1991, undertaken exclusively or mainly for the development and testing of new methods or products and not lasting for more than one year.

Czech Republic and Slovak Republic

Prepared for the European Bank for Reconstruction and Development and the
Commission of the European Communities by
White & Case*

1. Overview

1.1 The Guidelines

1.1.1 Background

Investments in the Czech Republic and the Slovak Republic are subject to many legal and economic requirements. This document focuses specifically on those compliance, operational and liability issues which arise from environmental protection measures and affect investments.

The Guidelines are intended to enable investors to familiarise themselves with the basic environmental regulatory regime relating to commercial and industrial greenfield site developments, joint venture operations or company acquisitions in the Czech Republic and Slovak Republic.

The Guidelines review institutional arrangements for environmental control, legislative requirements and procedures, time implications for permitting, public access to information, liability and sanctions. Because environmental policy, legislation and infrastructure in the Czech Republic and Slovak Republic are currently undergoing radical changes the review covers both current and proposed future arrangements.

Guidelines for the following CEE countries have been prepared on behalf of the European Bank for Reconstruction and Development and the Commission of the European Communities by Environmental Resources Limited and White & Case:

- Bulgaria;[1]
- Czech Republic and Slovak Republic;[1]

[1]   Guidelines prepared by White & Case.

*   White & Case acknowledges the valuable contribution in the preparation of the Investors' Environmental Guidelines: Czech Republic and Slovak Republic of Richard A. Horsch, Esq., Sophia Drewnowski, Esq., and Margaret Wachenfeld, Esq. of White & Case.
    White & Case would like to thank Professor Vaclav Mezricky, Dr. Eva Kruzikova, Dr. Anna Klimkova, Dr. Lubomira Zimanova, Dr. Bozena Gasparikova and Dr. Viera Bobrikova who acted as consultants to White & Case in its preparation of these Guidelines.

- Estonia;[1]
- Hungary;[1]
- Latvia;[2]
- Lithuania;[2]
- Poland;[1]
- Romania;[2]

These Guidelines present a description of the environmental regulatory framework as of February 1993. They provide a first step for investors in understanding environmental requirements but do not substitute for specific legal advice relating to particular sites.

Administrative and legal arrangements for environmental regulation are in a transition phase in the countries covered by these Guidelines. Requirements and implementation systems are subject to change. Investors are advised to discuss details of requirements with the authorities and check for any changes which may have taken place since February 1993.

1.1.2 Using the Guidelines

The Guidelines provide general guidance on environmental regulatory requirements applicable to foreign investment in commercial and industrial sectors of the economy. Some sections of the Guidelines, such as *Section 4* on Land Use Planning and *Section 5* on EIA are also applicable to other sectors of the economy such as agriculture, mining, forestry and fisheries. In relation to such types of activities however, it is advisable to review other applicable requirements which are outside the scope of the Guidelines.

Section 1 provides a quick reference to environmental regulatory requirements in two case studies, and in *Figure 1.1.2(a)* and *Figure 1.1.2(b)*. *Figure 1.1.2(b)* indicates how the Guidelines should be used by reference to the type of investment decision that has to be made.

The remainder of this section provides background information on the country and the following:

- Administrative structure;
- Legislative process and key items of legislation;
- Quick reference to the permitting process;
- Enforcement;
- Public participation.

Section 2 highlights the potential liabilities of investors. Liabilities potentially arising from past pollution to be taken into account at the time an investment is made and liabilities arising in the course of operating commercial and industrial facilities are presented separately. Additional details relating to specific sectors of control are provided in subsequent sections.

Section 3 identifies environmental auditing requirements and comments on the role of voluntary audits in achieving compliance.

Sections 4–11 provide guidance on permitting and related regulatory requirements for setting up and operating a commercial or industrial enterprise. Key aspects are presented at the beginning of each section for quick reference. Each section identifies the following:

---

[1]   Guidelines prepared by White & Case.
[2]   Guidelines prepared by Environmental Resources Limited.

Figure 1.1.2(a) Using the Guidelines: report structure

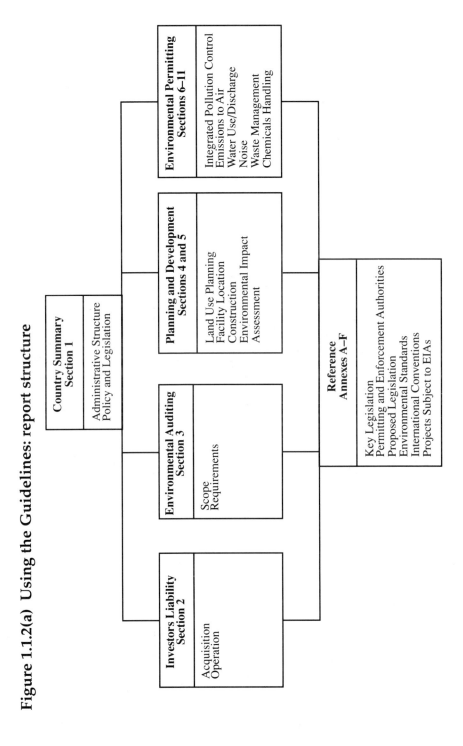

Figure 1.1.2(b) Using the Guidelines: summary by type of investment decision

Investment Decisions	Environmental Concerns	Sections in Guidelines
Choice of investment sector (eg commercial, services, manufacturing, energy)	Government and environmental bodies	1.4, 1.7, Annex B
	Existing and proposed legislation	1.5, Annex A & C
	Available forms of investment	1.2, 2.3.2
	Purchase of land	4.3
	Investments subject to EIA	5, Annex F
	Activities subject to permitting	6–11
	Permitting overview and examples	1.6
Development of a "greenfield site"	Government and environmental bodies	1.4, 1.7, Annex B
	Existing and proposed legislation	1.5, Annex A & C
	Purchase of land	4.3
	EIA requirements	5, Annex F
	Public participation	1.8
	Environmental standards	7, 8, 9, Annex D
Acquisition of existing facility and privatisation	Government and environmental bodies	1.4, 1.7
	Privatisation	1.2, 2.3.2
	Environmental liability	2
	Cleanup of contaminated sites	2.3
	Indemnification by government	2.3
	Environmental audits	3
	Environmental standards	7, 8, 9, Annex D
	EIA requirements (especially where modifications are made to existing facilities)	5, Annex F

Investment Decisions	Environmental Concerns	Sections in Guidelines
Redevelopment and expansion of commercial and industrial facilities	Government and environmental bodies	1.4, 1.7, Annex B
	Change of land use	4
	Construction permits	4
	EIA requirements	5, Annex F
	Permitting requirements	6–11
	Public participation	1.8
Operation of industrial and commercial facilities	Government and environmental bodies	1.4, 1.7, Annex B
	Environmental liability	2
	EIA requirements	5
	Public participation	1.8
	Integrated permitting	6
	Air requirements	7, Annex D
	Water requirements	8, Annex D
	Noise requirements	9, Annex D
	Waste management	10
	Chemical storage and handling	11
	Permitting overview and examples	1.6
	Compliance with international law	Annex E

- Key legislation;
- Activities covered;
- Requirements and Procedures;
- Timing;
- Public participation;
- Enforcement and sanctions.

Sections 4 and 5 outline requirements and procedures relating to land use planning, facility location and construction, and environmental impact assessment ("EIA"). *Section 6* indicates the extent to which environmental permitting is integrated.

Permitting and other regulatory requirements relating to air, water, noise, waste and chemicals are set out in *Sections 7–11*.

Annexes provide quick reference to existing and proposed legislation, contact points for the regulatory agencies, environmental standards, ratification of multilateral international conventions and investment projects subject to EIAs which are specifically identified in legislation.

1.2 The countries

The former Czechoslovakia peacefully ousted the communist government in the "Velvet Revolution" of 1989. As of 1 January 1993 the country split into two independent Republics.

The Czech Republic has a population of 10.37 million which covers a territory of 78,900 sq. km in Bohemia, Moravia and part of Silesia. It adopted a new *Constitution* on 16 December 1992.

The Slovak Republic has a population of 5.21 million and occupies 49,000 sq. km, in the territory of the former North Hungary. The Slovak Republic adopted a new Constitution on 1 September 1992.

After the communist government was ousted, the new government of the still unified country embarked on a privatisation programme to restructure its economy. The process, which included the "large privatisation" of major state enterprises and the small privatisation of retail shops and businesses, is currently being supervised by the Czech and Slovak Ministries of National Property Administration and Privatisation (in each case "Ministry of Privatisation") and the Republic National Property Funds.

On 16 December 1991, prior to the split into two Republics, the country signed an Association Agreement with the European Community ("EC") which was to establish free trade in goods, services and capital with the EC and to offset the fall in exports to the former COMECON countries. The accord was intended to lay the foundation for eventual full membership in the EC. As successor states to the former Federation, the Czech Republic and Slovak Republic will maintain individual associate memberships in the EC.

The Czech Republic and Slovak Republic have adopted all of the laws of the former Federation, including its environmental laws. The Slovak Republic is expected to amend some of the Federal environmental laws. Future environmental legislation and policies of the Republics are expected to be harmonised with the EC.

1.3 Administrative structure

The role of the Federal government was reduced in the summer of 1992 in preparation for the independence of the Czech Republic and Slovak Republic which took place on 1 January 1993. By that date, all Federal power-making authority and property had been divided between the two independent Republics.

1.3.1 Czech Republic

Most legislative and executive powers are concentrated at the central government level and lie with the Parliament of the Czech Republic and the Council of Ministers. On the regional level the country is organised into 76 Districts. The City of Prague has the status of a District. At the local level there are 6,000 self-governing Municipalities which also perform some administrative tasks assigned by law.

District Offices are an integral part of the state administrative structure and each has an environmental authority and a building authority that handle the administrative tasks assigned to them under environmental, land use and construction laws. District Office environmental authorities issue environmental permits in most of the environmental sectors.

Municipal Office environmental authorities have some power relating to the protection of natural resources and environmental law enforcement. Municipal Office building authorities issue construction permits if the District Offices specifically devolve that function to them.

1.3.2 Slovak Republic

Most legislative and executive powers are concentrated at the central government level and lie with the National Council of the Slovak Republic and the Council of Ministers.

On the regional level the country is organised into 38 Districts, 121 Sub-Districts and 2,826 independent, self-governing Municipalities. There are several separate specialised administrative structures, including a separate environmental administrative structure. The environmental structure consists of 38 District Offices of Environment and 121 Sub-District Offices of Environment which are supervised directly by the Ministry of Environment. These Environmental Offices are grouped into seven regions. They may inspect facilities, order remedial actions and assess penalties. The Sub-District Offices of Environment usually issue permits and make many of the decisions required under the environmental laws. They also perform certain functions under land use planning and construction laws. The District Offices of Environment act mainly as appeal bodies for decisions made at the Sub-District level.

The administrative structure in the environmental area is expected to change in the near future. The Slovak Republic intends to integrate District and Sub-District Offices of Environment into the general administrative system. Additional powers are expected to be transferred to the local self-governing Municipalities in 1994.

1.4 Government and environmental bodies

1.4.1 Ministries

Czech Republic

The Ministry of Environment has primary responsibility for the drafting of environmental legislation, the formulation of environmental policy and the enforcement of environmental laws in the following areas:

- Air;
- Water;
- Soil protection;
- Waste treatment and disposal;
- Nature protection;
- Landscape protection;
- Forestry;
- Protection of the Agricultural Land Fund;
- Protection of natural resources;
- Hunting and fishing;
- Geological surveys;
- Mining surveys;
- EIAs.

The Ministry of Environment's responsibilities include the maintenance of an information and monitoring system on the state of the environment. It is assisted in its enforcement responsibilities by the Czech Environmental Inspectorate as well as District and Municipal Offices.

The Ministry of Economy is responsible for land use planning as of 31 October 1992. This task was formerly carried out by the Ministry of Environment.

The Ministry of Privatisation is primarily responsible for the supervision and co-ordination of the privatisation process in the Czech Republic. It is assisted by the Czech National Property Fund, a body charged with disposition of state property.

The Ministry of Health is responsible for regulation of noise and toxic substances, as well as for general health and safety issues. It executes its responsibilities through Hygiene Offices on the District level.

The Ministry of Industry is responsible for energy policy.

Slovak Republic

The Ministry of Environment has primary responsibility for the drafting of environmental legislation, the formulation of environmental policy and the enforcement of environmental laws in the following areas:

- Nature protection;
- Water protection (though not water management);
- Air;
- Waste disposal and management;

- Territorial planning;
- Construction.

The Ministry of Environment executes its responsibilities through a network of District and Sub-District Offices of Environment. It is also assisted in its enforcement responsibilities by the Slovak Environmental Inspectorate.

The Ministry of Privatisation is primarily responsible for the supervision and co-ordination of the privatisation process in the Slovak Republic. It is assisted by the Slovak National Property Fund, a body charged with the disposition of state property.

The Ministry of Soil Management regulates water management, soil and forest protection and is assisted by four River Basin Authorities.

The Ministry of Health executes its responsibility for general health and safety matters through Institutes of Health on the District and Sub-District level. As the noise control structure in the Slovak Republic is currently being changed, it is unclear whether the Ministry of Health will be responsible for this area in the future. At present, the District Offices of the main state administration administer the noise laws with the assistance of the Institutes of Health.

1.4.2 Environmental bodies

Czech Republic

The Ministry of Environment enforces environmental laws through the Czech Environmental Inspectorate. The Environmental Inspectorate has 42 branches throughout the Republic. It has separate divisions for water, air, waste management, forestry and nature protection. It monitors compliance, issues administrative orders and imposes penalties in some sectors. Its powers are broadest in the air sector where it is authorised to issue permits.

In addition, the Ministry of Environment supervises the River Boards that manage and protect the river basins, carry out systematic monitoring of water quality and compliance and regulate water use.

The Ministry of Environment also supervises the activities of a number of environmental institutes:

- The Ecological Institute is currently training people to perform EIAs;
- The Hydrometeorological Institute provides weather forecasts and information on air pollution and climatic changes;
- The Water Management Institute conducts research on water supplies, sewage systems, water treatment, water sources and their protection and other water management issues.

Slovak Republic

The Ministry of Environment enforces environmental laws through the Slovak Environmental Inspectorate. The Environmental Inspectorate has two branch offices in the Republic. It monitors compliance with the laws governing soil and air protection and waste disposal. The Environmental Inspectorate also assesses penalties for violation of environmental regulations.

85

The Ministry of Environment supervises the activities of a number of environmental institutes:

- The Hydrometeorological Institute provides weather forecasts and information on air pollution and climatic changes;
- The Research Institute on Water Management carries out research and produces an annual report on water management issues;
- The Ecology and Biology Institute carries out research on environmental issues.

The Ministry of Soil Management supervises the four River Basin Authorities that issue water use permits and review water discharge permits.

1.4.3 Environmental Funds

Czech Republic

The Czech Republic has created a State Environmental Fund. The Fund derives its income from:

- Charges for waste water discharge, the use of groundwater, waste disposal and air emissions;
- Charges for the conversion of agricultural land for development;
- Payments for mining rights;
- Penalties for violation of environmental laws;
- State subsidies, tax revenues, loans and donations.

The Fund is to be used for:

- Protecting, improving, and monitoring the environment;
- Improving the functioning of streams and river catchments;
- Research and development, production and application of scientific and technological developments in environmental protection;
- Promoting environmental education.

Slovak Republic

The Slovak Republic has created a State Environmental Fund which is under the control of the Ministry of Environment. The Fund derives its income from:

- Charges for wastewater discharge, the use of groundwater, air emissions, and waste disposal;
- Penalties for violation of air protection and water laws;
- Donations.

Money from the Fund may be used only for the purpose of environmental protection and environmental education and can be disbursed as subsidies, grants or loans.

1.5 Environmental legislation

1.5.1 Legislative process

Czech Republic

The supreme legislative body in the Czech Republic is the Parliament. Under the new Czech *Constitution* the Parliament is divided into two chambers: the Chamber of Deputies and the Senate. The Senate does not actually exist at present. All basic social, economic and political questions are regulated by Acts. Other sources of legislation can be found in Decrees, Resolutions and Orders. Acts are the primary source of legislation and are adopted by the Parliament.

The process of passing an Act is commenced at the initiative of one of the following:

- Deputies of the Parliament;
- Council of Ministers.

Under the new *Constitution*, draft Acts in the environmental area are usually proposed by the Ministry of Environment. They are circulated to other Ministries for comment and revised, if necessary. A draft Act, which has been discussed and agreed upon by the Chamber of Deputies, is passed onto the Senate. The Senate discusses the draft Act and makes a decision upon it within thirty days. It can either approve or reject the draft Act or return it to the Chamber of Deputies with amendments or express an intention not to concern itself with it. If the Senate rejects a draft Act, the Chamber of Deputies votes once again. A simple majority vote of all Deputies is required to pass legislation. An Act becomes effective upon promulgation. It must be signed by the President of the Republic, the Prime Minister and the Chairman of the Chamber of Deputies. Thereafter it is published in *Sbirka zakonu (Sb.)*, the official law journal.

An Act may provide for the issuance of executive acts by the Council of Ministers or by individual Ministries. Executive acts, which are subordinate to Acts, take the form of Decrees if issued by the Council of Ministers.

Slovak Republic

The supreme legislative body in the Slovak Republic is the National Council of the Slovak Republic. All basic social, economic and political questions are regulated by Acts. Other sources of legislation can be found in Decrees, Resolutions and Orders.

Acts are the primary source of legislation and are adopted by the National Council.

The process of passing an Act is commenced at the initiative of one of the following:

- Deputies of the National Council;
- Committees of the National Council;
- Council of Ministers.

Draft Acts in the environmental area are usually proposed by the Ministry of Environment. They are circulated to other Ministries for comment and revised, if necessary. An absolute majority vote of all Deputies present in the National Council is required to pass legislation. An Act becomes effective upon promulgation. It must be signed by the Chairman of the National Council, the President of the Republic and the Prime Minister. Thereafter it is published in *Zbierka zakonov (Zb.)*, the official law journal.

An Act may provide for the issuance of executive acts by the Council of Ministers or by individual Ministries. Executive acts which are subordinate to Acts take the form of Decrees or Orders.

1.5.2 Legislation

At present, the principal environmental legislation in the Czech Republic and Slovak Republic was adopted by the former government of the Federation. This legislation is now in force in each of the Republics following implementing legislation passed by each Republic. As a result, although much of the basic environmental legislation in the Czech Republic and Slovak Republic is the same, its implementation differs. The *Act on the Environment, No. 17/1992* is the framework statute in the Czech Republic and Slovak Republic. It provides the legal basis for EIAs and contains environmental liability provisions. The main statute regulating air is the *Clean Air Act, No. 309/1991*, as amended by *Act No. 218/1992*. A new *Waste Act, No. 238/1991* regulates the generation, treatment, recycling and disposal of waste and introduces record-keeping requirements. The general structure of water protection is still contained in the *Water Act, No. 138/1973*.

The environmental legislation of the two Republics will diverge as they independently begin to replace old laws from the former regime. New laws are currently being drafted in both the Czech Republic and Slovak Republic on water and noise. In addition the Slovak Republic is working on a draft Act on Environmental Impact Assessments while the Czech Republic is preparing a draft Act on Contractual Environmental Liability Insurance.

1.6 Overview of permitting process and other regulatory requirements

The principal permits and approvals required by an investor intending to build and operate a commercial or industrial facility in the Czech Republic and Slovak Republic fall into three categories: land use and construction permits, EIAs and operational requirements.

Land use and construction permits are discussed in detail in *Section 4* below. EIAs which must be performed for projects identified in Appendices I and III of the *Act on the Environment, No. 17/1992*, are discussed in detail in *Section 5*. Operational requirements as regards air, water, noise, waste and chemical storage are discussed in detail in *Sections 6–10* below.

As regards operational requirements, permits are needed for air emissions, water use, wastewater discharge, noise, operation of waste management facilities, including the collection, accumulation, transport, storage and treatment of hazardous waste. There is no integrated permitting system in the Czech Republic or Slovak Republic.

The principal steps of the permitting and approval process are summarised in *Figure 1.6.1(a)* for the Czech Republic and *Figure 1.6.1(b)* for the Slovak Republic. The practical application of the permitting and approval process is illustrated in the two case studies discussed below.

Figure 1.6.1(a) Permitting Procedure — Czech Republic

Main Steps	*Authority*	*Timing*

Step 1. Permit for Change of Use of Land

Application to	District Office	30–60 days

Step 2. Environmental Impact Assessment

Application to	Ministry of Environment District Office	Not Fixed

Step 3. Location Decision

Application to	District or Municipal Office building authority	30–60 days

Step 4. Operating permits

Air Permit Application to	Environmental Inspectorate	30–60 days
Water Permits Application to	District Office	30–60 days
Noise Permit Application to	Hygiene Office	30–60 days
Waste Permit Application to	District Office	30–60 days

Step 5. Construction Permit

Application to	District or Municipal Office building authority	30–60 days

Step 6. Post-Construction Approval

Application to	District or Municipal Office building authority	30–60 days

Figure 1.6.1(b) Permitting Procedure — Slovak Republic

Main Steps	*Authority*	*Timing*
Step 1. Permit for Change of Use of Land		
Application to	District Office	30–60 days
Step 2. Location Decision		
Application to	Sub-District Office of Environment building authority	30–60 days
Step 3. Operating permits		
Air Permit Application to	Sub-District Office of Environment	30–60 days
Water Use Permit Application to	River Basin Authorities	30–60 days
Water Discharge Permit Application to	District Office with review by River Basin authorities	30–60 days
Noise Permit Application to	District Office	30–60 days
Waste Permit Application to	Sub-District Office of Environment	30–60 days
Step 4. Construction Permit		
Application to	Sub-District Office of Environment building authority	30–60 days
Step 5. Post-Completion Construction Approval		
Application to	Sub-District Office of Environment building authority	30–60 days

Steps of the permitting process

Czech Republic

- Pursuant to Section 25 of the *Federal Foreign Exchange Act, No. 528/1990*, as amended, and *Decree No. 611/1992 of the Ministry of Finance*, a foreign entity may not purchase land in the Czech Republic unless such a purchase falls within one of the exceptions to this provision which include the purchase of land as part of a privatisation project approved by the Czech government. A foreign entity may enter into a lease with a land owner, pursuant to the usual commercial procedures applicable in the Czech Republic, and obtain the right to construct on the land. A Czech entity (a Czech joint venture with foreign participation or a Czech limited liability company 100% owned by a foreign entity) however, can purchase land in the Czech Republic.
- If the proposed greenfield site is on agricultural land, the investor will have to obtain permission from the District Office environmental authority for a temporary or permanent exemption from agricultural land classification in order to use the land for industrial purposes. In practice, this type of permission may be very difficult to obtain.
- Where an EIA is required, it must be performed prior to the application for a location decision.
- After any necessary EIA is performed, the investor must obtain a location decision, then a construction permit from the District or Municipal building authority.
- Approval for the construction and operation of large and medium air pollution sources, the replacement of air pollution control equipment and the use of new fuels must be obtained from the Czech Environmental Inspectorate. The introduction of new technology involving large and medium air pollution sources requires the approval of the Ministry of Environment.
- The District Offices issue water use and water discharge permits, permits for the construction and operation of water treatment facilities, and the construction and operation of waste management facilities.
- The District Hygiene Offices issue noise permits, where necessary, and oversee compliance with the health laws on the safe handling of toxic and chemical substances.
- Once the facility is constructed and ready to be used, construction approval from the District or Municipal Office building authorities is required to commence facility operations.

Slovak Republic

- Pursuant to Section 25 of the Federal *Foreign Exchange Act, No. 528/1990*, as amended, and *Decree No. 465/1991 of the Ministry of Finance*, as amended, a foreign entity may not purchase land in the Slovak Republic unless such a purchase falls within one of the exceptions to this provision, which includes the purchase of land as part of a privatisation project approved by the Slovak government. A foreign entity may enter into a lease with a land owner, pursuant to the usual commercial procedures applicable in the Slovak Republic, and obtain the right to construct on the land. A Slovak entity with foreign participation may only purchase land with approval from the Ministry of Finance.
- If the proposed greenfield site is on agricultural land, the investor will have to apply to the Agricultural Land Fund supervised by the Ministry of Soil Management and then to the relevant District Office for a temporary or permanent exemption from agricultural land classification in order to use the land for industrial purposes.

91

- An EIA may be required, but the Slovak Republic has not yet adopted any legislation in this area.
- The investor must obtain a location decision, then a construction permit from the Sub-District Office of Environment building authority.
- Approval for the construction and operation of large and medium air pollution sources, the replacement of air pollution control equipment and the use of new fuels must be obtained from the Sub-District Office of Environment.
- The River Basin Authorities issue water use permits and the District Offices of Environment issue water discharge permits subject to approval by the River Basin Authorities.
- Permits from the Sub-District Office of Environment are required for the construction and operation of waste management facilities.
- Noise regulation and permitting is currently being changed.
- The Hygiene Institutes at District level oversee compliance with the health laws on the safe handling of chemical substances.
- Once the facility is constructed and ready to be used, construction approval from the Sub-District Office of Environment building authority is required to use the building.

At present the law does not require that operating permits be obtained in any special sequence. As regards the construction or redevelopment of facilities, the law requires that an EIA be performed before a construction permit is issued.

1.6.1 Case study 1

Foreign investor forming a joint venture with an existing company, with the joint venture acquiring two industrial plants and wishing to close one and refurbish the other to produce tyres.

Land use
Czech Republic:

A Czech joint venture with foreign participation wishing to purchase two industrial plants does not require approval from the Ministry of Finance in the Czech Republic. Depending on the scope of the refurbishment, a location decision may have to be obtained from the District or Municipal building authority.

Slovak Republic:

A Slovak joint venture with foreign participation wishing to purchase two industrial plants requires approval from the Ministry of Finance in the Slovak Republic. Depending on the scope of the refurbishment a location decision may have to be obtained from the Sub-District Office of Environment building authority.

Environmental Impact Assessments (EIAs)
Czech Republic:

No EIA appears to be required in the Czech Republic prior to the refurbishment of a plant to manufacture tyres.

Slovak Republic:

In the Slovak Republic an EIA may be required under future legislation.

Operating permits

The industrial plant which will manufacture tyres will require operating permits for the operation of any air pollution sources, the use of surface or groundwater, and wastewater discharge. Permits for the treatment, storage and disposal of hazardous waste must be obtained. In certain circumstances noise permits may be necessary.

In the Czech Republic these permits in each instance are issued as follows:

- The Ministry of Environment issues permits for the introduction of new technology involving air pollution sources. The Environmental Inspectorate issues permits for the operation of large and medium air pollution sources.
- The District Offices issue permits for water use and wastewater discharge.
- The District Offices issue all waste permits except those for the transboundary movement of waste which are issued by the Ministry of Environment.
- The Hygiene Offices at District Level issue noise permits, where necessary.

In the Slovak Republic these permits are issued as follows:

- The Sub-District Offices of Environment issue permits for the operation of air pollution sources and the introduction of technology large and medium air pollution sources.
- The River Basin Authorities issue permits for water use and approve permits for wastewater discharge issued by the District Offices of Environment.
- The Sub-District Offices of Environment issue permits for the operation of waste treatment facilities and the treatment of hazardous waste.
- The District Offices issue noise permits. The issuance of noise permits in the Slovak Republic in the future will be determined by new regulations.

Construction permits and approvals

The joint venture company will have to apply for a construction permit for the refurbishment of the second plant, provided such refurbishment is significant enough to fall within this requirement. A construction permit approval will also be required in that case before facility operations can be commenced.

The joint venture will be required to maintain the closed plant in reasonable condition. If it decides to tear the building down, a construction permit must be obtained.

1.6.2 Case study 2

Foreign company wishing to acquire a greenfield site and build a new paper mill.

Land use

In the Czech Republic and Slovak Republic the purchase of land by a foreign legal entity is not permitted under the Federal *Foreign Exchange Act of 1990, No. 528/1990*, as amended, unless such a purchase falls within one of the exceptions to that provision which includes the purchase of land as part of a privatisation project approved by the Czech government or Slovak government. In the Czech Republic the Ministry of Finance must be notified after any such purchase. In the Slovak Republic prior approval must be obtained from the Ministry of Finance. Foreign persons have been granted limited rights over land. Consequently, a foreign company can acquire the right to construct a building on a greenfield site from the owner of that site in accordance with the usual commercial requirements under Czech laws and Slovak laws. The foreign company must apply for a location decision and for approval of construction on the greenfield site. In the Czech Republic a location decision is obtained from the District or Municipal building authority. In the Slovak Republic Sub-District Office of Environment building authorities issue location decisions.

Environmental Impact Assessments (EIAs)

The construction and operation of a paper mill are subject to the EIA process in accordance with the Federal *Act on the Environment, No. 17/1992*, Appendix I, §6.3. An EIA must, therefore, be prepared and evaluated by the relevant Republic environmental authorities even before the company applies for a location decision.

In the Czech Republic, the relevant authority is the Ministry of Environment according to the Czech *Act on Environmental Impact Assessment*, Appendix 1, §5.1. As no EIA legislation has yet been adopted in the Slovak Republic, the Federal EIA provisions are not in force.

Operating permits

The paper mill will require the same categories of operating permits as the second industrial plant in *Case Study No. 1*.

Construction permits and approvals

A construction permit is required to build a new paper mill. In the Czech Republic an investor should apply for such a permit to the District or Municipal Office building authority. In the Slovak Republic the Sub-District Office of Environment building authorities issue construction permits. After the construction is complete, approval of the construction must be obtained from the relevant building authorities.

1.7 Enforcement of environmental legislation

Czech Republic

The Ministry of Environment is responsible for the enforcement of the environmental laws and acts through the Environmental Inspectorate. The District and Municipal Offices share responsibility for environmental enforcement.

In the air sector, the Environmental Inspectorate supervises compliance and imposes penalties and remediation orders on large and medium air pollution sources. The role of the District Offices is limited to notifying the Environmental Inspectorate of violations. Municipal Offices monitor compliance by small and mobile pollution sources.

In the water sector, the Environmental Inspectorate supervises compliance and issues administrative orders and imposes penalties. District Offices impose penalties and together with the Municipal Offices also supervise compliance and issue administrative orders.

In the area of waste management, the Environmental Inspectorate supervises compliance, issues administrative orders and imposes penalties and compliance orders. The District Offices also supervise compliance, impose penalties and issue administrative orders. They can halt operations if facilities fail to comply with the applicable requirements. The Municipal Offices can impose penalties and issue administrative orders in a limited range of cases.

In performing inspection activities, the authorities can enter a property to inspect a facility and any relevant books and records.

The Ministry of Environment acts as the final appeal body within the environmental structure.

Slovak Republic

The Ministry of Environment has overall responsibility for the enforcement of the environmental laws.

The Environmental Inspectorate is entitled to impose penalties for violation of the environmental laws. The District and Sub-District Offices of Environment also impose penalties but in addition, can order facilities to take remedial action.

The Environmental Inspectorate and District and Sub-District authorities are authorised to enter property for the purpose of inspecting and carrying out monitoring and otherwise supervising compliance with the law. If there is overlapping jurisdiction with respect to a particular violation, the Offices of the Environment have priority over the Environmental Inspectorate.

The Ministry of Environment is the final appeal body within the environmental structure.

1.8 Public participation

1.8.1 Public access to information

The Federal *Act on the Environment* provides for the public's right of access to true and accurate information about the state of the environment, activities which could affect the environment, and measures taken by the authorities to prevent or remedy environmental damage.

In addition, a number of the new environmental laws in specific areas also address public access to information. The Federal *Clean Air Act* requires public authorities to provide timely access to information on air quality and emissions from individual air pollution sources. Under the Federal *Water Act* persons showing a justified interest can have access to the register of water permits. Waste generators, waste transporters and operators of waste management facilities have an obligation to keep detailed records. It is unclear, at present, whether such records will eventually be made available to the public.

The Slovak Republic has begun working on a freedom of information law in the environmental area.

1.8.2 Provision of information

There is no general obligation on the government under the Federal *Act on the Environment* to disclose or report information to the public. Several environmental laws in specific areas, however, oblige authorities and polluters to report certain information to the public.

The Federal *Clean Air Act* obliges large and medium size air pollution sources to inform the public regarding emissions from sources of air pollution and action taken to reduce pollution generally and in emergency situations. Authorities in each Republic are required to promulgate warning and restriction measures during smog situations.

In the Slovak Republic public access to information about water management is provided through the publication of a yearly report.

The Federal *Waste Act* intends that the waste management plans of the authorities in each Republic will be made public.

The Czech and Slovak Ministries of Environment also publish a variety of materials discussing the state of the environment. For example, the Czech Ministry of Environment published the *Blue Books* in 1990 and the *Rainbow Programme* in 1991 reviewing the state of the environment and environmental law in the Czech Republic.

1.8.3 Public consultation

Consultation with the public is provided for in the areas of land use planning, EIAs and water permits. *See Sections 4, 5 and 7* below.

The Federal *Act on the Environment* gives citizens the right to "approach the relevant authority, and claim, in a prescribed manner, his or her legal rights," as provided under the environmental laws. It is unclear how this provision will be implemented.

2. Environmental liability

2.1 Summary

Liability of Investors for Past Pollution:	Under the Federal *Commercial Code* the purchaser of an enterprise assumes all the rights and liabilities of the enterprise.
	In the Czech Republic indemnifications are provided by the government to investors on a case-by-case basis. As regards enterprises whose privatisation projects were submitted after 29 February, 1992, the government's policy under *Resolution No. 455/1992* is to assume off-site environmental liabilities. The details of this policy are now being revised in the proposed Resolution No. 123/1993.
	In the Slovak Republic indemnifications are provided to investors on a case-by-case basis.

Investor Clean-up of Contaminated Sites:	The Czech and Slovak Ministries of the Environment have issued advisory opinions on soil and groundwater clean-up standards based on Dutch standards. These are non-binding.
Civil Liability:	Fault-based liability as well as strict liability of owners and operators of industrial facilities.
Administrative Liability:	Fines and administrative orders in cases of violation of environmental laws.
Criminal Liability:	Only natural persons are liable for crimes. Penalties for environmental crimes include fines and imprisonment.

2.2 Sources of legislation relating to environmental liability

Federal Law

- *Penal Code, No. 140/1961*, as amended;
- *Civil Code, No. 40/1964*, as amended;
- *Act on Land Use Planning and Construction, No. 50/1976*, as amended;
- *Commercial Code, No. 513/1991*, as amended;
- *Act on the Environment, No. 17/1992*;
- *Act on the Transfer of State Property to Other Persons, No. 92/1991*, as amended by *Act No. 92/1992 Amending and Transforming the Act on the Conditions of Transfer of State Property to Other Persons.*

Czech Republic

- *Czech Petty Offence Act, No. 200/1990*;
- *Resolution No. 455/1992 on Settlement of Environmental Liabilities of Enterprises pursuant to the Act on the Terms of Transfer of State Property to Other Persons*;
- *Methodical Instruction of the Ministry for the Management of State Property and Its Privatisation of the Czech Republic and the Ministry of the Environment of the Czech Republic of May 18, 1992 for Implementing Law No. 92 of February 18, 1992*;
- *Resolution No. 694/1992 regarding the Formation of Joint Ventures with Foreign Companies in the Automotive Industry in the Czech Republic*;
- Draft Resolution No. 123/1993 on the Settlement of Environmental Liabilities during the Privatisation Process.

Slovak Republic

- *Slovak Petty Offence Act, No. 372/1990*;
- *Methodical Instruction of the Ministry for Administration and Privatisation of the National Property of the Slovak Republic and of the Slovak Committee of Environment as of July 14, 1992 Regarding the Process of Assessment of Environmental Liabilities of an Enterprise within the Privatisation Project Presented by the Enterprise within the Second Wave Large-Scale Privatisation.*

2.3 Environmental liabilities for past pollution

2.3.1 Environmental liabilities and investment

An investor has to be aware of two types of potential environmental liabilities when making an investment in the Czech Republic and Slovak Republic:

- Liabilities arising from past environmental pollution caused by the former operation of Czech and Slovak state enterprises. These liabilities can encompass pollution at and migrating from the site of the enterprise, contamination migrating from off-site land-fills used by the enterprise and damage claims of employees and nearby residents.
- Liabilities associated with the current operations of a facility by the investor. These liabilities can encompass violations of law relating to permitting and other issues and liability for environmental damage under civil and criminal statutes.

An investor's exposure to environmental liabilities arising from past pollution is discussed herein in *Section 2.3*. Liabilities associated with the current operations of a facility are discussed below in *Section 2.4*.

The exact extent of an investor's liability for past pollution will depend on a variety of factors, including the form of the investment transaction, various environmental liability provisions and any indemnification provided to investors by the Czech government and Slovak government. Should the investor become responsible for the remediation of past pollution, the applicable environmental clean-up standards will have a bearing on the cost of such remediation.

2.3.2 Types of environmental liabilities

Investments in the Czech Republic and Slovak Republic may take a variety of forms. The Federal *Commercial Code* provides for the establishment of a number of business entities, including joint stock companies or limited liability companies incorporated under Czech or Slovak law. Joint ventures may be created with foreign participation. Foreign investors may also acquire stock in existing companies and purchase corporate assets.

Under Section 477 of the *Commercial Code* a purchaser of an enterprise assumes all the rights and liabilities of the enterprise, unless otherwise agreed to by the parties. The *Commercial Code* does not specifically address the question of environmental liabilities.

Section 486 of the *Commercial Code* provides that a purchaser shall be entitled to demand a reasonable discount off the purchase price "for missing or defective things". Under Section 484 the seller must notify the purchaser, at the latest in the contract of sale of an enterprise, of "all defects" of transferred things, rights and liabilities and other assets which the seller knew or should have known. The seller is liable for any damage which could have been prevented by such notification. It is unclear whether a seller's failure to notify a purchaser of pre-existing environmental pollution at the site of the enterprise of which the seller knew or should have known imposes liability on the seller under this provision. As the *Commercial Code* is so new, no caselaw or settled interpretations are available.

The large scale privatisation of state enterprises is governed by the *Act on the Transfer of State Property to Other Persons ("Large Privatisation Act")*. All liabilities of the enterprise are transferred to the new owner unless otherwise agreed in the purchase agreement between the purchaser of the state enterprise and the National Property Funds of the Czech Republic and Slovak Republic. The *Large Privatisation Act* does not specifically address the transfer of environmental liabilities. In practice, pre-existing environmental liabilities at the site of former state enterprises have been identified through environmental audits. Responsibility for such liabilities has been negotiated on a case-by-case basis between the seller (usually the Republic National Property Funds) and the buyer.

2.3.3 *Governmental indemnification of environmental liabilities*

Czech Republic
The Czech Republic has provided indemnification to investors for pre-existing environmental liabilities on a case-by-case basis. The indemnifications have been limited in amount and duration. In the case of strategic investments in important enterprises in the "first wave" of privatisation, the Czech Ministry of Privatisation and the National Property Fund have been willing to provide indemnification for environmental liabilities up to 100% of the purchase price of the enterprise and, in other cases, discounts have been given to the investor on the purchase price of the enterprise.

Resolution No. 455/1992 on the Settlement of Environmental Liabilities of Enterprises pursuant to the Act on the Terms of Transfer of State Property to Other Persons is applicable to all enterprises which submitted their privatisation projects after 29 February 1992. Under its provisions the Czech Republic has apparently agreed to assume the liabilities of these enterprises for off-site environmental damages arising from former operations. Since the language of *Resolution No. 455/1992* is not precise, it is unclear whether this provision also covers bodily injury to third parties caused by the former operations of the enterprise.

Resolution No. 455/1992 is currently being reviewed by the Czech Ministry of Environment and Ministry of Privatisation and is expected to be revised in 1993. A draft *Resolution No. 123/1993* is currently circulating for comment among various Czech Ministries.

Under *Resolution No. 694/1992* the Czech government has provided a limited environmental indemnity to the foreign joint venture partners in the Czech automotive industry.

Slovak Republic
To date the Slovak Republic has not formulated a policy on the indemnification of investors for the environmental liabilities of state enterprises arising from their past activities either in the context of a privatisation or where an investor becomes a joint venture partner. These issues are being dealt with on a case-by-case basis. It is generally known, however, that the Slovak National Property Fund has provided indemnification for environmental liabilities in the case of at least three privatised companies.

2.3.4 *Investor clean-up of contaminated sites*

Environmental clean-up standards
At present there are no legally binding clean-up standards either in the Czech Republic or the Slovak Republic pertaining to the remediation of contaminated soil and groundwater at the site of former state-owned enterprises.

The Ministries of Environment of the Czech Republic and the Slovak Republic have adopted advisory opinions concerning clean-up standards until binding legislation is enacted. The standards listed in the advisory opinions are modified versions of Dutch clean-up standards listing the permissible concentrations of a number of chemical substances in the soil and groundwater. *(See Annex D.)*

Escrow accounts

Some Central and East European governments have adopted escrow accounts as a financial mechanism in privatisation sales to help finance the cost of site remediation.

Resolution No. 455/1992 in the Czech Republic, provides for the setting aside of up to 50% of the purchase price of a qualified enterprise in a special account held by the State Fund for the Living Environment of the Czech Republic. Enterprises which qualify for this procedure must have submitted their privatisation projects to the Czech National Property Fund after 29 February 1992.

The procedure laid down by *Resolution No. 455/1992* requires the relevant environmental authority to impose a remediation order for clean-up within one year of the purchase and requires the new owner to prepare a remediation plan of site clean-up in response to the order. If the new owner's plan for site remediation is approved by the National Property Fund and the State Fund for the Living Environment, the State Fund reimburses the owner from the "escrow account" for clean-up costs properly incurred. According to the State Fund for the Living Environment, however, no money has been disbursed to date under the procedure in *Resolution No. 455/1992*.

There is no official governmental policy in the Slovak Republic to date regarding the setting aside of part of the purchase price of an enterprise to finance the cost of environmental remediation.

Environmental funds

Neither the Czech nor the Slovak Environmental Fund has specifically designated part of its income to finance the remediation of environmental pollution at the site of former state enterprises. It is unlikely, at least in the near future, that these Funds, with the limited amount of money they have, will finance the clean-up of contaminated sites undertaken by foreign investors.

Case examples

Investors who purchased enterprises in the so-called "first-wave" of privatisation (those enterprises for which privatisation plans were submitted before 29 February 1992), have individually negotiated with the Czech government the terms of environmental indemnifications for environmental liabilities arising from the past operations of those enterprises.

- Dow Chemical agreed to purchase 51% of the industrial chemicals company, Chemicke Zavody Sokolov and agreed to share with the Czech government the environmental liabilities associated with the previous operations of the enterprise.
- As regards other strategic companies in the "first-wave" of privatisation, the government has been willing to indemnify investors for environmental liabilities arising from

past activities of the enterprises up to an amount equivalent to 100% of the purchase price.

- As regards the indemnification of "second-wave" enterprises, the government has used the principles of *Resolution No. 455/1992* and a standard contract based on the *Resolution* as the starting point for its negotiations on environmental liability issues with investors.

2.4 Environmental liabilities arising from facility operation

2.4.1 Civil liability

At present, neither the Czech Republic nor the Slovak Republic has enacted comprehensive environmental legislation on civil environmental liability. Environmental liability provisions are found in legislation passed by the former Federal government.

Fault-based liability

Fault-based liability is governed by Section 420 of the Federal *Civil Code* which provides that a person who breaches a legal duty must provide compensation for any resulting damage.

Under Section 27 of the *Act on the Environment* anyone who causes damage to the environment is obliged to restore it to its original condition or, if this is not possible, to pay monetary compensation or both. Detailed regulations implementing this provision were to be enacted by each Republic.

Strict liability

Under Section 420a of the Federal *Civil Code* a person running an operation is strictly liable for damage caused to others through the running of the operation. The plaintiff has to prove the damage and a causal link between the damage and the operation of the enterprise. The operator is not liable in two situations:

- The damage was a result of force majeure (extraordinary circumstances beyond its control, external to the operation of the enterprise);
- The damage was due exclusively to the fault of the injured party.

Liability to compensate injured parties can arise even in cases where the activity is administratively permitted.

Unfair competition

Pursuant to Sections 41–55 of the Federal *Commercial Code*, endangering the environment is deemed unfair competition. Persons damaged by unfair competition may take legal action to halt the unfair practice and seek monetary compensation for damages and the forfeit of unjustified gains.

Statutes of limitation

The general statute of limitation under the *Civil Code* for contract and tort based claims is three years.

Remedies

The Federal *Civil Code* provides for monetary damages and injunctions, including the following remedies:

- Halting environmentally dangerous activities which can be ordered only by administrative authorities;
- Damages for personal injury and property damage;
- Damages for harm to natural resources.

Case examples

- In the 1980s several agricultural co-operatives were awarded damages for lost harvest by enterprises which had polluted agricultural land.

2.4.2 *Administrative liability*

Types of administrative liability

Administrative liability arises in the event of violations of environmental permits or statutes, regulations and legal requirements. The liability of a party under administrative laws does not preclude a civil law suit.

Fines

The Federal *Act on the Environment* authorises environmental authorities to impose the following fines on persons conducting business:

- Up to 1,000,000 Kcs for causing environmental damage by breaching legal obligations;
- Up to 500,000 Kcs for failure to take measures to avert a threat to the environment or environmental damage or failure to report the problem to the appropriate authorities.

There are specific administrative penalties associated with breaches of the environmental laws governing the various sectors.

Under the *Land Use Planning and Construction Act* the appropriate District, Subdistrict or Municipal Office building authorities in the Republics can impose fines on legal or natural persons that:

- Construct a small building or modify a building, or carry out maintenance work without the required notice to the building authorities;
- Construct a building, carry out ground modifications, make a change in a building or remove a building without the required permit;
- In constructing a building, fail to carry out any conditions imposed by state administrative authorities;
- Fail to maintain a building or carry out ordered modifications or safety measures;
- Supply improper construction materials or services;
- Engage a person to design the building who is not qualified;

- Exceed the time period for construction and thereby further contribute to environmental deterioration in the surrounding area;
- Use a building without the necessary construction approval.

The air protection authorities in each Republic may impose fines on operators of large and medium sized pollution sources that fail to:

- Comply with the smog regulations;
- Comply with remedies imposed by the air protection authorities where a violation has occurred;
- Operate a pollution source without a permit or operate a pollution source in violation of a permit;
- Abide by emission limits, keep records on emission or install monitoring equipment if required;
- Restrict activities or eliminate dangerous conditions during periods of endangerment to the air quality and to inform the public;
- Comply with remedies imposed by or other actions taken by authorities;
- Abide by the smog regulations.

The air protection authorities in each Republic can also impose penalties on persons who produce, import or sell fuel or mobile pollution sources that fail to meet the standards for fuel quality or emission limits imposed under separate regulations.

The Republic water management authorities may impose fines for:

- Use or discharge of water without a permit or in violation of permit conditions;
- Contamination of surface or groundwater;
- Damage to the public sewage system or the water supply;
- Breach of obligations imposed by the Federal *Water Act*.

The Czech District Offices and Slovak Sub-District Offices of Environment may impose fines on generators that fail to:

- Prepare waste management plans;
- Secure the proper collection, separation and storage of waste;
- Recycle or neutralise their waste;
- Maintain all necessary records;
- Report on the production and handling of special waste;
- Supply information with their products on how unused portions of the product and packaging can either be re-used or safely neutralised;
- Permit inspection authorities access to buildings and documents.

The Czech District Offices and Slovak Sub-District Offices of Environment may also impose fines on operators of waste storage, treatment or disposal facilities which:

- Operate without the necessary permits or approvals;
- Fail to publicise the types of waste the business collects or fail to accept the kinds of waste it publicly announced it will accept;

- Fail to securely store waste;
- Fail to give the inspection authorities access to buildings and documents;
- Fail to report to the authorities on the treatment of waste;
- Fail to treat waste where so requested by the authorities.

Administrative orders

The following administrative orders are generally available under environmental laws:

- Remedial orders;
- Temporary or permanent closure of facilities;
- Revocation of permits.

2.4.3 Criminal liability

Types of criminal liability

Under the Federal law of Czechoslovakia only natural persons could be criminally liable. This continues to be the case, in the Czech Republic and Slovak Republic.

There are two specific crimes in the environmental area:

- Intentional breach of the environmental protection laws resulting in serious environmental damage.;
- Negligent breach of the environmental protection laws resulting in serious environmental damage.

The statute of limitation for environmental crimes under the Federal *Criminal Code* is three to five years.

Lesser offences are regulated by the Czech *Petty Offence Act, No. 200/1990* and the Slovak *Petty Offence Act, No. 372/1990*. The provisions of these two Acts are identical with respect to environmental matters.

Under the Czech *Petty Offence Act*, the following acts are classified as petty offences:

- Breach of the environmental protection laws;
- Destruction of the forests, such as cutting down trees;
- Water management violations, such as washing cars too close to river bodies;
- Fishing or poaching game without a permit.

Penalties

Crimes are punishable with the following penalties:

- For intentional violations: imprisonment for between one to eight years depending on the severity of the damage caused or an order to terminate the activities causing the damage;
- For negligent violations: imprisonment for up to five years or a fine, or an order to terminate the activities causing the damage.

Petty offenses are punishable by fines of between 3,000–5,000 Kc/Sk and are subject to a one year statute of limitations.

3. Environmental audits

3.1 Summary

Sources of Legislation:	Audits are expressly required by the *Large Privatisation Act*, as amended, and the *Methodical Instructions* issued by the Ministries of Privatisation and Environment of each Republic but only during the privatisation process of enterprises in the "second wave" of privatisation. In practice, environmental audits are voluntarily performed by investors in most other investment situations.
Approved Requirements:	Under the *Large Privatisation Act*, as amended, an environmental evaluation is required of the current compliance status; the cost to bring the enterprise into compliance; a list of environmental charges and penalties paid by the enterprise; and an estimate of the environmental liabilities of the enterprise.
Clean-up Standards:	The Czech and Slovak Environmental Ministries have issued advisory opinions on soil and groundwater clean-up standards based on Dutch standards. These are non-binding in the Czech Republic and Slovak Republic.

3.2 Sources of legislation relating to environmental audits

Federal Law

● *Section 6a of Act No. 92/1992 Amending and Transforming the Act on the Conditions of Transfer of State Property to Other Persons* — amending *Act on the Transfer of State Property to Others, No. 92/1991.*

Czech Republic

● *Resolution No. 455/1992 of the Government of the Czech Republic on the Settlement of Environmental Liabilities of Enterprises Pursuant to Act No. 92/1991 on the Terms of Transfer of State Property to Other Persons,* as amended by *Act No. 92/1992;*
● *Methodical Instruction of the Ministry for the Management of State Property and Its Privatisation of the Czech Republic and the Ministry of Environment of the Czech Republic of May 18, 1992 for Implementing Section 6a of Law No. 92 of February 18, 1992.*

Slovak Republic

● *Methodical Instruction of the Ministry for Administration and Privatisation of the National Property of the Slovak Republic and of the Slovak Committee of Environment of July 14, 1992 Regarding the Process of Assessment of Environmental Liabilities of an Enterprise within the Privatisation Project Presented by the Enterprise within the Second Wave of Large-Scale Privatisation.*

3.3 Scope of activities subject to environmental audits and audit process

Federal Law

An amendment of 18 February 1992 to the Federal *Large Privatisation Act*, requires an environmental evaluation of any enterprise which submits a privatisation project after 29 February, 1992. This was generally understood to refer to enterprises in the so-called "second-wave" of privatisation.

The evaluation, which involves the performance of an environmental audit, must provide the following information:

- An environmental compliance review of the enterprise with an estimate of costs necessary to bring the enterprise into compliance with the environmental laws;
- A list of pollution charges, charges for natural resource use and any penalties paid by the enterprise within the last few years;
- An estimate of the environmental liabilities of the enterprise, including liabilities arising from past pollution.

Although, under the *Large Privatisation Act* environmental audits were only required in connection with "second-wave" privatisation sales, they have also been carried out by investors in other circumstances.

Czech Republic and Slovak Republic

The *Methodical Instructions* adopted in both the Czech Republic and Slovak Republic, provide further details about the scope and methodology of environmental audits.

3.4 Requirements relevant to environmental audits

Approved consultants

- *Czech Republic:*
  An Annex to the *Methodological Instruction* contains a list of environmental consulting firms in the Czech Republic which are qualified to perform environmental audits. Investors are not obliged to use one of the firms on the list. Many investors hire Western environmental consultants who often cooperate with their Czech counterparts.
- *Slovak Republic:*
  No list of approved consultants is provided in the *Methodical Instruction* but several Slovak environmental consulting firms have been established as a result of the new environmental audit requirements under the *Large Privatisation Act*. Foreign investors have tended to use Western consultants to carry out the audits.

Applicable clean-up standards

At present there are no legally binding clean-up standards in either the Czech Republic or the Slovak Republic pertaining to the remediation of contaminated soil and groundwater at the site of former state-owned enterprises.

The Ministries of Environment of the Czech Republic and the Slovak Republic adopted advisory opinions concerning clean-up standards until binding legislation is enacted. The standards listed in the advisory opinions are modified versions of Dutch clean-up standards listing the permissible concentrations of a number of chemical substances in the soil and groundwater.

Preparation and approval of remediation plans

- *Czech Republic:*

  As a practical matter, when environmental audits of enterprises are performed, the Czech Ministry of Privatisation, the Czech Environmental Inspectorate, and the Czech Ministry of Environment are consulted by the enterprise and the investor regarding remediation options at each site.

  Remediation plans for enterprises in "firstwave" privatisations and other enterprises outside the scope of *Resolution No. 455/1992* are being negotiated on a case-by-case basis with the Ministry of Privatisation, the National Property Fund and the Ministry of Environment.

  The preparation and approval of remediation plans for enterprises in "secondwave" privatisations are performed in accordance with the procedure set forth under *Resolution No. 455/1992*:

  (i)   The relevant District Office of Environment must order clean-up of the site of the purchased enterprise within one year of the acquisition;

  (ii)   The investor must prepare a technical remediation plan and provide remediation cost estimates in response to the remediation order;

  (iii)   The State Fund for the Living Environment approves the remediation plan and forwards its approval to the National Property Fund for review of the proposed expenditures;

  (iv)   If the remediation plan is accepted, the National Property Fund then transfers the necessary funds set aside from the purchase price paid by the new owner for the enterprise to the State Fund of the Living Environment. Reimbursement is made to the owner upon proof that expenditures have been incurred pursuant to the approved remediation plan.

- *Slovak Republic*

  Environmental audits of enterprises and proposed remediation options are reviewed by the District Office of Environment in co-operation with the Slovak Environmental Inspectorate.

  There is no specific procedure for review of remediation plans by the authorities, as is the case in the Czech Republic.

3.5 *National experience with environmental audits*

Pursuant to Section 6a of the Federal *Large Privatisation Act*, 1,247 environmental audits were submitted to the Ministry of Environment and of these, 1,035 audits were approved in the Czech Republic. The vast majority of the audits was performed by the enterprises themselves or by Czech environmental consultants. To date, only four audits have been conducted by foreign auditors and only two of the four audits have been approved. Only 80 out of 500 enterprises undergoing privatisation in the Slovak Republic under the provisions of the *Large Privatisation Act* have been the subject of environmental audits.

4. Land use planning

4.1 Summary

Types of Activity:	An investor must obtain a location decision, a construction permit and a construction approval in the event of any new construction, modification or extension to a building or the removal of a building.
Timing:	In principle 30 to 60 days.
Public Participation:	A public hearing is provided. Application documents are made available to the participants in the public hearing.

4.2 Sources of legislation relating to land use

Federal Law

- *Act on Land Use Planning and Construction, No. 50/1976*, as amended by *Act No. 262/1992*;
- *Decree on General Technical Requirements of Construction, No. 83/1976, as amended by Decree No. 376/1992*;
- *Decree on Land Use Data and Land Use Documentation, No. 84/1976, as amended by Decree No. 377/1992*;
- *Decree on More Detailed Regulation of Land Use Planning and Construction, No. 85/1976, as amended by Decree No. 378/1992*;
- *Foreign Exchange Act, No. 528/1990*, as amended.

4.3 Scope of activities subject to land use regulation

Investors planning to build new facilities on greenfield sites or to expand or redevelop existing facilities must comply with the land use and building regulations of the Czech Republic and the Slovak Republic. The principal law currently governing this area is the Federal *Act on Land Use Planning and Construction*.

Federal land use plans delineated the basic principles for the use and development of the territory of the former Czech and Slovak Federal Republic and set out the conditions for construction. Plans were prepared for large territorial units, residential areas and special zones for industry, agriculture, tourism, nature protection, etc.

Investors should be aware that, if they intend to construct on agricultural land, they may have to go through a procedure under the agricultural land laws to obtain an exemption from agricultural land classification.

Pursuant to Section 25 of the Federal *Foreign Exchange Act, No. 528/1990*, as amended, foreign individuals and companies may not purchase land in the Czech Republic and the Slovak Republic. The law provides for a number of exceptions including inheritance of land, purchase of land by members of the diplomatic corps and purchases of privatised enterprises together with the land on which they are situated, as part of the large privatisation programme governed by the *Large Privatisation Act*. Foreign investors may acquire other limited property rights, including limited rights to lease, occupy, use or build on land. Czech entities with foreign participation or Czech entities wholly- owned by foreign entities may purchase land in the Czech Republic. Notification to the Ministry of Finance is required after the purchase. Slovak entities with foreign participation wishing to purchase land must first obtain approval of the purchase price from the Slovak Ministry of Finance.

The siting and construction of a development project in the Czech Republic and Slovak Republic involves three steps: (i) obtaining a location decision; (ii) a construction permit; and (iii) construction approval. A location decision is required to obtain approval of the authorities with regards to the siting of the investment project and for changes in land use.

A construction permit is required for the construction, modification, maintenance or removal of any building regardless of its technical construction, purpose and duration of use, if not otherwise specified in the *Land Use Planning and Construction Act* or special regulations.

After construction is complete, if a construction permit was originally required for the construction of the building, a construction approval is required before the facility can commence operations. If the proposed structure is likely to affect interests protected by environmental regulations, the construction project can be approved only with the consent of the environmental authorities which can condition their approval on compliance with environmental requirements.

4.4 Permitting process

4.4.1 Authorities

Czech Republic

Location decisions, construction permits and construction approvals are issued by building authorities within the District Offices in the Czech Republic. The District Offices can assign the duties to the Municipal Offices, which is usually done if the Municipality has sufficient resources and expertise.

Slovak Republic

Location decisions, construction permits and construction approvals are issued by the building authorities within the Sub-District Offices of Environment.

4.4.2 *Application requirements*

Although the Federal *Land Use Planning and Construction Act* does not require it, applicants often visit the District or Municipal Office building authority to discuss their development project before submitting their application for permits in the Czech Republic and the Sub-District Office of Environment building authority in the Slovak Republic.

The detailed application requirements for the location decision, construction permit and construction approval are set out in the *Decree on More Detailed Regulation of Land Use Planning and Construction, No. 85/1976*, as amended. The discussion below lists the basic application documents for each process; further detailed documentation is required and in addition, supplementary documentation can be requested by the Czech District or Municipal Office building authorities and the building authorities of the Slovak Sub-District Offices of the Environment.

Location decisions

The application to obtain a location decision must include the following documentation:

- Name and address of the developer;
- Description of the proposed site for development;
- List and address of all parties which could be affected by the proposed construction;
- Description of the location of the proposed building;
- A plan of the construction;
- Necessary approvals or decisions from the government authorities.

If the proposed project requires an EIA and entails the development of a greenfield site, the EIA must be carried out before applying for the location decision *(see Section 5 below)*.

The application process is followed by a public hearing procedure discussed below. *(See Section 4.5.)*

Construction permits

An application for a construction permit must include the following information:

- Name and address of developer;
- Description of the proposed building;
- List and address of all parties which could be affected by the proposed construction;
- Description of the location of the proposed building;
- A plan of the construction;
- Evidence of the land ownership or the right to construct the building on land;
- Necessary approvals or decisions from other government authorities.

Construction approval

Once construction is complete, construction approval must be obtained from the Czech District or Municipal Office building authority or the Slovak Sub-District Office of Environment building authority before commencement of facility operations.

The basic application for the construction approval must include the following information:

- Description of the land and buildings;
- Expected term of completion of the construction and clearance of the site;
- Information on whether testing must be carried out on the building.

4.4.3 *Timing*

The Federal *Administrative Procedure Act* applies to location decisions, construction permits and construction approvals. It provides that decisions will be issued within 30 to 60 days. In practice it usually takes longer to obtain these decisions.

4.4.4 *Permit conditions*

Locations decisions, construction permits and construction approvals may be subject to numerous conditions to ensure that the necessary regulatory requirements are met and public interests are protected.

The Czech District or Municipal Office building authorities and the Slovak Sub-District Office of Environment building authorities must incorporate into the permits any comments presented by state administrative authorities, including the environmental authorities, during the public comment period. The building authorities must consider, but not necessarily incorporate, comments provided by the public.

4.5 *Public participation*

Federal Law

Under the Federal *Act on Land Use Planning and Construction* public participation is required during:

- Review of land use plans;
- Public hearings on location decisions;
- Public hearings on construction permits;
- Public hearings on construction approvals.

The *Act on Land Use Planning and Construction* was amended in April 1992. Its new public participation provisions provide for increased participation by the public. The public "participants" under the *Act* are neighbours, private individuals or businesses, which may be affected by the construction, and the concerned administrative authorities.

Land use plans for residential areas must be made available for public comment for a 30-day period. The land use planning authorities hold discussions with civic organisations and citizens which are published. Comments of public participants must be responded to in writing.

The new public participation provisions for a location decision, construction permit and construction approval are very similar.

Once the applicant has filed the appropriate papers and documentation with the Republic building authority, an announcement is made regarding the commencement of the relevant procedure to the relevant public participants. In practice, when the applicant files the application with the relevant building authority in each Republic, the applicant also sends a copy of the proposal and documentation directly to the public participants. An applicant can also arrange to meet each of the concerned administrative authorities to discuss any problems prior to each of the three proceedings.

The public comment period on an application for a location decision, a construction permit or a construction approval is one month. If the concerned administration authorities have questions about the application they can halt the proceedings until such questions are addressed, thus delaying the procedure. If an administrative authority does not provide for comments during the one-month comment period, it is presumed that it does not have any comments on the application.

The relevant authority then orders a public hearing on the application for a location decision, construction permit or construction approval. Usually, a local inspection is also ordered. Public participants may put forward objections to the project not later than the public hearing. Objections must be put forward at the earliest possible proceeding and will not be taken into account at later proceedings. The building authority may decide not to hold a public hearing if a decision on the application can be made on the basis of the documentation submitted. Public participants must still be notified of the period within which they can comment on the proposal.

In the event the participants cannot agree on the outcome of any of the proceedings, the building authority will refer the public participants and the applicant to court and suspend the proceedings. The building authority will also determine the deadline by which parties must submit evidence that the disputed matter has been submitted for resolution. If the parties fail to submit the matter for resolution within the allotted time, the relevant building authority will resolve the issue on its own.

Czech Republic

Public participation is limited to the submission of comments on the investment project and participation in the hearings during the three-step land use process. Appeals can be brought before the courts to challenge the procedural aspects of the decision-making process but not the decision itself.

Slovak Republic

Public participants may include anyone from the general public or any organisation, such as an environmental or a nature conservation group. Public participation is limited to the submission of comments on the investment project during the three-step land use process, participation in the hearings or a challenge to the procedural aspects of the decision-making process.

4.6 Enforcement

There are no penalties for failure to obtain a location decision. Under the Federal *Act on Land Use Planning and Construction* failure to secure construction permits or approvals and violations of the terms of a construction permit are subject to penalties of up to 20,000 Kcs for private individuals and up to 1,000,000 Kcs for companies. Czech District or

Municipal Office building authorities or Sub-District Office of Environment building authorities in the Slovak Republic can order:

- Necessary modifications by building owners;
- Removal of buildings constructed without a permit or which are not in compliance with the permit;
- Necessary repairs by building owners.

5. Environmental Impact Assessments (EIAs)

5.1 Summary

Scope of Activities:	Under Federal law, certain activities, technologies, buildings and projects listed in Appendices I and III of the *Act on the Environment* require EIAs. *See Annex F.* Under the Czech *Act on Environmental Impact Assessment*, activities listed in Annexes 1 and 2 require EIAs. *See Annex F.* No EIA legislation is in force in the Slovak Republic.
Public Participation:	The EIA study and application documents are made available to the public. Affected communities, concerned state administration authorities, civic associations with more than 500 members and the general public can submit comments and participate in public hearings.

5.2 Sources of legislation relating to the environmental impact of industrial and commercial developments

Federal Law

- *Act on the Environment, No. 17/1992.*

Czech Republic

- *Act on Environmental Impact Assessment, No. 244/1992;*
- *Decree on Qualifications in EIA Matters and the Manner of Proceeding in Public Hearings on the EIA Statement, No. 499/1992.*

Slovak Republic

- Draft Act on Environmental Impact Assessment.

5.3 Scope of activities subject to EIA process

Federal Law

Under the Federal *Act on the Environment, No. 17/1992*, EIAs are required for certain activities listed in Appendices I and III.

Appendix I of the *Act on the Environment* on activities with an impact on the territory of the Czech Republic and Slovak Republic covers activities in the following sectors which require an EIA:

- Agriculture and forestry;
- Food industry;
- Mining industry;
- Energy industry;
- Metallurgical industry;
- Wood and paper industry;
- Other industries;
- Infrastructure.

Appendix I identifies the specific projects in each of the above sectors which require an EIA. *(See Annex F.)*

The Federal *Act on the Environment* provides that each Republic must enact EIA legislation and appoint authorities to oversee the EIA process before the EIA provisions of the Federal *Act on the Environment* can come into force. The Czech Republic EIA Act came into force on 1 July 1992. The Slovak Republic expects to adopt EIA legislation in 1993.

Under the Federal *Act on the Environment* each Republic was explicitly permitted to expand the scope of activities listed in Appendix I.

Appendix III on activities which may have an impact beyond the borders of the Czech Republic and Slovak Republic covers the activities which require an EIA. These are listed in *Annex F* below.

Czech Republic

The Czech *Act on Environmental Impact Assessment, No. 244/1992* contains Annexes 1 and 2 which supplement the list of activities which require EIAs in the Federal *Act on the Environment* and, for the most part, fill in specific limit values.

Annex 1 lists buildings, activities and technologies in the following sectors which are subject to EIAs under the supervision of the Czech Ministry of Environment:

- Agriculture and forestry;
- Mining industry;
- Power industry;
- Metallurgy;
- Wood and paper industry;
- Other industries;
- Infrastructure.

A detailed description of the above is contained in *Annex F* below.

Annex 2 covers buildings, activities and technologies in the following sectors subject to EIAs under the supervision of Czech District Offices:

- Agriculture and forestry;
- Food industry;
- Power industry;
- Metallurgy;
- Wood and paper industry;
- Other industries;
- Infrastructure.

A detailed description of the above is contained in *Annex F* below.

Slovak Republic

The draft *Act on EIAs* includes the list of activities contained in Appendix III of the Federal *Act on the Environment*.

5.4 EIA process

5.4.1 Authority

Czech Republic

The Ministry of Environment supervises the EIA procedure for projects listed in Annex 1 of the *Act on Environmental Impact Assessments*. The District Offices supervise the EIA procedure for projects listed in Annex 2 of the Act.

Slovak Republic

Since the *Act on EIAs* is in draft form, it has not yet finally been decided which authority or authorities will be responsible for overseeing the EIA process.

5.4.2 Documentation

Federal Law

Where an EIA is required and the project entails the development of a greenfield site, the EIA procedure must be completed before applying for the location decision. If the project entails reconstruction of a building, the EIA must be completed before applying for a construction permit.

EIAs are required once plans to carry out the listed activities have been drawn up. Under Federal law, the details of the procedure for EIA approval are to be contained in legislation passed by the Czech Republic and Slovak Republic.

The Federal *Act on the Environment* sets out the information that must be included in an EIA application.

For activities in Appendix I and III, the Federal Act states that the EIA must include a description of:

- The planned activity and its goals, alternatives to the development plan and the corresponding impact of each alternative;
- The relevant environment and the impact on it;

- The measures taken to minimise the environmental impact of the project.

For activities in Appendix III the following additional information must be provided:

- A description of the methods used to arrive at the forecasted impact;
- A list of gaps in knowledge and uncertainties;
- A summary of the monitoring and control programmes and post-project analysis plans;
- A summary of a non-technical nature, if necessary.

Republic authorities were obliged to require at least the information specified in the Federal Act.

Czech Republic

The EIA procedure in the Czech Republic is initiated by the applicant. The applicant prepares the EIA and all necessary documentation, by submitting an initial statement to the Ministry of the Environment for projects in Annex 1 or the District Office for projects in Annex 2. Such a statement must contain:

- A basic description of the project, including the name of the applicant, the location, the date of commencement and termination of construction;
- A description of the technology to be used;
- Basic environmental data on the project including the amount of land, energy and raw materials used and the amount of pollution generated;
- An opinion of the District or Municipal Office building authority stating that the construction is in accordance with regional land use plans.

The statement must be presented together with the following information regarding the environmental impact of the activity, as described in Annex 3 of the *Act on Environmental Impact Assessment*:

- Data on the direct environmental impact on land, water, natural resources and energy and on transport and infrastructure;
- Data on emissions including air pollution, water effluent, waste, noise and vibrations, and radioactive and electromagnetic radiation;
- A complex description of the environmental impact on inhabitants, the ecosystem, its structure and function in the area, the anthropogenic systems and any major impact on the landscape;
- A description of any proposed measures to prevent, eliminate, minimise or compensate for the environmental impact;
- A description of the risks of the operation;
- An outline of the monitoring and management programme;
- A description of the methods used in preparing the EIA and any gaps or uncertainties.

Upon receipt of the EIA documentation the Ministry of Environment or the District Office will arrange for an expert opinion based on the documentation, public opinion, and the opinion of state administrative authorities.

The expert's opinion will discuss the following:

- Completeness of the documentation;
- Public opinion;
- Adequacy of evaluation of negative and positive impacts;
- Methods and data used;
- Proposed technical solutions;
- Alternative solutions;
- Proposals to mitigate the environmental impact.

Based on the expert opinion and the results of the public hearing and consultations the Ministry of Environment or the District Office will issue a decision on the EIA. This decision must approve or deny the project based on its environmental impact and must contain information set out in Annex 4 of the Act.

Slovak Republic
According to the draft EIA legislation, the applicant initiates the EIA procedure by filing an initial statement with the authorities. The initial EIA statement must include:

- A description of the principal characteristics of the project, including its size and location;
- Time period for completion;
- A description of the technical and technological processes to be used.

5.4.3 *Experts and consultants*

Czech Republic
An EIA study may only be prepared by persons holding a certificate of professional competence issued by the Ministry of Environment with the consent of the Ministry of Health. To obtain the certificate a person must have the relevant university education, six years of practical experience and have passed a special examination. The Ministry of Environment keeps a list of qualified persons.

Slovak Republic
Only persons who pass a special examination established by the Ministry of Environment can be listed with the Ministry as competent consultants. It is likely that only persons on this list will be entitled to carry out EIA studies.

5.4.4 *Timing*

Czech Republic
The public comment period on EIAs takes 50 days. Section 9 of the *Act on Environmental Impact Assessment* provides that an expert opinion will then be issued on the EIA within 60 days. This deadline may be extended in justified cases at the most for another 150 days. Thereafter, a public hearing on the expert opinion must take place within 30 days. A decision of the Ministry of the Environment or the District Office is made thereafter. Such a decision need not be rendered within the 30–60 day period normally applicable to administrative decisions.

Slovak Republic

It is anticipated that the entire process will take approximately seven months but the specific time frame is to be set forth in future regulations.

5.4.5 Standard of review

Federal Law

Section 22 of the Federal *Act on the Environment, No. 17/1992* states that the relevant authorities in each Republic shall review the environmental impact of investment projects with special regard to the following:

- Environmental tolerance of the location;
- Consequences of operations and possible accidents;
- Cumulative and synergistic phenomena based on various time horizons and taking into account irreversible consequences;
- Possible prevention, mitigation and compensation for any environmental impact;
- Opportunities for disposal or recycling after the completion of the project;
- Methods applied for evaluating the completeness of information;
- Comparison with the best available technologies.

Projects identified in Appendix III must be evaluated by reference to one or several of the following criteria: the volume of the environmental impact, the size of the area impacted and the nature of the consequences on the environment.

5.5 Public participation

Federal Law

Under Section 25 of the Federal *Act on the Environment* the EIA must be discussed by the Czech and Slovak EIA authorities with concerned state authorities and with communities whose territory will be affected and with the general public.

Czech Republic

The public may participate in the EIA procedure by submitting written comments and participating in a hearing. The "public participants" are deemed to include:

- Municipalities affected by the facility, activity or technology;
- Concerned state administrative bodies;
- Civic associations with 500 or more members who submit a written list of signatures supporting the association's opinion on the EIA;
- Members of the general public.

The environmental impact statement submitted by the applicant is subject to a public comment period. The public has 30 days after the publication of the documentation, the affected Municipalities have 44 days and the state administration authorities have 50 days within which to submit comments. The "concerned state administration authorities" are the Hygiene Offices, the Environmental Inspectorate and the District Offices.

The EIA authorities must appoint an expert to prepare an opinion on all aspects of the documentation within 60 days of the receipt of the public comments. The deadline may be extended for another 150 days where this is justified.

The expert's opinion will then be discussed in a public hearing within one month of its issuance. Civic groups, municipalities and concerned administrative authorities are to be notified of the time and place of the public hearing. A summary of the discussions at the hearing is distributed to the relevant parties.

The Ministry of Environment or the District Office then issues an opinion on the project, which may contain conditions or changes that must be met. No specific requirement currently exists with regard to the time in which the decision must be rendered. The opinion is not binding on the District or Municipal Office building authorities but construction permits and any other necessary permits cannot be issued unless the EIA procedure has been completed. It is expected that the building authorities will not give the go ahead to a project if an unfavourable opinion is rendered by the Ministry of Environment or the District Office.

Slovak Republic
Under the draft EIA legislation the applicant arranges for the preparation of the EIA report by an independent expert. The expert's report will then be discussed in a series of meetings with the public, the Sub-District Office of Environment building authorities and the other concerned state administrative authorities. The authorities must make the information from the EIA study accessible to the public. An independent committee prepares an expert opinion on the applicant's report.

A final opinion is prepared by the reviewing authority based on the expert committee opinion and the public's comments and discussions.

5.6 Enforcement

Czech Republic
If an investor fails to prepare an EIA where one is necessary, a location decision or a construction permit cannot be obtained.

Slovak Republic
The draft EIA legislation has not been enacted. In practice, it is expected that an investor's failure to prepare an EIA, where necessary, will prevent an investor from obtaining a location decision or a construction permit.

5.7 National experience with EIAs

Czech Republic
Almost 20 EIAs are in progress in the Czech Republic. One EIA for a proposed waste dump for spent nuclear fuel is near completion. The waste dump has engendered a great deal of public interest as reflected by the public's attendance at the public hearing.

Slovak Republic

The EIA legislation in the Slovak Republic has not yet been enacted. Consequently, there is no experience with EIAs in the Slovak Republic.

6. Integrated permitting requirements applicable to the operation of industrial and commercial facilities

6.1 Extent of integrated permitting

There is no integrated permitting system in the Czech Republic and the Slovak Republic. Individual permits must be applied for. For further information see *Sections 7–11*.

7. Air emission requirements applicable to the operation of industrial and commercial facilities

7.1 Summary

Permitting Authorities:	The Czech Ministry of Environment and Czech Environmental Inspectorate. The Slovak Ministry of Environment and the Slovak District and Sub-District Offices of Environment.
Permits:	Air permits are required for construction, modification and operation of "large" and "medium" air pollution sources; the manufacture, transport or import of equipment, material or products that may pollute the air; and any change of fuel or technology affecting air pollution sources.
Timing:	In principle 30 to 60 days.
Public Participation:	The authorities must provide information to the public about air quality and the effect of each air pollution source on air quality. Polluters must inform the public directly about measures taken to reduce air pollution.

7.2 Sources of legislation relating to air emissions

Federal Law

- *Clean Air Act, No. 309/1991*, as amended by *Act No. 218/1992*;
- *Air Measures of October, 1991 concerning Act No. 309/1991*;

- *Measures on Air Pollution, No. 84/1992;*
- *Act on Administration Procedure, No. 71/1967.*

Czech Republic

- *Act on Official Fees Collected by Administrative Authorities of the Czech Republic, No. 368/1992;*
- *Act on the State Administration of Air Protection and Charges for the Pollution of Air, No. 389/1991;*
- *Decree of the Ministry of Environment of the Czech Republic Establishing Regions Requiring Special Air Protection, and Establishing Principles for the Creation and Operation of Smog Regulation Systems and Other Measures for Protection of the Air, No. 41/1992.*

Slovak Republic

- *Act on the State Administration of Air Protection, No. 134/1992;*
- *Act on Charges for Air Pollution, No. 311/1992;*
- *Act on Administration Charges, No. 320/1992;*
- *Regulation which Specifies a List of Pollution Sources Categorization and List of Polluting Agents and Their Limits, and which Specifies Details on Assessment of Emission Limits in Existing Pollution Sources, No. 407/1992.*

7.3 Air protection zones

Federal Law

The Federal *Clean Air Act* provides for the establishment of special smog zones that require special air protection during periods of excessive smog. The required zoning and smog regulation system is the responsibility of each Republic.

Czech Republic

Decree No. 41/1992 Establishing Regions Requiring Special Air Protection, establishes the following special air protection zones:

- National parks;
- Protected areas of the countryside;
- Spas;
- Urban zones with limited operations of sources of pollution;
- Regions of cities and districts listed in Appendix No. 1 of the Decree.

Pollution sources in the zones requiring special protection will be subject to more stringent permit conditions than air pollution sources outside the special air protection zones and will be required to reduce emissions during smog emergencies.

Slovak Republic

The Ministry of Environment is working on a smog regulation system.

7.4 Scope of activities subject to air emission regulation

Federal Law

Under the Federal *Clean Air Act* the following air pollution sources are subject to regulation:

- Technological facilities containing stationary equipment for burning fuel;
- Equipment for technological processes;
- Coal quarries and other areas with possible spontaneous fire;
- Burning or emission of pollutants or areas on which work is being done which can cause air pollution;
- Storage and stock yards for fuel, raw materials, products and waste;
- Other facilities, equipment and activities for which approval or a similar decision was issued, on the basis of which a pollution source may be operated.

When in doubt whether an air pollution source is subject to regulation, a building office or another appropriate state administrative authority shall define the pollution source on the basis of a proposal of an air protection authority.

Under the Federal *Clean Air Act*, the above pollution sources are categorised (among other factors) by their heat output and the amount of pollution they generate into:

- Stationary sources which are classified as follows:
  - Large: thermal output > 5 MW
  - Medium: thermal output > 0.2 MW < 5 MW
  - Small: thermal output < 0.2 MW and other sources not included in "large" or "medium" category
- Mobile sources such as motor vehicles, trains, ships and airplanes.

The classification of air pollution was based on a country-wide Register of Emissions and Sources of Air Pollution ("REZZO").

Large and medium pollution sources are further categorised in Appendix No. 2 of the Federal *Measures on Air Pollution* into six categories:

- Fuel and power industry;
- Production and use of metals;
- Production of non-metallic mineral products;
- Chemical industry;
- Waste treatment;
- Other industry and equipment.

Czech Republic

The *Act on the State Administration of Air Protection and Charges for the Pollution of Air* implements the Federal *Clean Air Act*.

Decree No. 41/1992 contains a list of major air polluters in the Czech Republic which will be required to decrease their air emissions during smog emergencies according to special measures established by the Ministry of Environment.

Slovak Republic

The *Act on the State Administration of Air Protection, No. 134/1992* implements the Federal *Clean Air Act* and specifies the responsibilities of the Ministry of Environment, the Environmental Inspectorate and District and Sub-District Offices of Environment as regards air pollution control. The *Regulation on Air Pollution Sources, No. 407/1992* categorises pollution sources and lists pollutants and their limits and amends the Federal *Measure on Air Pollution*.

7.5 Standards

7.5.1 Ambient quality standards

Federal Law

Ambient air standards are listed in Appendix 4 of the Federal *Measures on Air Pollution*.

These standards were developed by reference to the relevant regulations of the EC, Germany and the recommendation of the World Health Organisation. They are given for the following pollutants:

- Fly dust;
- Sulphur dioxide;
- Nitrogen oxides;
- Carbon monoxide;
- Ozone;
- Lead in fly dust;
- Cadmium in fly dust;
- Odorous substances.

Most of the standards are expressed in average concentrations on an annual, daily, eight hour and 30 minute basis.

Special ambient air standards recommended during adverse weather conditions and periods during which there is increased air pollution are set forth in Annex 5 of the Federal *Measures on Air Pollution* for sulphur dioxide, nitrogen oxides, carbon monoxide, and flydust.

Czech Republic

Appendix No. 3 of *Decree No. 41/1992* sets out permissible concentrations of sulphur dioxides, nitrogen oxides and carbon monoxide in ambient air for the purpose of identifying smog emergency situations.

Slovak Republic

Currently, there are no Slovak ambient air quality standards.

7.5.2 Emission limit values

Federal Law

The Federal *Measures on Air Pollution* have set air emission limits for approximately 125 pollutants, categorised into the following groups:

- Basic pollutants;
- Pollutants with carcinogenic effect;
- Solid inorganic pollutants;
- Gaseous inorganic pollutants;
- Organic gases and vapours.

In addition, emission limits have been set for selected pollutants for the following industries and equipments:

- Solid, liquid and gaseous fuels combustion;
- Equipment for waste incineration.

These emission limits apply to new sources for which a permit was issued after 1 October, 1991 or to sources which will be put into operation after 31 December 1994. The list of pollutants and pollution limits can be made more stringent not earlier than five years after coming into effect and any changes or more stringent limitations must be announced three years before coming into effect. Sources of air pollution will have five years from the date on which the new measures become effective to come into compliance.

Czech Republic

Czech air emission standards are the same as those set in the Federal *Measures on Air Pollution.*

Slovak Republic

The revised Slovak air emission measures modify and expand the existing Federal emission limits. *Regulation No. 407/1992* makes some of the existing Federal limits stricter and establishes some new emission limits for selected polluting substances and certain technologies.

7.5.3 Technology based standards

Federal Law

Emission limits for selected polluting substances in selected technologies and equipment are set forth in Appendix 3 of the Federal Measures on *Air Pollution, No. 84/1991.*

New air pollution sources and modifications of existing sources must be constructed using the best available technology not entailing excessive cost.

Emission limits for existing sources will be established by the Republic air protection authorities by 30 June 1993 at the latest and will be based on the lowest attainable emissions under optimum operations given the state of the technological equipment and fuel used. Existing sources will have until 31 December 1998 at the latest to come into compliance with the emission limits established for new sources.

Czech Republic

The Environmental Inspectorate is responsible for establishing technology based standards for existing sources of air emissions.

Slovak Republic

The District Offices of Environment are responsible for establishing technology based standards for existing "large" sources and the Sub-District Offices of Environment are responsible for establishing emission limits for existing "medium" sources.

7.6 Permitting process

7.6.1 Authorities

The Federal *Clean Air Act* provided that certain categories of activities require permits issued by the air protection authorities in the Czech Republic and Slovak Republic.

Czech Republic

Permits for the construction, operation and modification of large and medium air pollution sources, as well as for any change in fuel or technology used by these sources, are issued by the Environmental Inspectorate. Permits for the introduction of new technologies in large and medium air pollution sources are issued by the Ministry of Environment.

Slovak Republic

Permits for the construction, operation and modification of large and medium air pollution sources are issued by Sub-District Offices of Environment, as are permits for the introduction of new technologies in large and medium air pollution sources.

7.6.2 Application requirements

Federal Law

Permits are required for a number of activities which may pollute the air including the operation of large and medium pollution sources, the introduction of new technologies or the change in fuel or technology used by these sources and the manufacture, import and transport of equipment, material and products that may pollute the air.

Czech Republic

No specific documentation is required, but a description of the air emission sources and other relevant information must be provided.

Slovak Republic

The application for an air emission permit must contain the following information:

- A description of the technological process and materials used;
- Results of emission measurements;
- A proposal for emission limits if the source is not in compliance with the emission limits set for new sources;
- A proposal for a technical solution for obtaining the emission limits with an economic breakdown and time schedule of how the emission limits will be met.

7.6.3 Timing

The general terms for granting permits in the environmental area in both the Czech Republic and Slovak Republic are governed by the Federal *Administrative Procedure Act* which states that permits should be issued:

- Without delay for simple administrative matters;
- Within 30 days from the start of the procedure in other cases;
- Within 60 days for particularly complex cases.

The appropriate appellate body can extend the periods if necessary.

7.6.4 Permit conditions

Federal Law

The necessary approvals issued by the Republic air protection authorities contain conditions that each pollution source must meet to ensure protection of the air. These conditions may include the installation of certain types of pollution control equipment.

7.6.5 Charges for emissions

Federal Law

Under the Federal *Clean Air Act* operators of pollution sources must pay charges assessed by the Republics. Pollution sources with a thermal output below 50 kW operated by private individuals and not regularly used for commercial activities do not pay charges.

Czech Republic

Operators of air emission sources must provide a calculation of the charges owed in respect of air emissions from each source to the appropriate authority by 15 February of each year together with data for the previous year as follows:

- Large sources submit calculations to the Environmental Inspectorate;
- Medium sources submit calculations to the District Office;
- Small sources submit calculations to the Municipal Office.

The air protection authorities verify the data and issue decisions concerning the definitive amount of charges owed. A surcharge is added if the limits established in air emission permits are exceeded.

Payment of air emissions charges will be phased in as follows: 30% of the charge is due in 1992 and 1993; 60% is due in 1994 and 1995; 80% is due in 1996; and 100% of the change is due by 1997 and thereafter. In addition, the air protection authorities can defer or waive 40% of the charges due if the operator demonstrably starts work on the reduction of emissions.

Slovak Republic

Operators of large and medium size air pollution sources are obliged to pay a charge to the State Fund of Environment according to the amount and type of pollutants emitted. A surcharge is added if the emission limits are exceeded.

Payment of air charges will be phased in as follows: 20% of the charge is due in 1992; 40% is due in 1993; 60% is due in 1994 and 1995; 80% is due in 1996 and 1997; and 100% of the charge is due by 1998 and thereafter.

7.6.6 Public participation

Federal Law

The Federal *Clean Air Act* does not provide for participation of the public in the air emissions permitting process.

It does, however, permit public access to information on the quality of the air and the effect of each pollution source on air quality. In addition, air protection authorities are obliged to inform the public of smog emergencies. Operators of large and medium air pollution sources must inform the public directly about measures taken to limit pollution generally and in cases of serious and imminent danger or impairment of air quality.

7.7 Enforcement

7.7.1 Compliance checking and monitoring

Federal Law

Under the Federal *Clean Air Act* large and medium size air pollution sources must monitor and keep a record of the quantity of discharged pollutants and provide the data to the respective authorities according to separate regulations which are to be adopted by the Czech Republic and Slovak Republic. In addition, operators of large and medium sources are obliged to permit air protection authorities to inspect and monitor emissions.

Czech Republic

Enforcement of air pollution laws in the Czech Republic is governed by the *Act on the State Administration of Air Protection and Charges for the Pollution of Air.*

Slovak Republic

Enforcement of air pollution laws in the Slovak Republic is governed by the *Act on the State Administration of Air Protection.*

7.7.2 Penalties and sanctions

Federal Law

Under the Federal *Clean Air Act* penalties range from 500 to 10,000,000 Kcs, depending on the seriousness of the violation, the quantity and kind of substance released, and the size of the source. Penalties may be doubled if the violation is repeated within a year.

The air protection authorities in each Republic can order any air pollution source which does not comply with air protection regulations to take whatever remedial action is necessary to bring the facility into compliance.

The air protection authorities designated by each Republic may restrict or terminate the operation of any large or medium pollution source if:

- An air pollution source poses a serious and imminent danger to or impairment of air quality;
- Emission limits are exceeded and the operator fails to take the compliance measures ordered;
- An operator of an air pollution source repeatedly violates the requirements of the *Clean Air Act* after a penalty has been imposed;
- A smog emergency exists and smog regulation measures have been announced.

Czech Republic

The Environmental Inspectorate monitors compliance and imposes penalties on large and medium-sized air pollution sources. In addition, the Environmental Inspectorate may shut down operations at large or medium-sized facilities that violate air protection requirements.

The District Offices supervise enforcement by the Municipal Offices and decide, together with the Municipal Offices, on the implementation of the smog regulation system. Municipal Offices monitor compliance by small air pollution sources, impose penalties on operators which do not comply with the smog warning system and on large and medium sources that do not comply with emission limits for dark smoke and may order operators of mobile pollution sources to submit to an inspection.

Slovak Republic

The Environmental Inspectorate ensures compliance with the technical operating parameters, emission limits and the smog regulation system. The Environmental Inspectorate imposes penalties for non-compliance and proposes remedial measures to the Environmental Offices.

The District and Sub-District Offices of Environment impose penalties on facility operators who violate air pollution obligations and may restrict or shut down operations at large and medium pollution sources that violate air protection requirements or impose remedial measures.

8. Water requirements applicable to the operation of industrial and commercial facilities

8.1 Summary

Water Requirements:	Czech District Offices and Slovak District Offices of Environment and River Basin Authorities supervised by the Slovak Ministry for Soil Management issue permits for water use and waste water discharge.
Timing:	In principle 30 to 60 days.

Public Participation:	In the Czech Republic, affected communities and water management authorities can participate in the water permitting procedure.
	In the Czech Republic persons who can justify an interest in a water permitting issue can have access to the permitting register once the permit has been issued.

8.2 Sources of legislation relating to water requirements

Federal Law

- *Water Act, No. 138/1973;*
- *Order on Charges in Water Management, No. 35/1979 in the Wording of Order No. 2/1989 for Surface and Groundwater Discharge, and Use of the Municipal Sewer System.*

Czech Republic

- *Act on the State Administration in Water Economy, No. 130/1974* as amended by *Act No. 23/1992 and Restated as Act. No. 458/1992;*
- *Act Which Modifies and Amends the Federal Order No. 35/1979 on Charges in Water Management, No. 281/1992;*
- *Order on Standards of Admissible Levels of Water Pollution, No. 171/1992;*
- *Order on the Protection of Surface and Groundwater Quality, No. 6/1977.*

Slovak Republic

- *Act on the State Administration of Water Management, No. 135/1974;*
- *Act on the State Administration of the Environment, No. 595/1990;*
- *Act on Transgressions, No. 372/1990, as amended by Act No. 524/1990;*
- *Order Determining the Indicators of Admissible Levels of Water Contamination, No. 30/1975;*
- *Order on the Protection of Surface and Groundwater Quality, No. 23/1977;*
- *Order on the Penalties for Breach of Liabilities in the Water Management Area, No. 31/1975;*
- *Methodical Instruction of the Ministry of Forest and Water Management of November. 28, 1977;*
- *Order on the Charges in Water Management, No. 35/1979 in the wording of Order No. 2/1989.*

8.3 Water management

8.3.1 Water management bodies

Czech Republic

Five River Boards manage the development and protection of river basins, carry out systematic water quality control, regulate the use of surface and groundwater, and monitor compliance with discharge requirements. The monitoring function is expected to be shifted to facilities which use and discharge water.

Slovak Republic
The Ministry of Soil Management has responsibility for water management and supervises the four River Basin Authorities.

8.3.2 Water quality categories

Federal Law
The Federal *Water Act* deals with water protection and sets out the conditions regulating water use and discharge. It provides for the creation of protected water management areas to safeguard drinking water supplies. Water quality categories are established by reference to six water quality parameters, namely:

- The oxygen regime;
- Basic physical and chemical parameters such as pH and temperatures;
- Supplementary chemical parameters and as the presence of calcium, magnesium and chlorides;
- Heavy metals such as mercury, cadmium, arsenic and lead;
- Biological and microbiological criteria;
- Radioactivity.

8.3.3 Activities subject to regulation

Federal Law
The Federal *Water Act* specifies certain activities which are subject to regulation:

- Water use;
- Discharge of waste water;
- Construction of facilities in or near water bodies or for the treatment of waste water;
- Extraction of any materials affecting water bodies;
- Use of the municipal sewage system.

Czech Republic
The *Act on the State Administration in Water Economy, No. 130/1974 as amended by Act No. 23/1992 and Restated as Act. No. 458/1992* regulates the administration of water management and protection and implements the Federal *Water Act*.

Slovak Republic
The *Act on the State Administration of Water Management, No. 135/1974* sets out the details of the administration of water management and protection and implements the Federal *Water Act*.

8.4 Standards

8.4.1 Ambient quality standards

Czech Republic
   Ambient quality standards are set in Category III of the *Order on Standards of Admissible Levels of Water Pollution, No. 171/1992* which provides ambient concentration values for a long list of substances in surface waters. Category II provides indicators for water quality, including biological indicators, smell and temperature.

Slovak Republic
   Ambient quality standards are set in the *Order Determining the Indicators of Admissible Levels of Water Contamination, No. 30/1975* which provides ambient concentration values for a long list of substances in surface waters. Other indicators, including biological indicators, smell and temperature are also given.

8.4.2 Discharge limit values

Czech Republic
   Category I of the *Order on Standards of Admissible Levels of Water Pollution, No. 171/1992* lists discharge limit values for communal and industrial waste waters. These limits must be reflected in permits for wastewater discharge or when conditions for the discharge of mine water into surface water are being set.
   Water quality criteria listed in Category II and III of *Order No. 171/1992* must be taken into account when issuing water discharge permits.

Slovak Republic
   Discharge limit values have not yet been set but are currently being drafted. At present, discharge limit values are negotiated on a case-by-case basis with each facility.

8.4.3 Technology based standards
   There are no technology based standards in the water area in either the Czech Republic or Slovak Republic.

8.5 Water use permitting process

8.5.1 Authorities

Czech Republic
   District Offices issue water use permits.

Slovak Republic
   The River Basin Authorities issue water use permits.

8.5.2 Application requirements

Federal Law

Permits from the designated Republic water management authorities are required for:

- Use of surface water;
- Use of groundwater.

Unless otherwise decided by the Republic water management authorities, water permits are automatically transferred to the next purchaser or user of the property as long as the property continues to be used in the manner for which the permit was granted. The new purchaser must notify the water management authority within two months of the transfer.

Czech Republic

Applications for water use permits must be accompanied by sufficient information to enable the authorities to determine the impact of the activity on water management. No specific forms are required.

Slovak Republic

Applications for water permits shall contain:

- Name and address of the applicant;
- Type, purpose, place and basic description of the use of water;
- List of participants in the procedure and their addresses known to the applicant;
- Time duration for which the permit is required.

8.5.3 Timing

The general terms for granting permits in the environmental area in both the Czech Republic and Slovak Republic are governed by the Federal *Administrative Procedure Act* which states that permits should be issued:

- Without delay for simple administrative matters;
- Within 30 days from the start of the procedure in other cases;
- Within 60 days for particularly complex cases.

The appropriate appellate body can extend the periods if necessary.

8.5.4 Permit conditions

The water authorities in each Republic can attach conditions and obligations to the permit if necessary to ensure that the permitted activity will be in compliance with the water laws.

8.5.5 Charges for water use

Under the Federal *Order on Charges in Water Management*, which has been implemented in both the Czech Republic and Slovak Republic charges are due for:

- Surface water withdrawal in excess of 15,000 m^3 per year or 1,250 m^3 per month;
- Use of surface water for power generation;

- Groundwater use;
- Supply of water from the public mains.

8.6 Water discharge permitting process

8.6.1 Authorities

Czech Republic
District Offices issue water discharge permits.

Slovak Republic
District Offices of Environment issue water discharge permits which must then be approved by the River Basin Authority for the water catchment area in question.

8.6.2 Application requirements

Federal Law
The Federal *Water Act* requires any person discharging wastewater into surface or groundwater to ensure that the water quality is not threatened.
Permits are needed for:

- Discharge of waste water and special water;
- Discharge of pre-treated water into the public sewage system.

Czech Republic
The application requirements are the same as those listed in *Section 8.5.2* above.

Slovak Republic
In addition to the information noted above in *Section 8.5.2*, the following data must be enclosed:

- Plans marking the place of discharge of water;
- The opinion of the River Basin Authority on compliance with the water management plan;
- Data concerning the water flow;
- Data concerning water quality of the water basin in the year preceding the permit application.

8.6.3 Timing
The timing for issuance of discharge permits in both the Czech Republic and Slovak Republic is the same as noted in *Section 8.5.3*.

8.6.4 Permit conditions

Czech Republic

In setting the permitted discharge limits in water discharge permits, the District Offices must follow the maximum permissible levels of pollution in discharged water contained in Category I of *Order No. 171/1992*. The indicators in Categories II and III must be taken into account but are not binding on the District Offices.

Slovak Republic

In setting the permitted limits in water discharge permits, the District Offices of Environment must follow the maximum permissible levels of pollution contained in the *Order No. 30/1975*.

8.6.5 Charges for water discharges

Charges are due for:

- Water discharge to surface or groundwater;
- Discharge of sewage and waste water to the public sewage system.

The charge depends on the amount of contaminants present in the waste water and the resulting rate of deterioration of water quality.

Czech Republic

The water management authorities can waive 60% of the water charges owed if the polluter completes the construction of a water treatment facility within a specified time.

8.6.6 Public Participation

Czech Republic

Parties to the permitting procedure are the applicant and affected municipalities, state administrative authorities and River Boards, but not the general public.

Anyone affected by water permitting decisions can request to see the authorities' records on permits, approvals, opinions and any other decisions issued. Information concerning compliance is confidential.

Slovak Republic

The general public is not allowed to participate in the application procedure for a water use or water discharge permit by an enterprise.

Public access to information concerning water management is provided in an annual report published by the Research Institute of Water Management. Information concerning compliance is confidential.

8.7 Enforcement

8.7.1 Compliance checking and monitoring

Czech Republic

District and Municipal Offices are obliged to ensure that facilities comply with water permit conditions and water protection laws.

Under the newly amended *Act on the State Administration in Water Economy*, the Municipal and District Offices may ask citizens' organisations involved in environmental protection to cooperate in water protection and may even assign some of the monitoring tasks to these organisations. The involvement of citizen's groups is likely to result in increased monitoring of the use and discharge of water by commercial and industrial facilities.

The Environmental Inspectorate is also involved in the supervision of wastewater discharges and protection of the surface and groundwaters.

Slovak Republic

The District Offices of Environment and the Slovak Hydrometeorological Institute are responsible for monitoring surface and groundwater use. Groundwater use is currently not monitored, however, due to lack of funds and appropriate equipment. Companies or persons using or discharging water have a general duty to monitor discharges. In addition those using groundwater have an express obligation to report their use to the Slovak Hydrometeorological Institute within 30 days. Users of water must provide the River Basin Authorities with data on the annual use of water for the purpose of calculating water charges which are owed.

8.7.2 Penalties and sanctions

Federal Law

Penalties can be imposed for breaching the Federal *Water Act*, for failure to obtain a necessary permit and for failure to comply with permit conditions.

The water management authorities in the Republics may impose remedial obligations on any person who breaches the duty to protect the quality of surface and groundwater.

Use of property or activities that threaten the water quality in protected zones can be prohibited by the water management authorities in the Republics.

Czech Republic

The Czech Environmental Inspectorate and the District Offices can assess penalties for:

- Drawing or using surface or groundwater without a permit or in breach of a permit;
- Discharges of waste water into surface or groundwater or the public sewage system without a permit or in breach of a permit;
- Pollution of surface or groundwater or causing penetration of contaminating substances into the public sewage system;
- Damaging the public water supply system or the sewage system;

● Breaching any duties in the water laws or regulations.

The size of the penalty depends on the nature of the violation, and any efforts made to mitigate the violation. The Czech *Act on the State Administration in Water Economy* provides a complex system for calculating the amount of the penalty for discharges in excess of permitted levels.

The District Offices, Municipal Offices and Environmental Inspectorates can impose compliance measures on persons or businesses within their sphere of competence. In addition, the Environmental Inspectorate can suspend operations endangering the environment until such operations come into compliance with environmental laws.

Slovak Republic

The Slovak Environmental Inspectorate and the District and Sub-District Offices of Environment can assess penalties from 3,000 to 1,000,000 Sk for violations of various provisions of water legislation including:

● Discharging waste water into surface or groundwater without or in breach of a permit;
● Contaminating surface or groundwater or threatening water quality by illegal discharges;
● Water use in the absence of or in breach of a permit;
● Damaging the public water supply or the sewage system.

9. Noise requirements applicable to the operation of industrial and commercial facilities

9.1 Summary

Noise Requirements:	The Czech District Hygiene Office issues noise permits. In the Slovak Republic the District and Sub-District Offices administrate the laws but the administration procedures are currently being revised.
Timing:	30 or 60 days.
Public Participation:	In the Slovak Republic the public can have access to information on noise levels at the Hygiene Office.

9.2 Sources of legislation relating to environmental noise

Federal Law

● *Act on Human Health Care, No. 20/1966;*
● *Regulation concerning the Safeguarding and Protection of Healthy Living Conditions, No. 45/1966,* as amended by *Act No. 548/1991.*

Czech Republic

- *Act on Human Health Care, No. 86/1992*, incorporating the *Federal Act on Human Health Care, No. 20/1966*;
- *Regulation on the Protection of Health against Harmful Effects of Noise and Vibrations, No. 13/1977.*

Slovak Republic

- *Act on Human Health Care, No. 96/1992* incorporating the *Federal Act on Human Health Care, No. 20/1966*;
- *Regulation on the Protection of Health against Harmful Effects of Noise and Vibrations, No. 14/1977*;
- *Act on Penalties for Breach of Legal Regulations Concerning the Creation and Protection of Healthy Environmental Conditions, No. 53/1975.*

9.3 Noise Zones

Noise zones may be determined in land use plans.

9.4 Activities subject to noise regulation

All industrial and commercial operations have an obligation to comply with the regulations setting noise and vibration levels and may be subject to noise control measures.

9.5 Standards

Czech Republic and Slovak Republic

Both Republics currently have the same noise standards, based on two identical regulations dating from the former Communist period.

Places of Work	*Day Time*
places of physical work	80–90 dB
general rule	85 dB
places of intensive intellectual work	50–75 dB
places of highly creative work	45 dB

137

Other Places	Day Time	Night Time
Hospitals	35 dB	25 dB
Homes	40 dB	30 dB
Lecture halls	45 dB	
Shops	60 dB	

External Spaces	Day Time	Night Time
Health centres, nature reserves	40 dB	30 dB
Recreational spaces in towns and schools	45 dB	35 dB
Housing estates in suburbs	50 dB	40 dB
Housing estates in towns	55 dB	45 dB
Mixed zones	60 dB	50 dB
Industrial zones, traffic zones, city centres	70 dB	60 dB

The Czech Republic and Slovak Republic are currently working on new noise laws.

9.6 Permitting process

9.6.1 Authorities

Czech Republic
The Hygiene Offices at District level are responsible for issuing noise permits.

Slovak Republic
The Hygiene Officers in the District Offices are responsible for issuing noise permits.

9.6.2 Application requirements

Czech Republic
Operators of facilities are required to submit documentation on noise levels to the District Hygiene Office for approval. Expert opinions on noise levels can be requested if the Hygiene Office considers it necessary.

Slovak Republic
Noise regulation procedures are currently being revised.

9.6.3 Timing
Under the Federal *Administrative Procedure Act* permits must be issued:

- Without delay for simple matters;
- Within 30 days in other cases;
- Within 60 days in particularly complex cases.

9.6.4 Permit conditions

The authorities may impose conditions within the permitting process to ensure compliance with noise regulations.

9.6.5 Public participation

Czech Republic

There is no provision for public access to information on noise.

Slovak Republic

The public has the right of access to information on noise and vibration held by the Hygiene Institutes.

9.7 Enforcement

9.7.1 Compliance checking and monitoring

Czech Republic

Facilities and equipment must be operated in compliance with the noise regulations and the best available technological standards.

Slovak Republic

Facilities and equipment must be operated in compliance with the noise regulations and the best available technological standards.

9.7.2 Penalties and sanctions

Czech Republic

If noise emission or ambient levels are breached, the Hygiene Offices at District level can order noise reduction measures to be taken within a designated period. Failure to comply with such an order may result in the imposition of a penalty.

Slovak Republic

If noise emission or ambient levels are breached, the Hygiene Officers in the District Offices can order noise reduction measures to be taken within a designated period.

If noise emission or ambient levels are breached, the Hygiene Offices at District level can order noise reduction measures to be taken within a designated period. Failure to comply with such an order may result in the imposition of a penalty.

10. Hazardous and non-hazardous waste management

10.1 Summary

Authorities:	Permits are issued by the Czech Ministry of Environment and District Offices and by the Slovak Ministry of Environment and the District and Sub-District Offices of Environment.
Permits:	Permits are required for constructing, establishing and operating waste treatment and disposal facilities; transporting hazardous waste; and operating a waste management business.
Timing:	30 or 60 days.
Public Participation:	The public can have access to the waste management plans of public authorities.

10.2 Sources of legislation relating to waste management

Federal Law

- *Waste Act, No. 238/1991;*
- *Provision on the Categorization and Cataloguing of Waste, No. 69/1991.*

Czech Republic

- *Act on the State Administration of Waste Management, No. 311/1991, as amended by Act No. 466/1992;*
- *Act on Charges for the Disposal of Waste, No. 62/1992;*
- *Public Notice on Waste Management Programmes, No. 401/1991;*
- *Decree on the Maintenance of Records on Waste, No. 521/1991;*
- *Order Specifying the Details Concerning Disposal of Wastes, No. 513/1992.*

Slovak Republic

- *Act on the State Administration of Waste Management, No. 494/1991;*
- *Act on the Charges for Disposal of Wastes, No. 309/1992;*
- *Regulation on Waste Management Programmes, No. 76/1992;*
- *Regulation No. 606/1992, adopted pursuant to Act No. 238/1991 on Waste.*

10.3 Categories of waste

Federal Law

The Federal *Provision on the Categorisation and Cataloguing of Waste, No. 69/1991* categorises waste into three types:

- Special waste which is harmful to human health or the environment;
- Hazardous waste is a special waste which is toxic, infectious, irritating, explosive, combustible, chemically harmful, carcinogenic, teratogenic and mutagenic or harmful to human health or the environment;
- Other waste.

Each waste category is further subdivided into small groups and individual types of waste, each of which is assigned a code. Assignment of a waste code and identification of the category to which the waste belongs is a necessary prerequisite to waste handling.

10.4 Waste storage and treatment

10.4.1 Generator requirements

Federal Law

According to the Federal *Waste Act*, generators of waste do not need permits to generate waste. They must, however, meet a number of obligations:

- Collect generated waste, separate it according to type, and store it safely;
- Collect hazardous waste separately according to its type, identify it, and treat it in accordance with special regulations;
- Report the generation, quantity, character and manner of use or treatment of special waste to the relevant waste management authorities in each Republic;
- Use the generated waste as secondary raw material;
- Provide for waste treatment if such use is not possible;
- Maintain and save records on the types and produced quantity of waste, its disposal and use;
- Give the inspection bodies access to documents and to the premises where waste is generated;
- Draft a waste management programme.

Republic waste management authorities may set special conditions until 1 August 1996 for:

- Generators which are not able to collect and store wastes separately and safely;
- Generators which cannot re-use waste or offer it to others for re-use or arrange for treatment.

Czech Republic

A generator must prepare a waste management plan if the facility generates on an annual basis more than 100 tons of waste or 50 kg of hazardous waste. The waste management plan must contain all the information specified in Appendix 1 to the *Public Notice on Waste Management Programmes* including:

- Identification of the generator and information on the production processes;
- Type and quantity of generated waste;
- Waste neutralization and disposal facilities;
- Waste management costs and records;
- Proposals for reducing waste generation and decontaminating and reclaiming waste dumps no longer in use;
- Location of relevant approvals and records concerning the facility.

The required reports, records and waste management programmes must be submitted to the District Offices. The public is granted access to the waste management programmes prepared by District Offices. There is no other public right of access to waste records.

Specific details on the storage of harmful wastes and the operation of incineration and neutralization equipment are given in *Order No. 513/1992*.

Slovak Republic

Regulation on Waste Management Programmes, No. 76/1992 imposes a duty on large-scale waste generators, District and Sub-District Offices, and the Ministry of Environment to prepare waste management plans that identify the wastes generated and the methods for waste recycling treatment and disposal. Generators of more than 100 kg of hazardous waste or 1 ton of special waste or 10 tons of other waste annually must prepare a waste management programme including the following information:

- Identification of the generator and information on the production process;
- Type and quantity of waste generated and waste disposal methods used;
- Proposals for reducing waste, confirmed by signature of the authorised representative of the generator;
- Annex showing the relevant decisions of state administration and inspection authorities.

The waste management programmes of the District and Sub-District Offices of Environment and of the Slovak Ministry of Environment for all of the Slovak Republic will be published.

Regulation No. 606/1992 adopted pursuant to Act No. 238/1991 on Waste contains detailed provisions regarding waste handling, treatment and disposal in the Slovak Republic.

10.4.2 Operator requirements

Federal Law

Operators of waste treatment facilities must meet the following requirements:

- Treat the waste according to operating rules approved by the waste management authorities in each Republic and prevent leakage or theft of the waste;
- Publicise a list of wastes the facility is authorised to treat;

- Maintain records on the quantity, types and origin of the waste taken in for treatment, the manner of treatment and its disposal at dumps;
- Report the quantity, character and manner of waste treatment to the relevant waste management authority in each Republic;
- In exceptional cases, treat waste as ordered by the waste management authority in each Republic;
- Give the inspection bodies access to the facilities and records.

State administrative authorities may set special conditions until 1 August 1996 for operators of waste treatment facilities that are not able to meet the obligations set out in the Federal *Waste Act*.

Legal or natural persons in the business of collecting, recycling or treating wastes must meet the following requirements:

- Specify and publicist the types of collected waste and the condition of their collection and recycling;
- Accept or redeem the publicised types of collected waste;
- Comply with all the requirements for waste generators except the preparation of a waste management programme.

Czech Republic

District Offices approve waste management plans, the operation of waste treatment, storage and disposal facilities, and can express opinions on the construction of such facilities required under the Federal *Waste Act*.

Order No. 513/1992 Concerning the Disposal of Waste provides details concerning the conditions for the treatment of waste and the operation of waste treatment equipment.

Approvals are issued without delay where a decision can be made on the documentation, within 30 days as a general rule and within 60 days in more complex cases.

Slovak Republic

The Sub-District Offices of Environment issue approvals for the operation of waste storage and treatment facilities, and maintain the required records on waste.

Approvals are issued without delay when a decision can be made on the documentation, within 30 days as a general rule and within 60 days in more complex cases.

Regulation No. 606/1992 adopted pursuant to Act No. 238/1991 on Waste contains detailed provisions regarding waste handling, treatment and disposal in the Slovak Republic.

10.5 Waste disposal

10.5.1 Generator requirements

Requirements applicable to waste disposal are the same as those addressed above in *Section 10.4*.

10.5.2 Operator requirements

Federal Law

Requirements applicable to waste disposal are the same as those addressed above in *Section 10.4*.

Czech Republic

The technical and operational requirements for managing a waste disposal site are specified in *Order No. 513/1992*. The Order describes the technical specifications for constructing different types of landfills, the types of wastes that can be dumped in landfills and rules governing the operation of landfills.

Disposal of hazardous waste requires approval of the District Office. The application for approval must include the following information:

- Address of the applicant;
- Composition and characteristic properties of dangerous waste which is to be disposed of;
- Description of the technical equipment in which the manipulation of the hazardous waste will be carried out, including the technological processes;
- Certificate of professional competence of the applicant to dispose of such hazardous waste.

Slovak Republic

To date the Slovak Republic has not issued any similar technical and operational requirements.

10.5.3 Charges

Czech Republic

The *Act on Charges for the Disposal of Waste, No. 62/1992* provides for a system of charges for different types of wastes disposed in landfills.

Charges are imposed on the operator of the waste dump, which then presumably passes on the charge to persons using the dump. The rate for waste is as follows:

- basic rate — 10 Kc/ton;
- solid communal waste — 20 Kc/ton;
- special waste — 40 Kc/ton;
- hazardous waste — 250 Kc/ton.

If the waste facility fails to meet the necessary technical requirements, an "additional charge" is applied that will increase almost six times for certain types of waste between 1992 and 1994. The additional charge for the disposal of hazardous waste starts at 3,000 kc/ton in 1992 and increases to 5,000 kc/ton in 1994.

Slovak Republic

The *Act on the Charges for Disposal of Waste, No. 76/1992* lays out the charges that must be paid for various types of wastes disposed in landfills.

Fees are charged by the operator per ton of waste accepted for disposal. The fees are then payable by the operators to the authorities. The basic fee is payable to the Municipality where the waste disposal site is located and an additional fee for the disposal of waste in dumps, not meeting current technical standards, is payable to the State Fund Environmental of the Slovak Republic.

The basic rates for various types of waste will increase over the period from 1992 to 1996.

10.6 Transport of waste

10.6.1 Labelling and containers

Federal Law

Transporters of hazardous waste are obliged to maintain records and report to the appropriate Republic waste management authority on the quantity and type of hazardous waste transported and the manner of its transport.

Czech Republic

The transport of hazardous waste requires approval from the District Office.

Containers used to store hazardous waste must be labelled with information regarding safety measures to be followed, toxicological data relating to the hazardous substance and the name of the owner.

Slovak Republic

The transport of hazardous waste requires approval from the District Office of Environment. If the transport of waste is across the territory of the Slovak Republic spanning more than one District approval of the Ministry of Environment is required.

10.6.2 Transboundary movement

Federal Law

A permit from the relevant waste management authority in each Republic is required for:

- Import of waste for re-use as a secondary raw material;
- Export of hazardous waste;
- Transit of waste across the territory of the Czech Republic or Slovak Republic.

Czech Republic

The Ministry of Environment is the body which grants authorisation for the transboundary movement of waste.

Slovak Republic

The Ministry of Environment is the body which grants authorisation for the transboundary movement of waste.

10.7 Recycling requirements

Generators of waste must use waste as a secondary raw material to the greatest extent possible and offer waste used not in such a manner to third parties who may be able to re-use it. Generators must also provide recycling and disposal information with their products.

10.8 Enforcement

10.8.1 Compliance checking and monitoring

Federal Law
Recordkeeping and reporting is required by:

- Generators and persons involved in the collection, recycling and treatment of waste;
- Transporters of hazardous waste;
- Operators of treatment facilities.

Czech Republic
The *Decree on the Maintenance of Records on Waste, No. 521/1991* details the record keeping requirements for generators and operators of waste treatment facilities.
Separate waste records are required for:

- Generation and treatment of waste;
- Generation and treatment of special and hazardous waste;
- Disposal of waste in dumps by operators of facilities for the treatment of waste;
- Transport of hazardous waste.

Slovak Republic
The *Act on Record Filings on Waste* provides the details of the recordkeeping requirements imposed by the Federal *Waste Act*.
Records must be kept by:

- Generators of waste;
- Persons authorised to collect, recycle or treat waste;
- Operators of waste treatment facilities;
- Transporters of waste.

The above persons are only required to maintain the records if they produce, handle or transport more than 100 kg of hazardous waste, 1 ton of special waste or 10 tons of other waste annually. In addition persons that generate, handle or transport any of the specific hazardous wastes listed in the Annex of the Act must keep the necessary records required by the Federal *Waste Act* regardless of the amount of those wastes handled.

10.8.2 Penalties and sanctions

Federal Law

Under the Federal *Waste Act* penalties for violations by generators of waste and operators of waste treatment, storage or disposal facilities range from 10,000 to 10,000,000 Kcs. The penalties can be doubled if violations are repeated within one year. The imposition of penalties under the Act does not preclude the imposition of additional penalties under the Federal *Civil Code* and *Commercial Code*.

If a generator fails to recycle the waste, or offer the waste to another party for re-use, or as a last resort, secure the safe treatment of the waste and the waste could produce serious environmental damage, the administrative authorities can prohibit the waste generating activities.

If an operator of a waste treatment facility fails to meet any of the obligations set forth in the *Waste Act* and that failure could cause serious environmental damage, the authorities can prohibit the operation of the facility.

Czech Republic

The Czech Environmental Inspectorate and the District Offices may impose penalties on any person who violates the applicable provisions of the Federal *Waste Act*. Municipal Offices are authorised to impose penalties ranging from 10,000 to 300,000 Kcs on persons who fail to prepare a waste management plan or fail to secure the appropriate storage of waste.

District Offices may order the facility shut down under the Federal *Waste Act*.

The District and Municipal Offices and the Czech Environmental Inspectorate may issue compliance orders as well as impose penalties. District Offices may order compliance measures to remedy violations of environmental law. Municipal Offices may order compliance measures in cases in which they can impose penalties.

A District Office may withdraw its approval for the operation of a waste storage, treatment or disposal facility if:

- The operator is not capable of ensuring that the facility is operated in a manner that does not damage the environment and any environmental violation is not remedied;
- The conditions of any approval are not complied with;
- Implementation of an approval has caused or may cause serious environmental damage.

An appeal from a decision of a Municipal Office is decided by the District Office; an appeal from a decision of a District Office or the Czech Inspectorate is decided by the Ministry of Environment.

Slovak Republic

Penalties under the Federal *Waste Act* may be imposed by the District or Sub-District environmental authorities or by the Environmental Inspectorate.

District and Sub-District Offices of Environment may restrict operations or shut-down facilities.

11. Chemicals storage, handling and emergency response

11.1 Summary

Requirements:	Hazardous substances must not be stored in such a manner as to cause pollution of water, soil or air. The construction of storage facilities for certain chemical substances such as natural gas, oil and pesticides is controlled.
Enforcement:	Enforcement of legal requirements is performed by the Czech Health Offices and Slovak Health Institutes at District level.

11.2 Sources of legislation relating to chemicals storage, handling and emergency response

11.2.1 Storage

Federal Law

- *Water Act, No. 138/1973*;
- *Act on Human Health Care, No. 20/1966*;
- *Act on the Protection and Use of Natural Resources, No. 44/1988*, as amended;
- *Clean Air Act, No. 309/1991*, as amended by *Act No. 218/1992*;
- *Waste Act, No. 238/1991*;
- *Act on the Environment, No. 17/1992*.

Czech Republic

- *Order on the Protection of Surface and Groundwater Quality, No. 6/1977*;
- *Order on Toxins and Certain Other Substances Harmful to Health, No. 206/1988*, as amended by *Order No. 232/1990 and No. 83/1992*;
- *Act on Environmental Impact Assessments, No. 244/1992*;
- *Act on the Protection and Use of Natural Resources, No. 44/1988*, as amended by *Czech Act No. 439/1992*;
- *Order specifying the Details Concerning the Disposal of Waste, No. 513/1992*.

Slovak Republic

- *Order on the Protection of Surface and Groundwater Quality, No. 23/1977*;
- *Order on Toxins and Certain Other Agents Harmful to Health, No. 206/1988*, as amended by *Order No. 232/1990* and *No. 83/1992*;

- *Act on the Protection and Use of Natural Resources, No. 44/1988,* as amended by *Slovak Act No. 498/1992* and *No. 439/1992.*

11.2.2 Handling
See Section *11.2.1* above.

11.2.3 Emergency response
See Section *11.2.1* above.

11.3 Regulatory requirements

Federal Law

The *Act on Human Health Care* contains only a general prohibition on the storage of hazardous substances in a manner that could result in the pollution of water, soil and air.

The construction of facilities for the storage and handling of certain chemical substances is controlled through the EIA procedure under Federal law.

The *Act on the Environment* requires the preparation of an EIA for:

- Natural gas surface storage facilities;
- Underground storage facilities for inflammable gases, crude oil, petrochemical and chemical products;
- Production and storage of poisons, pesticides, liquid fertilisers, pharmaceutical products, paints, varnishes and chemicals;
- Crude oil, crude oil products, petrochemical products and chemical storage.

Czech Republic

Toxic substances must be stored in closed and safe storage areas, separated according to type and secured against coming into contact with the air, leaking or unauthorised access. Extremely toxic substances may be stored in storage areas with only those non-toxic substances expressly designated for storage with such extremely toxic substances. Enterprises are obliged to issue safety instructions for the handling of toxic substances and procedures in emergency cases.

The *Order on the Protection of Surface and Groundwater Quality, No. 6/1977* provides further guidance on the handling and spill prevention of toxic substances such as crude oil, poisons, caustic agents, synthetic and natural fertilisers, insecticides and herbicides and wastes of all kinds. Toxic substances must be stored in adequate storage areas and containers and the enterprise must establish a control system and prepare an emergency response plan. In case of an accident, the person or enterprise responsible must report and liquidate the accident, monitor endangered groundwater sources and remediate the contaminated area.

The requirements of the Federal *Act on the Environment* have been adopted in the Czech Republic. The Czech *EIA Act* requires the preparation of an EIA for:

- Underground storage of natural gas and other gases with a capacity exceeding 1 million m^3; surface storage of natural gas and other gases with a capacity exceeding

100,000 m^3; storage of oil, oil products and chemicals with a capacity exceeding 1,000 m^3.

- The storage of poisons and pesticides in amount exceeding 1 ton, and the storage of pharmaceutical products, paints and varnishes exceeding 100 tons/year.

Under the *Order Specifying the Details Concerning the Disposal of Waste, No. 513/1992*, storage areas and storage containers for hazardous waste must be marked with an identification card which gives information on the type of waste, its hazardous properties, safety measures and measures to be taken in case of accident as fine, toxicological data and the name of the owner of the waste.

Slovak Republic

Regulations governing the storage of toxic chemicals in the Slovak Republic are very similar to those in the Czech Republic. No EIA legislation is in force in the Slovak Republic.

11.4 Public participation

Slovak Republic

Enterprises which sell chemical substances must provide information with the product concerning first aid and treatment in cases of poisoning and other accidents.

11.5 Enforcement

11.5.1 Compliance checking and monitoring

Czech Republic

The Ministry of Health, through the Hygiene Offices at District Level is responsible for supervising compliance with regulations governing toxic substances.

Slovak Republic

The Ministry of Health, through the Hygiene Institutes is responsible for supervising compliance with regulations governing toxic substances.

11.5.2 Penalties and sanctions

Czech Republic

The Hygiene Offices at District level enforce compliance with the regulations governing toxic substances.

Slovak Republic

The Hygiene Institutes enforce compliance with regulations governing toxic substances.

Annex A

List of Key Legislation

1. Overview

Federal Law

- *Act on the Environment, No. 17/1992;*
- *Clean Air Act, No. 309/1991,* as amended by *Act No. 218/1992;*
- *Waste Act, No. 238/1991;*
- *Water Act, No. 138/1973;*
- *Foreign Exchange Act, No. 528/1990,* as amended.

Czech Republic

- *Decree No. 61/1991 of the Ministry of Finance.*

Slovak Republic

- *Decree No. 465/1991 of the Ministry of Finance.*

2. Environmental liability

Federal Law

- *Act on the Environment, No. 17/1992;*
- *Civil Code, No. 40/1964,* as amended;
- *Commercial Code, No. 513/1991;*
- *Penal Code, No. 140/1961,* as amended;
- *Act on the Transfer of State Property to Other Persons, No. 92/1991,* as amended by *Act No. 92/1992 Amending and Transforming the Act on the Conditions of Transfer of State Property to Other Persons;*
- *Act on Land Use Planning and Construction, No. 50/1976,* as amended by *Act No. 262/1992.*

Czech Republic

- *Resolution No. 455/1992 on Settlement of Environmental Liabilities of Enterprises pursuant to the Act on the Terms of Transfer of State Property to Other Persons;*
- *Methodical Instruction of the Ministry for the Management of State Property and Its Privatisation of the Czech Republic and the Ministry of the Environment of the Czech Republic of May 18, 1992 for Carrying out the Provision §6a of the Law No. 92 of February 18, 1992;*
- *Resolution No. 694/1992 regarding the formation of joint venturers with foreign companies in the automotive industry in the Czech Republic.*

Slovak Republic

- *Methodical Instruction of the Ministry for Administration and Privatisation of the National Property of the Slovak Republic and of the Slovak Committee of Environment as of July 14, 1992 Regarding the Process of Assessment of Environmental Liabilities of an Enterprise within the Privatisation Project Presented by the Enterprise within the Second Wave Large-Scale Privatisation.*

3. Environmental audits

Federal Law

- *Section 6a of Act on the Transfer of State Property to Others, No. 92/1991*, as amended by *Act No. 92/1992 Amending and Transforming the Act on the Conditions of Transfer of State Property to Other Persons.*

Czech Republic

- *Resolution No. 455/1992 of the Government of the Czech Republic on the Settlement of Environmental Liabilities of Enterprises Pursuant to Act No. 92/1991 on the Terms of Transfer of State Property to Other Persons*, as amended by *Act No. 92/1992;*
- *Methodical Instruction of the Ministry for the Management of State Property and Its Privatisation of the Czech Republic and the Ministry of Environment of the Czech Republic of May 18, 1992 for Carrying Out Provision of Section 6(a) of Law No. 92 of February 18, 1992.*

Slovak Republic

- *Methodical Instruction of the Ministry for Administration and Privatisation of the National Property of the Slovak Republic and of the Slovak Committee of Environment as of July 14, 1992 regarding the Process of Assessment of Environmental Liabilities of an Enterprise within the Privatisation Project Presented by the Enterprise within the Second Wave of Large-Scale Privatisation.*

4. Land use planning

Federal Law

- *Act on Land Use Planning and Construction, No. 50/1976;*
- *Decree on General Technical Requirements of Construction, No. 83/1976,* as amended by *Decree No. 376/1992;*
- *Decree on Land Use Data and Land Use Documentation, No. 84/1976,* as amended by *Decree No. 377/1992;*
- *Decree on More Detailed Regulation of Land Use Planning and Construction Rules, No. 85/1976,* as amended by *Decree No. 378/1992;*
- *Foreign Exchange Act, No. 528/1990,* as amended.

5. Environmental Impact Assessments (EIAs)

Federal Law

- *Act on the Environment, No. 17/1992.*

Czech Republic

- *Act on Environmental Impact Assessments, No. 244/1992;*
- *Decree on Qualifications in EIA Matters and the Manner of Proceeding in Public Hearings on the EIA Statement, No. 499/1992.*

Slovak Republic

- *Act on Environmental Impact Assessment (under preparation).*

6. Air emission requirements

Federal Law

- *Clean Air Act, No. 309/1991,* as amended by *Act No. 218/1992;*
- *Air Measures of October 1991* concerning *Act No. 309/1991;*
- *Measures on Air Pollution, No. 84/1992;*
- *Act on Administration Procedure, No. 71/1967.*

Czech Republic

- *Act on the State Administration of Air Protection and Charges for the Pollution of Air, No. 389/1991;*
- *Decree of the Ministry of Environment of the Czech Republic Establishing Regions Requiring Special Air Protection, and Establishing Principles for the Creation and*

153

> *Operation of Smog Regulation Systems and Other Measures for Protection of the Air,
> No. 41/1992;*

- *Act on Official Fees Collected by Administrative Authorities of the Czech Republic,
  No. 368/1992.*

Slovak Republic

- *Act on the State Administration of Air Protection, No. 134/1992;*
- *Act on Charges for Air Pollution, No. 311/1992;*
- *Act on Administration Charges, No. 320/1992;*
- *Regulation which Specifies a List of Pollution Sources Categorization and List of Pol-
  luting Agents and Their Limits, and which Specifies Details on Assessment of Emission
  Limits in Existing Pollution Sources, No. 407/1992.*

7. Water requirements

Federal Law

- *Water Act, No. 138/1973;*
- *Order on Charges in Water Management, No. 35/1979 in the wording of Order No. 2/
  1989 For Surface and Groundwater Discharge, and Use of the Municipal Sewer System.*

Czech Republic

- *Act on the State Administration in Water Economy, No. 130/1974* as amended by *Act
  No. 23/1992* and restated as *Act. No. 458/1992;*
- *Act which Modifies and Amends Federal Order No. 35/1979 on Charges in Water
  Management, No. 281/1992;*
- *Order on Standards of Admissible Levels of Water Pollution, No. 171/1992;*
- *Order on the Protection of Surface and Groundwater Quality, No. 6/1977;*

Slovak Republic

- *Act on the State Administration of Water Management, No. 135/1974;*
- *Act on the State Administration of the Environment, No. 595/1990;*
- *Act on Transgressions, No. 372/1990, as amended by Act No. 524/1990;*
- *Order on the Charges in Water Management, No. 35/1979 in the wording of Order
  No. 2/1989;*
- *Order Determining the Indicators of Admissible Levels of Water Contamination,
  No. 30/1975;*
- *Order on the Protection of Surface and Groundwater Quality, No. 23/1977;*
- *Order on the Penalties for Breach of Liabilities in the Water Management Area,
  No. 31/1975;*
- *Methodical Instruction of the Ministry of Forest and Water Management of Nov. 28,
  1977.*

8. Noise requirements

Federal Law

- *Act on Human Health Care, No. 20/1966*;
- *Regulation concerning the Safeguarding and Protection of Healthy Living Conditions, No. 45/1966*, as amended by *Act No. 548/1991*.

Czech Republic

- *Act on Human Health Care, No. 86/1992*, incorporating the *Federal Act on Human Health Care, No. 20/1966*;
- *Regulation on the Protection of Health against Harmful Effects of Noise and Vibrations, No. 13/1977*.

Slovak Republic

- *Act on the Human Health Care, No. 96/1992*, incorporating the *Federal Act on Human Health Care, No. 20/1966*;
- *Regulation on the Protection of Health against Harmful Effects of Noise and Vibrations, No. 14/1977*;
- *Act on Penalties for Breach of Legal Regulations concerning the Creation and Protection of Healthy Environmental Conditions, No. 53/1975*.

9. Hazardous and non-hazardous waste management

Federal Law

- *Waste Act, No. 238/1991*;
- *Provision on the Categorisation and Cataloguing of Waste, No. 69/1991*.

Czech Republic

- *Act on the State Administration of Waste Management, No. 311/1991*, as amended by *Act No. 466/1992*;
- *Act on Charges for the Deposit of Waste, No. 62/1992*;
- *Public Notice on Waste Management Programmes, No. 401/1991*;
- *Decree on the Maintenance of Records on Waste, No. 521/1991*;
- *Order Specifying the Details Concerning Disposal of Waste, No. 513/1992*.

Slovak Republic

- *Act on the State Administration of Waste Management, No. 494/1991*;
- *Act on the Charges for Disposal of Waste, No. 309/1992*;

- *Regulation on Waste Management Programmes, No. 76/1992;*
- *Regulation No. 606/1992 adopted pursuant to Act No. 238/1991 on Waste.*

10. Chemicals storage, handling and emergency response

Federal Law

- *Act on the Environment, No. 17/1992;*
- *Act on Human Health Care, No. 20/1966;*
- *Act on the Protection and Use of Natural Resources, No. 44/1988,* as amended by *No. 439/1992;*
- *Clean Air Act, No. 309/1991,* as amended by *Act No. 218/1992;*
- *Water Act, No. 138/1973;*
- *Waste Act, No. 238/1991.*

Czech Republic

- *Order on Toxins and Certain Other Substances Harmful to Health, No. 206/1988,* as amended by *Order No. 232/1990* and *No. 83/1992;*
- *Order on the Protection of Surface and Groundwater Quality, No. 6/1977;*
- *Act on Environmental Impact Assessments, No. 244/1992;*
- *Act on the Protection and Use of Natural Resources No. 44/1988,* as amended by *Act No. 439/1992;*
- *Order specifying the Details Concerning the Disposal of Wastes, No. 5/3/1992.*

Slovak Republic

- *Order on Toxins and Certain Other Agents Harmful to Health No. 206/1988* as amended by *Order No. 232/1990.* and *No. 83/1992;*
- *Order on the Protection of Surface and Groundwater Quality, No. 23/1977;*
- *Act on the Protection and Use of Natural Resources No. 44/1988,* as amended by *Act No. 498/1992* and *No. 439/1992.*

Annex B

List of Permitting and Enforcement Authorities

Czech Republic
Ministry of Environment
Vrsovicka 65
100 10 Prague 10
Tel: (42 2) 712.1111
Fax: (42 2) 731.357

Regional Departments of the Ministry of Environment

Department for the Region of Central Bohemia
Zborovska 11
150 00 Prague 5
Tel: (42 2) 549.004
Fax: (42 2) 549.004

Department for the Region of Ceske Budejovice
Lidicka 2
270 81 Ceske Budejovice
Tel: (42 38) 384.65
Fax: (42 38) 384.65

Department for the Region of Plzen
Skroupova 18
301 36 Plzen
Tel: (42 19) 222.706
Fax: (42 19) 226.192

Department for the Region of Chomutov
Kochova ul. KORD II
430 01 Chomutov
Tel: (42 396) 59.62
Fax: (42 396) 51.52

Department for Region of Liberec
Trida 1. maje 108
P.O. Box 9
460 02 Liberec 2
Tel: (42 48) 225.71

Department for Region of Hradec Kralove
Susilova 1337
500 02 Hradec Kralove
Tel: (42 49) 612.632
Fax: (42 49) 617.482

Department for Region of Brno
Slovakova 2
602 00 Brno
Tel: (42 5) 753.241

Department for Region of Ostrava
Prokesovo nam. 8
701 00 Ostrava
Tel: (42 69) 225.343
Fax: (42 69) 212.061

Department for Region of Olomouc
Trida Miru 101
772 11 Olomouc-Neredin
Tel: (42 68) 412.23.21
Fax: (42 68) 414.467

Czech Environmental Inspectorate
Ministry of Environment
Vrsovicka 65
100 10 Prague 10
Tel: (42 2) 730.757
Fax: (42 2) 730.757

Air Protection Division Main Office
Czech Environmental Inspectorate
Trojska 13 A
182 00 Prague 8–Kobylisy
Tel: (42 2) 845.474
Fax: (42 2) 845.104

Water Protection Division Main Office
Czech Environmental Inspectorate
Italska 27
120 00 Prague 2
Tel: (42 2) 235.49.51
Fax: (42 2) 236.58.01

Waste Disposal Division Main Office
Czech Environmental Inspectorate
Pocernicka 96
108 03 Prague 10
Tel: (42 2) 772.606

Ministry of Privatisation
Lazarska 7
113 48 Prague 1
Tel: (42 2) 213.01.11
Fax: (42 2) 235.09.32

Ministry of Economy
100 10 Prague 10
Tel:
Fax: (42 2) 742.304

Ministry of Health
Palackeho Namesti 4
128 01 Prague 2
Tel: (42 2) 211.81.111
Fax: (42 2) 211.82.111

Slovak Republic
Ministry of Environment
Hlboka 2
812 35 Bratislava
Tel: (42 7) 492.451
Fax: (42 7) 311.368

Slovak Environmental Inspectorate
Trieda Ladislava Novomeskeho
842 22 Bratislava
Tel: (42 7) 727.969
Fax: (42 7) 723.181

Ministry of Privatisation
Drienova 24
820 09 Bratislava
Tel: (42 7) 299.71.11
Fax: (42 7) 294.536

Ministry of Soil Management
Dobrovicova 12
812 66 Bratislava
Tel: (42 7) 363.723
Fax: (42 7) 57.834

Ministry of Health
Spitalska 6
813 05 Bratislava
Tel: (42 7) 300.111
Fax: (42 7) 57.508

Annex C

List of Proposed Legislation

1. Environmental liability

Czech Republic

- Proposed Act on Contractual Insurance on Responsibility for Damages to the Environment.

2. Environmental impact assessments

Slovak Republic

- Act on Environmental Impact Assessments.

3. Air requirements

Czech Republic

- Decree on the Qualification of Persons Who Carry Out Air Inspections;
- Decree to Regulate the Import and Use of Freon.

Slovak Republic

- Regulation of the Ministry of Environment on the Smog Warning System;
- Act on Inspection of Air Pollution Sources.

4. Water requirements

Czech Republic

- Proposed New Water Act.

Slovak Republic

- Proposed New Water Act.

5. Noise requirements

Czech Republic

- Noise Act.

Slovak Republic

- Noise Act.

6. Hazardous and non-hazardous waste management

Czech Republic

- Act on Radioactive Waste.

7. Chemicals storage, handling and emergency response

Czech Republic

- Act on the Prevention and Liquidation of Accidents.

Slovak Republic

- Regulation of the Ministry of Environment on Conditions for Verification of the Professional Capacity of Persons Performing Expert Activities in the Environmental Sector.

Annex D

Environmental Standards

1. Environmental audits

Czech Republic

- *Standpoint of the Ministry of Environment of the Czech Republic concerning the Criteria and Standards for Contaminated Soil and Groundwater Cleanup annexed to the Methodical Instructions of the Ministry for the Management of State Property and Its Privatisation of the Czech Republic and the Ministry of the Environment of the Czech Republic of May 18, 1992 for Carrying out the Provision of Section 6a of the Law No. 92 of February 18, 1992.*

Slovak Republic

- *Recommendation of the Slovak Committee of Environment Regarding the Application of Criteria and Standards for Cleanup of the Contamination in Soil and Groundwater (from the Methodical Instruction of the Ministry for Administration and Privatisation of the National Property of the Slovak Republic and of the Slovak Committee of Environment as of July 14, 1992 Regarding the Process of Assessment of Environmental Liabilities of an Enterprise within the Privatisation Project Presented by the Enterprise within the Second Wave Large-Scale Privatisation).*

2. Air requirements

Federal Law

- *Air Measures of October 1991 concerning Act No. 309/1991;*
- *Measures on Air Pollution, No. 84/1992.*

Czech Republic

- *Decree No. 41/1991 of the Ministry of Environment of the Czech Republic Establishing Regions Requiring Special Air Protection, and Establishing Principles for the Creation and Operation of Smog Regulation Systems and Other Measures for Protection of the Air.*

161

Slovak Republic

- *Regulation which Specifies a List of Pollution Sources Categorization and List of Polluting Agents and Their Limits, and which Specifies Details on Assessment of Emission Limits in Existing Pollution Sources, No. 407/1992.*

3. Water requirements

Czech Republic

- *Order on Standards of Admissible Levels of Water Pollution, No. 171/1992;*
- *Order on the Protection of Surface and Groundwater Quality, No. 6/1977.*

Slovak Republic

- *Order Determining the Indicators of Admissible Levels of Water Contamination, No. 30/1975;*
- *Order on the Protection of Surface and Groundwater Quality, No. 23/1977.*

4. Noise requirements

Czech Republic

- *Regulation on the Protection of Health Against Harmful Effects of Noise and Vibration, No. 13/1977.*

Slovak Republic

- *Regulation of the Ministry of Health Regarding Health Protection Against Adverse Effects of Noise and Vibration, No. 14/1977.*

5. Hazardous and non-hazardous waste management

Federal Law

- *Provision on the Categorisation and Catalogue of Wastes, No. 69/1991.*

Annex E

International Conventions

- International Plant Protection Convention, 6 December 1951, 150 U.N.T.S. 67 (entered into force 3 April 1952).
- Convention on Long-Range Transboundary Air Pollution, 13 November 1979, 18 I.L.M. 1442 (entered into force 16 March 1983).
- Protocol on Long-Term Financing of the Co-operative Programme for Monitoring and Evaluation of the Long-Range Transmission of Air Pollutants in Europe, 28 September 1984, 24 I.L.M. 484 (entered into force 28 January 1988).
- Protocol to the Convention on Long-Range Transboundary Air Pollution on the Reduction of Sulphur Emissions or Their Transboundary Fluxes by at Least 30 Percent, 9 July 1985, U.N. DOC. ECE/EB.Air/7, annex 1.
- Protocol to the Convention on Long-Range Transboundary Air Pollution Concerning the Control of Emissions of Nitrogen Oxides or their Transboundary Fluxes, 31 October 1988, 28 I.L.M. 214 (entered into force 14 February 1991).
- Convention for the Protection of the Ozone Layer, 22 March 1985, 26 I.L.M. 1529 (entered into force 22 September 1988).
- Montreal Protocol on Substances that Deplete the Ozone Layer, 16 September 1987, 26 I.L.M. 1550 (entered into force 1 January 1989).
- Convention on Wetlands of International Importance, Especially as Waterfowl Habitat, 2 February 1971, 996 U.N.T.S. 245 (entered into force 21 December 1975).
- Convention Concerning Protection of the World Cultural and Natural Heritage, 16 November 1972, 1037 U.N.T.S. 151 (entered into force 17 December 1975).
- Convention on the Control of Transboundary Movements of Hazardous Wastes and Their Disposal, 22 March 1989, 28 I.L.M. 649 (entered into force May 1992).
- Convention on Environmental Impact Assessment in a Transboundary Context, 25 Febuary 1991, 30 I.L.M. 800.
- Convention on International Trade in Endangered Species of Wild Fauna and Flora, 3 March 1973, 993 U.N.T.S. 243 (entered into force 1 July 1975).

Annex F

Investment Projects Subject to EIAs

Appendix I of the *Act on the Environment* on activities with an impact on the territory of the Czech Republic and Slovak Republic covers activities in the following sectors which require an EIA:

Agriculture and forestry

- Large-capacity facilities for animal husbandry, including waste disposal.;
- Large-capacity facilities for storing agricultural products.;
- Land improvement projects (drainage, irrigation, anti-erosion soil protection, reallotment, technical improvements for forestry);
- Interference in the landscape that may cause substantial changes in biological diversity and in the structure and functions of ecosystems.

Food industry

- Breweries and malt plants;
- Slaughterhouses and meat processing combines;
- Starch manufacture;
- Sugar factories;
- Refrigerating plants;
- Distilleries;
- Fat industry and the production of detergents;
- Manufacture of dairy products;
- Canning industry.

Mining industry

- Coal and lignite underground and open-cast mining;
- Crude oil and natural gas exploration;
- Peat mining;
- Uranium ore mining and processing, waste banks, sludge beds, including reclamation;
- Mining and enrichment of metallic ore;
- Bituminous shale mining;
- Mining of industrial minerals;
- Surface industrial facilities for the mining and processing of coal, natural gas, bituminous shale and industrial minerals;
- Crude oil refineries, including plants for the regeneration of spent mineral-oils and facilities for the thermal and chemical processing of coal.

Energy industry

- Power plants and other fossil-fuel burning facilities;
- Other industrial facilities for the generation of electricity, steam and hot water;
- Nuclear power stations and other facilities equipped with nuclear reactors;
- Nuclear fuel conversion, enrichment and production facilities;
- Burnt nuclear fuel intermediate storage facilities;
- Processing and final deposit of highly radioactive waste;
- Processing and deposit of low and medium-level radioactive waste from the operation and closure of nuclear power stations and utilisation of radionuclides;
- Gas, steam and hot water conduits and their facilities (including pumping and changer stations, electric energy transmission by overhead circuits);
- Oil, gas and other product pipelines, including operational facilities;
- Natural gas surface storage facilities;
- Underground storage facilities for inflammable gases, crude oil, petrochemical and chemical products;
- Briquetting and coke plants;
- Hydro-electric power stations.

Metallurgical industry

- Ironworks and steelworks, including foundries, forges and rolling mills;
- Non-ferrous metallurgy works;
- Surface treatment of metals;
- Production and assembly of motor vehicles, train carriages and storage tanks;
- Shipyards;
- Facilities for construction and repair of aircraft.

Wood and paper industry

- Preservation of wood using toxic chemicals;
- Wood fibre board and plywood production;
- Cellulose and paper production;
- Furniture production.

Other industries

- Processing of asbestos and asbestos products;
- Textile preparation plants and dye houses;
- Tanneries;
- Glass works;
- Chemical and pharmaceutical industry;
- Utilisation or regeneration of chlorinated hydrocarbons;
- Production and storage of poisons, pesticides, liquid fertilisers, pharmaceutical products, paints, varnishes and chemicals;
- Storage, processing, neutralisation and deposit of hazardous wastes;
- Long-distance transport of radioactive and hazardous wastes;

- Crude oil and petrochemical products storage facilities;
- Cement works and lime works;
- Printing facilities.

Infrastructure

- Groundwater use;
- Wastewater treatment plants and sewage systems;
- Sludge beds and mud settling ponds;
- Facilities for communal waste treatment;
- Rendering plants, veterinary clearance facilities;
- Water reservoirs or dams rising to a height of over 3 m measured from the foundation joint or with the total storage capacity over 0.5 million cubic metres;
- Waterways regulation;
- Construction and reconstruction of highways and roads;
- Railways;
- Cableways;
- Water routes and ports for inland shipping;
- Airfields;
- Shopping centres with a built-in area over 3,000 square metres;
- Camping sites with over 200 places;
- Structures and activities which could affect interests protected by special regulations.

Appendix III on activities which may have an impact beyond the border of the Czech Republic and Slovak Republic covers the following activities which require an EIA:

- Crude oil refineries (with the exception of plants producing only lubricants from crude oil) and facilities for gasifying and burning coal and bituminous shales with a daily capacity of 500 tons and more;
- Thermal power stations and other combustion facilities, classified as "large" environmental pollution sources according to special regulations (§3a) of the *Clean Air Act No. 309/1991*;
- Nuclear power stations and other facilities equipped with nuclear reactors (with the exception of research facilities for the production and conversion of nuclear fuel and nuclear fuel raw materials, the maximum capacity of which does not exceed 1 kWh of constant thermal load);
- Facilities for the production or enrichment of nuclear fuel, the reprocessing of radioactive nuclear fuel, or the collection, storage and processing of nuclear waste;
- Facilities for the primary production of cast iron and steel and production of non-ferrous metals with an annual capacity of over 30,000 tons;
- Facilities for obtaining, processing and revising asbestos and asbestos products, for annual production of asbestos cement products exceeding 20,000 tons, for friction materials with an annual production exceeding 50 tons, and for other uses of asbestos exceeding 200 tons a year;
- Complex chemical facilities where two or more combined chemical or physical processes are used for the production of olefins from crude oil products, sulfuric acid, nitric acid, hydrofluoric acid, chlorides or fluorides;

166

- First-class roads, highways, national railways and airports with the main take-off and landing runways longer than 2,100 metres;
- Long-distance crude oil pipelines with pipes having an inner diametre of more than 500 millimetres and gas transmission lines with an inner diametre exceeding 300 millimetres;
- Facilities for the neutralisation of toxic and hazardous waste, underground storage sites and surface storage sites for toxic and dangerous wastes;
- Dams and reservoirs with dams rising to a height of more than 10 metres above the foundation joint or with a total capacity of the reservoir exceeding 10 million cubic metres;
- Facilities for the withdrawal of groundwater in case the annual volume of withdrawal equals or exceeds 10 million cubic metres;
- Cellulose and paper production with a daily output of 200 tons or more, with air drying;
- Inland water routes and ports for inland navigation, which enable the navigation of ships with a tonnage exceeding 1,350 tons;
- *Insitu* mining, preparation and refinement of ores, magnetite and all types of coal, with an annual capacity exceeding 100,000 tons;
- Large capacity storage facilities for storing crude oil (over 200,000 cubic metres), crude oil products (exceeding 50,000 cubic metres) and chemicals (over 2,000 cubic metres);
- Changes in land utilisation relating to large-scale felling of forests exceeding an area of 5 hectares.

Annex 1 lists buildings, activities and technologies subject to EIAs under the supervision of the Czech Ministry of Environment:

Agriculture and forestry

- Deforestation of an area exceeding 5 hectares.
- Land improvement (such as drainage, protection against soil erosion) on areas exceeding 500 hectares;

Mining industry

- Extraction and processing in situ of: ore, magnesite, coal exceeding
- 100,000 t/year, stone, gravel, bituminous shale and industrial minerals exceeding 200, 000 t/year, natural gas exceeding 100 million m^3/year, and peat;
- Extraction and processing of uranium ore, waste banks and sludge beds including recultivation;
- Extraction and refining of crude oil, including plants for regeneration of used mineral oils, facilities for thermal and chemical processing of coal and shale.

Power industry

- Electric power plants, other industrial facilities for the production of electricity, steam and hot water and other facilities with an installed output exceeding 100 MWt;
- Hydroelectric power plants with a peak output over 50 MWe;

- Nuclear power plants and other facilities with nuclear reactors;
- Facilities for converting, enriching and producing nuclear fuel;
- Interim storage facilities for spent nuclear fuel;
- Processing and final deposit of highly radioactive waste;
- Processing and deposit of low and medium radioactive waste from nuclear power plant operation and the shut-down of nuclear power plants and from facilities using radionuclides;
- Long-distance gas, oil, steam, hot water and other pipelines, including their facilities (pumping, exchange and compressor stations). Long-distance power transmittal grids (110 kw and over);
- Underground storage of natural gas and other gases with a capacity exceeding 1 million m^3, surface storage of natural gas and other gases with a capacity exceeding 100000 m^3, storage of oil, oil products and chemicals with a capacity exceeding 1 000 m^3.

Metallurgy

- Production and processing of crude iron, cast iron and steel with a capacity exceeding 30,000 t/year, production and processing of non-ferrous metals (non-ferrous metallurgy) with a capacity exceeding 3,000 t/year;
- Surface processing of metals with a capacity exceeding 10 million m^2/year of processed surface.

Wood and paper industry

- Production of cellulose and paper.

Other Industries

- Processing of asbestos and asbestos products;
- Cement factories and lime works with a capacity exceeding 100 000 t/year;
- Chemical production with a capacity exceeding 200 t/year;
- Production of toxics, pesticides and pharmaceutical products in an amount exceeding 1 t/year;
- Facilities for processing, neutralising and incinerating hazardous waste in an amount of 1,000 t/year and over and facilities for storing and disposing hazardous waste in the amount of 10 t and over.

Infrastructure

- Construction of highways, first class roads, railways, airports, permanent racing tracks for motor vehicles races with hardened surface, water ways, including ports;
- Water dams and water reservoirs if the height of the dam exceeds 10 m above the footing bottom or if the total volume exceeds 10 million m^3 of water;
- Facilities for ground water withdrawal if the annual volume of withdrawn water exceeds 10 million m^3;
- Facilities for municipal waste treatment with a capacity exceeding 100,000 t/year.

Annex 2 covers buildings, activities and technologies subject to EIAs under the supervision of the Czech District Offices:

Agriculture and Forestry

- Facilities for animal production, including waste deposits, for cattle breeding facilities with a capacity exceeding 100 animals, for pig breeding facilities with a capacity exceeding 200 pigs, poultry farms with a capacity exceeding 25,000 broilers or 25,000 hens;
- Storage facilities for agricultural products with a capacity exceeding 20,000 tons;
- Amelioration activities (drainage, irrigation, protection against soil erosion, land alterations, technical forestry amelioration) on an area from 10 to 500 hectares;
- Landscape interventions which may cause fundamental changes in the biological diversity, and in the structure and function of eco-systems.

Food Industry

- Breweries, malting houses and non-alcohol drinks production with a capacity exceeding 10,000 hl/year;
- Slaughter houses and meat processing works with a production capacity exceeding 5,000 t/year of products;
- Starch production plants with a capacity exceeding 50,000 t/year of processed potatoes;
- Sugar refineries with a capacity exceeding 15,000 t/year of processed raw material;
- Frozen food factories with a capacity exceeding 100,000 t/year of frozen products;
- Distilleries with a capacity exceeding 1000 t/year;
- The oil industry (production of vegetable oil and grease) and production of detergents with a production capacity exceeding 20,000 t/year of products;
- Dairies and milk production facilities with a capacity exceeding 100,000 t/year of processed milk;
- Canning factories with a capacity exceeding 100,000 t/year of products.

Power industry

- Electric power plants, other industrial facilities for the production of electricity, steam and hot water, and other facilities burning fossil fuel, with an installed output ranging from 20 to 100 MWt;
- Hydroelectric power plants with a peak output ranging from 10 to 50 MWe.

Metallurgy

- Surface processing of metals with a capacity from 5 to 10 million m^2/year of processed surface;
- Machinery and electrotechnical production on a production area larger than 5,000 m^2;
- Production and assembly of motor vehicles, railway carriages and tanks with a capacity exceeding 1,000 pcs/year;
- Production of passenger and cargo ships for river transport;
- Production and repair of airplanes with a capacity exceeding 100 pcs/year.

Wood and Paper Industry

- Impregnation of wood with toxic chemicals in an amount exceeding 1,000 t/year;
- Production of fiberboard and plywood with a production capacity exceeding 50,000 m^2/year of products;
- Production of furniture with capacity exceeding 10,000 m^3 of processed raw material per year.

Other Industries

- Processing of textiles and dye works with a consumption of chemicals exceeding 10,000 t/year;
- Tanneries with a capacity exceeding 50,000 m^2/year of processed raw material;
- Production of glass and glass fibres with a capacity exceeding 50,000 t/year;
- Use and recycling of contaminated chlorinated hydrocarbons in an amount exceeding 10 t/year;
- Polygraphic facilities with a consumption of chemicals exceeding 1 t/year;
- Storage of toxins and pesticides in an amount exceeding 1 t/year and of liquid fertilisers, pharmaceutical products, paints and lacquers exceeding 100 t/year;
- Production of construction materials with a capacity exceeding 100,000 t/year;
- Asphalt production with a capacity exceeding 10,000 t/year.

Infrastructure

- Facilities for withdrawing water of an annual volume of withdrawn water exceeding 3 million m^3;
- Waste water treatment plants and sewerage with a capacity exceeding 100 000 inhabitant equivalents.
- Sludge basins and sludge beds with a capacity exceeding 100,000 m^3 and others with an embankment height over 10 m above the footing bottom;
- Facilities for municipal waste treatment with a capacity ranging from 10,000 to 100,000 t/year;
- Rendering plants and veterinary decontamination plants;
- Modifications of water courses that fundamentally change the character of the water course and the nature of the landscape;
- Cableways, a part of which is the construction of ski pistes, covering an area exceeding 5 hectares;
- Trade and storage complexes covering a total built-on area exceeding 3,000 m^2;
- Camp sites, sports and military shooting ranges affecting interests protected by separate regulations;
- Airports and permanent racing tracks for motor vehicles without a hardened surface.

Estonia

Prepared for the European Bank for Reconstruction and Development and the
Commission of the European Communities by
Environmental Resources Limited*

1. Overview

1.1 The Guidelines

1.1.1 Background

Investments in Estonia are subject to many legal and economic requirements. This document focuses specifically on those compliance, operational and liability issues which arise from environmental protection measures and affect investments.

The Guidelines are intended to enable investors to familiarise themselves with the basic environmental regulatory regime relating to commercial and industrial greenfield site developments, joint venture operations or company acquisitions in Estonia.

The Guidelines review institutional arrangements for environmental control, legislative requirements and procedures, time implications for permitting, public access to information, liability and sanctions. Because environmental policy, legislation and infrastructure in Estonia are currently undergoing radical change the review covers both current and proposed future arrangements.

Guidelines for the following CEE countries have been prepared on behalf of the European Bank for Reconstruction and Development and the Commission of the European Communities by Environmental Resources Limited and White & Case:

- Bulgaria;[1]
- Czech Republic and Slovak Republic;[1]
- Estonia;[2]

---

[1]   Guidelines prepared by White & Case.
[2]   Guidelines prepared by Environmental Resources Limited.

*   Environmental Resources Limited acknowledges the valuable contribution in the preparation of the
     Investor's Environmental Guidelines: Estonia of Dr. David Gilbert of Environmental Resources Limited and
     Peter Zigalvis Esq.

- Hungary;[1]
- Latvia;[2]
- Lithuania;[2]
- Poland;[1]
- Romania.[2]

These Guidelines present a description of the environmental regulatory framework as of February 1993. They provide a first step for investors in understanding environmental requirements but do not substitute for specific legal advice relating to particular sites.

Administrative and legal arrangements for environmental regulation are in a transition phase in the countries covered by these Guidelines. Requirements and implementation systems are subject to change. Investors are advised to discuss details of requirements with the authorities and check for any changes which may have taken place since February 1993.

1.1.2 Using the Guidelines

The Guidelines provide general guidance on environmental regulatory requirements applicable to foreign investment in commercial and industrial sectors of the economy. Some sections of the Guidelines, such as *Section 4* on Land Use Planning and *Section 5* on EIA are also applicable to other sectors of the economy such as agriculture, mining, forestry and fisheries. In relation to such types of activities however, it is advisable to review other applicable requirements which are outside the scope of the Guidelines.

Section 1 provides a quick reference to environmental regulatory requirements in two case studies, and in *Figure 1.1.2(a)* and *Figure 1.1.2(b)*. *Figure 1.1.2(b)* indicates how the Guidelines should be used by reference to the type of investment decision that has to be made.

The remainder of this section provides background information on the country and the following.

- Administrative structure;
- Legislative process and key items of legislation;
- Quick reference to the permitting process;
- Enforcement;
- Public participation.

Section 2 highlights the potential liabilities of investors. Liabilities potentially arising from past pollution to be taken into account at the time an investment is made and liabilities arising in the course of operating commercial and industrial facilities are presented separately. Additional details relating to specific sectors of control are provided in subsequent Sections.

Section 3 identifies any environmental auditing requirements and comments on the role of voluntary audits in achieving compliance.

Sections 4–11 provide guidance on permitting and related regulatory requirements for setting up and operating a commercial or industrial enterprise. Key aspects are presented at the beginning of each section for quick reference. Each section identifies the following:

- Key legislation;
- Activities covered;

---

[1] Guidelines prepared by White & Case.
[2] Guidelines prepared by Environmental Resources Limited.

Figure 1.1.2(a) Using the Guidelines: report structure

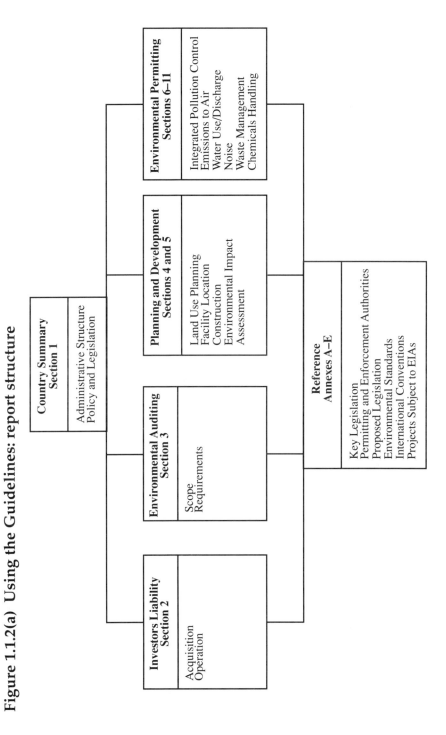

Figure 1.1.2(b) Using the Guidelines: summary by type of investment decision

Investment Decisions	Environmental Concerns	Sections in Guidelines
Choice of investment sector (eg commercial, services, manufacturing, energy)	Government and environmental bodies	1.4, 1.7, Annex B
	Existing and proposed legislation	1.5, Annex A & C
	Available forms of investment	1.2, 2.3.2
	Purchase of land	4.3
	Investments subject to EIA	5
	Activities subject to permitting	6–11
	Permitting overview and examples	1.6
Development of a "greenfield site"	Government and environmental bodies	1.4, 1.7, Annex B
	Existing and proposed legislation	1.5, Annex A & C
	Purchase of land	4.3
	EIA requirements	5
	Public participation	1.8
	Environmental standards	7, 8, Annex D
Acquisition of existing facility and privatisation	Government and environmental bodies	1.4, 1.7, Annex B
	Privatisation	1.2
	Environmental liability	2
	Cleanup of contaminated sites	2.3
	Indemnification by government	2.3
	Environmental audits	3
	Environmental standards	7, 8, Annex D
	EIA requirements (especially where modifications are made to existing facilities)	5

Investment Decisions	Environmental Concerns	Sections in Guidelines
Redevelopment and expansion of commercial and industrial facilities	Government and environmental bodies	1.4, 1.7, Annex B
	Change of land use	4
	Construction permits	4
	EIA requirements	5
	Permitting requirements	6–11
	Public participation	1.8
Operation of industrial and commercial facilities	Government and environmental bodies	1.4, 1.7, Annex B
	Environmental liability	2
	EIA requirements	5
	Public participation	1.8
	Integrated permitting	6
	Air requirements	7, Annex D
	Water requirements	8
	Noise requirements	9
	Waste management	10
	Chemical storage and handling	11
	Permitting overview and examples	1.6
	Compliance with international law	Annex E

- Requirements and procedures;
- Timing;
- Public participation;
- Enforcement and sanctions.

Sections 4 and 5 outline requirements and procedures relating to land use planning, facility location and construction, and environmental impact assessment. *Section 6* indicates the extent to which environmental permitting is integrated. Permitting and other regulatory requirements relating to air, water, noise, waste and chemicals are set out in *Sections 7–11*.

Annexes provide quick reference to existing and proposed legislation, contact points for the regulatory agencies, environmental standards, and ratification of international conventions.

1.2 The country

1.2.1 Background

Estonia has 1.5 million inhabitants and approximately 70% are citizens of Estonia. The non-citizens, as in Latvia and Lithuania, are chiefly Russian speaking and make up a high percentage of the industrial work force.

The Republic of Estonia has become a Parliamentary democracy and joined the United Nations on 17 September 1991. It is currently in transition from a centrally planned economy to a market economy. The Riigikogu (Estonian Parliament) and the new Republic of Estonia Constitution were launched on 20 September 1990, with the elections the National Assembly and the Supreme Council were held under the Estonian Soviet Socialist Republic and USSR Constitutions. The Estonian crown (kroon) was introduced in the summer of 1992, finalising Estonia's exit from the ruble zone (Kroons 19.5 = £1 sterling at 2/4/93).

1.2.2 Investment

The Estonian government faces the major task of rebuilding the economy whilst also protecting the environment as privatisation and land reform, including de-nationalisation of land and buildings, develop. A particular challenge currently facing Estonia is to carry out land reform so as not to endanger nature reserves and national parks.

Regional co-operation with the countries of the Baltic Sea is Estonia's highest priority in seeking to align to international environmental developments. Estonia plans to develop legislation that is in line with the European Community. The Estonian government applies the "polluter pays" principle and since 1991 natural resource charges and pollution taxes have been used as a way of balancing "command and control" regulation with economic incentives for pollution reduction. The *Regulation on the System of charges and Taxes in Nature Management of 13 February 1990* has been periodically updated taking into account feedback from the field. However, the state industry remains dominant and responds little to market and profit making pressures, making the economic incentives inevitably less effective than they would be in a fully free market economy.

Estonia uses tax credits as an economic incentive for pollution control. Enterprises which invest in pollution reduction measures and reduce waste by at least 25% are given a pollution tax credit of 1.5 times their pollution control investment. There are tax incentives in Estonian law for foreign investment. Guidelines issued by the Finance Ministry authorise the reduction of tax rates for "environment friendly" enterprises manufacturing or providing equipment for monitoring, metering, or recycling wastewater treatment and sanitary purposes. The environmental agencies are given authority to exempt enterprises which have made an investment in pollution abatement from paying pollution fees up to the amount of the investment made.

Estonia is the only one of the three Baltic countries with a centralised privatisation organisation, the Estonian Privatisation Company which is modelled on Germany's Treuhand.

260 large industries and 2,500 smaller enterprises are scheduled for sale by the Privatisation Company in the next two and a half years. Estonia is more oriented towards obtaining foreign investment in privatisation than Baltic neighbours Latvia and Lithuania. All of Estonia's industry is to be sold with the exception of the following:

● Energy;
● Railways;
● Telecommunications;
● Paper;
● Cement.

1.3 Administrative structure

Estonia is a centralised country divided into 15 Districts, with six towns outside Districts and 193 Municipalities. The Ministry of the Environment, located in the capital city of Tallinn, is the central environmental authority. There are 19 district Environmental Protection Departments (EPDs) which are part of the local government structure at District and Town level.

1.4 Government and environmental bodies

1.4.1 Ministries

The main authority for environmental protection is the Ministry of the Environment with its subdivisions, the district Environmental Protection Departments, the Forest Department, and the Fisheries Department. The Ministry of the Environment is responsible for:

● Developing environmental legislation and standards;
● Developing environmental policy and strategy;
● Co-ordinating management of natural resources, environmental protection activities and scientific research;
● Organising environmental monitoring;
● Carrying out environmental impact assessment of nationally significant projects;
● Managing protected nature areas;
● Organising the training and education of staff;

- Promoting environmental education;
- Co-ordinating international co-operation in the field of environmental protection.

The staff of the Ministry are located in the following departments (1992 figures):

- National office in Tallinn, 40;
- Environmental Management Scientific Information Centre, 15;
- Hydrometeorology Institute, 350;
- Central Laboratory, 40;
- Sea Inspectorate, 25;
- Forestry Board, 40;
- Fisheries Board, 20.

1.4.2 Environmental bodies

District Environmental Protection Departments (EPDs) are funded by the Ministry of the Environment but have been relatively independent from the Ministry since 1990. The EPDs are divisions of district/town governments and not directly subordinate to the Ministry of the Environment. The 19 district EPDs are responsible for:

- Issuing licences and permits for natural resource use;
- Issuing permits concerning pollutant discharges;
- Imposing and collecting emissions charges;
- Administering local environmental budgets into which a percentage of the charges are paid;
- Controlling polluters within their territory;
- Controlling Environmental Impact Assessment (EIA) within their areas of jurisdiction.

The largest district EPD is that of Tallinn with a staff of approximately 50. Some of the other EPDs are much smaller and staff are supplemented by volunteers.

1.4.3 Environmental Funds

The Environmental Protection Fund receives charges assessed for environmental damages and production losses and is used to finance local and central government environmental improvement projects. In 1991, 75% of the Fund's expenditures were for the control of water pollution.

Resource charges go to the national and regional budgets and taxes on pollution which exceeds set limits go to the regional budget.

Resource charges are collected for the use of mineral resources:

- Oil shale (50% to the national budget, 50% to local budgets);
- Peat, sand, and gravel use (30% to the national budget, 70% to local budgets);
- Water use (80% to the National budget, 20% to local budgets);
- Timber (100% to the State Forestry Board).

Part of the Fund is known as the Fisheries Fund and receives charges for issuing fishing licences.

The Ministry of the Environment is entitled to the seat of Chairman on the Fund's Board of Directors. Other Board members are representatives of the Ministry of Finance, the Supreme Council's (and now the National Assembly's) Standing Commission on the Environment, and the 19 district EPDs.

1.5 Environmental legislation

1.5.1 *Legislative process*

Environmental legislation was passed by the Supreme Council until 20 September 1992, when the National Assembly was elected under Estonian law (the Supreme Council was elected under ESSR and USSR law with the participation of foreign military and non-citizens). The new legislative process has not yet been set out. It will be defined in the *Law on the National Assembly By-Laws.*

Currently draft legislation may be submitted to the Supreme Council ("SC") by:

- Parliamentary commissions;
- Individual Members of the Riigikogu (Parliament);
- Parliamentary factions;
- The government.

Drafts are first submitted to the appropriate SC commission for review.

When a draft has its first reading in the Supreme Council, the author of the draft and a member of the commission that reviewed the draft, report on the proposal and answer questions. The first reading of the draft law ends with voting if neither the appropriate commission nor any faction rejects it. At least two weeks, but not more than a month, after the first reading of the draft, a second reading is given.

The commission must collaborate with the author or authors of the draft to prepare an edited version, including suggestions submitted for amendments and written corrections from Riigikogu Members. When the draft is presented to the session in the second reading, further changes can only be proposed to those clauses which have been rewritten after the first reading. The draft law as a whole is then voted on by the SC.

Two readings of a proposed law are required for acceptance unless a third reading is requested by a faction, commission, or a quarter of all MPs. The President will have the power of veto.

It is possible to call for a speeded-up process of legislative discussion. Discussion takes place in the first reading, but the following readings are held during the same or subsequent session. Changes to current laws are carried out using this process.

1.5.2 *Legislation*

In the new Constitution of the Republic of Estonia, approved on 27 June 1992, Article 53 sets the general duty that:

Everyone shall be obliged to preserve the human and natural environment and to compensate for damages caused by him or her to the environment. The procedures for compensation shall be determined by law.

179

The framework for environmental legislation is provided by the *Law on Environmental Protection in Estonia of 23 February 1990.* Regulations of the former USSR are still in force in many areas providing they do not conflict with the Constitution.

Other key items of environment related legislation are as follows.

- *Law on Land Reform;*
- *Law on Economic Zone;*
- *Law on the Protection of Nature 1990;*
- *Law on Municipal Government 1989;*
- *Order on the Protection of Coastal Areas;*
- *Order on Environmental Impact Assessment 1992;*
- *Temporary Distribution Order for Permission to Utilise the Environment and Natural Resources 1991;*
- *Temporary Order of Possession and Allotment of the Environment, Natural Resources and Objects submitted to the Competence of the Executive Body of the Primary Administrative Unit of Local Government 1991;*
- *Provision Order on Use of the Environment, Natural Resources and Objects within the Competence of Local Government 1991;*
- *Provisional Order on Permitting the use of Environment and Natural Resources 1991;*
- *Act of Fisheries 1991;*
- *Fishing Regulations 1992;*
- *Resolution No. 16 on the Approval of Standards for Air Emissions 1991;*
- *Regulation on the System of Charges and Taxes in Environmental Management of 13 February 1990,* as amended;
- *Regulation on the System of Charges and Taxes in Environmental Management of 20 November 1990;*
- *Sanitary Norms for Inhabited Areas, No. 3077-84, passed on 3.08.1984;*
- *Aviation: Allowable Noise Levels for Inhabited Areas, Gost 22283-88;*
- *Waste Law 1992;*
- *Order on the Licensing of Hazardous Waste Treatment 1992;*
- *Order Approving the Classification of Waste 1991.*

USSR Regulations that remain in force in Estonia include:

- OND 1-84 with supplements No. 3 and No. 6;
- SNIP Construction Regulations and Requirements;
- Sanitary Regulations, which regulate safety requirements.

Laws are currently being drafted on:

- Protected areas;
- Construction;
- Land planning;
- Property;
- District planning;
- Water;
- Forest management.

1.6 Overview of permitting process and other regulatory requirements

1.6.1 General

Sectoral environmental permits are currently required in Estonia for the operation of industrial and commercial facilities. Environmental permitting is closely linked to the EIA process and it is anticipated that an integrated permitting system will be introduced in the future. Because there has been little foreign investment in Estonia to date experience in the environmental permitting process is very limited.

For any commercial or industrial activity an investor must prepare a Technical Economic Calculation (TEC) and submit it to the municipality. The TEC includes information relating to site location, and environmental information which is required for the purposes of an Environmental Impact Assessment (EIA).

The TEC is then passed to the district Environmental Protection Department (EPD) which determines whether, for environmental purposes the project is of local or national significance.

For projects considered to be of only local significance the application for a construction permit is reviewed by the district EPD in consultation with the appropriate national authorities, ie Ministries of Environment, Planning, Fisheries, Sanitation and Mining. The construction applications for projects deemed to be of national significance, are reviewed by the national authorities as appropriate. In addition, for proposals for the construction of harbours, and for mining, telecommunications, energy production and distribution activities, the TEC is passed for review to the Ministry of Economy.

Once approval of the construction application has been received from the appropriate authorities the municipality may issue a construction permit. There is no time-limit for issue of the permit. Construction may not begin however, until approval of the EIA has been granted.

The EIA part of the TEC is reviewed by the district EPD for projects of only local significance. A standard review period of one month is prescribed, although this may be extended when applications require further information from the investor, or extensive consultation between environmental authorities.

Approval of the EIA provides the basis for sectoral environmental permits for air, water and waste as appropriate, based on information presented by the investor. Sectoral permits may be issued with different time durations of between one and five years.

A summary of the environmental permitting procedure is given in *Figure 1.6.1(a)*.

1.6.2 Case study 1

For a foreign investor acquiring a greenfield site for development of a new paper mill, the permitting procedure would involve the following steps.

First, an investor would have to confirm with the local authority that the site is appropriate for industrial use (eg not a protected area). After receiving approval for the requested land-use, and advice on whether an EIA is needed, the investor must produce a design of the proposed project and complete a TEC. The TEC is submitted to the municipality, and the EIA section is passed to the EPD. If the municipality and EPD grant general approval for the development, then further details eg predicted emissions are requested from the investor for the purposes of setting standards and issuing environmental sectoral permits. Once the EIA has been approved and environmental permits issued, the municipality may issue a construction permit.

A summary of the environmental permitting procedure for a proposed facility on a greenfield site is given in *Figure 1.6.1(a)*.

1.6.3 Case study 2

For a foreign investor forming a joint venture with an existing company, acquiring two factories, closing one and refurbishing the other to produce tyres, the permitting procedure would involve the following steps.

In order to close the factory, the issues arising would have to be resolved with the Ministry of Industry, Ministry of Labour, and the appropriate municipal government. There would be no barriers to closure from environmental authorities. The refurbishment of the other factory would be treated as a new project and the investor would need to complete a TEC and follow the steps outlined in *Case Study No. 1*.

The environmental permitting procedure for closure and modification to existing facilities is thus similar to the procedure for a proposed facility, as summarised in *Figure 1.6.1(a)*.

1.7 Enforcement of environmental legislation

The body ultimately responsible for the enforcement of environmental legislation is the Chief Inspector of Environmental Protection in the national Ministry of the Environment, who is appointed by the Supreme Council for a fixed term of seven years. The staff of the Environmental Protection Inspectorate, a branch of the Ministry of the Environment consists of approximately 20 employees. Many of the day to day enforcement tasks are delegated to the district Environmental Protection Department (EPDs). The main duty of the Chief Inspector's Office is to inspect and arbitrate the decisions of the EPDs.

The Chief Inspector has the right to close down enterprises or levy fines according to the Estonian Administrative Violation Code.

In addition to administrative sanctions, pollution discharges, in excess of norms will result in pollution charges under the *Regulation on the System of Charges and Taxes in Environmental Management 1990*.

1.8 Public participation

1.8.1 Public access to information

The *Law on Environmental Protection 1990* makes general provision for information on the environment to be made available to the public but no detailed provisions exist. There are no specific provisions on access to information.

1.8.2 Provision of information

The *Order on Environmental Impact Assessment 1992* requires that the proceedings of EIAs are made public by the competent authority. The authority must determine the

Figure 1.6.1(a) Environmental permitting procedure

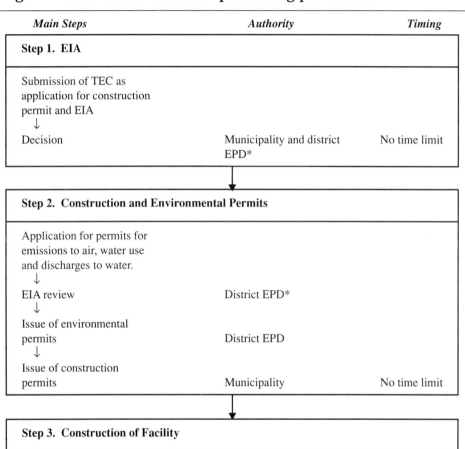

Main Steps	*Authority*	*Timing*
Step 1. EIA		
Submission of TEC as application for construction permit and EIA ↓		
Decision	Municipality and district EPD*	No time limit
Step 2. Construction and Environmental Permits		
Application for permits for emissions to air, water use and discharges to water. ↓		
EIA review ↓	District EPD*	
Issue of environmental permits ↓	District EPD	
Issue of construction permits	Municipality	No time limit
Step 3. Construction of Facility		

* National authorities for projects for national significance.

method of making information public, announce places and times of consultations and discussions, and determine the method of collecting information from the public.

1.8.3 Public consultation

The *Order on Environmental Impact Assessment 1992* states that comments from
citizens will have to be taken into account by environmental authorities. As yet there are
no specific procedures or requirements for consultation. The authority must determine
methods to announce places and times of consultations and discussions, and the method of
collecting information from the public.

2. Environmental liability

2.1 Summary

Note:	New liability legislation is currently being prepared in the form of a new civil code and privatisation laws. The following presents the existing situation.
Environmental Liabilities of Investors:	Legislation has not yet specifically addressed liability relating to investment.
Successor Liability:	Under the *Civil Code* liability is transferred with the property unless there is a contractual agreement to the contrary.
Investor Clean-up of Contaminated Sites:	No standards exist either which specifically trigger a clean-up obligation or for restoration levels.
Civil Liability:	In principle, civil liability currently operates through a system of fault-based liability. There is no strict liability at present.
Administrative Liability:	The *1992 Administrative Code* lists environmental violations. Remedies include fines and permit revocation.
Criminal Liability:	The *1992 Criminal Code* lists environmental violations. Penalties include fines and imprisonment.

2.2 Sources of legislation relating to environmental liability

Estonia is in the early stages of preparing an entirely new *Civil Code* which is expected
to be finalised in 1997. In the meantime, *Civil Code* sections will replace the sections of
the Soviet Civil Code which have been part of the planned economy. The *Law on Environmental Protection 1990* sets out general provisions for compensation for environmental
damage.

The Civil Code is only used to exact compensation for damage. The *Administrative* and *Criminal Codes* are used to remedy violations of environmental laws and regulations.

2.3 Environmental liabilities for past pollution

2.3.1 Types of environmental liabilities

Provisions relating to environmental liability for past pollution are not as yet well developed. There have been no cases of private companies being held liable in the courts for environmental damage. Legislation in this area is currently being developed.

The question of liability for on-site pollution arising from past operations has not yet been clarified in Estonia's privatisation laws. Whoever currently owns the property is considered liable under the Civil Code as long as there has been a legal transfer. There may however be a contractual agreement between the buyer and vendor to absolve one of the parties of liability.

Before an enterprise goes out of business or an organisation is liquidated, newspaper notices are publicised stating that all obligations must be settled. All requests for payment of an obligation must be submitted within two months. After this period has passed, neither the previous owner nor the new owner will be liable. The same process would apply where a government enterprise sold its facilities and went out of business.

2.3.2 Government indemnification of environmental liabilities

There are no provisions for government indemnification of investors regarding environmental liabilities. Indemnification is a question for the new privatisation legislation. In the ESSR, it was assumed that an organisation that announced its liquidation publicly and then settled its accounts with all creditors, claimants etc, was indemnified from liability.

2.3.3 Investor clean-up of contaminated sites

There are no special standards or requirements for the clean-up of contaminated land. Although there have been some clean-up operations of sites formerly occupied by the Soviet Military, attention is focused mostly on assessment of environmental damage rather than remediation. No large-scale clean-up operations have been undertaken.

2.4 Environmental liabilities arising from facility operation

2.4.1 Civil liability

The *Law on Environmental Protection 1990* states that there must be compensation for all environmental damages. In the ESSR all compensation was paid to the state but, since 1990, it has been paid to the Estonian Nature Protection Fund (ENPF). Damages are now available for owners or users of natural resources.

The *Law on Environmental Protection 1990* states that a citizen can sue a violator of environmental law or regulations but in practice, only owners, users (of the natural resource), and the Ministry of the Environment have been allowed to bring suits.

If a contractual agreement were made to leave environmental liability with the vendor, it may (theoretically) be possible to sue in the Civil Court.

Fault Based Liability

In principle, current civil liability operates through a system of fault-based liability ie intention or carelessness. However, according to the *Law on Environmental Protection 1990* if a violator cannot be found, the state will be responsible for damages. This provision was introduced prior to privatisation whereas according to the *Waste Law 1992*, if it is impossible to determine the polluter, the liability falls on the land owner.

Strict liability

There is no strict liability at present.

Statutes of limitation

The statute of limitations in Estonia is one year for cases between organisations and three years for cases involving a private citizen.

2.4.2 Administrative liability

Types of administrative liability

The new Administrative Violation Code was adopted by the Republic of Estonia on 1 August, 1992. The Code lists over 30 causes of administrative action as given in *Table 2.4.2(a)*.

Remedies

Penalties under the Administrative Code are directed at individuals rather than companies and other organisations. Breach of the code may result in fines, loss of rights or imprisonment. The maximum fine, based on the statutory minimum wage, is 200 days wages. Violators may be imprisoned for up to 30 days. Facilities may be shut down and permits withdrawn under the *Law on Environmental Protection 1990*.

Case examples

A recent example is a spill of oil products into the Gulf of Finland due to a railway incident. There is an investigation under way to identify the responsible railway worker. The punishment is likely to be an administrative fine, but criminal charges may also be brought.

In 1991 the Mardu chemical plant in Estonia was completely closed for emitting water and air pollution in excess of limits. An individual production process at Tallinn's Pulp and Paper Mill was also closed down in 1991.

Another example is the case of a Tallinn factory which emitted a noxious odour and a negligent worker was fined 10 Estonian Kroons.

Until recently, the company has always been state-operated so sanctions have been against individuals. At the time of writing no examples of sanctions against private operators have been identified.

Table 2.4.2a   Administrative offences

- Violation of Property Rights.

- Violation of Water Rights.

- Violation of Ownership Rights to Forests.

- Failure to Return Land Used Under a Land-Use Agreement on the Due Date or to Restore it in a State Adequate For Its Projected Use.

- Unauthorised Disregard of the Projected Use of a Land Area.

- Damaging Boundary Marks on Projected Land Use Areas.

- Violation of Land Surveying Regulations.Violation of Rules Applying to the Use and Protection of Natural Resources and Land Deposits.

- Violation of Rules Governing the Protection and Use of Inland and Territorial Water and the Economic Zone.

- Violation of Rules Governing Protection and Use of Water in Cases Where No Water Ownership Rights Have Been Violated.

- Violation of Fishing Rules.

- Storage, Transportation and Use of Substances Dangerous to Human Health or the Environment and Violation of Rules Requiring the Reporting and Registration of Operations Involving Such Substances.

- Damaging Installations or Equipment for Water Protection and Water Supply.

- Violation of Regulations Concerning Supply of Timber and Other Forestry-Based Products or Other Forest Utilisation Rules.

- Illegally Cutting or Otherwise Damaging Forests or Individual Trees or Bushes, Forest Cultures, Environmental Protection Work, Forestry Installations, or Markings.

- Violation of Reforestation Regulations.

- Violation of Regulations and Requirements Governing the Use and Protection of Air.

- Violation of Waste Handling Rules.

- Causing Noise in Excess of Permitted Levels.

- Disregarding Orders Issued by Officials Controlling the Protection and Use of Natural Environment and Natural Resources to Stop Violation of Regulations On the Protection and Use of the Environment and Natural Resources.

- Violation of Regulations and Requirements Pertaining To Natural Objects Under Special Government Protection (National Parks and Other Protected Areas, Protected Plant and Animal Species, and Natural Monuments.

- Acceptance of Illegally Obtained Natural Resources (Fish, Wild Animals, Forest Materials etc) For Sale, Processing, or Storage.

2.4.3 *Criminal liability*

Types of criminal liability
   The Criminal Code was adopted on 1 June 1992. Environmental violations are as follows.

- Violation of land and soil regulations;
- Violation of mineral resource use and protection regulations;
- Illegal cutting of timber;
- Intentional destruction or damage of forests;
- Negligent destruction or damage of forests;
- Damage of fields or plantations;
- Poaching and illegal collection of plants;
- Pollution and littering of air and water;
- Destruction of fishing resources.

Penalties
   Sanctions under the Criminal Code include fines and imprisonment. Fines equivalent to US$30 may be imposed and prison sentences of approximately one year.
   At the time of writing no examples relating to sanctions against private operators have been identified.

3. Environmental audits

3.1 *Sources of legislation relating to environmental audits*

   There are no legal requirements to undertake pre-acquisition audits. Such requirements are subject to discussion amongst environmental officials but there are no definite plans for legislation on this issue.
   Modification of an existing facility, however, may require that an environmental impact assessment is undertaken which would include assessment of compliance with environmental standards and other regulatory requirements, ie an audit.
   The investor should consider carrying out a pre-acquisition audit to determine that the facility is in compliance and whether any liability exists and discuss potential liability issues with the authorities.

3.2 *National experience with environmental audits*

   It is expected that projects sponsored by financial institutions such as the IFC and EBRD would include requirements for some form of environmental audit to be undertaken. A certain number of audits are being carried out to ascertain the degree of environmental damage being left by the USSR Army.

4. Land use planning

4.1 Summary

Authorities:	District Environmental Protection Department (EPD) and Ministry of Economy.
Types of Activity:	*EPD* — All activities except those covered by Ministry of Economy. *Ministry of Economy* — Harbours, mining, telecommunications and energy facilities.
Permits:	Construction permit.
Timing:	No fixed time.
Public Information:	The *Law on Environmental Protection 1990* makes general provision for information on the environment to be made available to the public but no detailed provisions exist.
Public Consultation:	There is currently no legal requirement for public participation. A general requirement for public participation exists for the EIA process.

4.2 Sources of relevant land use legislation

The control of land use planning is currently undergoing considerable change with the shift towards privatisation. Several new items of legislation have been introduced recently and further laws and orders are in draft.

- *Law on Land Reform;*
- *Law on Economic Zone;*
- *Law on Environmental Protection 1990;*
- *Law on Municipal Government 1989;*
- *Order on the Protection of Coastal Areas;*
- *Order on Environmental Impact Assessment 1992;*
- *Rule of Regulation Concerning the Extraction of Mineral Resources 1991;*
- *Order of Granting Permissions for Exploration and Extraction of Mineral Resources 1991;*
- *Law on Lähemaa National Park.*

Draft legislation is being developed as follows:

- Draft Law on Protected Areas;
- Draft Law on Construction;
- Draft Government Order on Land Planning;

- Draft Law on Property;
- Draft Law on District Planning;
- Draft Law on Water;
- Draft Law on Forest Management.

A number of sets of regulations of the former USSR relating to land use process remain in force:

- OND 1-84, with supplements No. 3 and No. 6;
- SNIP Construction Regulations and Requirements;
- Sanitary Regulations, which regulate safety requirements.

4.3 Scope of activities subject to land use regulation

The construction or modification of a facility for any commercial or industrial activity requires a permit for construction.

The new system of approval for land use when fully implemented will be primarily based on:

- *Order on Environmental Impact Assessment 1992*;
- Draft Order on Land Planning;
- Draft Law on Construction.

The Estonian government will decide which forest lands, water bodies and nature protection areas are to remain under state ownership. It is expected that decisions on state ownership will be resolved in 1993.

4.4 Permitting process

4.4.1 Authorities

Permission for land use/development is controlled by the Municipalities in consultation with the appropriate national authorities, ie Ministries of Environment, Planning, Fisheries, Sanitation, Mining.

The Ministry of the Economy is responsible for granting planning permission to construct harbours, and for mining, telecommunications, energy production and distribution activities.

4.4.2 Application requirements

Foreign investors cannot purchase land but can lease it for an unrestricted period of time. To obtain a permit for construction, the investor must prepare a Technical/Economic Calculation (TEC) on a standard form. The TEC includes information relating to site location, and environmental information which is required for the purposes of an Environmental Impact Assessment (see *Section 5*).

For projects deemed by the district EPD to be of national significance, the municipality cannot make decisions before it receives approval from the national environmental, land, health-sanitary inspection, and construction authorities. The projected environmental impact of the proposed development is to be taken into account in the review process.

The decision-making process is set out in the *Law on Municipal Government 1989*. This however was adopted under the old Constitution and it has not yet been decided how much of this system will remain, on the introduction of new legislation.

4.4.3 Fees
Fees are not charged for permitting.

4.4.4 Timing
The time-frame for the permitting process is not prescribed.

4.4.5 Permit conditions
Permit conditions are derived from the following former USSR regulations.

- OND 1-84, with supplements No. 3 and No .6;
- SNIP Construction Regulations and Requirements;
- Sanitary Regulations, which regulate safety requirements.

4.5 Public participation

4.5.1 Public access to information
The *Order on Environmental Impact Assessment 1992* includes general provisions on public access to information regarding new economic activities. This may include information from the construction permitting process.

The *Law on Environmental Protection 1990* makes general provision for information on the environment to be made available to the public but no detailed provisions exist. There are no specific provisions on access to information.

4.5.2 Provision of information
The *Order on Environmental Impact Assessment 1992* requires that the proceedings of EIAs are made public by the competent authority. The authority must determine the method of making information public, and announcing places and times of consultations and discussions.

4.5.3 Public consultation
There are no requirements for public consultation in relation to the construction permit application. The application is closely linked to the EIA process and there is a general provision for public consultation in the EIA process.

The *Order on Environmental Impact Assessment 1992* states that comments from citizens will have to be taken into account by environmental authorities. As yet there are no specific procedures or requirements for consultation. The authority must determine methods to announce places and times of consultations and discussions, and the method of collecting information from the public.

4.6 Enforcement

The municipal authorities can halt construction activities where it is a breach of the construction permit.

5. Environmental impact assessments (EIAs)

5.1 Summary

Note:	The following summary outlines *proposed* requirements.
Authorities:	Ministry of the Environment or its regional offices.
Types of Activity:	Specified activities including manufacturing and processing industries; waste disposal; change in land use; storage and transport of hazardous waste.
Permits:	EIA approval.
Timing:	One month unless extended.
Public Information:	The *Law on Environmental Protection 1990* makes general provision for information on the environment to be made available to the public but no detailed provisions exist. Information on releases to the environment may be obtained by the public from the Ministry of the Environment's Information Centre.
Public Consultation:	A general provision requires public consultation in the EIA process. Detailed provisions have yet to be introduced.

5.2 Sources of legislation relating to the environmental impact of industrial and commercial developments

The following legislation is relevant.

- *Order on Environmental Impact Assessment 1992;*
- *Temporary Distribution Order for Permission to Utilise the Environment and Natural Resources 1991;*
- *Temporary Order of Possession and Allotment of the Environment, Natural Resources and Objects submitted to the Competence of the Executive Body of the Primary Administrative Unit of Local Government 1991.*

5.3 Scope of activities subject to EIA process

The development of facilities which are required to carry out an EIA are prescribed by the *Order on Environmental Impact Assessment 1992*. The Order indicates which authority the EIA must be submitted to. Facilities for which an EIA is dealt with by the district EPD are listed in *Table 5.3(a)*.

Projects and economic plans which according to the *Order on Environmental Impact Assessment 1992* must be presented to the national Ministry of the Environment are listed in *Table 5.3(b)*.

5.4 EIA process

The EIA process currently predicts whether a planned activity will remain within pollution norms, before permission to proceed is granted. The Ministry of the Environment and the local government have power to withhold permission for a planned activity to proceed, if norms are not adhered to.

In the past EIA were all for state enterprises and were carried out and paid for by the state. Very few private enterprises have financed their own EIAs. The recent *Order on Environmental Impact Assessment 1992* requires enterprises to pay for their own EIAs. The form of EIA is set out in detail in the 1992 Order.

5.4.1 Authority
EIA applications are made to the EPD or the Ministry of the Environment as indicated in *Tables 5.3(a) and 5.3(b)*.

5.4.2 Documentation
Environmental protection measures must be outlined in the technical/ economic calculation (TEC) documentation which constitutes the application for a construction permit. The TEC is then used for the EIA. The focus of the EIA is ensuring that environmental quality standards for pollutants are not exceeded.

The main steps in the EIA process are as follows.

- Application to municipality for a permit for construction;
- If there is an impact on the environment the district EPD or national Ministry of the Environment carries out EIA review. Project is reviewed on the basis of projected pollution discharges;
- Binding EIA conclusion;
- Final decision on the project by local government.

5.4.3 Experts and consultants
Experts and consultants involved in carrying out EIAs must be licensed by the Ministry of the Environment.

5.4.4 Timing
The process is to take one month, but may be extended if further information is required.

5.4.5 Standards of review
The project is reviewed prior to a decision at either district EPD or national Ministry level. If an EIA is reviewed at the district level, then the EPD can ask for assistance from the Ministry if necessary.

The specialists entrusted with the review of the project, do so on the basis of the projected pollution discharges. If the projected discharges exceed national standards then the project will not be allowed to proceed without modifications.

Table 5.3(a) Facilities requiring EIA, reviewed by District EPD

- Nuclear industry.

- Industry and activities using radioactive materials.

- Biochemistry, biotechnology, and pharmacy.

- Chemical industry.

- Production and use of mutagenic, including carcinogenic, substances.

- Energy distribution networks.

- Research, where hazardous substances, pathogens, high level electromagnetic radiation, radioactive matter, or environmentally hazardous substances are used.

- Production, storage, and use of mineral and organic fertilisers, pesticides, and poisonous substances in areas with environmental protection restrictions.

- Production, using natural resources; eg cement, glass and cellulose.

- Mining and processing of mineral resources.

- Processing agricultural products.

- Waste disposal.

- Storage, transportation and disposal of hazardous waste.

- Storage of oil products with capacity higher than 5 m^3; technical service centres.

- Activities causing noise, vibration, and electromagnetic fields, including high capacity communications.

- Microelectronics industry.

- Activities, causing erosion and deterioration or changes to the shores of water-bodies.

- Flow regulation of natural waterbodies and amelioration.

- Fish-breeding in natural waterbodies.

- Use of forests and other reproducible natural resources.

- Activities changing landscape and recultivation.

- Changing land use.

- Changing sanitary conditions of recreation areas as well as the natural condition of nature conservation areas.

Table 5.3(b)   Facilities Requiring EIA, Reviewed by National Ministry of the Environment

- State and branch concepts, programmes, and general plans as well as designs, including the use of the fund of land, economic plans of water management and forests management and other reproducible resources, district waste management, or towns in connection with the utilisation of the environment in Estonia.

- General and regional plans of regions and administrative units.

- General planning of regions and administrative units.

- Industrial regional planning and Republic town traffic schemes.

- The planning of holiday resorts and recreational areas of Republic-level importance.

- Creation of nature conservation areas and zoning.

- Establishing communication and production objectives; planning their settlements; making changes in the ownership of land, its use and in the purposes of land use; mining.

- Selection of project location as well as state communication network projects (gas, communication, electric transmission lines of 110 KW and more), railways and roads, airports and ports.

- Dredging in the Baltic Sea, Lake Peipsi, and Pihkva, as well as in other water bodies belonging to the state.

- Oil terminals with a capacity in excess of 5,000 m³.

- Water mains and water body regulation projects of regional and State importance.

- Projects for the disposal and storage of hazardous substances, including radioactive waste.

- Inter-state and inter-district plans for nature utilisation and conservation.

- Electric power stations with capacity in excess of 50 MW and atomic power stations.

- Projects for the establishment, reconstruction and liquidation of enterprises utilising natural resources on a large scale.

- Projects which produce environmentally hazardous or waste abundant products.

- Projects which introduce new technological schemes.

- Mining projects and projects utilising natural resources of state importance.

- Groundwater intake structures in groundwater layers of state importance.

- Projects of waste disposal and experimental wastewater purification equipment.

- Plans for liquidation of the consequences of large scale accidents.

- Products and packages which do not have quality certificates guaranteed by the state.

- Projects connected to changing the gene pool of livestock.

The Ministry of the Environment acts as arbitrator if an EIA decision by the EPD is contested by an investor. However, a decision to refuse approval by the district EPD will not be changed if there is good reason to refuse.

5.5 Public participation

5.5.1 Public access to information

The *Order on Environmental Impact Assessment 1992* includes general provisions on public access to information regarding new economic activities.

The *Law on Environmental Protection 1990* makes general provision for information on the environment to be made available to the public but no detailed provisions exist. There are no specific provisions on access to information.

5.5.2 Provision of information

The *Order on Environmental Impact Assessment 1992* requires that the proceedings of EIAs are made public by the competent authority. The authority must determine the method of making information public, and announcing places and times of consultations and discussions.

5.5.3 Public consultation

The *Order on Environmental Impact Assessment 1992* states that comments from citizens will have to be taken into account by environmental authorities. As yet there are no specific procedures or requirements for consultation. The authority must determine methods to announce places and times of consultations and discussions, and the method of collecting information from the public.

5.6 Enforcement

5.6.1 Compliance checking

The *Order on Environmental Impact Assessment 1992* makes it an offence to provide false information in relation to the EIA.

5.6.2 Sanctions

An investor providing false information may be subject to administrative sanctions resulting in a fine.

5.7 National experience with EIAs

Since the introduction of the *Order on Environmental Impact Assessment 1992* several EIAs have been initiated but as yet no major ones completed. Examples of current EIAs include the following:

- An oil terminal reconstruction has been proposed at a site which is already contaminated. The first stage of the process will be to examine the existing levels of pollution which is expected to take three weeks.
- At Muga port a proposal has been developed to construct four separate oil terminals. In each case first stage of the assessments, ie a general review of the proposals have been approved. It is expected that the final stage which examines predicted emissions to the environment in detail will take one month to complete.
- The reconstruction of a cement manufacturing facility which is a joint venture involving a local presence and a US company is part way through the EIA process. In this case, the key feature of the assessment is the assessment of changes to releases to the environment. The project is at the first stage of the assessment process.

6. Integrated permitting requirements applicable to the operation of industrial and commercial facilities

6.1 Summary

> The current permitting procedure is sectoral rather than integrated. However, there are plans to develop an integrated system.

6.2 Permitting process

Environmental permitting is carried out on a sectoral basis with separate permits required for air emissions, water use and discharge, and for waste generation and waste management. A permit is not required in relation to noise.

Information provided by the investor for the permit application will rely heavily on information provided for the EIA, which takes account of discharges to the environment.

Plans for an integrated permitting system are being developed but details have yet to be decided.

7. Air emission requirements applicable to the operation of industrial and commercial facilities

7.1 Summary

Authorities:	District Environmental Protection Department (EPD).
Types of Activity:	Determined on the basis of the content and volume of emissions.
Permits:	Air emission source permit.

Timing:	Permit issued after the one month EIA period and within 2 weeks of application.
Public Information:	The *Law on Environmental Protection 1990* makes general provision for information on the environment to be made available to the public but no detailed provisions exist. Information on releases to the environment may be obtained by the public from the Ministry of the Environment's Information Centre.
Public Consultation:	There is no specific provision for consultation in relation to air emissions. General provisions for consultation exist in relation to EIAs.

7.2 Sources of legislation relating to air emissions

Law on Environmental Protection 1990;

- *Provisional Order on Use of the Environment, Natural Resources and Object within the Competence of Local Government 1991;*
- *Provisional Order on Permitting the Use of Environment and Natural Resources 1991;*
- *Resolution No. 16 on the Approval of Standards for Air Emissions 1991;*
- *Regulation on the System of Charges and Taxes in Natural Management of 13 February 1990* as amended;
- *Regulation on the System of Charges and Taxes in Natural Management of 20 November 1990.*

7.3 Air protection zones

"Non-conforming" zones have been established in which levels of environmental pollutants exceed prescribed standards. In these zones, facilities can only obtain temporary, annual permits. It is anticipated that emission limits will be stricter each year thereby reducing overall emissions until the zones conform with environmental quality standards.

7.4 Scope of activities subject to air emission regulation

Activities required to be permitted for emission to the atmosphere are determined according to composition and volumes of emissions as set out in the *Resolution No. 16 on the Approval of Standards for Air Emissions 1991*. The resolution lists 152 substances.

7.5 Standards

7.5.1 Ambient quality standards

Air pollution control is based on the Maximum Permissible Concentrations (MPC) system of the former USSR which controls the concentration of pollutants in the air. Ambient air quality standards apply to over 800 pollutants. They specify 30 minute and 24 hour averages for MACs which are based on concentrations of chemical substances or chemical combinations which do not affect respiratory reflex actions in rural locations within 20–30 minutes. Standards for over 150 substances are set in Estonian *Resolution No. 16 on the Approval of Standards for Air Emissions 1991*. Examples of standards are given in Annex D.

The application of standards has proved difficult in practice because of the excessive detail. The MPCs are seen also as being too strict, making their attainment unachievable in many cases, which can lead to disrespect for standards overall.

Estonia aims to achieve ambient air quality which meets EC standards in all areas of the country. Existing standards will be revised and made more practical, with the possibility of increasing their strictness as technology allows. A commitment has also been made to the concept of permissible amounts of pollutants per unit of production.

7.5.2 Emission limit values

Emission limit values are set according to the former USSR system and written into facility permits. The Maximum Permissible Emission (MPE), is the maximum permissible amount of a pollutant that can be discharged into the atmosphere by a stationary source per time unit, which does not exceed the established near-the-surface maximum allowable concentrations (MAC).

Where it is not possible for a facility to achieve the MPE, Temporary Permissible Emissions (TPE) are determined and written into the permit. TPEs are set for a limited time period, eg 12 months after which the limit is reviewed.

7.5.3 Technology based standards

In cases where it is not technically possible for an enterprise to achieve emission standards because pollution control equipment is inadequate, temporary permits setting emission standards based on existing technology are issued.

7.6 Permitting process

7.6.1 Authorities

District Environmental Protection Departments (EPDs) are responsible for atmospheric emissions permitting.

7.6.2 Application requirements

The air emission source permitting process begins with preparation of the Technical/Economic Calculation for the construction permit and EIA applications. As part of the TEC, the investor must prepare MPE standards for proposed emissions. MPE standards are derived from the Maximum Allowable Concentration (MAC) set in former USSR air quality standards using simplified dispersion algorithms. Standards derived by the operator must be agreed by the EPD.

In a case where a facility proposes to emit a substance for which an MAC (or an approximate harmless level) has not been determined, the enterprise must apply to the appropriate scientific organisation to establish the value and to evaluate the overall impact of discharge of the substance. The enterprise must then submit a copy of its application to the appropriate district EPD and a TPE standard is determined.

When determining MPE standards for harmful substances, it is necessary to take into account the background concentration created by neighbouring sources. When assessing the background values by means of calculation, only the emissions overlapping the impact zone of the enterprise in question are taken into account. The list of enterprises, parameters of sources of pollution, and the volumes of emissions needed to make these calculations are provided by the district EPD.

7.6.3 Fees

There are no charges for permitting.

7.6.4 Timing

A permit application must be determined within two weeks of application.

7.6.5 Permit conditions

Emission limits for each pollutant are set in the permit. Operators are required to monitor and record emissions. Permits are issued for between one and five years.

7.7 Charges for emissions

Charges for air emissions were established by the *Regulation on the System of Charges and Taxes in Environmental Management of 13 February 1990* as amended and the *Regulation on the System of Charges and Taxes in Environmental Management of 20 November 1990*. Air pollution charges are calculated taking into account not only the pollutant produced but also the characteristics of the area being polluted. The area is calculated as that of a circle with a radius of 80 fold the height of the pollution source.

Charges on pollutants are calculated on the basis of their Maximum Permissible Concentrations (MPC) using the former USSR standards and are written into permits. Increased charges are imposed as fines for emission of pollutants in excess of limits are intended to encourage the reduction of emissions. The current levels of charges are very low, largely due to inflation and proposals are being developed to introduce a new range of charges early in 1993.

7.8 Public participation

7.8.1 Public access to information

The *Law on Environmental Protection 1990* makes general provision for information on the environment to be made available to the public but no detailed provisions exist. Information on releases to the environment may be obtained by the public from the Ministry of the Environment's Information Centre. There are no specific provisions on access to information.

7.8.2 Provision of information

As yet there are no requirements for the authorities to provide information except where it is requested. With regard to the development or modification of facilities, the *Order on*

Environmental Impact Assessment 1992 requires that the proceedings of EIAs are made public by the competent authority. The authority must determine the method of making information public, and announcing places and times of consultations and discussions.

7.8.3 Public consultation

In relation to the development or modification of facilities the *Order on Environmental Impact Assessment 1992* states that comments from citizens will have to be taken into account by environmental authorities. As yet there are no specific procedures or requirements for consultation. The authority must determine methods to announce places and times of consultations and discussions, and the method of collecting information from the public.

7.9 Enforcement

7.9.1 Compliance checking and monitoring

Enforcement is largely carried out by the district EPD. Compliance checking is based on data provided by the operator and spot checks by the EPD.

7.9.2 Sanctions

The EPD may levy fines or, in certain cases, shut down a facility and withdraw the permit. The decision to close may be subject to an appeal to the Ministry of the Environment or the appropriate district council. The final decision on the closure will be made by the Ministry of the Environment Chief Inspector. Fines are adjusted according to the hazard index of the pollutant in question. Because there are very few privately operated facilities fines have been imposed on individuals and are based on the rates of daily pay.

8. Water requirements applicable to the operation of industrial and commercial facilities

8.1 Summary

Authorities:	District Environmental Protection Department (EPD).
Types of Activity:	Facilities using more than $10m^3$ per day of water for commercial or industrial purposes. Facilities discharging commercial or industrial wastewater.
Permits:	Water use permit. Wastewater discharge permit.
Timing:	One month unless extended, following the EIA process.
Public Information:	The *Law on Environmental Protection 1990* makes general provision for information on the environment to be made available to the public but no detailed provisions exist. Information on releases to the environment may be obtained by the public from the Ministry of the Environment's Information Centre.

Public Consultation:	There is no specific legal requirement for public consultation in relation to water permitting. General provisions for consultation exist in relation to EIAs.

8.2 Sources of legislation relating to water requirements

- *Law on Environmental Protection 1990;*
- *Provisional Order on Use of the Environment, Natural Resources and Object within the Competence of Local Government 1991;*
- *Provisional Order on Permitting the Use of Environment and Natural Resources 1991;*
- *Resolution No. 16 on the Approval of Standards for Air Emissions 1991;*
- *Regulation on the System of Charges and Taxes in Environmental Management of 13 February 1990, as amended;*
- *Regulation on the System of Charges and Taxes in Environmental Management of 20 November 1990;*
- *Draft Law on Water Quality.*

8.3 Water management

8.3.1 Water quality categories

Water quality standards are defined in terms of the "maximum permissible concentrations" for household/service sector water use, for recreational water use, and for fishery use. The following sources of water are differentiated:

- Sub-surface water (groundwater, artesian);
- Surface water (differentiated into lakes and rivers);
- Drinking water.

8.3.2 Water management bodies

Water management is the responsibility of the Ministry of the Environment and district authorities. Permits for water use and wastewater discharge are issued by district EPDs.

8.4 Activities subject to water use and discharge regulation

8.4.1 Water use

All facilities using more than 10 m³ per day for commercial or industrial purposes are required to obtain a water use permit.

8.4.2 Water discharge

All facilities discharging commercial or industrial wastewater must obtain a wastewater discharge permit.

8.5 Standards

8.5.1 Ambient quality standards

Water quality is based on the "maximum permissible concentrations" (MPC) system of the former USSR concerning the concentration of pollutants in water. In Estonia, the MPCs are seen as being too strict, making their attainment impossible to achieve in many cases, which can lead to disrespect for overall standards. Examples of standards are given in *Annex D*.

The pollutants regulated are listed in Table 8.5.1(a).
Standards will be revised and made more practical with the possibility of increasing their strictness as technology allows. A commitment has also been made to the concept of permissible amounts of pollutants per unit of production. The draft Law on Water Quality is currently under consideration.

Table 8.5.1(a)   Regulated Water Pollutants

• suspended solids	• phenol
• chloride	• fluoride
• sulphate	• methanol
• BOD$_{21}$	• formaldehyde
• COD	• sulphite, thiosulphate, sulphide
• nitrate, nitrite	• active chloride
• ammonia, phosphate	• cyanide
• detergents (eugenic, non-eugenic)	• acrylonitrile
• iron	• chromium III and VI
• Caprolactam	• nickel
• fat substances	• cadmium
• tannin	• copper
• lignosulphanic acids	• zinc
• furfurol (C$_4$H$_3$O)	• manganese
• oil products	• lead

8.5.2 Discharge limit values

Discharge limit values are developed case-by-case, based on ambient quality standards and are written into permits.

8.5.3 Technology based standards

Where existing wastewater treatment technology at a facility is not adequate to meet discharge limits derived from water quality standards, a temporary permit may be issued based on the capability of the existing equipment.

8.6 *Water use permitting process*

8.6.1 *Authorities*

District Environmental Protection Departments (EPD) are responsible water use permitting.

8.6.2 *Application requirements*

Permitting requirements are set out in the *Provisional Order on Permitting the Use of Environment and Natural Resources 1991*. Following the EIA process an application is made to the district EPD. Information provided with the application is largely based on the data provided for the EIA.

8.6.3 *Fees*

Fees are not imposed for water use permits.

8.6.4 *Timing*

The authority is required to respond to a permit application within one month. This period can be extended for example where more information is required.

8.6.5 *Permit conditions*

Limits on the volume of water used may be written into the permit. The limits are based on data of predicted water use provided for the EIA process.

8.7 *Water discharge permitting process*

8.7.1 *Authorities*

Wastewater discharge permits are obtained from the district Environmental Protection Departments (EPD).

8.7.2 *Application requirements*

Permitting requirements are set out in the *Provisional Order on Permitting the Use of Environment and Natural Resources 1991*. Following the EIA process an application is made to the district EPD. Information provided with the application is largely based on the data provided for the EIA.

The investor must prepare a calculation of the maximum discharge which will not result in water quality standards being exceeded in the receiving waters. The maximum discharge must be agreed by the EPD.

In cases where the enterprise is discharging a substance into the water for which a maximum allowable concentration (or an approximate harmless level) has not been determined, the enterprise must apply to the appropriate scientific organisation to establish these values and to evaluate the overall impact of the discharge of the substance. The enterprise must then submit a copy of its application to the district EPD. The maximum permissible discharge standard is then determined based on the existing situation.

In cases where it is technically impossible for an enterprise to achieve discharge standards because of the absence, or low capacity of, wastewater treatment equipment temporary discharge standards are applied until ways to meet MPE standards are introduced.

8.7.3 Fees
Fees are not charged for permitting.

8.7.4 Timing
The authority is required to respond to a permit application within one month. This period can be extended for example where more information is required.

8.7.5 Permit conditions
The discharge limits in permits are worked out after negotiations with the discharging facility. They are based on the capabilities of existing water treatment technology. Permits can be valid for a period of one to five years.

8.8 Water charges

8.8.1 Water use

Charges for water use were established by the *Regulation on the System of Charges and Taxes in Environmental Management, of 13 February 1990*, as amended and the *Regulation on the System of Charges and Taxes in Environmental Management of 20 November 1990*. The current levels of charges are very low, largely due to inflation. Proposals are being developed to introduce a new range of charges early in 1993.

8.8.2 Water discharge
Water pollution charges based on the volume of pollutants discharged have been established for the following pollutants:

- BOD total;
- Suspended solids;
- Oil products;
- Phenols;
- Total phosphorus;
- Total nitrogen;
- Sulphates;
- Fats.

Increased charges are imposed as fines for the discharge of pollutants in excess of limits and are intended to encourage the reduction of emissions. The current levels of charges are currently very low, largely due to inflation and proposals are being developed to introduce a new range of charges early in 1993.

8.9 Public participation

8.9.1 Public access to information

The *Law on Environmental Protection 1990* makes general provision for information on the environment to be made available to the public but no detailed provisions exist. Information on releases to the environment may be obtained by the public from the Ministry of the Environment's Information Centre. There are no specific requirements on access to information.

8.9.2 Provision of information

As yet there are no requirements for the authorities to provide information except where it is requested. With regard to the development or modification of facilities, the *Order on Environmental Impact Assessment 1992* requires that the proceedings of EIAs are made public by the competent authority. The authority must determine the method of making information public, and announcing places and times of consultations and discussions.

8.9.3 Public consultation

In relation to the development or modification of facilities the *Order on Environmental Impact Assessment 1992* states that comments from citizens will have to be taken into account by environmental authorities. As yet there are no specific procedures or requirements for consultation. The authority must determine methods to announce places and times of consultations and discussions, and the method of collecting information from the public.

8.10 Enforcement

8.10.1 Compliance checking and monitoring

Enforcement is carried out by the district EPDs. Compliance checking is based on data provided by the operator and spot checks by the district EPD.

8.10.2 Sanctions

The district EPD may levy fines or, in certain cases, shut down a facility and withdraw the permit. The decision to close may be subject to an appeal to the Ministry of the Environment or the appropriate district council. The final decision on the closure will be made by the Ministry of the Environment Chief Inspector. Fines are adjusted according to the hazard index of the pollutant in question.

9. Noise requirements applicable to the operation of industrial and commercial facilities

9.1 Summary

Authorities:	District EPD.
Types of Activity:	All commercial and industrial operations.

Permits:	EIA permit.
Timing:	One month.
Public Information:	The *Law on Environmental Protection 1990* makes general provision for information on the environment to be made available to the public but no detailed provisions exist. Information on releases to the environment may be obtained by the public from the Ministry of the Environment's Information Centre.
Public Consultation:	There is currently no specific legal requirement for public consultation. A general duty to consult the public applies in mention to EIAs.

9.2 Sources of legislation relating to environmental noise

- Sanitary Norms for Inhabited Areas, No. 3077–84 1984;
- Aviation: Allowable Noise levels for Inhabited Areas, GOST 22283-88 1988.

9.3 Noise zones

All air fields are obliged to submit documents showing noise zones which have been co-ordinated with local government health protection services. The following must be set out:

- Equivalent noise level;
- Maximum noise level;
- Night noise level.

Noise zones (except where they are part of general sanitary zones) do not exist for factories or streets.

9.4 Activities subject to noise regulation

All commercial and industrial operations may be subject to noise control.

9.5 Standards

All former USSR standards have been adopted and remain in force until their repeal or replacement. The following legislation applies.

- Sanitary Norms for Inhabited Areas, No. 3077-84, passed on 3 August1984.
- Aviation: Allowable Noise Levels for Inhabited Areas, GOST 22283–88.

There are approximately 20 standards and methods in force from former USSR legislation including the following:

- GOST 23337-78 Noise: methods of noise measurement in residential areas and in the rooms of residential, public, and community buildings.
- GOST 15116-79 Noise: methods of sound insulation measurement of inner enclosures of buildings.
- GOST 20444-85 Noise: traffic flows; methods of noise characterisation and measurement.

9.6 Permitting process

9.6.1 Authorities
The District Environmental Protection Departments are responsible for noise regulation.

9.6.2 Application requirements
A permit relating specifically to noise is not required for new or modified facilities. Noise is taken into account in the EIA process as described in Section 5.

9.7 Public participation

9.7.1 Public access to information
The *Order on Environmental Impact Assessment 1992* includes general provisions on public access to information regarding new economic activities which may include information from the construction permitting process.

The *Law on Environmental Protection 1990* makes general provision for information on the environment to be made available to the public but no detailed provisions exist. There are no specific provisions on access to information.

9.7.2 Provision of information
The *Order on Environmental Impact Assessment 1992* requires that the proceedings of EIAs are made public by the competent authority. The authority must determine the method of making information public, and announcing places and times of consultations and discussions.

9.7.3 Public consultation
The *Order on Environmental Impact Assessment 1992* states that comments from citizens will have to be taken into account by environmental authorities. As yet there are no specific procedures or requirements for consultation. The authority must determine methods to announce places and times of consultations and discussions, and the method of collecting information from the public.

9.8 Enforcement

9.8.1 Compliance checking and monitoring
Enforcement is carried out by the district Environmental Protection Departments.

9.8.2 Sanctions
Operators creating noise in excess of permitted levels may be subject to fines under the *Administrative Violation Code.*

10. Hazardous and non-hazardous waste management

10.1 Summary

Authorities:	District Environmental Protection Departments (EPD) and Ministry of Economy.
Types of Activity:	Generating, transporting, processing, storage and disposal of wastes.
Permits:	Permit for waste disposal. Permit for waste treatment. Licence for hazardous waste.
Timing:	Not specified.
Public Information:	The *Law on Environmental Protection 1990* makes general provision for information on the environment to be made available to the public but no detailed provisions exist. Information on releases to the environment may be obtained by the public from the Ministry of the Environment's Information Centre.
Public Consultation:	There is currently no legal requirement for public participation.

10.2 Sources of legislation relating to waste management

- *Relevant legislation includes the following:*
- *Waste Law 1992;*
- *Order on the Licensing of Hazardous Waste Treatment 1992;*
- *Law on Environmental Protection 1990;*
- *Regulation on the System of Charges and Taxes in Environmental Management of 13 February 1990,* as amended;
- *Regulation on the changes in the Regulation the System of Charges and Taxes in Environmental Management of 8 January 1993;*

- *Order Approving the Classification of Waste 1991;*
- *Order on Procedures for export, import and transit movements of hazardous and other wastes 1992;*
- *Order on Procedures for issuing Waste Permits 1992;*
- *Order on Procedures for Labelling Hazardous Wastes 1992.*

10.3 Categories of waste

Classes of waste are determined by the Order Approving the Classification Waste 1991. Wastes are classified as either inert (non-hazardous) wastes or as hazardous wastes. Hazardous wastes are further sub-divided into four classes:

- Class 1 — Especially hazardous substances;
- Class 2 — Hazardous substances;
- Class 3 — Moderately hazardous substances;
- Class 4 — Waste of low hazard.

10.4 Waste storage and treatment

10.4.1 Generator permits and other requirements

A waste permit is required under the *Law on Waste 1992* for a facility which generates, transports, processes, stores, or disposes of wastes. The operator must submit an application for a waste permit to the district EPD. A special licence is required in the case of hazardous wastes.

The waste permit sets out limits for the amount of waste which can be generated from a manufacturing process and stored.

The *Waste Law* states that all hazardous waste producers must:

- Carry out statistical calculations of the generation and treatment of waste connected with their activities;
- Make reports about their activities to local authorities;
- Draw up waste programmes if required by local authorities.

Reports of waste volume and activities must be made on an annual basis to the district EPD. The amount and content of these are determined by regulations on statistical information. The waste report is submitted by producers and enterprises involved in the generation, storage, recycling, or disposal of wastes to:

- The Ministry of the Environment;
- Local authorities;
- The Estonian Statistics Board.

The following information is required:

- The name of the waste;
- The Estonian Waste Classification code;
- The nature of the waste;

- Quantity of waste generated and disposed of;
- Storage data.

The report is based on the level existing as of 31 December of its publication year. The responsibility for the accuracy of the report and for its submission on time lies with the CEO of the enterprise, who signs the report and appoints an executor whose name and contact telephone number must be included.

Data on the quantities of useful or hazardous components of waste are calculated on the basis of the whole amount of waste and the given chemical composition. A quarterly assessment of waste storage taxes is submitted to the district or town executive.

The national government enacts the procedure for waste collection while the local authority carries out the following:

- Governs waste management within its administrative territory;
- Arranges collection, sorting, transportation, processing, storage, and disposal of household and inert wastes.

10.4.2 Operator permits and other requirements

A waste permit is required under the *Law on Waste 1992* by a facility which generates, transports, processes, stores, or disposes of wastes. Requirements for permitting and reporting are as set out in *Section 10.4.1*.

10.5 Waste disposal

10.5.1 Generator permits and other requirements

A waste disposal permit is required under the *Law on Waste 1992* by a facility which processes, stores or disposes of wastes. Requirements for permitting and reporting are as set out in *Section 10.4.1*.

10.5.2 Operator permits and other requirements

A waste disposal permit is required under the *Law on Waste 1992* by a facility which processes, stores or disposes of wastes. Requirements for permitting and reporting are as set out in *Section 10.4.1*.

10.6 Transport of waste

10.6.1 Labelling and containers

Classes of hazards are determined by documents enacted by the Ministries of the Environment and Public Health, or provisionally on the basis of the former USSR Ministry of Public Health and State Science and Technical Committee Guidelines No. 4186–87, 1987.

10.6.2 Transboundary movement

Estonia has ratified the Basel Convention which entered into force in Estonia on 19 October 1992. Corresponding national legislation was approved in December 1992, as the

Order on Procedures for Export, Import and Transit Movements of Hazardous and other Wastes 1992. Under this legislation, the import of hazardous waste into Estonia is prohibited.

10.7 Waste charges

Taxes are charged according to the *Regulation on the System of Charges and Taxes in Environmental Management of 13 February 1990* as amended on 8 January 1993 relating to the generation of wastes in accordance with their toxicity level (there are five different levels according to hazard that they represent). Taxes are currently very low, largely due to inflation. Proposals are being developed to introduce a new range of charges early in 1993.

Incentives are also given for investments in environmentally friendly technology. For example, investments that lead to a minimum 25% decrease in waste result in pollution tax credits of 1.5 times their pollution control investment.

If pollution exceeds the permitted volume, the dumping of waste is taxed on a progressive basis according to its toxicity level.

10.8 Recycling requirements

There are recycling facilities in Estonia but there are no requirements to recycle.

10.9 Public participation

10.9.1 Public access to information

The *Law on Environmental Protection 1990* makes general provision for information on the environment to be made available to the public but no detailed provisions exist. Information on releases to the environment may be obtained by the public from the Ministry of the Environment's Information Centre. There are no specific requirements on access to information.

10.9.2 Provision of information

As yet there are no requirements for the authorities to provide information except where it is requested. With regard to the development or modification of facilities, the *Order on Environmental Impact Assessment 1992* requires that the proceedings of EIAs are made public by the competent authority. The authority must determine the method of making information public, and announcing places and times of consultations and discussions.

10.9.3 Public consultation

In relation to the development or modification of facilities the *Order on Environmental Impact Assessment 1992* states that comments from citizens will have to be taken into account by environmental authorities. As yet there are no specific procedures or requirements for consultation. The authority must determine methods to announce places and times of consultations and discussions, and the method of collecting information from the public.

10.10 Enforcement

10.10.1 Compliance checking
Enforcement is carried out by district EPDs.

10.10.2 Sanctions
Prohibition notices, administrative fines, permit withdrawal/facility shut down and criminal sanctions are available under the *Waste Law 1992*.

If waste storage taxes are not paid on time, a penalty of 0.5% is assessed for every day of non-payment. If the tax is not paid by the start of the next term, the storage licence may be suspended.

11. Chemicals storage, handling and emergency response

11.1 Summary

> There is no specific environmental legislation on chemicals storage, handling or emergency response. These issues may be covered in part, by the EIA system for new or modified facilities.

11.2 Legislation relating to chemicals storage, handling and emergency response

- *Waste Law 1992;*
- *Law on Environmental Protection 1990.*

11.2.1 Storage and handling
Storage and secondary containment of chemical substances is at present primarily controlled by USSR technical safety measures, not environmental regulations. Environmental regulations only cover the emission of pollutants into the environment. However, the *Waste Law of the Republic of Estonia* states that the generator of hazardous wastes is responsible for safe storage of them until they are delivered to a waste treatment enterprise that has a license for hazardo us waste treatment.

11.2.2 Emergency response
All former USSR standards have been adopted and remain in force until their repeal or replacement. There is no specific law on chemicals and environmental protection.

The *Law on Environmental Protection 1990* requires facility operators to inform the district EPD and the Ministry of the Environment where any environmental damage occurs. Further, the *Waste Law 1992* states that waste treatment enterprises must have an emergency action plan which has been approved by local authorities.

11.3 Regulatory requirements

There are no specific regulatory requirements relating to chemicals safety and the environment.

11.4 Public participation

11.4.1 Public access to information

The *Law on Environmental Protection 1990* makes general provision for information on the environment to be made available to the public but no detailed provisions exist. Information on releases to the environment may be obtained by the public from the Ministry of the Environment's Information Centre. There are no specific requirements on access to information.

11.4.2 Provision of information

As yet there are no requirements for the authorities to provide information except where it is requested. With regard to the development or modification of facilities, the *Order on Environmental Impact Assessment 1992* requires that the proceedings of EIAs are made public by the competent authority. The authority must determine the method of making information public, and announcing places and times of consultations and discussions.

11.4.3 Public consultation

In relation to the development or modification of facilities the *Order on Environmental Impact Assessment 1992* states that comments from citizens will have to be taken into account by environmental authorities. As yet there are no specific procedures or require- ments for consultation. The authority must determine methods to announce places and times of consultations and discussions, and the method of collecting information from the public.

11.5 Enforcement

11.5.1 Compliance checking

Enforcement is primarily carried out by the Ministry of Health and the Department of Technical Safety. The Ministry of the Environment and district EPDs carry out control of the EIA process and discharges into the environment.

11.5.2 Sanctions

Administrative and criminal sanctions are available for damage to the environment aris- ing from the storage and handling of chemical substances under the *Administrative* and *Civil Codes*.

Annex A

List of Key Legislation

1. Environmental liability

- *Law on Nature Protection 1990;*
- *Administrative Violation Code 1992;*
- *Criminal Code 1992.*

2. Land use planning

- *Law on Land Reform, which sets out the state principles on state minicipal, and private lands;*
- *Law on Economic Zone;*
- *Law on Environmental Protection 1990;*
- *Law on Minicipal Government 1989;*
- *Order on the Protection of Coastal Areas;*
- *Order on Environmental Impact Assessment 1992;*
- *Rule of Regulation Concerning the Extraction of Mineral Resources 1991;*
- *Order of Granting Permission for Exploration and Extraction of Mineral Resources 1991;*
- *Law on Lähemaa National Park.*

3. USSR Regulations

- OND 1-84, with supplements No. 3 and No. 6;
- SNIP Construction Regulations and Requirements;
- Sanitary Regulations, which regulate safety requirements.

4. Environmental Impact Assessments (EIAs)

- *Order on Environmental Impact Assessment 1992;*
- *Temporary Distribution Order for Permission to Utilise the Environment and Natural Resources 1991;*
- *Temporary Order of Possession on Allotment of the Environment, Natural Resources and Objects submitted to the Competence of the Executive Body of the Primary Administrative Unit of Local Government.*

5. Air emission requirements applicable to the operation of industrial and commercial facilities

- *Law on Environmental Protection 1990;*
- *Provisional Order on Use of the Environment, Natural Resources and Object within the Competence of Local Government 1991;*
- *Provisional Order on Permitting the Use of Environment and Natural Resources 1991;*
- *Resolution No. 16 on the Approval of Standards for Air Emission 1991;*
- *Regulation on the System of Charges and Taxes in Environmental Management of 13 February 1990 as amended;*
- *Regulation on the System of Charges and Taxes in Environmental Management of 20 November 1990.*

6. Water requirements applicable to the operation of industrial and commercial facilities

- *Law on Environmental Protection 1990;*
- *Provisional Order on Use of the Environment, Natural Resources and Object within the Competence of Local Government 1991;*
- *Provisional Order on Permitting the Use of Environment and Natural Resources 1991;*
- *Resolution No.16 on the Approval of Standards for Air Emission 1991;*
- *Regulation on the System of Cgarges and Taxes in Environmental Management of 13 February 1990, as amended;*
- *Regulation on the System of Charges and Taxes in Environmental Management of 20 November 1990.*

7. Noise requirements applicable to the operation of industrial and commercial facilities

- *Sanitary Norms for Inhabited Areas, No. 3077–84 1984;*
- *Aviation: Allowable Noise Levels for Inhabited Areas, GOST 22283–88 1988.*

8. Hazardous and non-hazardous waste management

- *Waste Law 1992;*
- *Order on the Licensing of Hazardous Waste Treatment 1992;*
- *Law on Environmental Protection 1990;*

- *Regulation on the System of Charges and Taxes in Environmental Management of 13 February 1990;* as amended;
- *Regulation on charges in the Regulation on the System of Charges and Taxes in Environmental Management of 8 January 1993;*
- *Order Approving the Classification of Waste 1991;*
- *Order on Procedures for Export, Import and Transit Movements of Hazardous and other Wastes 1992;*
- *Order on Procedures for Labelling Hazardous Wastes 1992.*

9. Chemical storage, handling and emergency response

- *Waste Law 1992;*
- *Law on Environmental Protection 1990.*

10. Other sectors

- *Act on Fisheries 1991;*
- *Fishing Regulations 1992.*

There is no specific legislation on the following:

- *Environmental audits;*
- *Integrated permitting.*

Annex B

List of Permitting Enforcement Authorities

Regional Environmental Protection Departments (EPD)

1.	Lääne Maavaitsuse Keskkonaamet EE 170 Haapsalu, Uus 21	44 255 44 355
2.	Harjumaa Looduskaitseamet EE 103 Tallinn, Roosikrantsi 12	77 12 37 77 14 57 42 11 66
3.	Hiiumaa Looduskaitse Valitsus 203200 Kärdla, Kôrgessaare mnt 18	91 633
4.	Jôgeva Loodusamet 202350 Jôgeva, Suur 3 42 855	22 855
5.	Järva Maavalitsuse Keskkonnaosakond 202810 Türi, Tallinna 8	8 238 78 115 79 890
6.	Ida-Viru Maavalitsuse Keskkonnakaitse osakond 202020 Kohtla Järve, Pargi 15	23362650 62 302
7.	Narva Looduskaitse Valitsus 202000 Narva, Peetri 3–9	33 196
8.	Pärnumaa Looduskaitse Valitsus 203600 Pärnu, Kerese 4	43 187 41 341
9.	Pôlva Keskkonnaamet 202611 Räpina, Apteegi 14	92 000 90 904
10.	Lääne-Virumaa Looduskaitse Talitus 202100 Rakvere, Narva tn 25	8 232 40 496 43 751 40 496
11.	Rapla Maavalitsuse Loodushoisuosakond 203500 Rapla, Tallinna mnt 14	56 382 55 807

12.	Saare Maavalitsuse	
	Keskkonnaamet	59751
	203300 Kuressaare	59 692
	Pargi 1 p/k 224	
13.	Tartu Linnavalitsuse	30 103
	Looduskaitse Amet	
	202300 Tartu, Akadeemia 4	30 417
14.	Tartumaa Looduskaitse Amet	30 017
	202300 Turtu Akadeemia 4	
15.	Tallinna Keskkonaamet	44 06 66
	200001 Tallinn	601
	Sulevimagi 10	44 09 07
16.	Valga Maavalitsuse	43 907
	Looksuskaitse Osakond	43 865
	202500 Valga, Keske 16	
17.	Viljandi Maavalitsuse	
	Keskkonnaamet	54 211
18.	Vôru Maa Keskkonnaamet	31 841
	202710 Vôro, Karja 17 a	
19.	Sillamäe Looduskaitse Valitsus	76 606
	202010 Sillamäe, Kirovi 27	

Other authorities

1.	National Board of Forestry	45 29 82
	Toompuiestee 24	
	EE 0100 Tallinn	
2.	National Board of Fisheries	682 760
	Liivalaia 14	
	EE 0100 Tallinn	

Annex C

List of Proposed Legislation

Legislation is being developed on the following subjects

- Protected areas;
- Construction;
- Land planning;
- Property
- District planning;
- Water;
- Forest management.

Annex D

Environmental Standards

Environmental quality standards for emission to air

The following examples are taken from former USSR standards:

Substance	24 h Maximum allowable concentration (mg/m³)
SO_2	0.50
NO	0.085
Particulates	0.050
Lead	0.003
Nickel	0.001
Cadmium	0.003
Mercury	0.003
Cobalt	0.001
Copper	0.002
Tungsten	0.001
Chlorine	0.100
Fluorine	0.02
Acetone	0.35

Annex E

International Conventions

Estonia participates in the following.

- Ronneby Conference;
- Baltic Sea Environmental Declaration (1990);
- Convention on the Protection of the Marine Environment of the Baltic Sea Area;
- International Atomic Energy Agency;
- Intergovernmental Oceanographic Commission;
- Convention on the Protection and Use of Transboundary Watercourses and International Lakes;
- Convention on the Transboundary Effects of Industrial Accidents;
- Convention on Fishing and Conservation of the Living Resources of the Baltic Sea and Belts;
- Convention on the International Council for Exploration of the Sea.

Estonia has signed bi-lateral agreements of co-operation for environmental protection with Sweden, Denmark, Germany, and Finland and plans adopt international conventions on sustainable development.

Hungary

Prepared for the European Bank for Reconstruction and Development and the
Commission of the European Communities by
White & Case*

1. Overview

1.1 The Guidelines

1.1.1 Background

Investments in Hungary are subject to many legal and economic requirements. This document focuses specifically on those compliance, operational and liability issues which arise from environmental protection measures and affect investments.

The Guidelines are intended to enable investors to familiarise themselves with the basic environmental regulatory regime relating to commercial and industrial greenfield site developments, joint venture operations or company acquisitions in Hungary.

The Guidelines review institutional arrangements for environmental control, legislative requirements and procedures, time implications for permitting, public access to information, liability and sanctions. Because environmental policy, legislation and infrastructure in Hungary are currently undergoing radical changes the review covers both current and proposed future arrangements.

Guidelines for the following CEE countries have been prepared on behalf of the European Bank for Reconstruction and Development and the Commission of the European Communities by Environmental Resources Limited and White & Case:

- Bulgaria;[1]
- Czech Republic and Slovak Republic;[1]

---

[1] Guidelines prepared by White & Case.

* White & Case acknowledges the valuable contribution in the preparation of the *Investors' Environmental Guidelines: Hungary* of Richard A. Horsch, Esq., Sophia Drewnowski, Esq. and Katherine Simonetti, Esq. of White & Case.
    White & Case would like to thank Dr. Gyula Bandi who acted as a consultant to White & Case in its preparation of these Guidelines.

- Estonia;[2]
- Hungary;[1]
- Latvia;[2]
- Lithuania;[2]
- Poland;[1]
- Romania.[2]

These Guidelines present a description of the environmental regulatory framework as of February 1993. They provide a first step for investors in understanding environmental requirements but do not substitute for specific legal advice relating to particular sites.

Administrative and legal arrangements for environmental regulation are in a transition phase in the countries covered by these Guidelines. Requirements and implementation systems are subject to change. Investors are advised to discuss details of requirements with the authorities and check for any changes which may have taken place since February 1993.

1.1.2 Using the Guidelines

The Guidelines provide general guidance on environmental regulatory requirements applicable to foreign investment in commercial and industrial sectors of the economy. Some sections of the Guidelines, such as *Section 4* on Land Use Planning and *Section 5* on EIA are also applicable to other sectors of the economy such as agriculture, mining, forestry and fisheries. In relation to such types of activities however, it is advisable to review other applicable requirements which are outside the scope of the Guidelines.

Section 1 provides a quick reference to environmental regulatory requirements in two case studies, and in *Figure 1.1.2(a) and Figure 1.1.2(b)*. *Figure 1.1.2(b)* indicates how the Guidelines should be used by reference to the type of investment decision that has to be made.

The remainder of this section provides background information on the country and the following:

- Administrative structure;
- Legislative process and key items of legislation;
- Quick reference to the permitting process;
- Enforcement;
- Public participation.

Section 2 highlights the potential liabilities of investors. Liabilities potentially arising from past pollution to be taken into account at the time an investment is made and liabilities arising in the course of operating commercial and industrial facilities are presented separately. Additional details relating to specific sectors of control are provided in subsequent sections.

Section 3 identifies environmental auditing requirements and comments on the role of voluntary audits in achieving compliance.

---

[1] Guidelines prepared by White & Case.
[2] Guidelines prepared by Environmental Resources Limited.

Figure 1.1.2(a) Using the Guidelines: report structure

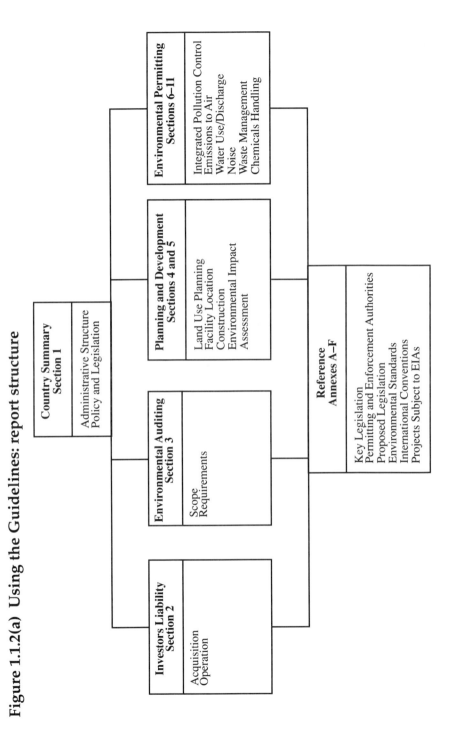

Country Summary
Section 1

Administrative Structure
Policy and Legislation

Investors Liability
Section 2

Acquisition
Operation

Environmental Auditing
Section 3

Scope
Requirements

Planning and Development
Sections 4 and 5

Land Use Planning
Facility Location
Construction
Environmental Impact
Assessment

Environmental Permitting
Sections 6–11

Integrated Pollution Control
Emissions to Air
Water Use/Discharge
Noise
Waste Management
Chemicals Handling

Reference
Annexes A–F

Key Legislation
Permitting and Enforcement Authorities
Proposed Legislation
Environmental Standards
International Conventions
Projects Subject to EIAs

Figure 1.1.2(b) Using the Guidelines: summary by type of investment decision

Investment Decisions	Environmental Concerns	Sections in Guidelines
Choice of investment sector (eg commercial, services, manufacturing, energy)	Government and Environmental bodies	1.4, 1.7, Annex B
	Existing and proposed legislation	1.5, Annex A & C
	Available forms of investment	1.2, 2.3.2
	Purchase of land	4.3
	Investments subject to EIA	5, Annex F
	Activities subject to permitting	6–11
	Permitting overview and examples	1.6
Development of a "greenfield site"	Government and Environmental bodies	1.4, 1.7, Annex B
	Existing and proposed legislation	1.5, Annex A & C
	Purchase of land	4.3
	EIA requirements	5, Annex F
	Public participation	1.8
	Environmental standards	7, 8, 9, Annex D
Acquisition of existing facility and privatisation	Government and Environmental bodies	1.4, 1.7
	Privatisation	1.2, 2.3.2
	Environmental liability	2
	Cleanup of contaminated sites	2.3
	Indemnification by government	2.3
	Environmental audits	3
	Environmental standards	7, 8, 9, Annex D
	EIA requirements (especially where modifications are made to existing facilities)	5, Annex F

Investment Decisions	Environmental Concerns	Sections in Guidelines
Redevelopment and expansion of commercial and industrial facilities	Government and environmental bodies	1.4, 1.7, Annex B
	Change of land use	4
	Construction permits	4
	EIA requirements	5, Annex F
	Permitting requirements	6–11
	Public participation	1.8
Operation of industrial and commercial facilities	Government and environmental bodies	1.4, 1.7, Annex B
	Environmental liability	2
	EIA requirements	5, Annex F
	Public participation	1.8
	Integrated permitting	6
	Air requirements	7, Annex D
	Water requirements	8, Annex D
	Noise requirements	9, Annex D
	Waste management	10
	Chemical storage and handling	11
	Permitting overview and examples	1.6
	Compliance with international law	Annex E

Sections 4–11 provide guidance on permitting and related regulatory requirements for setting up and operating a commercial or industrial enterprise. Key aspects are presented at the beginning of each section for quick reference. Each section identifies the following:

- Key legislation;
- Activities covered;
- Requirements and Procedures;
- Timing;
- Public participation;
- Enforcement and sanctions.

Sections 4 and 5 outline requirements and procedures relating to land use planning, facility location and construction, and environmental impact assessment ("EIA").

Section 6 indicates the extent to which environmental permitting is integrated. Permitting and other regulatory requirements relating to air, water, noise, waste and chemicals are set out in *Sections 7–11*.

Annexes provide quick reference to existing and proposed legislation, contact points for the regulatory agencies, environmental standards, ratification of multilateral international conventions and investment projects subject to EIAs which are specifically identified in legislation.

1.2 The country

The Republic of Hungary has a population of 10 million and covers a territory of 93,033 sq km. Hungary was the first country in the CEE to implement market reforms with the introduction of the "New Economic Mechanism" in 1968. Since the Communist regime remained in control of the country, however, a significant proportion of Hungary's trade continued to be with the former Soviet Union and the CEE countries.

During the late 1980s, the political system in Hungary underwent dramatic changes. In 1990, following the first free elections since 1947, a multi-party democratic government was formed. Hungary established a programme of privatisation and reform to restructure its economy. Central to this programme was the creation of the State Property Agency ("SPA") in 1990 and the enactment of *Acts No. VII and VIII of 1990* on the administration, utilisation and transfer of state-owned enterprises. This legislation was materially amended and updated in 1992 primarily by *Act No. LIII of 1992*, which created a new state entity to operate state-owned companies, *Act No. LIV of 1992 on the Sale, Utilisation and Protection of Assets Temporarily Owned by the State and Act No. LV* which amended previous privatisation-related statutes (together the *"Privatisation Laws"*).

In September 1990, the Ministry for Environment and Regional Policy ("Environment Ministry") launched a national programme of environmental protection calling for significant changes in legislative and administrative structures. The new programme targets five priority areas for action:

- Air quality improvement;
- Treatment and safe disposal of hazardous wastes;

- Protection of drinking water supplies from contamination;
- Conservation of threatened natural areas;
- Development of regional solutions to environmental problems.

Hungary is pursuing political and economic integration with Western Europe. In December 1991, Hungary signed an Association Agreement with the European Community ("EC") which will gradually establish free trade in goods, services, capital and labor between Hungary and the EC countries within ten years. Environmental laws, regulations and policies are likely to change as Hungary seeks to harmonise its legislation with that of the EC. For example, Hungary expects to conform its vehicular emission standards to those of the EC by 1994.

1.3 Administrative structure

Hungary is a centralised country consisting of 19 Counties and approximately 3,200 Municipalities. Hungary's capital, Budapest, has the same status as a County, unless otherwise specified by law.

The administrative framework of each County comprises a Representative Assembly, a Clerk and a Mayor. In general, Counties are granted a limited number of administrative powers, most of which do not relate to environmental matters.

Each Municipality has a Representative Assembly, a Clerk and a Mayor. Since 1992, Municipalities have been self-governing. Municipal building authorities are responsible for land use planning and development projects. They also draft regulations regarding local matters, including matters of an environmental nature.

All actions of Counties and Municipalities are reviewed by eight Commissioners of the Republic, nominated by the Prime Minister and appointed by the President. Each Commissioner is charged with overseeing the Counties and Municipalities within a defined territory. The Commissioners ensure that the actions of Counties and Municipalities are within the law.

Decisions of Municipalities, which fall within the scope of local government, may be appealed to the Municipal Representative Assembly or challenged in court. Decisions which fall within the Municipality's role as a representative of central government, however, must be appealed to a Commissioner or to the appropriate central government authority, depending upon the circumstances of the case. In general, cases which require substantial technical knowledge will be appealed to the central government authority. The decision of the Commissioner or central government authority may then be appealed in court.

1.4 Government and environmental bodies

1.4.1 Ministries
Environmental decision-making is carried out principally by the central government. With respect to environmental protection, the most significant central government institution is the Environment Ministry. The Environment Ministry has overall responsibility for

environmental policy-making and the drafting of environmental legislation. Its responsibilities encompass:

- Air pollution;
- Water pollution;
- Noise abatement;
- Waste management;
- Regional planning;
- Construction permits;
- Forest protection;
- Nature conservation;
- Landscape protection;
- Management of public and historic monuments;
- Supervision of meteorological services;
- Radiation.

The Environment Ministry acts in the territory of Hungary through the National
Environmental Protection Inspectorate and its 12 offices, the Regional Environmental
Inspectorates.

The Department of Construction Administration at the Environment Ministry (in addition to municipal building authorities) is responsible for matters relating to the construction of buildings (in addition to Municipal building authorities).

The Ministry of Transport, Telecommunication and Water Management is responsible
for water management and use. It is assisted by the National Water Management Authority
and by the National Water Directorate. Vehicular emissions testing is carried out and
enforced by six Transportation Inspectorates which assist the Ministry.

The Ministry of Public Welfare and Health, assisted by its National Public Health
Service, is responsible for regulating any type of pollution affecting public health and for
setting ambient air pollution standards.

The Ministry of Agriculture and its Land Registries are responsible for land use, soil
protection and forest management.

The Ministry of Housing and Construction is responsible for land use and construction
regulations.

The Ministry of Interior Affairs is responsible for waste management in general.
Although the Environment Ministry is legally responsible for household waste, all hazardous waste matters fall within the responsibility of the Ministry of Interior Affairs.

Hungary does not have a Privatisation Ministry. The SPA (working with the Hungarian
State Asset Management Company established in 1992) is charged with the implementation of the privatisation process, including, in certain cases, the preparation of privatisation programmes determined by the government and the valuation of property. The SPA is
supervised by a Minister without Portfolio.

1.4.2 Environmental bodies

The National Environmental Protection Inspectorate, headed by the Inspector General
of Environmental Protection, is responsible for, among other things, the issuance of air

and water discharge permits, the imposition of fines and penalties and the enforcement of regulations, including those relating to hazardous waste and sewage.

The National Water Directorate and its 12 regional Water Directorates issue water permits.

The Transportation Inspectorate conducts tests of vehicular emissions.

The Hungarian Standard Agency sets environmental pollution standards.

The National Public Health Service, supervised by the Ministry of Public Welfare and Health, issues permits for the manufacture, handling and transportation of toxic substances. It has regional and local branches. It also monitors and collects data related to the public health effects of pollution.

Land Registries, organised under and supervised by the Ministry of Agriculture, regulate changes in the use of arable land.

The Institute for Environmental Management, a scientific institution of the Environment Ministry, performs scientific research in the field of environmental protection, provides monitoring services and assists in environmental education. It can also perform research in specific areas at the request of third parties, such as potential investors.

Under draft environmental legislation, discussed in *Section 1.5.2* below, a proposal has been made to use the existing post of Ombudsman, a commissioner in charge of protecting citizens' rights, to further the goals of environmental protection. The Ombudsman would be authorised to initiate lawsuits to enforce environmental law and to call attention to issues necessary to protect the environmental interests of Hungarian citizens. An alternative proposal calls for a special Ombudsman, nominated by the President of the Republic and elected by Parliament, to initiate new government programmes and to propose legislation to the Environmental Committee of Parliament at the request of citizens or upon his or her own initiative.

1.4.3 Environmental Funds

There are a number of Environmental Funds in Hungary, including the Central Environmental Fund, the Regional Environmental Fund and the Water Fund. Some of the Funds' income is derived from the imposition of environmental charges and penalties.

Central Environmental Fund

The Central Environmental Fund is managed by the Environment Ministry. It is used by the government to finance environmental projects, currently amounting to HUF 550 million annually. 75% of the Fund is targeted for air pollution reduction programmes. Its income is collected from charges and state budget allocations. Grants and interest free loans may be obtained from the Central Environmental Fund. It will also reimburse up to 50% of the amount paid in penalties by a polluting company if the company undertakes to invest the money in environmental control technology to reduce emissions to permissible levels.

The procedure for obtaining loans, grants and reimbursements from the Central Environmental Fund is through a tender process. The terms of individual tenders are announced by the Environment Ministry. A tender offer should be submitted to the Regional Environmental Inspectorate depending on the location of the proposed environmental investment. The Inspectorate will then forward the tender offer to the Environment Ministry with its recommendation to fund the proposed investment. If the loan or grant requested from the Fund exceeds 5 million HUF, the Environment Ministry will establish a joint committee with the Ministry of Finance and the ministry responsible for the industry in which the investment would be made. The inter-ministerial committee takes account of the following considerations in determining whether to approve a loan or grant:

- Effect of the investment on national or regional environmental protection policies;
- Likelihood that the investment will reduce or eliminate the most harmful environmental pollution source in the area;
- Ability of the investment to meet all of the requirements of the relevant environmental authority;
- Investment's fulfillment of other environmental protection goals;
- Investment's effect on energy or raw material conservation.

Hungary recently introduced an environmental product tax on petrol. This income will be paid into the Central Environmental Fund.

Regional Environmental Fund

The Regional Environmental Fund provides grants for investments in certain areas of the country requiring assistance in the development of infrastructure, telecommunications, energy and waste treatment systems. Grants may also be provided from the Fund for the purpose of the rational redevelopment of agricultural land.

Grants from the Regional Environmental Fund may be provided following a tender held by the Environment Ministry. The Environment Ministry announces the terms of individual tenders. The applicant must attach the prior consent of the relevant Municipality and of the Environment Ministry or the Regional Environmental Inspectorate with responsibilities in the area of the investment.

Water Fund

The Water Fund provides grants and low interest or interest free loans for water management development projects, investments in water treatment and other facilities. Once a year, the Ministry of Transport, Telecommunication and Water Management announces in its official publication a tender for the making of grants or loans which includes all the relevant conditions of the application and the amount of such grants or loans.

1.5 Environmental legislation

1.5.1 Legislative process

The supreme legislative body in Hungary is the National Assembly, also known as the Parliament. All basic social, economic and political questions are regulated by Acts and Decrees. Other sources of legislation can be found in Ordinances, Resolutions and Orders.

Acts are the primary source of legislation and are adopted by the Parliament. The process of passing an Act is commenced at the initiative of any of the following:

- President of the Republic of Hungary;
- Council of Ministers;
- Committees of Parliament;
- Members of Parliament.

Draft environmental legislation is prepared within the Environment Ministry, together with the Ministry of Justice which has overall responsibility for legislation. A draft Act will be discussed by organisations representing interest groups affected by the proposed legislation. The draft Act is then submitted by the Environment and Justice Ministers to the Council of Ministers, who present it to the Environmental Committee of Parliament which issues an opinion recommending enactment.

A simple majority of votes of the Members of Parliament is required for the passage of an Act. Parliament decides at its own discretion whether to pass an Act after one or two readings. If the Act is likely to have a wide national impact, two readings usually take place. A draft Act is enacted once it is signed by the President of the Republic of Hungary and published in the *Magyar Közlöny*, the official law journal.

Government Decrees, issued by the Council of Ministers, typically deal with the execution of an Act. The government is also authorised to pass government Decrees within the scope of specific activities set forth in the *Constitution*.

Ministerial Decrees are passed by the Prime Minister, or one or more of the Ministers pursuant to authorisation in an Act or government Decree, in areas falling within the Prime Minister's or a Ministry's scope of responsibility.

Ordinances are issued by government bodies, other than Ministries, on subjects falling within their scope of responsibility.

Resolutions may be adopted by Parliament, the government and Counties or Municipalities. The subject matter of resolutions is limited to the issuing entity's sphere of authority.

Ministerial Orders are passed by Ministers to regulate activities of the governmental bodies directly under their control. For example, the Environment Minister can use a ministerial order to regulate the activity of the National Environmental Inspectorate.

Legal guidelines are published by Parliament or the government to clarify laws and regulations.

1.5.2 Legislation

The Hungarian *Constitution of 1949*, as amended, states that the Republic of Hungary shall recognise and enforce the right of all citizens to a healthy environment. The *Constitution* is the supreme law and other laws cannot be inconsistent with it.

The principal environmental statute in Hungary is *Act No. II of 1976 on the Protection of the Human Environment ("Environmental Protection Act")*. It contains the basic legal provisions relating to the protection of the environment and nature conservation. Implementing Decrees regulate the areas of air, noise and waste. The main statute in the water area is *Act No. IV of 1964 on Water*. Separate Acts and implementing Decrees regulate land use.

In October 1992, the Environment Ministry presented to the public a new draft Law on Environmental Protection ("draft Environmental Law"). The draft Environmental Law provides the foundation for Hungary's environmental policy. It establishes the following environmental objectives:

- Development of an EIA programme;
- Adherence to the "polluter pays" principle;
- Introduction of charges for the use of natural resources;

- Provision for a right of access to information on the state of the environment;
- Establishment of Central and Regional Environmental Protection Funds;
- Public participation in environmental protection decision-making;
- Provision for citizens' suits;
- Establishment of an environmental Ombudsman;
- Provision for third party insurance;
- Procedures for drafting and adopting environmental legislation;
- Allocation of the rights and responsibilities of the enforcement agencies;
- Enactment of environmental legislation in compliance with EC standards.

The draft Environmental Law is being circulated for discussion. It is predicted that it will be submitted to the Parliament shortly and will be adapted at the end of 1993.

1.6 Overview of permitting process and other regulatory requirements

The principal permits and approvals which must be obtained by an investor intending to build and operate a commercial or industrial facility in Hungary fall into two categories: (i) land use and construction permits; and (ii) operational requirements.

Land use and construction permits are discussed in detail in *Section 4* below. Operational requirements with respect to air, water, noise, waste and chemical storage are discussed in *Sections 6–10* below. There is no integrated permitting system in Hungary.

There is no legal requirement to perform EIAs in Hungary, although the Draft Environmental Law provides a foundation for future EIA legislation. A draft decree on EIAs ("draft EIA Decree") has also been prepared. Currently the environmental impact of investment projects is reviewed by concerned authorities, including the Regional Environmental Inspectorate, prior to the issuance of a construction permit.

Steps of the permitting process:

- If the construction is to take place on a "greenfield site", an approval from the relevant Land Registry is required.
- A permit for air emissions can be obtained from the Regional Environmental Inspectorate.
- Permits for water use and water discharge can be obtained from the Water Directorate.
- Permits for the operation of waste storage, treatment and disposal facilities are obtained from the Regional Environmental Inspectorate .
- A land use permit approving the siting of the development project and a construction permit must be obtained from the Municipal building authority.
- Once construction of the facility is complete, it must be approved before commencement of facility operations by the Municipal building authority.

The principal steps of the permitting and approval process are summarised in *Figure 1.6.1*. The practical application of the permitting and approval process is illustrated in the two case studies discussed below.

Figure 1.6.1 Environmental permitting procedure

Main Steps	*Authority*	*Timing*
Step 1. Permit for Change of Use of Land		
Application to	Land Registry	1 to 2 months
Step 2. Permit for Location and Use		
Application to	Municipal building authority	1 to 2 months
Step 3. Permit for Air Emissions		
Application to	Regional Environmental Inspectorate	1 to 2 months
Step 4. Permit for Water Use and Discharge		
Application to	Water Directorate	1 to 2 months
Step 5. Permit for Waste Storage, Treatment and Disposal		
Application to	Regional Environmental Inspectorate, Municipality	1 to 2 months
Step 6. Permit for Chemical Storage and Handling		
Application to	National Public Health Service	
Step 7. Construction Permit		
Application to	Municipal building authority	
Step 8. Post Completion Construction Approval		
Application to	Municipal building authority	

1.6.1 Case study 1

Foreign investor forming a joint venture with an existing company, with the joint venture acquiring two industrial plants and wishing to close one and refurbish the other to produce tyres.

Land use

A Hungarian joint venture with foreign participation may purchase real estate, without any government approval requirement based on foreign participation, provided that the purchase of land is made in connection with the business activity specified in the joint venture's articles of association. With respect to the first industrial plant which is to be closed down, no special land use procedures are mandatory. With respect to the second industrial plant which is to be refurbished, a permit must be obtained from the relevant Land Registry for any change in the use of the existing buildings or land in connection with the refurbishment.

Environmental Impact Assessments (EIAs)

EIAs are currently not required under Hungarian law, although they are provided for in the draft Environmental Law. The draft Decree on EIAs regulates EIA procedures, and requires an EIA to be performed before a construction permit can be issued.

Operating permits

Operating permits are needed for:

- New stationary air emission sources, to be obtained from the Regional Environmental Inspectorate;
- Water use and discharge of wastewater, to be obtained from the Water Directorate;
- Storage, treatment and disposal of hazardous waste, to be obtained from the Regional Environmental Inspectorate;
- Any activity involving toxic substances, to be obtained from the National Public Health Service.

No permits are needed for noise emissions except during construction.

Construction permits and approvals

- If buildings are to be destroyed at the first plant, a construction permit must be obtained from the Municipal building authority.
- If the refurbishment of the second plant entails modifications to the buildings, a construction permit must be obtained from the Municipal building authority.
- Construction permits may include noise emission limits to be observed during the construction of a facility.
- Once the construction is complete, approval of the construction must be obtained from the Municipal building authority prior to commencement of operations.

1.6.2 Case study 2
Foreign company wishing to acquire a greenfield site and build a new paper mill.

Change in use of land

Any change in the use of the land requires a permit from the Land Registry.

Land use

Under *Act No. I of 1987 on Land Use and Land Ownership*, foreign corporate entities and foreign individuals may not purchase land without obtaining a permit from the Ministry of Finance. Such a permit is not granted as a matter of course. Since there are no restrictions on the purchase of land by Hungarian entities, the foreign entity may wish to establish a Hungarian corporation or a joint venture with foreign participation in order to acquire a greenfield site and build a paper mill.

Location and use permits approving the siting of a new investment must be obtained from the Municipal building authority prior to construction.

Environmental Impact Assessments (EIAs)

EIAs are currently not required under Hungarian law. The draft Environmental Law and draft Decree on EIAs will require EIAs to be performed before construction permits can be issued.

Operating permits

Operating permits will be needed for:

- New stationary emission sources, to be obtained from the Regional Environmental Inspectorate;
- Water use and wastewater discharge, to be obtained from the Water Directorate;
- Storage, treatment and disposal of hazardous waste, to be obtained from the Regional Environmental Inspectorate;
- Any activity involving toxic substances, to be obtained from the National Public Health Service.

No permits are required for noise emissions except during construction.

Construction permits and approvals

After obtaining permits for location, use and any change in use of land, and the required operating permits, the company must obtain a construction permit from the Municipal building authority. Noise emission limits applicable during construction work are included within the construction permit. After the paper mill is completed, an approval for its use must be obtained from the Municipal building authority.

1.7 Enforcement of environmental legislation

The Environment Ministry, the Municipalities and the National Environmental Protection Inspectorate, with assistance from the Regional Environmental Inspectorates, responsible for the enforcement of environmental legislation in the areas of air, waste and noise.

With respect to the enforcement of any water protection regulation, the enforcement body is the Ministry of Transport, Telecommunication, and Water Management, which is assisted by the National Water Directorate and its 12 regional Water Directorates.

The decisions of the Regional Environmental Inspectorates are subject to administrative review by the Inspector General of Environmental Protection based in Budapest and to judicial review. All administrative decisions may be challenged in court. Prior to 1991, however, Hungary had a sparse practice of judicial review of administrative decisions.

The draft Environmental Law grants non-governmental environmental organisations ("NGOs") the right to demand enforcement measures to be taken by the appropriate environmental authorities. If the authority does not respond to these demands, the NGO may sue the alleged polluter. The NGO may also request a court to declare that the given activity is unlawful and to issue orders to halt the unlawful activity, to prohibit further unlawful activities and restore the environment to its former state.

1.8 Public participation

1.8.1 Public access to information

Chapter 1, Article 18 of the Hungarian *Constitution* states that: "the Republic of Hungary shall recognise and enforce the right of all to a healthy environment." The government can refuse to disclose information to the public if it determines:

- An absence of a recognisable legal right to that information;
- A need to protect the information in the interest of official secrecy.

There are no enforceable guidelines at present that would limit the right of the authorities in declaring a piece of information to be a state secret.

Act No. LXIII of 1992 on Protection of Personal Data, which will come into force on 27 April 1993 provides for public access to data of public interest. This Act states that: "...all data under the management of the central or local government is to be regarded as data of public interest, except such data which falls under the scope of personal data." Under this new legislation the government is obliged to provide accurate and timely information on all issues within its scope of responsibility. The new legislation details the claims procedure in the case of the government's refusal to disclose and establishes a post of Ombudsman for the protection of the right to disclose data of public interest.

The draft Environmental Law also provides for the right of access to information on the state of the environment, the state of human health, environmental risks and environmental protection activities. Governmental authorities, Municipalities and users of the environment are obliged to make public all data they may acquire on the state of the environment and human health, subject to certain exceptions based on a justifiable protection of interests.

1.8.2 Provision of information

Act No. XI of 1991 on Establishing the National Public Health Service, which was implemented by *Decree No. 7/1991 (IV.26.) of the Ministry of Public Welfare and Health*, provides that information regarding the effects of pollution on public health collected by the National Public Health Service must be available to the public. *Act No. XI of 1991* does not establish procedures for the public to enforce the obligations of the National Public Health Service to disclose the required information.

Information collected by the National Public Health Service is sent to:

- Environment Ministry;
- National Statistics Office;
- *Health Science*, a publication of the National Public Health Service.

The National Public Health Service currently lacks the funding necessary to monitor the entire country. Consequently, the information which it collects on a regular basis may not be comprehensive.

1.8.3 Public consultation

Article 36, Chapter VII of the Hungarian *Constitution* states that: "in the course of discharging its functions, the government shall co-operate with interested social organisations." Chapter IX, Article 42 thereof states in part: "local self-government means autonomous and democratic management of local affairs by the communities concerned and the exercise of local public authority in the interests of the population."

There is some legal basis in the *Act No. I of 1957 on Administrative Procedure* for the consultation of the public on environmental matters. Paragraph 2(4) thereof provides that: "the administrative procedure is based on the effective co-operation of the public authority, of the participating parties and of any other organs and persons participating in the procedure." Participating parties are guaranteed certain procedural rights to ensure that their views are at least considered by the relevant authorities. In practice, however, these parties have been government agencies, workers' associations and scientific institutes. This process resembles an internal governmental consultative process more than it does a public forum.

Under the *Act No. LXV of 1990 on Local Self-Government*, Municipalities were granted autonomy over a wide range of matters affecting the local population. *Act No. LXV* states that the local representative body is to hold public meetings. It further provides that citizens may examine the records of such meetings, except for those of closed meetings. Thus, the potential exists, if Municipalities do their duty, for a meaningful forum with good public participation on issues of local environmental importance. A meeting can be declared to be closed, however, by the representatives themselves for "justified" reasons.

2. Environment liability

2.1 Summary

Liability of Investors for Past Pollution:	A purchaser of stock in a state-owned enterprise undergoing privatisation or of substantial assets of such an enterprise assumes the liabilities of that enterprise.

Government Indemnification:	The policy of the SPA is to grant indemnifications to investors on a case-by-case basis.
Investor Clean-up of Contaminated Sites:	No standards exist which specifically trigger a clean-up obligation.
Civil Liability:	The law provides for fault based and strict liability.
Administrative Liability:	Violations of environmental laws can result in the imposition of penalties. Administrative orders can be issued to halt the polluting activity and to shut down a facility, and to remedy the consequences of the environmental damage.
Criminal Liability:	Penalties for petty offenses and environmental crimes include imprisonment and fines.

2.2 Sources of legislation relating to environmental liability

- *Act No. III of 1952 on Civil Procedure;*
- *Act No. IV of 1957 on Administrative Procedure;*
- *Civil Code, Act No. IV of 1959;*
- *Act No. II of 1976 on Protection of the Human Environment;*
- *Criminal Code, Act No. IV of 1978;*
- *Act XXIV of 1988 on Investments by Foreign Persons in Hungary;*
- *Act No. LIII of 1992 on the Management and Utilisation of Entrepreneurial Assets Permanently Remaining in State Ownership;*
- *Act No. LIV of 1992 on the Sale, Utilisation and Protection of Assets Temporarily Owned by the State;*
- *Act No. LV of 1992 on the Amendment of Legal Rules in Connection with Acts Concerning Entrepreneurial Property of the State;*
- Draft Environmental Law.

2.3 Environmental liabilities for past pollution

2.3.1 Environmental liabilities and investment

An investor has to be aware of two types of potential environmental liability when making an investment in Hungary:

- Liabilities arising from past environmental pollution caused by the operation of Hungarian state enterprises. These liabilities can encompass pollution at the site of the enterprise, contamination migrating from off-site landfills used by the enterprise and damage claims of employees and nearby residents.
- Liabilities associated with the current operations of a facility by the investor. These liabilities can encompass violations of law relating to permitting and related issues and liability for environmental damage under civil and criminal statutes.

An investor's exposure to environmental liabilities arising from past pollution is discussed herein in *Section 2.3*. Liabilities associated with the current operations of a facility are discussed below in *Section 2.4*.

The exact extent of an investor's liability for past pollution will depend on a variety of factors, including the form of the investment transaction and the commercial laws governing that transaction, various environmental liability provisions and any indemnification provided to the investor by the government. Should the investor become responsible for the remediation of past pollution, the applicable environmental clean-up standards will have a bearing on the cost of such remediation.

2.3.2 *Types of environmental liabilities*

Investments in Hungary may take a variety of forms. Hungarian legislation permits the purchase of stock or assets of former state-owned enterprises, the creation of joint ventures and the establishment of new corporations wholly or partially-owned by foreign investors.

The SPA was created in 1990 to oversee the privatisation of Hungary's state-owned enterprises. It is supervised by a Minister without Portfolio. The recent *Privatisation Laws* govern the privatisation process in Hungary. Section 35(2) of *Act No. LIV of 1992* states that the transformation plan of a state-owned enterprise must include a provision on how environmental damages caused by the operation of the former state enterprise will be apportioned. Prior to its privatisation, a state enterprise must be "corporatised" into either a joint stock or a limited liability company. The former state enterprise's obligations do not cease to exist with its transformation into corporate form. During this transformation process parts of the enterprise, which are not corporatised may be sold as assets. Assets may be acquired without assuming the liabilities of the former state enterprise, unless there is a sale of all or substantially all of the assets of the former state enterprise.

The principal legislation governing forms of foreign investment is *Act XXIV of 1988 Regarding Investments by Foreign Persons in Hungary*, as amended, (*"Foreign Investment Law"*). The *Foreign Investment Law* contains no specific provisions regarding environmental liability.

The transfer of property sections of the *Civil Code* and *Act No. LV of 1992* provide for a general transfer of liabilities upon the transformation or sale of an enterprise to a purchaser corporation, unless the transaction is structured as an asset purchase or the contract provides otherwise.

The *Draft Environmental Law* does not contain any provisions relating to the liability of new owners of former state enterprises for pollution arising from its past operations.

2.3.2 *Government indemnification of environmental liabilities*

In principle, environmental indemnification can be obtained by investors on a case-by-case basis to the extent that under Hungarian law contracting parties are free to agree on the specific terms of their agreement.

In practice, the SPA has recently agreed to indemnify a number of investors for liabilities arising from past pollution. The SPA issued a written statement to a meeting of environmental experts on 23 October 1992, stating that in the case of known environmental pollution, the SPA can either:

- Deduct the cost of clean-up from the purchase price, based on the estimated cost to remediate the past pollution, or
- Provide an indemnification for the past pollution.

It appears that the SPA's current indemnification policy is limited to the reimbursement of site clean-up costs. The SPA will generally pay such costs only if the pollution is discovered within three to five years after the closing of the transaction.

Under Paragraph 17 *of Act No. LIV of 1992*, the SPA must obtain approval of the Minister of Finance prior to any decision resulting in the SPA's assumption of any responsibility for a guarantee, security or warranty. Under a new policy announced on 10 December 1992 the SPA will have the discretion to indemnify investors for up to 500 million HUF.

The draft Environmental Law does not contain any provisions relating to the government's indemnification of investors for past environmental liabilities.

2.3.4 Investor clean-up of contaminated sites

Environmental clean-up standards

No environmental standards are in force which specifically trigger an obligation to clean up contaminated sites. In practice, Regional Environmental Inspectorates have broad discretion regarding the method of remediation to be adopted.

Escrow accounts

Some Central and East European governments have adopted escrow accounts as a financial mechanism in privatisation sales to help finance the cost of site remediation. In order to expedite the clean-up of contaminated sites in Hungary, a portion of the purchase price of a privatised company might be paid by an investor into a special escrow account. The funds could be made available to the investor if an acceptable site remediation plan is presented to the government and is carried out by the investor. To date, the Hungarian government has not adopted this approach.

Environmental Funds

It is unclear whether investors will have access to income from existing Environmental Funds to finance the clean-up of sites which formerly belonged to the state. It is unlikely, at least in the near future, that these funds, with their limited resources, will make funding available for the clean-up of contaminated sites undertaken by foreign investors.

2.3.5 Case examples

In March 1991, Electrolux, a large Swedish company, purchased the Lehel Refrigerator Plant. It was agreed that Electrolux would remediate the pollution on site and that the cost of the remediation would be off-set against the negotiated amount of the purchase price. The ensuing clean-up is now expected to cost an amount equal to the purchase price.

2.4 Environmental liabilities arising from facility operation

2.4.1 Civil liability

Fault-based liability

Article 339 of the *Civil Code* provides that a party whose unlawful conduct causes damage shall pay compensation to the injured party. The following defences are available:

- The party's conduct was acceptable under the given circumstances;
- Special extenuating circumstances exist;
- Liability may be reduced to the extent of the injured party's contributory liability.

Due to the lack of case law in this area, the extent to which fault based liability may apply to environmental damages is not clear.

Strict liability

Article 345 of the *Civil Code* provides for strict liability in civil law for "ultrahazardous activities". Article 345 specifically states that its provisions apply to persons who, through actions which constitute a threat to the environment, harm other persons.

Nuisance

Under Article 100 of the *Civil Code*, a property owner must avoid those activities which needlessly disturb others (particularly neighbours) or impede the exercise of the rights of others. Nuisance is not restricted to actions brought by immediate neighbours. There is uncertainty as to what conduct is needless, as neighbours are expected to tolerate some level of disturbance. Nuisance is subject to a strict liability standard.

Trespass

Under Article. 188 of the *Civil Code*, trespass is based on a theoretical right to undisturbed possession of property. As in the case of nuisance, disturbances must be examined on a case-by-case basis and balanced against locally acceptable levels of disturbance. Trespass is subject to a strict liability standard.

Damages

There is little case law or civil law on the different types of damages which may be assessed in environmental cases.

Under Hungarian law, compensation may be recovered for lost income as well as for direct loss actually incurred. The *Civil Code* also provides for compensation for pain and suffering. Hungarian law further provides for "general compensation" when the amount of damages is not ascertainable.

The draft Environmental Law defines the term "environmental damage" as:

- Damage to health, life and bodily integrity;
- Damage to property and lost profits;
- Damage and loss to the environment which may be determined from the cost of restoring the environment to its original state.

The draft Environmental Law provides that if damage to the environment cannot be determined under the above definition, it will be determined according to the general compensation provisions of the *Civil Code*.

In the event of a threat of imminent damage, any person threatened with such damage can request a court to issue an injunction prohibiting the dangerous action or ordering the defendant to take the appropriate measures to prevent any such damage from occurring and, if necessary, to post a bond.

Statutes of limitation

The statute of limitations for strict liability is three years. For fault based liability the statute of limitations is five years.

Case examples

Most of the cases dealing with environmental damages have concerned the use of chemicals in agriculture. Liability has been imposed based on the standard of strict liability for "ultrahazardous activities".

- In a 1985 Supreme Court decision (P.torv.I.20.919/1985), the court decided that the storage of chemicals near an apartment could infringe upon the rights of possession of the apartment dwellers if the storage adversely affected the use of the apartment or the health of the persons living there. The court protected the plaintiff's individual interest, noting that the protection of human beings from harm is a social interest of the highest priority.
- On 8 April 1992, the Wall Street Journal discussed a "class action" lawsuit brought by an environmental group called Green Future. The legal claims of this organisation are based on harm resulting from lead dust emissions at a state-owned metal-recycling plant. The lawsuit is apparently the first such suit against a state entity in Hungary.
- In 1991, Borsodchem, one of Hungary's largest chemical concerns, experienced a large spill of mercury which collected into a pool. As the mercury was not considered to be "waste", waste regulations did not apply and no penalties were imposed.

2.4.2 Administrative liability

Types of Administrative liability

Administrative liability arises in the event of violations of environmental permits, statutes, regulations and other legal requirements.

There are two types of administrative remedies: fines and administrative orders.

Fines

The most frequently used administrative sanction is the environmental fine. Under the *Environmental Protection Act*, all persons who pursue activities contrary to statutory provisions and official orders which serve to protect the environment, or fail to meet obligations prescribed thereunder, are subject to fines.

Fines are imposed for violations of regulations in the following areas:

- Land protection;
- Water pollution;

- Sewage treatment;
- Air pollution;
- Nature conservation;
- Hazardous waste;
- Noise or vibration.

Fines are calculated based on the extent of the pollution and danger to human health and the environment. In practice, the policy of levying fines has not been an effective deterrent. The fines collected are not close to the actual cost of remediating the environmental damage, as in many cases the full extent of damage remains undetected. Also, as industrial production has dropped in Hungary following the loss of export markets to the former Soviet Union and the CEE countries, the total amount of environmental fines levied has shrunk from HUF 400–500 million to HUF 200–300 million in the past year.

If a fine is paid, the polluter may still be subject to criminal, civil or other administrative penalties.

The imposition of a fine requires no proof of fault or negligence, except in the case of land protection fines.

The draft Environmental Law provides a general authorisation for the imposition of fines.

Administrative orders

Administrative remedies may include the following:

- Closure, suspension or cessation of an activity;
- Limitation of some aspect of an activity, such as the use of an energy source;
- Limitation of the distribution of products;
- Halting the importation of goods;
- Withdrawal or suspension of a permit.

Since 1989, the law provides for judicial review of administrative decisions.

2.4.3 Criminal liability

Types of criminal liability

Under Hungarian law only natural persons may be criminally liable. There are two types of criminal offences under Hungarian law: petty offences and crimes.

Fines are imposed to penalise negligent or intentional wrongdoing which falls within the category of petty offences.

In 1978 the *Criminal Code* introduced two environmentally related crimes:

- *Damage to the environment*:
  Pursuant to Article 280 of the *Criminal Code*, pollution or damage to protected areas, plants and animals is punishable with imprisonment for up to three years. If such an act endangers life, the punishment is imprisonment for up to five years.

  A person who negligently damages the environment shall be punished with imprisonment for up to one year and a fine. If this negligence endangers life, the punishment shall be imprisonment for up to three years.

245

- *Damage to nature*:
  Pursuant to Article 281 of the *Criminal Code*, a person damages the environment who:
  - Destroys or gathers protected plants or animals or eggs of such animals;
  - Significantly damages a protected cave or geological formation;
  - Diversely alters a nature conservation area.

The above acts are punishable with imprisonment for up to one year and a possible fine.

If the offender's acts are intentional and cause mass extinction of plants or animals, they are punishable with imprisonment for up to three years.

If the acts constitute negligence, they are punishable with imprisonment for up to one year or a fine.

Case examples

The prosecutor's office charged two workers at the Duna Co-operative in Taksony with "endangering life in the pursuit of professional activities". Chinoin, one of Hungary's largest pharmaceutical firms, privatised in 1990, contracted with the Duna Co-operative to have Chinoin's tanks cleaned. Residues of a chemical exported for use in producing chemical weapons were found in some tanks. Chinoin gave Duna no prior notice of this fact. During the cleaning process, several people were injured and flora and fauna in a nearby forest were damaged. Only two unskilled workers were prosecuted for this damage. The court imposed penalties on the two workers, but stated that responsibility for the damage lay with the managers of Chinoin, who either knew or should have known of the dangerous effects of the chemical. The actions of these managers, however, were not investigated by the police.

3. Environmental audits

3.1 Summary

Scope of Activities:	*Act No. LIV of 1992* requires an evaluation of damage and clean-up costs arising from past pollution by former state enterprises.
Approved Consultants:	The SPA and investors hire consultants to evaluate enterprises in the privatisation process. No individual licensing procedure exists for environmental consultants although the Environment Ministry keeps a list of approved consultants.
Applicable Clean-up Standards:	No specific standards exist which trigger an obligation to clean up contaminated sites.

3.2 Sources of legislation relating to environmental audits

- *Act No. LIV of 1992 on the Sale, Utilisation and Protection of Assets Temporarily Owned by the State;*
- Draft Environmental Law.

3.3 Scope of activities subject to environmental audits and audit process

There are currently no legal requirements specifically requiring the performance of environmental audits in Hungary. Paragraph 35 (2)(f) of *Act No. LIV of 1992*, however, requires an estimate of environmental damages and clean-up costs when former state enterprises are "corporatised" prior to privatisation. This estimate is frequently provided without conducting any environmental audit.

The current position of the SPA, which is charged with overseeing the sale of former state enterprises to investors, appears to be that mandatory environmental audits would unduly delay the already prolonged privatisation process. As a practical matter, environmental audits are conducted by investors on a voluntary basis in the context of privatisation.

The draft Environmental Law provides for surveys of the state of the environment with respect to operations of existing facilities which have considerable impact on the environment. Under Paragraph 39 of the draft Environmental Law, the fact, extent and nature of environmental damage discovered as a result of an environmental audit must be recorded in the register at the relevant Land Registry. In addition, the extent of existing and contingent environmental liabilities must be recorded in the company register of the enterprise.

3.4 Requirements relevant to environmental audits

Approved consultants

The Environment Ministry maintains a list of approved environmental experts. The SPA uses the services of several consultants selected through tender.

Applicable clean-up standards

No clean-up standards have been drafted specifically for contaminated sites. Some clean-ups have taken place since the enactment of Hungary's new investment and privatisation legislation. Standards are set following discussions with Regional Environmental Inspectorates and Water Directorates.

Preparation and approval of remediation plans

At present no procedure has been developed by the Environment Ministry or the SPA regarding the preparation and approval of remediation plans relating to contaminated sites, and in particular sites contaminated by the operations of former state enterprises.

Remediation plans should be discussed with Regional Environmental Inspectorates and Water Directorates.

3.5 National experience with environmental audits

In practice, environmental audits are mostly conducted by investors contemplating the purchase of Hungarian companies during the privatisation process.

4. Land use planning

4.1 Summary

Permits Required:	Approval for the purchase of land by a foreign entity must be obtained from the Ministry of Finance. Approval for the conversion of arable land to commercial or industrial use must be obtained from the Land Registry. Land use approval for the siting of the development project and a construction permit for new buildings or expansions must be obtained from the Municipal building authority.
Timing:	Two to twelve months.
Public Participation:	Local land use plans must be made available to the public for comment.
Enforcement:	If no construction permit is obtained or its conditions or other legal provisions regarding construction are violated, the construction may be prohibited or an order to destroy the building may be issued.

4.2 Sources of legislation relating to land use

- *Act No. III of 1964 on Housing and Construction*, governs building permits;
- *Act. No. I of 1987 on Land Use and Land Ownership;*
- *Decree No. 30/1964 (XII.2.)*, implementing Act No. III of 1964;
- *Decree No. 1/1968 (I.II.), of the Ministry of Construction and Urban Development*, sets forth procedures for land use permits;
- *Decree No. 29/1971 (XII.29.) of the Ministry of Construction and Urban Development*, on construction procedure;
- *Decree No. 17/1981 (VI.19.) of the Ministry of Housing and Construction*, sets forth fines for violation of building and construction regulations;
- *Decree No. 2/1986 (II.27.) of the Ministry of Housing and Construction;*
- *Decree No. 12/1986 (XII.30.) of the Ministry of Housing and Construction*, sets forth the procedure for obtaining land use and construction permits;

- *Decree No. 8/1987 (IX.1.) of the Ministry of Agriculture,* implementing Act No. 1 of 1987;
- *Decree No. 26/1987 (VII.30.) of the Ministry of Agriculture,* implementing Act No. 1 of 1987;
- *Decree No. 171/1991 (XII.27.) on the Acquisition of Immoveable Property by Foreigners;*
- *Decree No. 23/1992 (I.28.),* gives the Environment Ministry, the Ministry of Industry and Trade and the Ministry of Transport, Telecommunication and Water Management permitting authority for construction insofar as it implicates their respective spheres of responsibility.

4.3 Scope of activities subject to land use regulation

Investors planning to build new facilities on greenfield sites or to expand existing facilities will have to comply with Hungarian land use and construction legislation. Land use is governed by *Act No. 1 of 1987 on Land Use and Land Ownership*, as implemented by *Decree No. 26/1987 and Decree No. 8/1987.*

Land use plans delineate the basic principles for the use and development of Hungary's territory. They are prepared at national, regional and local levels. Regional plans are prepared by the Environment Ministry. Municipalities are authorised to prepare local land use plans in which zoning regulations are set forth. The siting of a development project must comply with the land use plan for that part of the country.

The acquisition of real property in Hungary by foreign individuals and companies is regulated by *Act No. I of 1987 on Land Use and Land Ownership and by Decree No. 171/1991 (XII.27).* A foreign person wishing to purchase real estate in Hungary must obtain a permit from the Ministry of Finance. Agricultural land and national conservation areas may not be purchased by foreign entities under any circumstances. A Hungarian corporate entity may purchase real estate without a permit, even if it is wholly-owned by a foreign entity, providing that the land is used in connection with the business activity of the company as stated in its articles of association.

The *Act No. I of 1987 on Land Use and Land Ownership* classifies land into four categories:

- Arable land;
- Developed land;
- Land set aside for special purposes, eg, for military use or nature conservation;
- Land unsuitable for use.

All arable land must be used for agricultural purposes. The conversion of arable land from agricultural use to other uses must not diminish the land's potential for cultivation.

Construction activities must meet the criteria outlined in *Decree No. 2/1986 (II.27.)* ("*National Building Rules*"). The *National Building Rules* set forth certain construction requirements with respect to fire protection, public health and environmental protection.

A new Construction Act which will conform to EC standards is expected to be enacted.

4.4 Permitting Process

4.4.1 Authorities

Change of use of land

The withdrawal of arable land from cultivation requires a permit from the Land Registry.

When an investor intends to refurbish an existing commercial or industrial facility, a permit must be obtained from the Land Registry for any change in the use of buildings or land.

Location and use

Municipal building authorities grant land use permits, approving the location of the investment, which must be obtained before a construction permit is issued. Prior to granting a land use permit, the Municipality consults with the Regional Environmental Inspectorate regarding the potential environmental impact of the investment project. The procedure for obtaining this permit is set forth in *Decree No. 1/1968*.

Construction permits

Construction permits must be obtained from the Municipal building authority for virtually all industrial and commercial development, including the erection of new buildings and the modification, expansion or destruction of existing structures.

Before a construction permit is issued, the approval of several authorities is required:

- National Public Health Service, as regards air pollution;
- Ministry of Transport, Telecommunication and Water Management, as regards water use and wastewater discharge;
- Ministry of Agriculture, as regards pollution and the effect of the investment on soil;
- Ministry of Industry and Trade, as regards energy use;
- Regional Environmental Inspectorate, as regards waste disposal.

The Ministry of Transport, Telecommunication and Water Management, the Ministry of Justice, the Ministry of Agriculture and the Ministry of Finance are authorised to promulgate rules necessary to implement *Act No. 1 of 1987 on Land Use and Land Ownership* in their respective spheres of activity.

4.4.2 Application requirements

Change in use of land

Permits for change in use of arable land are granted by the Land Registry either for the temporary (up to a five-year period) or permanent withdrawal of land from cultivation. The application must contain a map and plan for the proposed land use. If a permit for a change in land use is required for an investment project which will also require a land use permit, additional items must be submitted with the application.

Decisions of the Land Registry at the Municipal level may be appealed to the County Office of the Land Registry. Should any environmental questions arise, the Regional Environmental Inspectorate may be asked to issue an opinion on the environmental impact of the change in use of the land.

Location and use

Municipal building authorities grant use permits and approve the siting of proposed development projects. Applications must contain detailed information about the location of the development project and the proposed activity.

Construction permits

Prior to the submission of an application for a construction permit, it is common for an informal consultation to take place between the developer and the Municipal building authority.

A developer must first seek approval from the Municipal building authority for an outline planning permission to determine the feasibility of the proposed project. This application is far less detailed than the application for a full construction permit. Legal regulations governing such permissions vary among Municipalities.

When an outline planning permission is granted, the applicant may proceed to apply for the full construction permit.

An application for a construction permit must be filed with the Municipal building authority or, in the case of some smaller villages, with the nearest Municipal building authority. The content and form of the application depends upon the Municipality's regulations. Suggested standard forms of application have recently been published by the *Economic and Legal Publishing Company*. The application must be accompanied by plans prepared by a qualified architect and complying with environmental regulations, and, in some instances, an administrative fee.

Under the draft Environmental Law an EIA will in certain circumstances have to be performed before a construction permit is issued.

4.4.3 *Timing*

Change in use of land and location and use permits

Pursuant to the *Act No. IV of 1957 on Administrative Procedure*, decisions of the Land Registry regarding permits for location, use and change in use of land permits must be completed within 30 days from submission of the permit application. If the case is complex, the time may be extended by another 30 days.

Construction permits

The time required to obtain planning permission varies according to the scale of the development. The granting of construction permits for major industrial installations usually takes between six to twelve months, while the approval of smaller projects can be obtained in two to three months.

4.4.4 *Permit conditions*

Construction permits

Construction permits contain all the conditions related to the carrying out of the project. The law provides for a fee of 400 to 1,000 HUF for the issuance of such permits.

Construction must begin within two years and be completed within three years of the issuance of a construction permit. This deadline may be continuously extended by one-year periods.

4.5 Public participation

There are no legal provisions for public participation in the land use or planning process, except with respect to the drafting of land use plans. Article 6 of *Act No. III of 1964 on Housing and Construction* provides that local land use plans must be made public and the public may submit its comments. If the Municipality does not heed the public comments, it must provide an explanation for its decision.

The draft Environmental Law provides that citizens may establish associations which have a right to participate in the following:

- Preparing the regional policy and environmental protection plan for their territory;
- Participating in the administrative process for new construction if it would affect environmental protection;
- Participating in procedures defining sites for developments and capital investments which are of material concern to their members.

4.6 Enforcement

The Municipal building authorities are charged with the enforcement of regulations relating to construction.

Sanctions for failure to follow construction regulations range from orders to modify or destroy the building to payment of damages to injured neighbours.

In addition, fines of up to 50% of the value of the building, depending on the type and location of the building, may be imposed.

5. Environmental Impact Assessments (EIAs)

5.1 Summary

Scope of Activities:	EIAs are currently not required under Hungarian law.
Procedure:	An Appendix to the draft EIA Decree lists activities which may require EIAs in the future.
Experts:	The draft EIA Decree makes no provision for experts.
Public Participation:	The draft EIA Decree requires public participation.

5.2   Sources of legislation relating to the environmental impact of industrial and commercial developments

- *Hungarian Standard No. MI 1345/1990: Technical Guidelines of the Environment Ministry on EIAs;*
- Draft Environmental Law;
- Draft EIA Decree.

5.3   Scope of activities subject to EIA process

EIAs are not formally required under Hungarian law. Currently an environmental impact review is conducted by various authorities, including the Regional Environmental Inspectorate and the National Public Health Service, prior to the issuance of construction permits.

Pursuant to Section 51 of the draft Environmental Law, a notification by the investor to the Regional Environmental Inspectorate is required if a proposed investment or activity may have an impact on the environment. The draft Environmental Law sets forth a list of matters which must be examined in all EIAs.

The draft EIA Decree to be issued under the *Environmental Protection Act* is expected to be passed by April 1993. An Appendix to the draft EIA Decree lists the types of operations and investments where EIAs must be performed. This list will be reviewed by the government every two years and may be amended and expanded. See *Annex F.*

5.4   EIA process

5.4.1   Authority

Under the draft EIA Decree, the Regional Environmental Inspectorate will determine whether an EIA is required. Once an EIA statement is submitted by an investor to the Regional Environmental Inspectorate, the Inspectorate can grant or refuse permission for the investment, or request further details.

5.4.2   Documentation

The draft EIA Decree provides for a preliminary and a detailed EIA. A preliminary EIA shall be submitted to the Regional Environmental Inspectorate in every case which falls within one of the categories listed in the Appendix to the draft EIA Decree.

A preliminary EIA must contain:

- A description of purpose and the technological feasibility of the investment;
- A description of the expected environmental pollution;
- A list of those questions which require further examination.

If the Regional Environmental Inspectorate determines that the information contained in the preliminary EIA is insufficient to issue the required opinion, it may request a detailed EIA. A detailed EIA must contain:

- A forecast of the environmental impact as a result of the proposed activity;
- The possible means and procedures for limiting the pollution;

- Plans for a pollution monitoring system;
- A list of the applicable scientific literature;
- A map of the relevant area;
- Sources of related environmental studies prepared in connection with the EIA;
- A short summary of the EIA.

An investor should submit the required information to the Regional Environmental Inspectorate.

It seems that the Inspectorate has no discretionary power to demand an EIA in the cases not provided for in the Appendix to the draft EIA Decree.

5.4.3 Experts and consultants

Neither the draft Environmental Law nor the draft EIA Decree make any provision with regard to the choice of experts and consultants to be used in preparing an EIA.

5.4.4 Timing

Under the draft EIA Decree, the Regional Environmental Inspectorate must make a decision on the EIA statement, either approving it, rejecting it or requiring more information, within 30 days.

5.4.5 Standard of review

Although there is currently no EIA legislation in force, *Hungarian Standard MI 1345/ 1990: Technical Guidelines on EIAs*, detail technical procedures to be used in performing an EIA. The *Technical Guidelines* have the status of standards which are currently not legally binding under Hungarian law.

5.5 Public participation

Pursuant to the draft EIA Decree the permitting authority must hold a public hearing on the EIA process. The public hearing must be held prior to the issuance of the necessary permits for the construction or operation of the new facility. The hearing is held at the offices of the relevant Municipal building authority. The participants are the investor or operator, the Municipality and civic and environmental organisations. The public must receive 15 days' notice of the hearing. The draft EIA Decree states that any comments made as a result of the hearing must be considered in the permitting procedure.

5.6 Enforcement

Pursuant to the draft Environmental Law an operational permit cannot be granted for a new facility unless an EIA has been performed.

5.7 National experience with EIAs

An EIA is being prepared in connection with the construction activities related to World EXPO, 1995.

6. Integrated permitting requirements applicable to the operation of industrial and commercial facilities

6.1 Extent of integrated permitting

There is no integrated permitting system in Hungary. Individual permits must be applied for. For further information see *Sections 7–11*.

7. Air emission requirements applicable to the operation of industrial and commercial facilities

7.1 Summary

Air Requirements:	Permits must be obtained by individual facilities for new stationary sources of air emissions from the Regional Environmental Inspectorate. There are no charges payable for air emissions.
Timing:	In principle, 30 to 60 days.
Public Participation:	No public participation is provided for in the administrative decision making process of present. The draft Environmental Law provides for the right of access to information and for public participation in the environmental permitting procedure.
Enforcement:	Regional Environmental Inspectorates and Municipalities can impose fines for violations of air protection laws and air emission standards. The Regional Environmental Inspectorates and the Municipalities can issue orders to halt or terminate activities which cause pollution. Regional Environmental Inspectorates can require operators to install or modernise air pollution control equipment.

7.2 Sources of legislation relating to air emissions

- *Act No. II of 1976 on the Protection of the Human Environment, paras. 23–26;*
- *Decree No. 21/1986 (VI.2.);*
- *Ordinance No. 4/1986 (VI.2.) of the President of the National Office for the Protection of the Environment and Nature Conservation, as amended by Decree*

255

No. 9/1990 (IV.30.) of the Minister of Environment and Regional Policy, implements Decree No. 21/1986;

- *Decree No. 3/1988 (VI.10.) of the Environment Ministry;*
- *Decree No. 5/1990 (XII.6.) of the Ministry of Public Welfare and Health;*
- *Decree No. 6/1990 (IV.12.) of the Ministry of Transport, Telecommunication and Water Management;*
- *Decree No. 18/1991 (XII.18.) of the Ministry of Transport, Telecommunication and Water Management on the Abatement of Air Pollution Arising from Vehicular Traffic;*
- *Decree No. 11/1991 (V.16.) of the Environment Ministry;*
- *Hungarian Standard MSZ 21854-1990: Requirements of Cleanliness of Ambient Air.*

7.3 Air protection zones

Under *Decree No. 21/1986 (VI.2.)*, which relates to air protection, Hungary's territory is classified into three types of protected categories:

Highly protected areas, such as summer resorts and recreation areas, determined by the Environment Ministry, along with the Ministry of Agriculture, Ministry of Public Welfare and Health and the Municipality;

- Category I protected areas;
- Category II protected areas.

Categories I and II are determined by Municipalities, together with the Regional Environmental Inspectorates.

The emission of certain air pollutants in any quantity in highly protected areas is prohibited. The use of certain fuels in those areas is restricted. *Decree No. 3/1988 (VI.10.)* contains detailed regulations on highly protected areas.

7.4 Scope of activities subject to air emission regulation

Hungarian regulations govern the level of pollutants in ambient air as well as the permissible level of emissions of pollutants into air. *Decree No. 21/1986 (VI.2.)* distinguishes between harmful and dangerous air pollution. Air pollution is harmful in excess of permissible ambient standards. It is dangerous when it reaches levels which seriously endanger human health or the environment.

Hungarian law distinguishes two types of air pollution sources:

- Stationary sources;
- Mobile sources generated by combustion engines.

Emissions from stationary sources are regulated by reference to standards applicable to the industry in question. The most recent focus of air protection policy has been on mobile sources of air emissions, specifically the environmental impact of vehicular emissions. Compulsory vehicle emission testing has been introduced recently in Hungary. The government hopes that the introduction of market mechanisms, such as an energy tax on petrol, tax incentives for the conversion of vehicle engines from two to four cycles, and the use of catalytic converters, will promote energy conservation and environmental compliance. Hungary is planning to introduce EC standards for vehicle emissions by 1994.

7.5 Standards

7.5.1 Ambient quality standards

Decree No. 5/1990 (XII.6.) sets the ambient air quality standards for the following four substances:

- Nitrogen dioxide;
- Carbon monoxide;
- Sulphur dioxide;
- Dust.

The *Decree* lists maximum permissible concentrations in the air in different areas of the country and over a period of 30 minutes, a period of 24 hours and on an annual basis.

Ambient quality standards are also set forth in the *Hungarian Standard MSZ 21854-1990 on the Requirements of Cleanliness of Ambient Air.* These Requirements establish permissible concentration levels in ambient air for a long list of substances. The substances are classified into four categories depending on the level of possible harm ranging from extremely dangerous to slightly dangerous. Three levels of "air pollution alertness" are defined by reference to the concentration levels of those substances.

7.5.2 Emission limit values

Emission limit values are determined pursuant to the *Ordinance No. 4/1986 (VI.2.) of the President of National Office of Environmental Protection and Nature Conservation*, as amended by *Decree No. 9/1990(IV.30.) of the Minister of Environment and Regional Policy*. The emission limits are determined by reference to multipliers which are calculated from ambient air standards in accordance with mathematical formulas. The formulas are defined separately for three categories of pollution:

- Point sources;
- Building sources;
- Open field sources (such as strip mines).

The Ordinance contains an extensive list of localities in Hungary. Multipliers are calculated separately for each locality and apply to:

- Nitrogen dioxide;
- Carbon monoxide;
- Sulphur dioxide;
- Dust;
- Other substances.

Decree No. 6/1990 (IV.12.) of the Ministry of Transport, Telecommunication and Water Management regulates vehicular emission limits. Hungary expects to conform its vehicle emission standards to EC standards by 1994.

7.5.3 Technology based standards

Decree No. 11/1991 (V.16.) of the Environment Ministry sets technology based standards for air emissions resulting from waste incineration.

7.6 Permitting process

7.6.1 Authorities

Air permits may be obtained from Regional Environmental Inspectorates, which set emission limits of individual air emission sources in the particular regions under their control.

7.6.2 Application requirements

Under *Decree No. 4/1986* and *Decree No. 21/1986*, air discharge permits are required for all new stationary air emission sources.

7.6.3 Timing

Under the *Act No. IV of 1957 on Administrative Procedure*, air emission permits must be issued by the Regional Environmental Inspectorate within thirty days. The time period may be extended by another thirty days.

7.6.4 Permit conditions

Air emission permits may be issued for a limited period. Permits may impose certain conditions on the facility relating to pollution control.

7.6.5 Charges for emission

There are no provisions currently in effect which provide for the payment of charges for the emission of air pollutants not exceeding standards set in air emission permits.

The Draft Environmental Law contains a general authorisation for user charges. It provides for an environmental user charge payable for air emissions falling short of pollution, with further details to be set forth in separate legislation.

7.6.6 Public participation

There is no right of public participation in the air permitting process. The National Public Health Service, an agency organised under the auspices of the Ministry of Public Welfare and Health, monitors and collects data related to the public health effects of pollution and plays a role in determining air pollution standards insofar as the pollution affects public health. Its functions in this regard are set forth in *Decree No. 5/1990 (XII.6.)*. This information is available to the public and the National Public Health Service is required to publicise its data. *See Section 1.8 above.*

7.7 Enforcement

7.7.1 Compliance checking and monitoring

In the case of new industrial or commercial facilities, the Municipal building authority must ensure that land use plans meet air pollution requirements.

Regional Environmental Inspectorates, which keep a record of all air polluting sources, may require an operator to install or modernise air pollution control equipment and to monitor its own air emissions.

Reporting requirements for stationary sources are set forth in Article 9 of *Ordinance No. 4/1986*. Operators of air emission sources must report to the Regional Environmental Inspectorate within 30 days any modifications which result in a change in air emissions.

Vehicular emission testing is carried out and enforced by the police and by six Transportation Inspectorates which assist the Ministry of Transport, Telecommunication and Water Management. *Decree No. 18/1991 (XII.18.)* sets forth detailed regulations for vehicle emission testing.

The Environment Ministry operates approximately 8,000 monitoring stations covering about 25,000 sources of air pollution. The Institute for Environmental Management also manages certain monitoring stations. The methodology employed by the Ministry and the Institute is that recommended by the World Meteorological Organisation.

7.7.2 Penalties and sanctions

With respect to existing stationary sources, Regional Environmental Inspectorates or Municipalities impose fines if air pollution standards are violated. With respect to vehicular emissions, the Transport Pollution Inspectorate, organised under the Ministry of Transport, Telecommunication and Water Management, imposes fines for violations of emission limits.

The *Ordinance No. 4/1986* provides for the imposition of fines on entities emitting in excess of the defined emission limits. Fines are assessed every three months. The fines are calculated according to complex formulas. The *Ordinance* establishes progressive rates of fines in relation to the amount of pollutant in excess of permissible levels. In addition, the law provides for increased fines in the second and subsequent years where emissions are in excess of permissible levels. Where a polluter violates a standard for five years, the resulting fine will be more than double the original fine. The additional penalty can be eliminated if the polluter has taken steps to avoid further pollution. The amount of fines is different for substances in each of the four categories defined in the *Hungarian Standards MSZ 21854-1990: Requirements on the Cleanliness of Ambient Air.*

8. Water requirements applicable to the operation of industrial and commercial facilities

8.1 Summary

Water Requirements:	Permits for water use and water discharge can be obtained from Water Directorates. Charges are payable for water use but not for water discharge.
Timing:	In principle, 30 to 60 days.

Public Participation:	No public participation is provided for in the present administrative decision-making process. The draft Environmental Law provides for the right of access to information and for public participation in the environmental permitting procedure.
Enforcement:	Regional Environmental Inspectorates can issue orders to halt or terminate activities in case of imminent danger of contamination or harmful pollution. Regional Environmental Inspectorates impose fines for water and sewage system pollution.

8.2 Sources of legislation relating to water requirements

- *Act No. IV of 1964 on Water, amended by Act No. I of 1984;*
- *Act No. II of 1976 on the Protection of the Human Environment, paragraphs 16–22;*
- *Decree No. 32/1964 (XII.13.), as amended by Decree No. 40/1969 and Decree No. 10/ 1984, implementing Act No. IV of 1964;*
- *Joint Decree No. 1/1970 (XI.18.) of the President of the National Water Management Authority and Price Office, sets forth fees for the use of water sources;*
- *Joint Decree No. 3/1970 (XII.18.) of the President of the National Water Management Authority and Price Office, regulates the industrial use of water;*
- *Decree No. 5/1970 (XII.31.) of the President of the National Water Management Authority, sets forth the administrative authority of local water management;*
- *Decree No. 4/1981 (IV.4.) of the President of the National Water Management Authority, sets forth the technical principles and requirements of any water related construction;*
- *Decree No. 3/1982 (VI.I.) of the President of the National Water Management Authority;*
- *Decree No. 1/1992 (I.6.) of the Environment Ministry;*
- *Ordinance No. 3/1984 (II.7.) of the President of the National Water Management Authority;*
- *Ordinance No. 4/1984 (II.7.) of the President of the National Water Management Authority;*
- *Hungarian Standard MI-10-172/3-85: Classification of Water Quality.*

8.3 Water management

8.3.1 Water management bodies

The Ministry of Transport, Telecommunication and Water Management has overall responsibility for water management. It is assisted by the National Water Management Authority which supervises 12 Water Directorates. The National Water Management Authority is also responsible for drafting regulations concerning water use.

Water Directorates are responsible for:

- Issuing water use and wastewater discharge permits;

- Granting permission for construction work which may affect water;
- Controlling water pollution;
- Taking steps to eliminate damage caused by water.

8.3.2 *Water quality categories*

Water quality categories are determined by reference to certain water quality parameters set forth in *Hungarian Standard MI-10-172/3-85: Classification of Water Quality* and by an evaluation of water use.

A national water management plan, developed by the Ministry of Transport, Telecommunication and Water Management ranks water use as either residential, industrial or agricultural.

Water is classified as follows:

- Class I: requiring little or no treatment;
- Class II: requiring treatment but not harmful in environmental terms;
- Class III: polluted and harmful to the environment.

8.3.3 *Activities subject to regulation*

Act No. IV of 1964 on Water, as amended, and various Decrees issued thereunder, regulate water use and wastewater discharge and construction affecting water bodies. Permits from the Water Directorate are required for any use of water or wastewater discharge. Permits are also required to construct anything which might impede the natural flow of water.

8.4 *Standards*

8.4.1 *Ambient quality standards*

Hungarian Standard MI-10-172/3-85 provides limits for three lists of parameters, including temperature, pH and dissolved oxygen in surface waters. Parameters enumerated in list I are to be monitored with a high frequency. Parameters on lists II and III are to be monitored with low frequency and, parameters on list III only occasionally.

8.4.2 *Discharge limit values*

Ordinance No. 3 of 1984 (II.7.) of the President of National Water Management Authority establishes discharge limit values for the discharge of 19 polluting substances and 13 toxic substances (mainly heavy metals) into surface waters and sewers. The limits are determined separately with respect to each of the following six water areas:

- Highly protected areas;
- Sources of potable water and recreational areas;
- Industrial areas;
- Reservoirs used for irrigation;
- Waters of the rivers Danube and Tisza excluding highly protected waters;
- Other waters.

8.4.3 *Technology based standards*

There are no technology based standards in the water area.

8.5 Water use permitting process

8.5.1 Authorities
Permits from the Water Directorates are required for water use and any construction affecting the flow of water.

8.5.2 Application requirements
Applications for permits for water use must provide relevant information regarding the quantity of water which is likely to be used and its purpose.

The content of an application for a construction permit affecting water is listed in *Decree No. 3/1982* and must include the following information:

- Description of the proposed construction activity;
- Effect of the proposed construction on water bodies.

8.5.3 Timing
According to the *Administrative Procedure Code* the general processing time is 30 days. This period may be extended by an additional 30 days.

8.5.4 Permit conditions
Water use permits are issued either for a limited period of time or indefinitely. They may be subject to certain conditions regarding pollution control.

8.5.5 Charges for water use
Charges are payable for water use. They are calculated based on the quantity of water used and its purpose.

All water use charges are paid into a Water Fund which helps to finance water management projects such as the construction of water treatment centers.

8.6 Water discharge permitting process

8.6.1 Authorities
Permits from the Water Directorate are required for wastewater and sewage discharge.

8.6.2 Application requirements
Relevant information regarding expected wastewater and sewage discharges must be provided by the applicant to the Water Directorate.

8.6.3 Timing
Wastewater permits are issued within 30 days. This period may be extended by an additional 30 days.

8.6.4 *Permit conditions*

Individual discharge limits can be increased or reduced by Water Directorates with respect to specific activities. The Water Directorates can further modify these individual discharge limits. Facilities are required to develop plans for emergency situations and must inform the Water Directorate if the sewage system is endangered.

8.6.5 *Charges for water discharge*

There are no charges for wastewater discharge which does not exceed the discharge limits specified by *Ordinance No. 3/1984*.

8.6.6 *Public participation*

There is no provision under Hungarian law for public participation in the water permitting process.

The Draft Environmental Law provides for the right of access to information and for public participation in environmental permitting procedures.

8.7 *Enforcement*

8.7.1 *Compliance checking and monitoring*

Discharges into surface waters and sewers by facilities are measured at the discharge plant at least twice a year either by Water Directorates or Regional Environmental Inspectorates. Facilities may be required to perform monitoring on a more frequent basis to demonstrate compliance. If on-site inspection by the authorities indicates that pollutants are being discharged into surface water or sewers in excess of permissible discharge limit values, a report of the findings will be prepared by the authorities and sent to the facility operator within thirty days of the inspection. When wastewater discharges are contaminated with bacteria, a report by the National Public Health service shall be included. If the facility operator does not object to the findings of this report within 15 days of its receipt, a pollution fine will be assessed and imposed on the facility.

8.7.2 *Penalties and sanctions*

Fines are assessed by Regional Environmental Inspectorates when discharges exceed limits set forth in Annex 1 to *Ordinance No. 3/1984*. The discharge limits and corresponding penalties are different for each of the six water quality areas and depend on whether the discharge is into sewers or surface water.

Where a violation is continuous, the Water Directorate can over time increase the fine up to five times the original amount. The imposition of fines does not preclude the obligation to build water treatment facilities or any potential civil or criminal liability.

The Regional Environmental Inspectorate may refrain from imposing increased penalties if the polluter has implemented pollution control measures.

In addition to penalties, Regional Environmental Inspectorates are authorised to suspend industrial activity in case of imminent danger of contamination or harmful pollution.

9. Noise requirements applicable to the operation of industrial and commercial facilities

9.1 Summary

Noise Requirements:	Noise standards exist with regard to construction and industrial operations. Limits for noise emissions from individual facilities are incorporated within construction permits.
Timing:	In principle, 30 to 60 days.
Public Participation:	No public participation is provided for in the administrative decision-making process at present. The draft Environmental Law provides for the right of access to information and for public participation in environmental permitting procedures.
Enforcement:	Fines may be assessed and imposed by Municipalities with respect to service industry facilities which violate noise regulations. The Regional Environmental Inspectorates can assess and impose fines on non-service industry facilities and facilities comprising both service and non-service activities. In addition, Regional Environmental Inspectorates can halt activities that violate regulations or have the potential to directly or seriously harm the environment.

9.2 Sources of legislation relating to environmental noise

- *Act II of 1976 on the Protection of the Human Environment;*
- *Decree No. 12/1983 (V.12.)*, as amended by *Decree No. 88/1990 (IV.30.)*, sets forth regulations concerning harmful vibrations and noise;
- *Decree No. 4/1984 (I.23.) of the Ministry of Public Welfare and Health*, sets forth limits for vibration and noise emissions;
- *Ordinance No. 2/1983 (V.25.) of the President of the National Office for the Protection of Environment and Nature Conservation*, modified by *Decree No. 12/1990 (V.23.) KVM of the Environment Ministry*, sets forth fines for violations of noise emission limits;
- *Hungarian Standard MSz 18150/1-83 measuring noise;*
- *Hungarian Standard MSz 1816312-83 measuring vibration;*
- *Hungarian Standards MSz 13-111-85 determining noise levels.*

9.3 Noise zones

Counties or Municipalities can establish noise zones with the consent of the National Environmental Protection Inspectorate and the National Public Health Service. "Quiet belts" may also be established around residential areas and health resorts.

9.4 Activities subject to noise regulation

The principal legislation governing environmental noise is the *Environmental Protection Act*. Under its provisions, it is forbidden to cause noise or vibrations which can cause harm or endanger human health. Paragraph 41 of the *Environmental Protection Act* prohibits the operation of machinery, appliances and vehicles which cause harmful or endangering noise, shaking, vibrations or oscillations in residential areas. The production, storage, transportation, treatment and use of biological, chemical and ionising and vibrating materials are permitted only in accordance with the law.

The provisions of the *Environmental Protection Act* as regards environmental noise are implemented by various Decrees and Ordinances.

9.5 Standards

Ordinance No. 4/1984 sets ambient noise standards to be observed by commercial and industrial facilities during construction and in the course of their operations.

Ambient standards are determined in decibels and depend on the zone affected, the type of activity and the time of day.

Standards for industrial activities

Zones	Day	Night
Hospitals, resorts etc	45 dB	35 dB
Residential areas	50 dB	40 dB
Inner cities	55 dB	45 dB
Populated area with industrial facilities	60 dB	50 dB

Standards for construction activities (exceeding 1 year in duration)

Zones	Day	Night
Resorts, hospitals, etc.	50 dB	35 dB
Residential areas	55 dB	40 dB
Inner cities	60 dB	45 dB
Populated area with industrial facilities	65 dB	50 dB

Hungary has also established several standards for noise levels related to different products and technologies. Hungary will join the European standardisation system in 1993. Harmonisation with specific EC directives on economic and market competition will dictate the regulations on noise in this area.

9.6 Permitting process

9.6.1 Authorities

With respect to service industries, regulation and enforcement in the noise area is entrusted to Municipalities. Agriculture, manufacturing and construction are generally classified as service industries.

Municipalities have the following responsibilities in connection with environmental noise:

- Defining noise zones;
- Drafting local noise and vibration regulations;
- Limiting or prohibiting any activity if it violates noise limits;
- Defining noise limits for new or existing plants;
- Defining and imposing fines for violation of noise limits.

With respect to non-service industries or industries comprised of both service and non-service activities, the National Environmental Protection Inspectorate and its Regional Environmental Inspectorates are entrusted with the following responsibilities:

- Defining noise and vibration limits for new or existing facilities;
- Defining noise and vibration limits for construction of airports, roads or railways;
- Developing and implementing requirements for noise reduction equipment to be used in road, railway and airport construction;
- Limiting or prohibiting an activity if it exceeds noise limits;
- Defining and imposing fines for violation of noise limits.

9.6.2 Application requirements

Individual construction permits will provide permissible vibration and noise limits applicable during construction work. There is no separate noise emission permit. The application for a construction permit must describe all likely sources of noise, the surrounding environment, the technology used to maintain noise levels within the required limits and any other relevant information. No noise permits are required once construction is complete and the commercial and industrial facility commences operations. Thereafter, the facility must comply with ambient noise standards.

Pursuant to *Decree No. 12/1983*, paragraph 13(1), any increase in noise levels from the defined level must be reported to the Regional Environmental Inspectorate within 30 days.

No fees are charged since there is no separate noise emission permit.

9.6.3 Timing

Construction permits, which incorporate noise emission limits, are issued within 30 days. This period can be extended by an additional 30 days.

9.6.4 Permit conditions

A construction permit which incorporates noise emission levels may require the taking of specific measures during construction activities to limit noise emissions.

9.6.5 Public participation

There are no legal provisions providing for public participation in the administrative decision-making process.

The draft Environmental Law provides for the right of access to information on the state of the environment and public participation in the environmental permitting process.

9.7 Enforcement

9.7.1 Compliance checking and monitoring

The Environment Ministry establishes the method of checking and monitoring compliance with noise standards.

9.7.2 Penalties and sanctions

Municipalities can assess fines for violations of regulations relating to noise. Repeat violators can incur fines up to double the stated penalty. Appeals regarding fines imposed by Municipalities may be made to the appropriate Regional Environmental Inspectorate.

Regional Environmental Inspectorates are authorised to suspend or limit any activity that violates regulations or has the potential to directly or seriously harm the environment.

10. Hazardous and non-hazardous waste management

10.1 Summary

Waste Handling Requirements:	Waste is classified into three types: household, industrial and hazardous.
	Permits are required from the Regional Environmental Inspectorate to treat, store and dispose of hazardous waste. Disposal or storage of liquid non-hazardous waste must be approved by the Municipality, together with the Regional Environmental Inspectorate and the Water Directorate.
	A permit must be obtained from the Environment Ministry to import hazardous waste into Hungary.
Timing:	In principle, 30 to 60 days.
Public Participation:	The draft Environmental Law provides for the right of access to information on the state of the environment and public participation in the permitting process.

Enforcement:	The Regional Environmental Inspectorates enforce legislation on waste and may impose fines for violations of waste regulations.

10.2 Sources of legislation relating to waste management

- *Act No. II of 1976 on the Protection of the Human Environment,* paragraphs 17, 18, 23, 25, 32, and 42;
- *Ordinance No. 2/1981 (XI.18.) of the President of the National Office for the Protection of Environment and Nature Conservation,* sets forth the method of calculating fines for violations of hazardous waste regulations;
- *Decree No. 56/1981 (XI.18.),* as amended by *Decree No. 27/1992 (II.10.),* sets forth rules regarding waste treatment and disposal;
- *Decree No. 55/1987 (X.30.MT.);*
- *Decree No. 11/1991 (V.16.) of the Environment Ministry.*

10.3 Categories of waste

Under Hungarian law, waste is classified into three types:

- Household waste;
- Industrial waste;
- Hazardous waste.

Municipalities are authorised to adopt regulations in connection with the disposal of household waste.

If industrial waste is non-hazardous, it can be disposed of as household waste. If industrial waste is hazardous, it must be regulated as a hazardous waste.

Hazardous wastes include any materials or residue from manufacturing or other activities which may have a direct or indirect, latent or immediate harmful effect on human health or the environment. Hazardous wastes are listed in the Appendix to *Decree No. 56/1981.*

The Environment Ministry, together with the Ministry for Public Welfare and Health, is responsible for further classifying hazardous waste according to the degree of danger posed. Any waste which has been previously unknown or which is the result of a new industrial process is considered hazardous until there is evidence to the contrary.

10.4 Waste storage and treatment

10.4.1 Generator requirements

Generators of waste must follow certain record-keeping guidelines set out in Annex 2 of *Decree No. 56/1981.* In particular, records must be kept of all temporary waste storage facilities.

If a generator of hazardous waste does not reuse or sell the waste, it must treat the waste to make it harmless. Permits are issued by the Regional Environmental Inspectorate for incineration or any other method of waste treatment. Such permits must be approved by the National Public Health Service. Permits are generally issued within 30 days. This period may be extended for another 30 days.

10.4.2 Operator requirements
An operator of hazardous waste storage facilities or waste treatment facilities must obtain a permit from the Regional Environmental Inspectorate. Permits are generally issued within 30 days. This period may be extended for another 30 days.

10.4.3 Charges
No charges for waste storage and treatment exist at present.

10.4.4 Public participation
The draft Environmental Law provides for the right of access to information on the state of the environment and public participation in the permitting process.

10.5 Waste disposal

10.5.1 Generator requirements
Generators of hazardous waste must submit reports to the Regional Environmental Inspectorate as regards the following:

- Type of waste generated;
- Daily and annual quantity of waste generated;
- Any changes in reported data regarding any hazardous waste generated.

Generators must also maintain records of all hazardous wastes generated and of all temporary waste storage facilities.

Permits are required for the disposal of wastes. Hazardous waste disposal permits are obtained from Regional Environmental Inspectorate. The National Public Health Service and the fire prevention authorities each have a role in approving permits issued by the Regional Environmental Inspectorate. The Municipality issues permits for the disposal of non-hazardous waste. The time frame for the issuance of permits is the same as set forth in *Section 9.4.1* above.

10.5.2 Operator requirements
Disposal or storage sites for liquid non-hazardous waste must be approved by the Municipality, together with the Regional Environmental Inspectorate and the Water Directorate.

Preliminary consent must be obtained from the Regional Environmental Inspectorate prior to the establishment of hazardous waste disposal or storage sites. *Decree No. 11/1991* sets forth the technical standards for waste incineration. The procedure for obtaining a disposal site permit is set forth in *Decree No. 56/1981*. The time frame for the issuance of permits is the same as set forth in *Section 9.4* above.

10.5.3 Charges

No charges for waste disposal exist at present.

10.5.4 Public participation

The draft Environmental Law provides for the right of access to information on the state of the environment and public participation in the permitting process.

10.6 Transport of waste

10.6.1 Labelling and containers

The transport and temporary storage of wastes is regulated by *Decree No. 56/1981*, as amended.

10.6.2 Transboundary movement

Hungary is a party to the *Basle Convention on the Control of Transboundary Movements of Hazardous Wastes and their Disposal*. The *Basle Convention*, which is intended to restrict trade in hazardous wastes, permits transboundary movement of wastes only in limited circumstances, for example where the importing country will recycle the waste.

Hazardous waste may be imported into Hungary with a special permit of the Environment Ministry. A permit is granted only if the imported wastes can be reused or recycled. The procedure for obtaining such permits is set forth in *Decree No. 55/1987 (X.30.MT.)* Those who violate import rules are required to restore the environment in the event of damage or to make the waste harmless.

10.7 Recycling requirements

Decree No. 56/1981, as amended, provides that a waste generator must either render hazardous waste harmless or recycle it. There are no detailed recycling regulations at the present time.

10.8 Enforcement

10.8.1 Compliance checking and monitoring

Regional Environmental Inspectorates license and monitor hazardous waste treatment facilities, establish collection methods, and enforce restrictions on the operation of hazardous waste facilities, suspending operations if necessary.

There is no comprehensive record of hazardous waste sites in Hungary.

10.8.2 Penalties and sanctions

Under *Decree No. 56/1981*, as amended, fines are imposed by Regional Environmental Inspectorates for violation of hazardous waste regulations, collection and treatment regulations and transport and temporary disposal regulations. The method of calculating the fines is set out in *Ordinance No. 2/1991 (XI.18)*. The amount of the fine is based on the quantity and class of the hazardous waste and the degree of danger posed by the violation. Repeated violations give rise to higher penalties.

11. Chemicals storage, handling and emergency response

11.1 Summary

Types of Activity:	Any regulated activity involving toxic substances, including manufacture, use and transportation, requires a permit from the National Public Health Service.
Emergency Response:	There are no specific regulations governing emergency response, but a draft Emergency Response Code is being prepared.
Public Participation:	No public participation is provided for in the present administrative decision-making process. The National Public Health Service, which monitors and collects data related to the public health effects of pollution, is required to publicise its data.
Enforcement:	The Ministry of Public Welfare and Health has the authority to suspend or limit any activity in violation of chemical substance regulation and to impose fines for violations of such regulations.

11.2 Sources of legislation relating to chemical storage, handling and emergency response

11.2.1 Storage

- *Decree No. 26/1985 (V.11.)* as supplemented by *Decree No. 46/1988(XII.22.) of the Ministry of Public Welfare and Health;*
- *Decree No. 16/1988 (XII.22.) of the Ministry of Public Welfare and Health,* which executes *Decree No. 26/1985 (V.II.),* lists toxic substances and sets forth detailed regulations on the storage of toxic substances.

11.2.2 Handling

- *Joint Decree No. 1/1975 (XII.5.) of the Ministry of Transport and Postal Service and the Ministry of Interior Affairs,* sets forth general traffic regulations which must be observed in the transportation of toxic substances;
- *Decree No. 26/1985 (V.11.),* sets forth general regulations concerning the storage and handling of toxic substances and is implemented by *Decree No. 46/1988(XII.22.) of the Ministry of Public Welfare and Health;*

- *Decree No. 12/1989 (XII.5.) of the Ministry of Transport, Communication and Water Management*, sets forth regulations regarding transport routes for toxic substances.

11.2.3 Emergency response

- Draft Emergency Response Code.

11.3 Regulatory requirements

11.3.18 Storage and handling

Decree No. 16/1988 regulates the storage of toxic substances. Appendix 6 of the Decree contains detailed provisions regarding the storage, handling and labelling of toxic substances.

The manufacture, handling and transportation of toxic substances requires a permit from the National Public Health Service. The procedure for obtaining permits is set forth in *Decree No. 16/1988.*

11.3.2 Transportation

Joint Decree No. 1/1975 and *Decree No. 12/1989* set forth detailed regulations for the transport of toxic substances.

11.3.3 Emergency response

The Ministry of Interior Affairs is currently preparing a draft Emergency Response Code regarding chemical spills.

11.4 Public participation

The National Public Health Service monitors and collects data related to the public health effects of pollution. It is required to publicise its data.

11.5 Enforcement

11.5.1 Compliance checking and monitoring

The Ministry of Public Welfare and Health is responsible for monitoring the storage and handling of toxic substances. Officials of the Ministry have a right to enter any buildings or facilities to obtain necessary information.

11.5.2 Penalties and sanctions

The Ministry of Public Welfare and Health has the authority to suspend or limit any activity in violation of regulations governing chemical substances or which can seriously harm the environment. It can assess fines for the violation of regulations.

Annex A

List of Key Legislation

1. Overview

- *Act XX of 1949, Constitution of the Republic of Hungary,* as amended;
- *Act No. I of 1957 on Administrative Procedure;*
- *Act No. IV of 1964 on Water,* as amended;
- *Act No. II of 1976 on the Protection of the Human Environment;*
- *Act No. I of 1987 on Land Use and Land Ownership;*
- *Act No. LXV of 1990 on Local Self-Government;*
- *Act No. LXIII of 1992 on Protection of Personal Data;*
- *Decree No. 1/1990 (XI.13.) of the Environment Ministry on the duties and scope of authority of the Environmental Inspectorates, Inspector General and the Municipalities in connection with environmental protection;*
- *Decree No. 4/1990 (X.24.) of the Ministry of Transport, Telecommunication and Water Management on the duties and scope of authority of the National Water Management Authority;*
- *Decree No. 43/1990 (IX.15.) on the duties and scope of authority of the Environment Ministry;*
- *Decree No. 44/1990 (IX.15.) on the duties and scope of authority of the Ministry of Transport, Telecommunication and Water Management;*
- *Act No. XI of 1991 on establishing the National Public Health Service; executed by Decree No. 7/1991 (IV.26) of the Ministry of Public Welfare and Health;*
- *Act No. LIV of 1992 on the Sale, Utilisation and Protection of Assets Temporarily Owned by the State;*
- *Act No. VII and VIII of 1990 on the Administration, Utilisation and Transfer of State-owned Enterprises;*
- *Act No. LIII of 1992 on the Management and Utilisation of Entrepreneurial Assets Permanently Remaining in State Ownership.*

2. Environmental liability

- *Act No. III of 1952 on Civil Procedure;*
- *Act No. IV of 1957 on Administrative Procedure;*
- *Civil Code, Act No. IV of 1959;*
- *Act No. II of 1976 on Protection of the Human Environment;*
- *Criminal Code, Act No. IV of 1978;*

273

- *Act XXIV of 1988 Regarding Investments by Foreigners in Hungary*, as amended;
- *Act No. LIII of 1992 on the Management and Utilisation of Entrepreneurial Assets Permanently Remaining in State Ownership;*
- *Act No. LIV of 1992 on the Sale, Utilisation and Protection of Assets Temporarily Owned by the State;*
- *Act No. LV of 1992 on the Amendment of Legal Rules in Connection with Acts Concerning Entrepreneurial Property of the State.*

3. Environmental audits

- *Act No. LIV of 1992 on the Sale, Utilisation and Protection of Assets Temporarily Owned by the State.*

4. Land use planning

- *Act No. III of 1964 on Housing and Construction, governs building permits;*
- *Act. No. I of 1987 on Land Use and Land Ownership;*
- *Decree No. 30/1964 (XII.2.),* implementing *Act No. III of 1964;*
- *Decree No. 1/1968 (I.II.) of the Ministry of Construction and Urban Development;*
- *Decree No. 29/1971 (XII.29.) of the Ministry of Construction and Urban Development;*
- *Decree No. 17/1981 (VI.19.) of the Ministry of Housing and Construction,* sets forth fines for violation of building and construction regulations;
- *Decree No. 2/1986 (II.27.) of the Ministry of Housing and Construction;*
- *Decree No. 12/1986 (XII.30.) of the Ministry of Housing and Construction;*
- *Decree No. 8/1987 (IX.1.) of the Ministry of Agriculture,* implementing *Act No. 1 of 1987;*
- *Decree No. 26/1987 (VII.30.) of the Ministry of Agriculture,* implementing *Act No. 1 of 1987;*
- *Decree No. 171/1991 (XII.27.) on the acquisition of immoveable property by foreigners;*
- *Decree No. 23/1992 (I.28.).*

5. Environmental Impact Assessments (EIAs)

- *Hungarian Standard No. MI 1345/1990: Technical Guidelines of the Environment Ministry on EIAs.*

6. Air emission requirements applicable to the operation of industrial and commercial facilities

- *Act No. II of 1976 on the Protection of the Human Environment, paragraphs 23–26;*
- *Decree No. 21/1986 (VI.2.);*
- *Ordinance No. 4/1986 (VI.2.) of the President of the National Office for the Protection of the Environment and Nature Conservation,* as amended by *Decree No. 9/1990 (IV.30.) of the Minister of Environment and Regional Policy, implements Decree No. 21/1986;*
- *Decree No. 3/1988 (VI.10.) of the Environment Ministry;*
- *Decree No. 5/1990 (XII.6.) of the Ministry of Public Welfare and Health;*
- *Decree No. 6/1990 (IV.12.) of the Ministry of Transport, Telecommunication and Water Management;*
- *Decree No. 18/1991 (XII.18.) of the Ministry of Transport, Telecommunication and Water Management on the Abatement of Air Pollution Arising from Vehicular Traffic;*
- *Decree No. 11/1991 (V.16.) of the Environment Ministry;*
- *Hungarian Standard MSZ 21854-1990: Requirements of Cleanliness of Ambient Air.*

7. Water requirements applicable to the operation of industrial and commercial facilities

- *Act No. IV of 1964 on Water,* amended by *Act No. I of 1984;*
- *Act No. II of 1976 on the Protection of the Human Environment, paragraphs 16–22;*
- *Decree No. 32/1964 (XII.13.),* as amended by *Decree No. 40/1969 and Decree No. 10/1984,* implementing *Act No. IV of 1964;*
- *Joint Decree No. 1/1970 (XI.18.) of the President of the National Water Management Authority and Price Office;*
- *Joint Decree No. 3/1970 (XII.18.) of the President of the National Water Management Authority and Price Office;*
- *Decree No. 5/1970 (XII.31.) of the President of the National Water Management Authority;*
- *Decree No. 4/1981 (IV.4.) of the President of the National Water Management Authority;*
- *Decree No. 3/1982 (VI.I.) of the President of the National Water Management Authority;*
- *Decree No. 1/1992 (I.6.) of the Environment Ministry;*
- *Ordinance No. 3/1984 (II.7.) of the President of the National Water Management Authority.;*
- *Ordinance No. 4/1984 (II.7.) of the President of the National Water Management Authority;*
- *Hungarian Standard MI-10-172/3-85: Classification of Water Quality.*

8. Noise requirements applicable to the operation of industrial and commercial facilities

- *Act II of 1976 on the Protection of the Human Environment;*
- *Decree No. 12/1983 (V.12.),* as amended by *Decree No. 88/1990 (IV.30.);*
- *Decree No. 4/1984 (I.23.) of the Ministry of Public Welfare and Health;*
- *Ordinance No. 2/1983 (V.25.) of the President of the National Office for the Protection of Environment and Nature Conservation, modified by Decree No. 12/1990 (V.23.) KVM of the Environment Ministry,* sets forth fines for violations of noise emission limits;
- *Hungarian Standard MSz 18150/1-83 measuring noise;*
- *Hungarian Standard MSz 1816312-83 measuring vibration;*
- *Hungarian Standards MSz 13-111-85 determining noise levels.*

9. Hazardous and non-hazardous waste management

- Act No. II of 1976 on the Protection of the Human Environment, paragraphs 17, 18, 23, 25, 32, and 42;
- *Ordinance No. 2/1981 (XI.18.) of the President of the National Office for the Protection of Environment and Nature Conservation;*
- *Decree No. 56/1981 (XI.18.),* as amended by *Decree No. 27/1992 (II.10.);*
- *Decree No. 55/1987 (X.30.MT.);*
- *Decree No. 11/1991 (V.16.) of the Environment Ministry.*

10. Chemicals storage, handling and emergency response

- *Joint Decree No. 1/1975 (XII.5.) of the Ministry of Transport and Postal Service and the Ministry of Interior Affairs;*
- *Decree No. 26/1985 (V.11.),* supplemented by *Decree 46/1988 (XII.22.) of the Ministry of Public Welfare and Health;*
- *Decree No. 16/1988 (XII.22.) of the Ministry of Public Welfare and Health;*
- *Decree No. 12/1989 (XII.5.) of the Ministry of Transport, Communication and Water Management.*

Annex B

List of Permitting and Enforcement Authorities

Környezetvédelmi és Területfejlesztési
Minisztérium
Ministry for Environment and Regional
Policy
Fő utca 44-50.
1011 Budapest I.
Telephone: (1) 201-2964

Környezetvédelmi Főfelügyelőség
National Environmental Protection
Inspectorte
Alkotmany u. 29
1054 Budapest
Telephone: (1) 132-9940, 2787

National Bureau for Nature Conservation
Költő utca 21
1121 Budapest
Telephone: (1) 156-2130

Építésügyi Igazgatási Főosztály
Department of Construction
Administration
Fő utca 44-50.
1011 Budapest
Telephone: (1) 201-2416

Földmüvelésügyi Minisztérium
Ministry of Agriculture
Kossuth L. tér 11
1055 Budapest
Telephone: (1) 153-3000

Land Registry
(Information available from Ministry of
Agriculture)

Ipari és Kereskedelmi Minisztérium
Ministry of Industry and Trade
Mártírok Utca 85.
1024 Budapest
Telephone: (1) 156-5566

Népjóléti Minisztérium
Ministry of Public Welfare
Arany János u. 6-8.
1361 Budapest
Telephone: (1) 132-3100

Állami Népegészségügyi és Tisztiorvosi
Szolgálat
National Public Health Service
Váci Út 174
1138 Budapest
Telephone: (1) 129-0490

Magyar Szabaványügyi Hivatal
Hungarian Standard Agency
Üllői Út. 25
1091 Budapest
Telephone: (1)118-3011

Közlekedési, Hírközlési és Vízügyi
Minisztérium
Ministry of Transport, Telecommunica-
tion, and Water Management
Dob utca 75/81
1077 Budapest
Telephone: (1) 122-0220, 9620

Országos Vízügyi Főigazgatóság
National Water Management Authority
Fő utca 44-50.
1011 Budapest
Telephone: (1) 201-4133

Ministry of Interior Affairs
József Attila utca 2/4
1051 Budapest
Telephone: (1) 112-0600

Regional Environmental Inspectorates

North-Transdanubian Inspectorate
Győr, Árpád u. 28-32.
H-9021
Tel: (96) 15-687

West-Transdanubian Inspectorate
Szombathely, Vörösmarty u. 3.
H-9700
Tel: (94) 28-188

Central-Transdanubian Inspectorate
Székesfehérvár, Balatoni u. 8.
H-8000
Tel: (22) 319-339

South-Transdanubian Inspectorate
Pécs, Kulich Gyula u. 13.
H-7623
Tel: (72) 12-511

Central Danube Basin Inspectorate
Budapest, Rákóczi út 41.
H-1088
Tel: (1) 113-0452

Lower Danube Basin Inspectorate
Baja, Bajcsy Zsilinszky u. 10.
H-6500
Tel: (79) 25-385

Upper Tisza Region Inspectorate
Nyiregyháza, Széchenyi u. 2.
H-4400
Tel: (42) 10-155

Lower Tisza Region Inspectorate
Szeged, Felső-Tiszapart u. 17.
H-6720
Tel: (62) 312-513

Central Tisza Region Inspectorate
Szolnok, Ságvári krt. 32.
H-5000
Tel: (56) 378-422

North Hungarian Inspectorate
Miskolc, Mindszent tér 4.
H-3530
Tel: (46) 356-412

Transtiszanian Inspectorate
Debrecen, Piac u. 9/b.
H-4024
Tel: (52) 12-653

Körös Region Inspectorate
Gyula, Városház u. 36.
H-5700
Tel: (66) 361-365

Water Directorates (followed by regions within scope of authority)

North Transdanubian Water Directorate
9021 Győr
Árpád u. 28-32
Telephone: (96) 15-067

Győr-Moson, Komárom-Esztergom,
Sopron,
Portions of Vas and Veszprém

West Transdanubian Water Directorate
9700 Szombathely
Vörösmarty u. 2.
Telephone: (94) 11-280

Vas, Zala,
Portions of Veszprém, Somogy and
Győr-Moson-Sopron

Central Transdanubian Water Directorate
8000 Székesfehérvár
Balatoni u. 6.
Telephone: (22) 315-370

Fejér, Veszprém, Tolna,
Portions of Somogy, Baranya and Bács-Kiskun

South Transdanubian Water Directorate
7623 Pécs
Köztársaság tér 7.
Telephone: (72) 26-311

Pécs, Baranya, Somogy,
Portion of Tolna

Central Danube Basin Water Directorate
1088 Budapest
Rákóczi út 41.
Telephone: (1) 113-1690

Budapest, Pest, Nógrád,
Portion of Heves

Lower Danube Basin Water Directorate
6500 Baja
Széchenyi u. 2/C.
Telephone: (79) 21-233

Bács-Kiskun,
Portion of Baranya

Upper Tisza Region Water Directorate
4400 Nyíregyháza
Széchenyi u. 19.
Telephone: (42) 10-155

Szabolcs-Szatmár-Bereg,
Portions of Hajdu-Bihar and Borsod-
Abaúj-Zemplén

Central Tisza Region Water Directorate
5000 Szolnok
Ságvári krt. 4.

Jász-Nagykun-Szolnok,
Portions of Heves, Bács-Kiskun, Békés,
Borsod-
Abaúj-Zemplén, Pest and Csongrád

Lower Tisza Region Water Directorate
6720 Szeged
Tanácsköztársaság u. 4.
Telephone: (62) 312-933

Szeged-Csongrád,
Portions of Békés, Bács-Kiskun and Jász-
Nagykun,
Szolnok

North Hungarian Water Directorate
3530 Miskolc
Vörösmarty u. 77.
Telephone: (46) 350-611

Miskolc, Bosod-Abaúj-Zemplén, Heves,
Portions of Szabolcs-Szatmár-Bereg,
Hajdu-Bihar and Jász-Nagykun,
Szolnok

Trans Tiszanian Water Directorate
4025 Debrecen
Hatvan u. 8-10.
Telephone: (52) 10-677

Debrecen, Hajdu-Bihar,
Portions of Békés, Szabolcs-Szatmár-
Bereg,
Borsod-Abaúj-Zemplén and Jász-
Nagykun, Szolnok

Kőrös Region Water Directorate
5700 Gyula
Városház u. 20.
Telephone: (66) 361-455

Békés,
Portions of Hajdu-Bihar and Jász-
Nagykun, Szolnok

Annex C

List of Proposed Legislation

1. Overview

- Draft Law on Environmental Protection;
- Draft Decree on EIAs.

2. Land use planning

- Draft Construction Act.

3. Environmental impact assessments (EIAs)

- Draft Decree on EIAs.

4. Chemicals storage, handling and emergency response

- Draft Emergency Response Code.

Annex D

Environmental Standards

1. Air quality

- *Decree No. 21/1986 (VI.2.)*, sets forth the protection of the clean air, amended by *Decree No. 49/1986 (VI.5.);*
- *Ordinance No. 4/1986 (VI.2.) of the President of the National Office for Environmental Protection and Nature Conservation*, amended by *Decree No. 9/1990 (IV.30.) of the Minister of Environment and Regional Policy*, implements *Decree No. 21/1986;*
- *Decree No. 5/1990 (XII.6.) of the Ministry of Public Welfare and Health*, setting forth airquality standards and defining monitoring and control programmes;
- *Decree No. 6/1990 (IV.12.) of the Ministry of Transport, Telecommunication and Water Management*, defining vehicular air emission limits (paragraphs 15–16);
- *Decree No. 11/1991 (V.16.) of the Environment Ministry*, on the best available control technology for waste incineration;
- *Hungarian Standards MSZ 21854-1990*, on cleanliness requirements of environmental air.

2. Water quality

- *Ordinance No. 3/1984 (II.7.) of the President of the National Water Management Authority*, defining the limit and method of calculating fines for polluting rivers, lakes, public canals and groundwater;
- *Ordinance No. 4/1984 (II.7.) of the President of the National Water Management Authority*, defining the limit and method of calculating fines for polluting canal and water purification systems.

3. Environmental noise

- *Decree No. 4/1984 (I.23.) of the Ministry of Public Welfare and Health*, setting forth limits for vibration and noise emissions.

Annex E

International Conventions

- Protocol on Long-Term Financing of the Co-operative Programme for Monitoring and Evaluation of the Long-Range Transmission of Air Pollutants in Europe, 28 September 1984, 24 I.L.M. 484 (entered into force 28 January 1988).
- Protocol to the Convention on Long-Range Transboundary Air Pollution on the Reduction of Sulfur Emissions or Their Transboundary Fluxes by at Least 30 Percent, 9 July 1985, U.N. DOC. ECE/EB.Air/7, annex 1.
- Protocol to the Convention on Long-Range Transboundary Air Pollution Concerning the Control of Emissions of Nitrogen Oxides or Their Transboundary Fluxes, 31 October 1988, 28 I.L.M. 214 (entered into force 14 February 1991).
- Protocol to the Convention on Long-Range Transboundary Air Pollution Concerning the Control of Emissions of Volatile Organic Compounds or Their Transboundary Fluxes, opened for signature 18 November 1991, Int'l Envtl. Rep. (BNA) 21:3061.
- Convention for the Protection of the Ozone Layer, 22 March, 1985, 26 I.L.M. 1529 (entered into force 22 September 1988).
- Montreal Protocol on Substances that Deplete the Ozone Layer, 16 September 1987, 26 I.L.M. 1550 (entered into force 1 January 1989).
- Convention on the Control of Transboundary Movements of Hazardous Wastes and Their Disposal, 22 March 1989, 28 I.L.M. 649 (entered into force May 1992).
- Convention on Environmental Impact Assessment in a Transboundary Context, 25 February 1991, 30 I.L.M. 800.

Annex F

Investment Projects Subject to EIAs

- The draft EIA Decree to be issued under the *Environmental Protection Act* is expected to be passed by April 1993. An Appendix to the draft decree lists the types of operations and investments where EIAs must be performed including the following:

Mining industry

- Strip mines;
- Subterranean mines;
- Processing of minerals;
- Mine dumps with a capacity of more than 100,000 m^3;
- Ore processing;
- Coal processing and briqueting plants;
- Coke production;
- Crude oil and natural gas processing plants;
- Underground storage tanks for inflammable gases.

Energy industry

- Nuclear power plants;
- Nuclear reactors with a thermal output of more than 1 KW;
- Nuclear fuel production and enrichment plants as well as nuclear fuel rod production plants;
- Plants for the recycling of irradiated nuclear fuel rods;
- Facilities for the handling and storage of radioactive materials;
- Storage of spent nuclear fuel;
- Laboratories for the manufacture of A-type isotopes;
- Thermoelectric power plants with a capacity of 50 MW;
- Hydroelectric power plants;
- Electric power lines with a capacity greater than 120 KV.

Metallurgy

- Iron works and steel works, including foundries;
- Forges (iron, steel, aluminum, non-ferrous metals);
- Bauxite processing.

Engineering industry

- Works for the refurbishing of industrial machines and railway equipment of a capacity of 50 or more at any given time;
- Manufacture of engines and machines;
- Manufacture of railway equipment;
- Manufacture of car batteries;
- Plants for the surface treatment of metals (anodising, de-greasing) capable of treating more than 20,000 m^2.

Construction industry

- Plants for the manufacture of fireproof bricks, insulation and asphalt with a yearly production rate of more than 2,000 tons;
- Cement manufacturing;
- Manufacture of asbestos and asbestos products;
- Fine ceramics manufacturing with an annual production rate of more than 5,000 tons;
- Glass manufacturing with an annual production rate of more than 20,000 tons.

Chemical industry

- Refineries;
- Fossil oil-based lubricant manufacturing with a production rate of more than 15,000 tons;
- Coal processing and coal distillation;
- CO_2 natural gas processing and its technological use;
- Nitric acid and sulphuric acid production;
- Electrolysis;
- Ammonia production;
- Phosgene production;
- Pesticide production;
- Polyurethane and paint manufacturing plants with an annual production rate of more than 5,000 tons;
- Production of gunpowder, explosives and ammunition;
- Production of chemicals used in the construction industry with a yearly output of more than 100 tons;
- Synthetic coal and graphite manufacturing;
- Plants for developing photographic film with an annual output of more than 15,000 m^2, or plants for the manufacture of photographic paper with an annual output of more than 5,000 m^2;
- Production of fertilisers;
- Production of plastics;
- Production of synthetic strands of cellulose;
- Processing of plastics;
- Production of rubber;
- Production of pharmaceuticals;
- Plants for the production of detergents and cleaning materials with an annual output of 5,000 tons.

Light industry

- Plants for painting and lacquering;
- Manufacture of cellulose and paper;
- Manufacture of asbestos-containing materials;
- Tanneries and leather processing plants.

Food industry

- Slaughterhouses;
- Plants for meat processing with an annual output of more than 5,000 tons;
- Animal-fat processing plants with an hourly output of more than 2 tons;
- Animal protein processing plants;
- Sugar manufacturing;
- Manufacture of vegetable oils;
- Distilleries and alcohol processing plants;
- Manufacture of starch and yeast.

Agriculture and forestry

- Complete improvement of flatlands and hilly areas greater than 500 ha;
- Partial improvement or hilly areas greater than 500 ha;
- Industrial water drainage of more than 1,000 ha.

Transportation, mail and telecommunications

- Railroads;
- Railroad stations;
- Expressways and thruways;
- First class roadways;
- Second class roadways, roadways that cut through forests (forests of greater than 50 ha;
- Bus terminals;
- Subways;
- Ports and shipping docks;
- Commercial airports;
- Crude oil, natural gas and petroleum pipelines.

Water management

- Reservoirs of more than 1 million m^3 capacity or having a dam height of more than 2 m;
- Dams;
- Back-water and stagnant river regulation;
- Regulation of riverbed longer than 3 km;
- Regulation of main running waters longer than 5 km in hilly areas;
- Water permeability, if the permeability is 5% or more than the water volume;

- Regulation of main water canals longer than 5km in flatland areas;
- Sewage treatment plants with a capacity of 20,000 m^3/d;
- Sewage treatment farms larger than 100 ha;
- Exploitation of underground water reservoirs larger than 20,000 m^3/d;
- Regulation of streams longer than 500 m.

Other economic activities

- District-heating plants of a capacity of more than 50 MW.

Military installations and other activities

- Military training areas larger than 50 ha;
- Barracks and facilities for the storage of weapons and machinery that are larger than 5 ha;
- Military airports.

Waste management
Solid Waste Management:
- Waste dumps;
- Carrion pits;
- Incinerators.

Liquid waste management:

- Sewage treatment plants with a daily capacity of more than 50 m^3;
- Sewage treatment farms greater than 5 ha;
- Sludge pits.

Hazardous waste management:

- Temporary storage facilities for hazardous waste;
- Plants for the initial treatment of hazardous waste;
- Storage facilities for hazardous waste;
- Hazardous waste incinerators;
- Incinerators not specifically designed for, but burning hazardous waste at a daily rate of more than 1 ton;
- Other facilities for the treatment of hazardous waste.

In certain areas of national importance EIAs are required without regard to the quantitative criteria included in some of the above categories (output etc.).

The following projects, if undertaken in areas of national importance, require an EIA:

- Game breeding farms;
- Animal breeding farms;
- Wild game reserves;
- Roads in continuous use;
- Railroads for use by agriculture and forestry;
- Radio and television broadcasting stations;

- Reservoirs and fishing areas;
- Downhill skiing and sledding areas;
- Geothermic power stations;
- Fisheries;
- Reed growing lakes, fish breeding lakes;
- Airports other than for commercial use;
- Flood prevention;
- Surface irrigation canals;
- Long distance aqueducts;
- Sewage carrying pipes;
- Air carrying pipes;
- Areas of tourism and recreation.

This list will be reviewed by the government every two years and may be amended and expanded.

Latvia

Prepared for the European Bank for Reconstruction and Development and the
Commission of the European Communities by
Environmental Resources Limited*

1. Overview

1.1 The Guidelines

1.1.1 Background

Investments in Latvia are subject to many legal and economic requirements. This document focuses specifically on those compliance, operational and liability issues which arise from environmental protection measures and affect investments.

The Guidelines are intended to enable investors to familiarise themselves with the basic environmental regulatory regime relating to commercial and industrial greenfield site developments, joint venture operations or company acquisitions in Latvia.

The Guidelines review institutional arrangements for environmental control, legislative requirements and procedures, time implications for permitting, public access to information, liability and sanctions. Because environmental policy, legislation and infrastructure in Latvia are currently undergoing radical change the review covers both current and proposed future arrangements.

Guidelines for the following CEE countries have been prepared on behalf of the European Bank for Reconstruction and Development and the Commission of the European Communities by Environmental Resources Limited and White & Case:

- Bulgaria;[1]
- Czech Republic and Slovak Republic;[1]
- Estonia;[2]

---

[1] Guidelines prepared by White & Case.
[2] Guidelines prepared by Environmental Resources Limited.

* Environmental Resources Limited acknowledges the valuable contribution in the preparation of the Investors' Environmental Guidelines: Latvia of Dr David Gilbert of Environmental Resources Limited and Peter Zilgalvis Esq.

- Hungary;[1]
- Latvia;[2]
- Lithuania;[2]
- Poland;[1]
- Romania.[2]

These Guidelines present a description of the environmental regulatory framework as of February 1993. They provide a first step for investors in understanding environmental requirements but do not substitute for specific legal advice relating to particular sites.

Administrative and legal arrangements for environmental regulation are in a transition phase in the countries covered by these Guidelines. Requirements and implementation systems are subject to change. Investors are advised to discuss details of requirements with the authorities and check for any changes which may have taken place since February 1993.

1.1.2 Using the Guidelines

The Guidelines provide general guidance on environmental regulatory requirements applicable to foreign investment in commercial and industrial sectors of the economy. Some sections of the Guidelines, such as *Section 4* on Land Use Planning and *Section 5* on EIA are also applicable to other sectors of the economy such as agriculture, mining, forestry and fisheries. In relation to such types of activities however, it is advisable to review other applicable requirements which are outside the scope of the Guidelines.

Section 1 provides a quick reference to environmental regulatory requirements in two case studies, and in *Figure 1.1.2(a) and Figure 1.1.2(b)*. *Figure 1.1.2(b)* indicates how the Guidelines should be used by reference to the type of investment decision that has to be made.

The remainder of this section provides background information on the country and the following.

- Administrative structure;
- Legislative process and key items of legislation;
- Quick reference to the permitting process;
- Enforcement;
- Public participation.

Section 2 highlights the potential liabilities of investors. Liabilities potentially arising from past pollution to be taken into account at the time an investment is made and liabilities arising in the course of operating commercial and industrial facilities are presented separately. Additional details relating to specific sectors of control are provided in subsequent sections.

Section 3 identifies any environmental auditing requirements and comments on the role of voluntary audits in achieving compliance.

---

[1] Guidelines prepared by White & Case.
[2] Guidelines prepared by Environmental Resources Limited.

Figure 1.1.2(a) Using the Guidelines: report structure

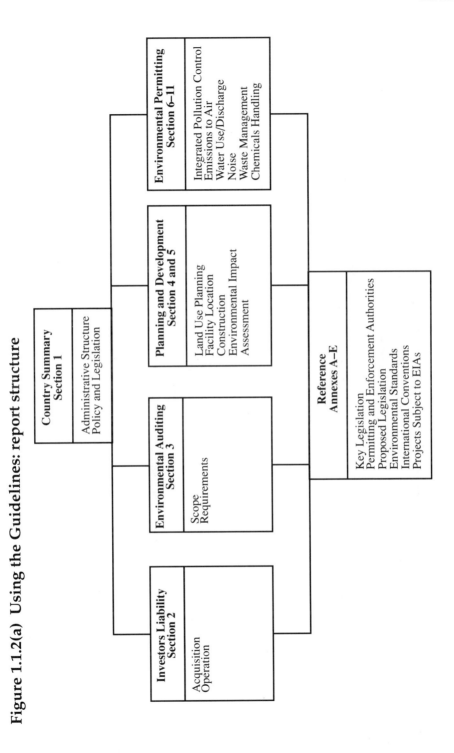

Figure 1.1.2(b) Using the Guidelines: summary by type of investment decision

Investment Decisions	Environmental Concerns	Sections in Guidelines
Choice of investment sector (eg commercial, services, manufacturing, energy)	Government and environmental bodies	1.4, 1.7, Annex B
	Existing and proposed legislation	1.5, Annex A & C
	Available forms of investment	1.2, 2.3.2
	Purchase of land	4.3
	Investments subject to EIA	5
	Activities subject to permitting	6–11
	Permitting overview and examples	1.6
Development of a "greenfield site"	Government and environmental bodies	1.4, 1.7, Annex B
	Existing and proposed legislation	1.5, Annex A & C
	Purchase of land	4.3
	EIA requirements	5
	Public participation	1.8
	Environmental standards	7, 8, Annex D
Acquisition of existing facility and privatisation	Government and environmental bodies	1.4, 1.7, Annex B
	Privatisation	1.2
	Environmental liability	2
	Cleanup of contaminated sites	2.3
	Indemnification by government	2.3
	Environmental audits	3
	Environmental standards	7, 8, Annex D
	EIA requirements (especially where modifications are made to existing facilities)	5

Investment Decisions	Environmental Concerns	Sections in Guidelines
Redevelopment and expansion of commercial and industrial facilities	Government and environmental bodies	1.4, 1.7, Annex B
	Change of land use	4
	Construction permits	4
	EIA requirements	5
	Permitting requirements	6–11
	Public participation	1.8
Operation of industrial and commercial facilities	Government and environmental bodies	1.4, 1.7, Annex B
	Environmental liability	2
	EIA requirements	5
	Public participation	1.8
	Integrated permitting	6
	Air requirements	7, Annex D
	Water requirements	8
	Noise requirements	9
	Waste management	10
	Chemical storage and handling	11
	Permitting overview and examples	1.6
	Compliance with international law	Annex E

Sections 4–11 provide guidance on permitting and related regulatory requirements for setting up and operating a commercial or industrial enterprise. Key aspects are presented at the beginning of each section for quick reference. Each section identifies the following:

- Key legislation;
- Activities covered;
- Requirements and procedures;
- Timing;
- Public participation;
- Enforcement and sanctions.

Sections 4 and 5 outline requirements and procedures relating to land use planning, facility location and construction, and environmental impact assessment. *Section 6* indicates the extent to which environmental permitting is integrated. Permitting and other regulatory requirements relating to air, water, noise, waste and chemicals are set out in *Sections 7–11*.

Annexes provide quick reference to existing and proposed legislation, contact points for the regulatory agencies, environmental standards, and ratification of international conventions.

1.2 The country

1.2.1 Background

The Republic of Latvia renewed its independence on 4 May 1990, and was accepted into the United Nations in 1991. The country has 2.6 million inhabitants, approximately 75% are citizens of Latvia and 34% of the population lives in the capital city, Riga.

After its inclusion in the USSR, Latvia was industrialised and between 1945 and 1985, the number of industrial workers increased by 370%, chiefly as a result of immigration from Russia. Until 1989, the country had the highest population growth in Europe due almost entirely to immigration. The natural growth of population saw a continuous decline from the late 1950s to the 1980s. The currency is the Latvian ruble (183 rubles = £1 sterling as of 2 April 1993).

1.2.2 Investment

The chief goal of the Latvian Government is the transition to a sovereign, market economy. Government policy is focused on the re-orientation of the economy towards the use of local resources and a reduction in imports. Latvia is dependent on foreign energy sources with domestic electricity meeting only half of the country's demand.

Latvia has a decentralised privatisation programme and individual ministries will be selling off the enterprises under their jurisdiction. Foreign investors can own up to 100% of an enterprise, they cannot own land, but can lease it for up to 99 years.

In Latvia, as in Estonia and Lithuania, foreign investors are guaranteed protection against nationalisation and expropriation of their property, and are guaranteed compensation for any such loss. The Latvian *Investment Law* allows investors to refer back to the legislation that was in effect when their investment was made for up to ten years. Tax incentives are available for foreign investment.

A system of privatisation vouchers is planned for Latvian citizens and permanent residents. The draft legislation for privatisation vouchers has been accepted by the Supreme

Council and vouchers for both citizens and permanent residents are expected although the calculation criteria differ. Because of the high number of non-Latvians in the industrial workforce, the decision on citizenship will have a great effect on the political attitude towards the closing of industry for environmental or economic reasons.

1.2.3 Environmental Protection

Latvia has introduced the "polluter pays" principle and imposed environmental charges for natural resource use and pollution discharges in order to reduce pollution. Natural resource charges are collected for the use of, and discharge to, surface water and groundwater, and for emissions to air and minerals exploitation.

The National Report of Latvia to UNCED 1992 states that Latvia's main strategic aim is the achievement of sustainable development. The most important tasks to be undertaken in order to achieve sustainable development are seen as the following:

- The replacement of environmentally damaging technologies in traditional Baltic industries, eg wood processing, building materials, light industry, food processing, technical appliances.
- Implementation of economic incentives for pollution reduction in conjunction with the development of free market mechanisms.
- Compulsory fulfilment of environmental requirements (command and control).
- Development of local production facilities and crafts with strict environmental enforcement.

Latvia aims to follow the EC regulatory approach, but there are difficulties because of the economic, financial, and social disparities existing between Latvia and the EC. The Latvian Environment Protection Committee (EPC) has two formal aims in this regard:

- To continue developing regulations based on Latvian Law passed since 4 May 1990.
- To create the pre-conditions necessary for the introduction of EC standards.

1.3 Administrative structure

Latvia has a centralised administrative system in which certain tasks are delegated to the regional offices of national ministries. The national Environmental Protection Committee (EPC) is the key agency for the development and implementation of environmental legislation. The EPC is supported by nine regional EPCs, each responsible for three to four districts. An exception to this is the Ogre regional EPC which is responsible only for the Ogre District. This is an experimental arrangement to test the possibility of attaching an EPC to every district government.

1.4 Government and environmental bodies

1.4.1 Ministries

Latvia's central environmental authority is the Environmental Protection Committee (EPC) which was established by the *Law on the Environmental Protection Committee of*

295

the Republic of Latvia 1990. It is expected that after the parliamentary elections in 1993 under the *Constitution*, the EPC will become a Ministry.

The EPC functions as the central Latvian state executive and overseeing body for all environmental protection and natural resource matters within its competence. Its main functions are as follows:

- To formulate and implement, together with other government agencies, a unified policy for environmental protection and natural resource use;
- To perform State Environmental Impact Assessments and establish environmental protection requirements;
- To oversee environmental protection and natural resource use throughout Latvia's territory, the continental shelf, and that area of the Baltic Sea comprising the Latvian economic zone.

1.4.2 Environmental Bodies

The nine regional branches of the EPC (Daugavpils, Jelgava, Liepaja, Madona, Ogre, Rezekne, Riga, Valmiera, Ventspils) implement EPC policy throughout Latvian territory. Their functions include permitting inspections, monitoring, enforcement and liaison with the Hydrometeorlogical Agency. Eight of the regional EPCs cover three to four districts each, while only the Ogre EPC covers the Ogre district alone.

Each regional EPC is sub-divided as follows:

- Inspectorate;
- Laboratory;
- Statistics department;
- EIA department.

The following administrative bodies are also responsible for implementation of environmental policy on particular issues:

- Baltic Sea Protection State Inspectorate;
- Forest and Hunting State Control Inspectorate;
- Water Reservoir and Ground Soil Protection Inspectorate.

A number of bodies contribute to policy development and information collection and dissemination:

- The State Standard Centre (part of the Council of Ministers, executive branch) is responsible, along with the EPC, for the formulation of environmental standards. The regional EPCs are responsible for the majority of permitting and enforcement tasks.
- Forests are administered by the Ministry of Forests and the Ministry of Agriculture, which has jurisdiction over forests found on the property of the collective farms (which will be privatised). The Ministry of Forestry also manages the Gauja National Park.
- The Hydrometeorlogical Agency, a Latvian Council of Ministers Institution, is responsible for collection, analysis, and dissemination of meteorological, hydrological, and environmental data. It has a central laboratory and six regional laboratories. It coordinates its work with the Latvian EPC and publishes annual reports on freshwater and coastal water conditions.

- The Standing Commission on the Environment in the Latvian Supreme Council is made up of Members of the Latvian Saeima (Parliament) who review and work on proposed environmental legislation.

1.4.3 Environmental Funds

The *Law on Environmental Protection 1991* provides for an environmental protection and natural resources fund which is to be used for environmental improvement. Charges from activities which might have harmful effects on the environment, eg releases to air and water, and natural resources use, will be used for the fund. Detailed provisions have yet to be introduced. The fund will be controlled by the Council of Ministers.

1.5 Environmental legislation

1.5.1 Legislative process

The laws currently in force have been passed on the basis of the Latvian Soviet Socialist Republic (LSSR) Constitution. On 5 and 6 June 1993, Latvia will fully rein-state its *1992 Constitution* when it elects its first Parliament under Latvian Law. Because of this, Laws, Regulations and Institutions will have to be modified to conform with the Constitution. For instance, the Environmental Protection Committee will not be able to remain in the parliamentary structure, and sections of laws may have to be modified or annulled.

The investor should therefore be aware that although the environmental requirements indicated in these Guidelines are unlikely to change substantively in themselves, the legal and institutional context may change. The requirement to carry out an Environmental Impact Assessment, for example, is unlikely to change, but the institution to which it is submitted, and the nature of the approval process, may change.

Environmental legislation in Latvia is passed by the Supreme Council (SC) after it has been sent to the floor by the Supreme Council's Standing Committee on the Environment. The EPC drafts environmental legislation. Drafts of legislation may be submitted by:

- Members of Latvian Saeima (Parliament);
- The SC Presidium;
- SC standing commissions;
- SC factions;
- The Government;
- Regional and city councils;
- Public organisations.

The present legislative authority, the Republic of Latvian Supreme Council was elected under USSR law with the participation of the Soviet military and non-Latvian citizens, and is therefore seen as a transitionary body. Two institutions in Latvia are responsible for the drafting of environmental regulations and standards:

- The Latvian Environmental Protection Committee;
- The State Standard Centre (part of the Council of Ministers, the executive branch).

Debate and acceptance of proposed legislation is regulated by the *Decree on the Procedure of the Consideration of Draft Laws of June 19, 1990*. It states that drafts of legislation are to be submitted to the Supreme Council Presidium, which is then to submit the draft to the appropriate SC standing commission for review. After the standing commission and the legislative commission approve the draft, it is presented to the plenary session. The decision on when the draft is presented is at the discretion of the SC Presidium.

Three readings are required for the passage of a law. After approval of the first reading, basic changes in the concept of the draft are not allowed. In the second reading, the draft is debated and voted on paragraph by paragraph. In the third reading, only editorial changes may be made.

There is a fast track process for the passage of legislation considered to be urgent in which a law can be passed in two readings. This process may be initiated by a standing commission or, 20 or more deputies.

1.5.2 Legislation

The fundamental principles of Latvian environmental policy are set out in the *Law on Environmental Protection 1991*. Other environmental legislation passed since 1990 is as follows:

- *Law on State Environmental Impact Assessments 1990*;
- *Law on Natural Resource Taxes 1990*;
- *Law on the Environmental Protection Committee of the Republic of Latvia 1990*;
- *Regulation on the Environmental Protection Inspectorate 1990*;
- *Regulation on the State Specially Protected Cultural/Historical Territory "Livod Randa" 1991*;
- *Regulation on the Baltic Sea and Gulf of Riga Coastal Protection Regime 1990*;
- *Regulation on the creation of Northern Vidzeme's Regional Nature Protection Complex and Activities for the Organisation of Biosphere Reserve 1990*;
- *Regulation on Private Home Construction in Connection with the Emergency Ecological Situation 1990*.

Draft legislation and standards in preparation cover the following topics:

- Hazardous waste;
- Chemical substances;
- Use of water resources;
- Exploitation of underground resources;
- Soil protection;
- Air protection;
- Specially protected nature objects;
- Drinking water standards;
- Methods for the calculation of damages for water pollution.

1.6 Overview of permitting process and other regulatory requirements

1.6.1 General

Sectoral environmental permits are currently required in Latvia for the operation of industrial and commercial facilities. Environmental permitting is closely linked to the EIA process and it is anticipated that an integrated permitting system will be introduced in the future. Because there has been little foreign investment in Latvia to date, experience in the environmental permitting process is very limited.

The following permits are required for any proposed industrial development:

- A construction permit;
- An air emissions permit;
- A water use and discharge permit.

A summary of the permitting procedure is given in *Figure 1.6.1(a)*. First, an investor must complete a Technical Economic Calculation (TEC) and submit it to the municipality or, for developments deemed by the regional Environmental Protection Committee (EPC) to be of national significance, to the State Construction Committee. A timeframe of three months is specified.

An Environmental Impact Assessment (EIA) for proposed facilities or modifications to existing facilities provides the focus of the permitting process. The EIA document is submitted to the regional EPC and is reviewed over a period of three months by an Expert Commission appointed by the EPC. Certain cases may be referred by the regional EPC for review by the national EPC. In all cases, and on the basis of the information provided, the EPC produces a State EIA report which includes the EPC's and experts' conclusions and recommendations to the developer.

Permitting for emissions to air, water use and wastewater discharge, is integrated with the EIA procedure. Applications are submitted with the EIA documentation and permits are issued by the regional EPC largely on the basis of information in the EIA. For proposed developments, permits are therefore issued within the same three-month timeframe as the EIA. Separate permits for noise and chemical storage are not required, but these issues must be addressed in the EIA.

According to *proposed* legislation, a declaration of any activities involving hazardous waste would then be made to the regional EPC, and a decision on whether to issue a permit, made within 15 days.

Following construction of the facility, approval must be given by the local fire department.

Two case study examples are given below to illustrate the key steps in the permitting process. Because very little foreign investment has taken place in Latvia to date, the case studies are based more on theory than practice.

1.6.2 Case study 1

For a foreign investor acquiring a greenfield site for development of a new paper mill, the permitting procedure would involve the following steps.

First, the investor must apply to the municipality for a construction permit. A decision on this must be made within three months.

Parallel to this application, the EIA process can be carried out. Firstly, advice must be sought from the regional EPC as to the scope of the EIA (extent of surveying, monitoring etc). The EIA itself is then carried out by the investor and must include:

- An evaluation of the predicted environmental impact of the facility;
- A declaration of measures to be taken to guarantee environmental quality.

The complete EIA is submitted to the regional EPC for approval. During the three months available for review of the EIA, the investor must discuss the project with representatives of local interest groups and residents although a specific mechanism for consultation has not as yet been prescribed. The EIA is reviewed by an Expert Commission appointed by the EPC. A decision on the EIA must be issued within three months unless further information is requested, which can extend the time period.

Applications for the various sectoral environmental permits are made to the regional EPC at the same time as application for EIA approval. The permits may be issued with conditions and standards attached, on the basis of the EIA. Permits for water use, wastewater discharge and emissions to air must be issued within the same three-month period as the EIA. Separate permits for noise and chemical storage are not required, but these issues must be addressed in the EIA.

Proposed legislation would require that a declaration of any activities involving hazardous waste is then made to the regional EPC which must make a decision on issue of a permit within 15 days.

One final approval must be sought from the local fire department once the paper mill has been built.

The main steps of this procedure are summarised in *Figure 1.6.1(a)*.

1.6.3 Case Study 2

For a foreign investor forming a joint venture with an existing company, acquiring two factories, closing one and refurbishing the other to produce tyres, the permitting procedure would involve the following steps.

The permitting procedure would be essentially the same as described in Case Study 1 for development of a greenfield site. In summary:

- **Step 1** : Application for construction permit for change in land use. Decision within three months.
- **Step 2** : Application for approval of EIA and for sectoral permits. Decisions within three months.
- **Step 3** : Declaration of any activities involving hazardous waste (*proposed legislation*). Decision within 15 days.
- **Step 4** : Construction of facility.
- **Step 5** : Application for fire safety approval and decision.

1.7 Enforcement of environmental legislation

Enforcement of environmental laws and standards in Latvia is carried out by the EPC State Environmental Protection Inspectorate (EPSI). Inspectors control compliance with environmental protection laws relating to the following:

- Land use planning;
- The choice of locations for new construction;
- Construction, expansion, reconstruction;
- Facility operation;
- Increases in production volume and modifications for new types of production.

300

Responsibilities of the Inspectorate are set out in the *Regulation on the Environmental Protection Inspectorate 1990.*

Charges for exceeding discharge limits are calculated according to the *Law on Natural Resource Taxes 1990.* Taxes on pollution and resource use in excess of prescribed limits are assessed at a penalty rate of three times the basic rate. For every day that the payment of taxes is late, a penalty of 0.1% of the tax sum is added.

The submission of fraudulent data or registers, or the concealment of required data or registers may result in administrative or criminal liability according to the Criminal Code and Administrative Violation Code of the LSSR. These remain in force in Latvia until the new legislation is introduced to replace them.

Where permits for effluent discharge are breached on thermal or bacteriological pollution limits, or in the event of the release of toxic wastewater, the EPC *Resolution on Water Use Permits 1990* requires increasing payments in order to reduce pollution and improve water quality to acceptable levels. If discharge levels set out in the permit for wastewater are exceeded threefold, then regional EPCs can impose charges to cover damage to the environment. If the data submitted by the water user does not correspond to the data collected by the state, payments will be calculated according to state data for a maximum of six months. Regional EPCs have the right to withdraw, supplement, change, or annul permits.

Further penalties for the violation of environmental laws which do not carry criminal liability are calculated according to the *Administrative Violation Code.*

The penalty sums in the *Administrative Violation Code* (calculated in Rubles) have become inadequate due to hyperinflation. Consequently new penalties are being drafted by the national EPC.

The Environmental Protection Chief State Inspector and the regional unit EP Chief State Inspectors (or, in their absence, their deputies) can issue and revoke permits for the following:

- Emission of polluting substances into the environment;
- Activities which cause artificial changes to the air, and for the utilisation of air for production;
- Special water use, and activities in water or coastal zones;
- Activities which are connected to harmful physical, biological, or other effects on the environment;
- Use of, or geological exploration of, soil;
- Introduction of wild plants, animals or water organisms not native to Latvia, its interior and territorial waters, continental shelf, or the Latvian Baltic Sea economic zone or which are native but their dissemination and acquisition has been for various reasons interrupted;
- Acquisition of rare or rapidly disappearing wild plants or animals, or the acquisition, trade, and export of animals and water organisms, which are not hunting or fishing objects;
- Use of plants or animals in specially protected territories, and the use of photo, film, sound recording, and video apparatus in such territories;
- Disposal of industrial, communal or other wastes on land or at sea.

The Hygiene Centre and its local Sanitary–Epidemiological Inspectorates are the primary enforcement organisations in the fields of drinking water, recreational water, and occupational health and safety.

The Baltic Sea Basin Fishery Protection and Fish Stock Regulation Board deals with Baltic Sea fishing issues.

1.8 Public participation

1.8.1 Public Access to Information

Under the *Law on Environmental Protection 1991* citizens and public organisations may demand information on the environmental effects of any proposed facilities or facilities under construction, from state institutions, and where an EIA has been carried out (new or modified facilities) demand the publication of the EIA statement and inquiry results.

1.8.2 Provision of Information

Environmental protection institutions have a duty to regularly inform inhabitants about the condition of the environment.

1.8.3 Public Consultation

Where an EIA is to be carried out, ie new or modified facilities, the *Law on State Environmental Impact Assessment 1990* requires the investor to discuss the project concept and its potential environmental effects with the representatives of social organisations and citizens. A detailed procedure for public consultation has not yet been introduced.

Citizens may request the courts to repeal or restrain resolutions and actions on environmental issues of administrative institutions and their officials which ignore the rights of inhabitants and local organisations.

2. Environmental liability

2.1 Summary

Note:	Liability law is in a transitional phase. Revision of existing legislation and new legislation, particularly on privatisation is expected to address liability issues in more detail.
Environmental Liabilities:	The regulation on land reform states that new investors are not liable for past pollution.
Successor Liability:	The previous owner remains liable and the successor can claim from him the cost for remediation works.
Investor Clean-up of Contaminated Sites:	No standards exist which either trigger a clean-up obligation or for restoration levels.

Civil Liability:	Civil liability operates largely on the basis of fault-based liability. Strict liability is applied to "extremely hazardous" activities.
Administrative Liability:	The *Administrative Violation Code* lists environmental violations. Remedies include fines, permit revocation or the closing of a facility.
Criminal Liability:	Penalties for breach of the *Criminal Code* include fines, confiscation and imprisonment. The Code is currently under revision.

2.2 Sources of legislation relating to environmental liability

Liability law is in a transitional phase in which the 1937 Republic of Latvia Civil Code is being renewed but the 1963 LSSR Code (derived from the USSR), which was established temporarily as the Latvian *Civil Code*, still remains partially in force. The LSSR Civil Code was amended in 1990 by the *Law on Amendments and Supplements to the LSSR Administrative Violation Code 1990*.

Environmental Liability is also covered by the *Law on Environmental Protection 1991* and the *Administrative* and *Criminal Codes*.

The methodology to calculate damages comes from USSR instructions with the exception of the *Council of Ministers Resolution No. 1, on Compensation for Damage Caused by Air Pollution from Stationary Sources Operating Without a Permit or While Exceeding State Emissions Standards of 7 May 1992*.

2.3 Environmental liabilities for past pollution

2.3.1 Types of environmental liabilities

Privatisation and environmental legislation

With regard to private transactions (in practice public/private for most cases), the majority of contracts are placing the environmental liability on the previous owner. If the investor is held responsible for previous pollution, he can sue the previous owner to recover costs. An operator can sue the previous owner for reimbursement of clean-up costs in a civil or commercial court.

The change in the status of the Civil Codes and reforms undertaken on the 1937 Code are expected to affect this issue whereby responsibility will rest with the new owner unless otherwise agreed. The new owner will assume all responsibility for the property.

Past environmental liabilities

The question of liability for on-site pollution arising from past operations will need clarification in Latvia's future laws, primarily those concerning privatisation. At present, the regulation on land reform states that the previous owner, under whose ownership the damage occurred, is responsible for its remediation. If the investor repairs the damage, he can make a financial claim from the previous owner.

Current environmental liabilities

Theoretically, an operator could be found liable for off-site landfills if the site had been classified as a source of an "increased level of danger" or if the landfills are currently in use and in violation of the law. For the most part, however, such cases have not been pursued.

Theoretically, the violator or owner of a source of an "increased level of danger", is liable for third party claims arising from past actions to all who are harmed.

Under *Law on Environmental Protection 1991* a citizen (or resident) can submit a complaint to the courts, if the EPC or Latvian Prosecutor have not already done so, and demand that any activity or inactivity which harms the environment or health is remedied.

2.3.2 Governmental indemnification of environmental liabilities

Privatisation sales

Government indemnification is not available for investors. The question will be addressed by new privatisation legislation and the revised Latvian Civil Code. In the LSSR, indemnification from liability was available for an organisation that announced its liquidation publicly and then settled its accounts with all creditors, claimants etc.

There are no requirements for operators to hold private insurance against environmental damage.

2.3.3 Investor clean-up of contaminated sites

Environmental clean-up standards

No clean-up standards have been drafted specifically for contaminated sites. It is expected that in practice recommendations would be made by the EPC or the Sanitary Service for restoration to pollution levels acceptable under USSR or Latvian standards.

Escrow accounts

There are no provisions for escrow accounts. This is likely to be a subject for future legislation but as yet the authorities have not announced any plans.

Environmental funds

A general provision for an environmental protection and natural resources fund is established by the *Law on Environmental Protection 1991*. The fund will be resourced by pollution and natural resource use. Details of the operation of the fund have not been developed. The Law states that the fund will be used for environmental improvement but it has not been determined whether this will relate to investor operations.

2.3.4 Case examples

At the time of writing no examples of legal cases relating to environmental liabilities of investors have been identified.

2.4 Environmental liabilities arising from facility operation

2.4.1 Civil liability

Civil actions for environmental liability are instituted in civil or commercial courts. The Latvian 1937 Civil Code has been renewed with regard to inheritance and property rights, but the section that contains obligation rights is scheduled to be re-instituted and reformed.

The methodology to calculate damages comes from USSR instructions with the exception of the Council of Ministers *Resolution No. 1, on Compensation for Damage Caused by Air Pollution from Stationary Sources Operating Without a Permit or While Exceeding State Emissions Standards of 7 May 1992.*

An example of the USSR methodology still in force is the 1983 "Methods for Calculating Damages Which Result from Water Quality Regulation Violations". However, it is expected that new instructions on water quality damages will replace this USSR methodology.

Council of Ministers resolutions are also used to calculate damages. For example, the *Resolution on the Calculation of Losses to Forestry*, enacted in place of the LSSR Resolution on the same subject.

Fault based liability

Current civil liability operates largely on the basis of fault-based liability. According to the *Law on Environmental Protection 1991* operators, as companies and individuals, in breach of environmental protection legislation and causing damage to the environment may be liable to repair the damage, or where this is not possible, to pay compensation.

Strict liability

The concept of strict liability is not widely used in current civil law. An exception is found in the doctrine of the "increased level of danger". Under the *Law on Environmental Protection 1991* environmental damage from activities which are "extremely hazardous", which is not defined, may result in strict liability. This doctrine is also set out in the Civil Code.

Statutes of limitation

Before the passage of the *Law on Environmental Protection 1991* the LSSR Civil Code established limitations of one year for cases between organisations, and three years for those involving a private citizen. Article 56 of the 1991 Law has removed the statute of limitations for environmental liability.

Remedies

Provisions relating to remedies will be undergoing fundamental changes with the re-institution of the obligation rights section of the 1937 Latvian Civil Code. The present situation under the Latvian–LSSR Civil Code is as follows.

The current *Civil Code* provides only for the reimbursement of direct costs:

- Arising from material losses, calculated as to the financial value of the property damaged or lost;
- For expenses related to the renewal of the object that was damaged;
- For lost earnings.

The remedy may be financial or by return of the object itself. Remedies such as revocation of a permit have been extremely difficult for an ordinary citizen to achieve and virtually never occurred. In the case of an on-going nuisance, the citizen has repeatedly to seek damages.

The *Law on Environmental Protection 1991* provides for claims by citizens for damage to health and property resulting from environmentally hazardous activities.

Case examples

In the case of the Getlini waste disposal site, the City of Riga was found liable for groundwater contamination caused by the dump even though the City's only connection with its operation was ownership. The City was fined 1 million Latvian rubles in the civil court, with the money designated to pay for the clean-up of the site.

The Baldone waste disposal site case was resolved with the City of Riga giving apartments in the city to the two families residing near the site plus a nominal sum of money for the loss of their gardens.

2.4.2 *Administrative liability*

Types of administrative liability

The Administrative Violation Code lists over 30 causes of administrative offence, as given in *Table 2.4.2(a)*.

Article 28 of the *Law on Parish Municipal Government* states that the Parish Council has the right to confirm regulations and to provide for administrative liability dealing with the following matters:

- Buildings in inhabited areas;
- Maintenance of parish land, forest, water, and specially protected nature and culture objects;
- Weed eradication, chemical and mineral fertilizer use and storage on parish territory;
- Commerce in public areas;
- Buildings and their territory; the maintenance of public buildings;
- Maintenance of sanitary cleanliness in inhabited areas;
- Organisation of public services and facilities in inhabited areas, green belt maintenance, general water use and landscape protection;
- Other matters not conflicting with Latvian laws.

Article 25 of the *Law on District Municipal Governments* states that the district council has the right to confirm regulations and to provide for administrative liability for their violation, if such liability is not stated in Latvian laws.

Remedies

Remedies available are permit revocation and fines, typically ranging between 2,000 and 5,000 Latvian rubles. State environmental inspectors can halt any activity presenting a threat to human health or the environment.

Table 2.4.2a   Administrative Violations

- Non-fulfilment of obligatory land protection undertakings (anti-erosion measures and water protection to be carried out by land-users).
- Non-return by the due date of land allotted for use for a stated period of time, or not fulfilling the duties imposed on the land owner by the conditions stated for the use of the land.
- Arbitrary non-conformance with state land plans, leading to negative ecological consequences.
- Soil protection regulation violations.
- Geological exploration regulation violations.
- Damage or destruction of an object of nature.
- Environmental pollution or littering.
- Emission of a polluting substance into the air or water in excess of environmental quality standards or in violation of said standards.
- Water resource protection regime violations in water basins.
- Non-fulfilment of regulations on activities involving hazardous materials or mixtures registered in ship documents.
- Violation of water protection or utilisation regulations.
- Destruction or damage of man-made objects influencing the environment.
- Violation of water collection regulations.
- Violation of natural resource or pollution emission recording regulations.
- Violation of forestry procedure regulations.
- Violation of forest renewal requirements.
- Violation of water treatment plant regulations.
- Violation of waste handling regulations.
- Violation of specially protected natural objects' protection regimes or interior procedural regulations.
- Violation of the Baltic Sea Latvian economic zone, territorial or interior sea water protection and regime regulations.
- Artificial island formation or setting up instruments or structures in violation of regulations.
- Failure to report the release of hazardous substances.
- Failure to observe land use procedure when a cultural monument is found on the land.
- Damage to sand dunes.
- Emission of hazardous substances or the failure to carry out a control action during inclement weather.
- Submission of fraudulent information or the failure to submit information regarding an ecological situation.
- Failure to observe project documentation coordination regulations.
- Knowingly submitting fraudulent information in project documentation regarding its adherence to environmental protection standards or regulations.
- Violation of industrial or communal waste dump site regulations.
- Production, or utilisation of chemical substances in violation of environmental quality standards.
- Violation of ecological certificate regulations.
- Arbitrary reactivation or continued activity of an enterprise or other object after it has been closed by environmental protection officials.
- Failure to carry out instructions of state environmental protection or state sanitary supervision institution officials.
- Damage of cultural monuments or the violation of their protection regulations.
- Violation of cultural monument restoration, conservation, repair, research, or archaeological dig regulations.
- Causing damage to the territory, protection zone, or visual appreciation zone of a cultural monument.

Case examples
In today's economic situation, almost no economic activity is being shut down. Fines levied for administrative violations are the most common sanctions.

2.4.3 Criminal liability

Types of criminal liability
The Latvian (formerly LSSR) *Criminal Code* is currently in force. Proposals are being collected for the revisions of the Code, including the section "Crimes Against Nature and the Irrational Use of Natural Resources".

Penalties
Breach of the *Criminal Code* can result in fines (typically in the region of 300 rubles) confiscation, and imprisonment.

Case examples
In 1992, 25 suspected criminal cases were investigated. Most of the cases involved ecosystem destruction or poaching. There have been no cases relating to environmental damage from commercial or industrial operations.

3. Environmental audits

3.1 Sources of legislation relating to environmental audits

There are no legal requirements to undertake pre-acquisition audits. Such requirements are subject to discussion amongst environmental officials but there are no definite plans for legislation on this issue.

Modification of an existing facility however, may require that an environmental impact assessment is undertaken which would include assessment of compliance with environmental standards and other regulatory requirements, ie an audit.

The investor should consider carrying out a pre-acquisition audit to determine that the facility is in compliance and whether any liability exists and discuss potential liability issues with the authorities.

3.2 National experience with environmental audits

It is expected that projects sponsored by financial institutions such as the IFC and EBRD would include requirements for some form of environmental audit to be undertaken. For example, audits of power and energy facilities have been undertaken by EBRD as part of the Emergency Energy Investment Project.

4. Land use planning

4.1 Summary

Authorities:	Municipality or Council of Ministers.
Types of Activity:	*Municipality* All developments. *Council of Ministers* Developments deemed by regional Environmental Protection Committee to be of national significance require an additional permit from the Council of Ministers.
Permits:	*Construction Permit* for construction or conversion from one land use to another.
Timing:	Three months.
Public Information:	Citizens and public organisations may request that state institutions publish information on the environmental effects of any proposed facilities or facilities prior to or during construction.
Public Consultation:	The developer has a duty to discuss the project and its environmental effects with the public.

4.2 Sources of relevant land use legislation

The control of land use planning in Latvia is undergoing significant change with the shift towards privatisation. The USSR regulations are still in force but two new Latvian Laws have been introduced:

- *Law on Parish Municipal Government of 5 February 1992;*
- *Law on District Municipal Governments of 5 February 1992.*

The most significant former USSR land use regulations, concentrating largely on approval of proposed construction, are:

- OND 1-84, with supplements No. 3 and No. 6;
- SNIP Construction Regulations and Requirements;
- Sanitary Regulations, which regulate safety requirements.

The Council of Ministers *Regulation No. 73 of March 22, 1990, on the Procedure for the Allotment of Water Objects for Separate Utilisation, and Withdrawal from Separate Utilisation*; governs the use of lakes, rivers, etc. There is also a register of protected nature territories which cannot be privatised.

4.3 Scope of activities subject to land use regulation

Construction and conversion from one land use to another are the primary cases requiring a construction permit. An investor is required to obtain a government permit if the investment is in a state enterprise or if he obtains control over an enterprise with assets in excess of US$ 1 million. The exception is agriculture where permitting is a question of land reform, which involves a separate set of issues.

Under the USSR system, industrial zones were planned to meet the needs of industry in urban areas. These zones were established by the appropriate project institute in co-ordination with the state Architecture, Construction, and Nature Committees, and the appropriate local authority. The zone was confirmed by the State Plan which was developed by the Council of Ministers. Generally, the Chairman of the State Plan was the Vice-Chairman of the Council of Ministers.

In future, local planning is to be carried out by local government (district and municipal) in consultation with the appropriate state authorities such as the regional EPC. The *Law on Parish Municipal Government of 1992* and the *Law on District Municipal Government 1992* regulate the rights and responsibilities of municipal and district governments.

Foreign investors cannot purchase land, but leases for up to 99 years are available. To start a new industrial facility, the following permits are necessary:

- For a facility of local significance, permission from the local municipality;
- For a facility of national significance, an additional permit from the Council of Ministers. The regional Environmental Protection Committee (EPC) determines whether a planned facility is of national significance.

The project must be co-ordinated with the following organisations:

- The Ministry of Construction and Architecture;
- The Fire Department;
- If necessary, with the Sanitary Inspectorate;
- The appropriate institutions if there are specific construction requirements.

4.4 Permitting process

4.4.1 Authorities
The municipal authority is responsible for determining applications for construction permits except where the facility is deemed by the EPC to be of national significance, in which case the Council of Ministers is responsible for the decision.

4.4.2 Application requirements
To obtain a permit for construction, the investor must prepare a Technical/Economic Calculation (TEC) on a standard form, which is reviewed by the municipality, or for proposals of national significance by the State Construction Committee. The TEC is the fundamental document for land use regulation.

The following example is from a proposal to build a compost factory in Riga:

- The enterprise "Resurss" submitted their technical council's protocol on the necessity of building such a factory;
- The City of Riga Executive Committee issued an instruction supporting the project;
- The task of completing a TEC was given to a project institute;
- The instructions on the procedure for the completion of the TEC were confirmed by the Ministry of Construction and Architecture.

The *Law on State Environmental Impact Assessment 1990* also requires the completion of an Environmental Impact Assessment (EIA) for certain major industrial investments or developments. This is submitted to the regional EPC, or where the project is nationally significant or especially complex, to the national EPC. EIA requirements are set out in *Section 5*.

4.4.3 Fees
There are no fees for construction permits.

4.4.4 Timing
A decision on the application must be given within three months although this period may be extended, for example, if further information is required by the authority.

4.4.5 Permit conditions
Permit conditions are derived from the following regulations of the former USSR:

- OND 1-84, with supplements No. 3 and No. 6;
- SNIP Construction Regulations and Requirements;
- Sanitary Regulations, which regulate safety requirements.

4.5 Public participation

4.5.1 Public access to information
Under the *Law on Environmental Protection 1991* citizens and public organisations may demand information on the environmental effects of any proposed facilities or facilities under construction.

4.5.2 Provision of information
There are no specific requirements to provide information on construction permits.

4.5.3 Public consultation
Under the USSR system, there was no public participation and there are no requirements in land use legislation relating to public participation. Under the *Law on State Environmental Impact Assessment 1990*, however, the developer is required to discuss the project and its environmental effects with social organisations and residents, and this may cover information included in the construction permit application.

The EPC is taking steps to include the public in significant land use questions. An example is the current search for a location for a hazardous waste treatment and disposal site in Latvia. There have been meetings with representatives of municipal government and the community in Jelgava, Ogre and Olaine.

4.6 Enforcement

Cases of unauthorised construction are reviewed by the EPC. In the past it has been difficult for authorities to impose significant administrative sanctions, although the State and regional EPCs have the power under the *Regulation on the Environmental Protection Inspectorate 1990* to halt or shut down environmentally dangerous activities.

For violations by industry, a typical fine would be 50–100 rubles imposed on the chief engineer.

5. Environmental impact assessment (EIAs)

5.1 Summary

Authorities:	Regional Environmental Protection Committee (EPC) or National EPC and Supreme Council Standing Commission on the Environment (SCSCE).
Types of Activity:	*Regional EPC* All industrial projects, other "economic facilities" which the EPC determines and those developments for which the SCSCE orders a second EIA. *National EPC* Developments which are referred to it by the regional EPC.
Permit:	Approval of EIA
Timing:	Three months
Public Information:	Citizens and public organisations may request that state institutions provide information on the environmental effects of any proposed facilities or facilities prior to or during construction and make the EIA available.
Public Consultation:	There is no formal process of public participation. The developer has a duty to discuss the project and its environmental effects with the public.

5.2 Sources of legislation relating to the environmental impact of industrial and commercial developments

The following legislation concerns Environmental Impact Assessments (EIAs):

- *Law on the Environmental Protection Committee of the Republic of Latvia 1990*;
- *Law on State Environmental Impact Assessments 1990*;
- *Law on Environmental Protection 1991*;
- *Regulation on the Environmental Protection Inspectorate Regulation 1990*;
- Confirmed Instruction. *"The Rational Use of Natural Resources and Protection Projects In Melioration."* Prepared by the EIA Department and Latvia's Melioration Planning Institute;
- *Council of Ministers Resolution on the State Specially Protected Cultural/Historical Territory "Livod Rānda" Regulation Confirmation 1991*;
- *Council of Ministers Resolution on the Baltic Sea and Gulf of Riga Coastal Protection Regime 1990*;
- *Law on Natural Resource and Pollution Charges 1990*;
- *Environmental Protection Committee Resolution on Water Use Permits 1991*.

5.3 Scope of activities subject to EIA process

Under the *Law on State Environmental Impact Assessment 1990* investors must carry out an EIA for all new industrial projects and modifications to existing facilities. The national and regional EPCs have the right to determine when an EIA is required for other projects, although local government may request the EPC to initiate an EIA. The legislation does not state that the EPC must comply with such a request. The Supreme Council Standing Commission on the Environment has the power to order the EPC to undertake a second EIA.

The EIA process in Latvia is principally concerned with compliance with existing legislative norms, although the EIA law is not specific on this. The law sets the requirement to "evaluate the effects of economic facilities" impact on the surrounding environment.

Land use and planning concerns fall primarily to local government. There is no legal requirement for the regional EPC and the local government to co-operate in co-ordinating land use/zoning and environmental requirements.

5.4 EIA process

5.4.1 Authority

The regional Environmental Protection Committee (EPC) is the authority responsible for approving environmental impact assessments. At the discretion of the regional Committee, the EIA of a major project may be referred to the national EPC.

313

5.4.2 Documentation

Project developers are responsible for the organisation, financing and carrying out of scientific research and planning needed for evaluating a proposed activity's environmental impact.

The scope of any assessment work must first be approved by the regional EPC, for example surveying activities and geological research may not be allowed in protected areas. After this, the investor submits documentation characterising the activity's level of potential environmental impact. There is no requirement for the investor's evaluation to be carried out by independent experts.

The scope of an EIA must include the following:

• An evaluation of the planned activity's impact on:
   (i)   the surrounding environment;
   (ii) public health;
   (iii) public living conditions;
• A Declaration of Environmental Effects, which describes the measures that the developer will take to guarantee environmental quality during the period of activity.

According to a policy statement, a foreign investor must provide a record of acceptable environmental safety from the environmental protection agency of its native country. The Standing Committee would verify the information with the foreign environmental protection institutions. There is no agreed format for this assessment although an evaluation of the company's performance by the environmental protection agency of its country of origin would be assessed by the Standing Committee. As yet there is no legal requirement for this assessment.

Several additional permits and reports are required:

• A Technical/Economic Calculation (TEC) form must be submitted to the EPC. The form must be confirmed by the investing company's director or assistant who deals with construction issues. The form deals with details of construction, and there is a section on environmental protection measures planned by the investor. State affiliated institutions can assist with the compilation of the form;
• A report on the characteristics of the land on which the construction is to take place; for example, whether it contains roads, trees, buildings etc;
• A fire safety approval from the local fire department;
• Contracts with the relevant public utilities.

5.4.3 Experts and consultants

It is not necessary for experts and consultants engaged in preparing material for an EIA to be approved by the authorities.

5.4.4 Timing

A decision on the application must be given within three months although this period may be extended, eg if further information is required.

5.4.5 Standard of review

EIA documentation submitted to the regional EPC may be reviewed by the EPC itself or, for complex proposals, by an expert commission which is selected by the EPC.

Members of the commission may include Latvian and foreign scientists, specialists, and representatives of government agencies, local governments, social organisations, and society at large. The EPC is responsible for the membership of the expert commission and the qualifications of its members, which must be appropriate to the level of complexity of the assessment.

After reviewing the materials, the EPC prepares a State EIA, which is approved by the EPC's Chair, or the First Vice-Chair if the former is absent. The conclusion of this review as to whether or not to approve the EIA, hinges on whether the proposed activity will comply with Latvian environmental standards and legislation. If there is non compliance on some points, approval may be given on the condition that the deficiencies will be corrected within a specified time period.

The State EIA report must include:

- Individual experts' evaluations of specific questions;
- The EPC's report on the experts' conclusions;
- Recommendations to the developer and to interested organisations regarding the requirement for economic activity.

EPC State EIAs are not subject to appeal although a second assessment can be demanded by the Supreme Council.

5.5 Public participation

5.5.1 Public access to information

The *Law on State Environmental Impact Assessment* 1990 aims to ensure public access to information about the EIA process. It states that one of the basic principles of the State EIA is openness and that the EPC is responsible for ensuring the openness of the assessment.

5.5.2 Provision of information

Under the *Law on Environmental Protection 1991* citizens and public organisations may demand that state institutions provide information on the environmental effects of any proposed facilities or facilities under construction, and publish Environmental Impact Assessment Statements and inquiry results.

5.5.3 Public consultation

The EPC has the right to publish materials in the media regarding the EIAs undertaken by the state. However, as yet there are no provisions on the legislation relating to the manner in which information should be provided. There is no formal method for public participation in the EIA process.

It is the responsibility of the investor under the *Law on State Environmental Impact Assessment 1990* to discuss the project concept and its potential environmental effects with the representatives of social organisations and local residents. Procedures for such discussions have not yet been determined.

315

5.6 Enforcement

Under the *Administrative Code*, it is a violation to knowingly submit fraudulent information in project documentation regarding adherence to environmental protection standards or legislations.

5.7 National experience with EIAs

EIAs are required for all new or modified industrial facilities. In practice, depending on the nature of proposed developments, there are variations in the complexity of the EIA. A simple modification of an existing facility may be carried out with co-ordination of the planned activity with the local EPC, while a complex industrial project may require the formation of a special expert commission determined by the national EPC to analyse the EIA.

The simple EIA carried out in co-ordination with the regional EPC usually takes about three weeks. A complex industrial project which requires the formation of an expert commission may take up to three months, although this period can be extended, notably when a regional EPC requests more information or asks for help from the national EPC.

6. Integrated permitting requirements applicable to the operation of industrial and commercial facilities

6.1 Summary

> The Permitting procedure is in part an integrated system. Once a construction permit has been issued, permitting focuses on the EIA procedure. Applications for all other permits are submitted with the EIA documentation, and their issue is based largely on information in the EIA. However, individual permits (eg for emissions to air, water use etc) may have a different period of validity and their renewal will therefore be made individually. In this respect the permitting system is not integrated.

6.2 Extent of integrated permitting

The privatisation programme in Latvia is at a very early stage and as yet there is no practical experience of permitting of major facilities. The permitting process is therefore somewhat theoretical at this stage.

Application for a construction permit is made to the municipality and it is expected that consideration of the application will be made in co-operation with the regional EPC. An application for all other environmental permits is then made to the regional EPC.

The main focus for the permitting process is the Environmental Impact Assessment (EIA). Data and information prepared by the investor for the EIA application provide the basis for other necessary permits eg emissions to air, water use and discharge.

Following application for the construction permit, an application for all other permits, is submitted with the EIA documents; and separate applications are not needed.

Permits for air, water etc may be issued for different time periods in which case applications for renewals would be made individually. In this respect the permitting system is not integrated.

7. Air emission requirements applicable to the operation of industrial and commercial facilities

7.1 Summary

Authorities:	Regional Environmental Protection Committee (EPC).
Types of Activity:	Facilities emitting 200 t/yror more of prescribed substances.
Permits:	A temporary permit is issued initially for all facilities. Facilities located within areas not conforming with air quality standards may only be issued with a temporary permit. A regular permit is issued once a facility's compliance with the temporary permit has been confirmed and a maximum permissible emission (MPE) has been prescribed.
Timing:	Three months.
Public Information:	Citizens and public organisations may request that state institutions provide information on the environmental effects of any proposed facilities or facilities under construction and make the EIA available.
Public Consultation:	There is no formal process of public participation. Where an EIA is required, the developer has a duty to discuss the project and its environmental effects with the public.

7.2 Sources of legislation relating to air emissions

• *Council of Ministers Resolution No. 337 of August 14 1992.*

7.3 Air protection zones

Two "non-conforming" zones, Riga and Ventspils, have been established in which levels of environmental pollutants exceed prescribed standards. In these zones, facilities can only obtain temporary, annual permits. It is anticipated that emission limits will be stricter in each annual permit thereby reducing overall emissions until the zones conform with environmental quality standards.

7.4 Scope of activities subject to air emission regulations

Facilities require a permit for emissions to air if the total cumulative emission of substances listed in the USSR air quality standards, exceeds 200t/yr. For certain prescribed substances considered to be particularly toxic, the emission standard is more stringent. (Further details are given in *Annex D*.)

7.5 Standards

7.5.1 Ambient quality standards

The *Council of Ministers Resolution No. 337 of August 14 1992*, states that all former USSR standards and technical standards have been adopted and remain in force until their repeal or replacement, providing they do not conflict with Latvian Law or Council of Ministers Resolutions. There are 99 USSR–LSSR documents regulating air quality currently in force in Latvia.

USSR ambient air quality standards, specifying 30 minute and 24 hour averages for Maximum Air Concentrations (MACs) apply to over 800 pollutants. MACs are based on concentrations of chemical substances or chemical combinations which do not affect respiratory reflex actions in rural locations within 20–30 minutes. Examples of environmental quality standards are given in *Annex D*.

The following legislation is currently being drafted.

- Resolution "On Normative Maximum Allowable Pollution Substance Emission into the Atmosphere and Harmful, Physical Impact on That".
- Resolution "On Temporary Permit Issue for the Discharge of Pollutants in the Air, On Permit Co-ordination Terms, and Sanctions for Enterprise Activity Without a Permit and Exceeding Stated Standards".
- "Recommendations for Enterprise Maximum Permissible Emissions (MPE) Normative Project Preparation and Contents."

7.5.2 Emission limit values

Emission limits are derived from ambient quality standards on a case by case basis and are included as conditions of the permit. Specific air emission limits (based on the former USSR regulations) are set for factories using simplified dispersion algorithms employed in the former USSR.

The procedural document, "On the Procedure for Determining Environmental Pollution Standards and the Issue of Permits for the Utilisation of Natural Resources", was accepted by the EPC in January 1991. This document defines two classes of emissions standards:

- Maximum Permissible Emissions (MPE), defined as the maximum permissible amount of pollutants that can be discharged into the atmosphere by a stationary source

per time unit, which does not exceed the established near-the-surface maximum allowable concentrations (MAC);
- Temporary Permissible Emissions (TPE).

In determining air quality standards, the Environmental Protection Committee (EPC) has taken into account the recommendations outlined in the 1979 Geneva Convention on Long-Range Transboundary Air Pollution. Because economic realities make compliance unrealistic in the short run, the EPC has created the TPE, temporary permissible emission levels, based on the quantities currently discharged and the present level of technology.

The EPC has begun a comprehensive program for the attainment of MPE levels, based on annual reviews of activities and emissions until MPE has been attained.

The following steps have been taken in Latvia to protect air quality:

- A commitment has been made to implement the requirements of the Geneva Convention on long-range transboundary air pollution by utilising less sulphurous (up to 2.5%) petroleum, and where possible, natural gas (lack of hard currency may hinder this commitment);
- Implementation of already established requirements for the introduction of treatment facilities in thermoelectric power plants;
- Phasing out the use of ozone depleting substances by 1995, replacing them with safer alternatives (eg CFC 22).

All major thermal power plants are being required to install filters for sulphur dioxides and nitrogen oxides. However, the capital required may not be available.

7.5.3 Technology based standards

Technology based standards are not prescribed but consideration of a permit application may take account of pollution control equipment and permitting may require fitting of specified equipment on a case-by-case basis.

7.6 Permitting process

7.6.1 Authorities

Permit applications are made to the regional EPC.

7.6.2 Application requirements

There are two types of permits available:

- Temporary permits;
- Regular permits.

For any modifications to a facility or changes in emissions, an entirely new permit is required.

The application procedure for all point sources begins with the registration of the point source of emissions. The next step differs, depending on whether the facility is proposed or existing.

319

For a proposed source, the emission volume "inventory" is calculated using theoretical methods. For a source already in operation, the "inventory" is calculated based on monitoring data.

If the operation in question is a small one, then the temporary permit can be issued quickly. There is a prescribed form for the permit that sets out the allowable emissions. For larger operations the data on the hazardous substance pollution level (dispersal) are computerised. The results are then analysed.

If the facility does not conform to the standards or if it is located in an area that does not conform to quality standards (eg Riga, Ventspils), then a temporary permit will be issued for a year. The permit for the following years will reduce emissions, thereby reducing pollution progressively until it reaches the standard. Measures to reduce the pollution level to the permitted level are determined and included in the permit documents.

If the facility is projected to conform then a MPE norm can be worked out and a regular permit issued. The standards and all the details of the case are contained in the facility permit record (ie a book of emissions data).

7.6.3 Fees

There is no charge for the application.

7.6.4 Timing

A decision must be made within three months of the application.

7.6.5 Permit conditions

The specific emission limits for facilities are set using simplified dispersion algorithms employed in the former USSR based on ambient quality standards. General emissions monitoring and reporting requirements are set in air quality legislation. Every enterprise has the duty to measure and record emissions, and to report them to air quality authorities. Emissions charges are based on this reported information.

7.7 Charges for emissions

Charges for air emissions are found in the *Law on Natural Resource Taxes 1990*. The Law establishes charges for the emission of pollutants into the air within normative limits and sanctions for emissions in excess of normative limits. Charges are levied per tonne of discharges based on five hazard classifications (non-toxic substances, medium hazard substances, hazardous substances, very hazardous substances, and extremely hazardous substances) and range from 20–65,000 rbl/t.

If emissions exceed the limit specified in the permit, the charges are multiplied by a factor of three. The penalty is levied from the enterprise's disposable income after all other taxes have been paid.

7.8 Public participation

7.8.1 Public access to information

Under the *Law on Environmental Protection 1991* citizens and public organisations may request that state institutions provide information on the environmental effects of any proposed facilities or facilities under construction, and in relation to new or modified facilities, EIA Statements and inquiry results.

7.8.2 Provision of information

Environmental protection institutions have a duty to regularly inform inhabitants about the condition of the environment.

7.8.3 Public consultation

Where an EIA is to be carried out, ie new or modified facilities, the *Law on State Environmental Impact Assessment 1990* requires the investor to discuss the project concept and its potential environmental effects with the representatives of social organisations and citizens. A detailed procedure for public consultation has not yet been introduced.

7.9 Enforcement

7.9.1 Compliance checking and monitoring

The regional EPCs are responsible for enforcement which is chiefly governed by the *Regulation on the Environmental Protection Inspectorate 1990*. Inspectors can check compliance using monitoring data produced by the operator and can carry out their own monitoring of releases to the environment.

7.9.2 Sanctions

Operating without a permit or breach of permit conditions can result in administrative fines, facility shut down, permit withdrawal or criminal sanctions.

The procedural document on methodology for calculating damages "On Compensation for Damages Caused by Air Pollution from Stationary Sources Operating Without a Permit or While Exceeding State Standards", was accepted on 7 May, 1992.

8. Water requirements applicable to the operation of industrial and commercial facilities

8.1 Summary

Authorities:	Issued by the regional Environmental Protection Committee and approved by the Municipality.
Types of Activity:	All commercial and industrial activities.

Permits:	One permit covers both water use and wastewater discharge.
Timing:	One to three months.
Public Information:	Citizens and public organisations may request that state institutions publish information on the environmental effects of any proposed facilities or facilities under construction and make the EIA available. The Hydrometeorlogical Department issues bulletins dealing with water quality monitoring. The Hydrology Department issues a bulletin on groundwater quality.
Public Consultation:	There is no formal process of public participation. Where an EIA is required, the developer has a duty to discuss the project and its environmental effects with the public.

8.2 Sources of legislation relating to water requirements

Latvia has introduced the following legislation regarding water quality:

- *Environmental Protection Committee Resolution No. 3 of 29 November 1991, Water Pollution Hazard Categories and their Maximum Allowable Concentrations in Above-Ground Water Objects and Wastewater Discharge Sites;*
- *Resolution on Water Use Permits of 29 November 1991.*

Water use and discharge reporting instructions are given in State Statistical Report No. 2 — Water, Reporting Instructions.
The following texts are currently being drafted.

- Drinking Water Standards;
- Methods for the Calculation of Damages.

8.3 Water management

8.3.1 Water quality categories

Water quality standards are defined in terms of the maximum permissible concentrations (MPCs) for household/service sector water use, for recreational water use, and for fishery use. The following sources of water are differentiated in *EPC Resolution No. 3 1991*:

- Sub-surface water (groundwater, artesian water);
- Surface water (interior — lakes and rivers, sea);
- Reservoirs;
- Watermill lakes;
- Small hydro-electric reservoirs;
- Drinking water.

8.3.2 *Water management bodies*
Water management falls within the remit of the regional Environmental Protection Committees.

8.4 *Activities subject to water use and discharge regulation*

8.4.1 *Water use*
All commercial and industrial water users are required to obtain a permit for water use. The water use permit also covers discharges to water and sewer.

8.4.2 *Water discharge*
All commercial and industrial operations discharging wastewater from their operations are required to obtain a permit. Discharges and water use are covered by the same permit.

8.5 *Standards*

8.5.1 *Ambient quality standards*
All former USSR standards have been adopted and remain in force, to the extent that they do not conflict with Latvian Law, until their repeal or replacement. Maximum Permissible Concentration standards for water have been translated from Russian to Latvian, English and German.

The pollutants regulated are listed in *Table 8.5.1(a)*.

Table 8.5.1(a)   Regulated Water Pollutants

- suspended solids;
- chloride;
- sulphate;
- BOD21;
- COD;
- nitrate, nitrite;
- ammonia, phosphate;
- detergents (eugenic, non-eugenic);
- iron;
- Caprolactam;
- fat substances;
- tannin;
- lignosulphanic acids;
- furfurol (C_4H_3O);
- oil products.
- phenol;
- fluoride;
- methanol;
- formaldehyde;
- sulphite, thiosulphate, sulphide;
- active chloride;
- cyanide;
- acrylonitrile;
- chromium III and VI;
- nickel;
- cadmium;
- copper;
- zinc;
- manganese;
- lead.

8.5.2 Discharge limit values

Discharge limit values are developed case-by-case based on ambient quality standards and are written into permits.

8.5.3 Technology based standards

The legislation does not prescribe technology standards for wastewater treatment but details of such treatment must be given in the permit application and may be taken into account by the EPC in granting the permit. Issue of the permit may depend on the fitting of equipment prescribed on a case-by-case basis by the EPC.

8.6 Water use permitting process

8.6.1 Authorities

Permits are issued by regional Environmental Protection Committees (EPCs) and must be approved by the municipal government.

8.6.2 Application requirements

The *EPC Resolution On Water Use Permits 1991* regulates the use of interior and sea waters, and sets out the procedure for obtaining water use permits. The application must provide details of water abstraction use including source and volume.

8.6.3 Fees

There are no fees for permitting.

8.6.4 Timing

Permits must be issued within one month of the application assuming the application documentation is adequate. In the case of a new or modified facility, the application would be submitted as part of the EIA process which takes three months.

8.6.5 Permit conditions

The operator must observe limits for the use of water set out in the EIA. The volume of water used must be monitored and recorded.

8.7 Water discharge permitting process

8.7.1 Authorities

The regional EPC is the permitting authority.

8.7.2 Application requirements

The water use permit covers use and discharge to water and sewer. The investor must include in the permit application details of sources of wastewater and sewage, the drainage system, volume, composition, pollutant concentration and volume of the discharge.

8.7.3 Fees

There are no fees for permitting.

8.7.4 Timing

It takes one month, from the submission of the application, to obtain a permit assuming the application documentation is adequate. In the case of a new or modified facility, the application would be submitted as part of the EIA process which takes three months.

8.7.5 Permit conditions

Permit conditions are based on environmental quality standards. The permit sets out the permissable pollution load (per second and annually).

The limits on pollution concentration, content and volume are determined according to ambient quality standards and the capabilities of existing water treatment technology, using both a system of calculations based on dispersion algorithms, and the EIA conclusions. Permits can be valid for a period of one to five years.

Wastewater discharges must be monitored and recorded by the operator including details of quantity and quality.

8.8 Water charges

8.8.1 Water use

Charges are set out in the *Law on Natural Resource Taxes 1990* which establishes a charge system for the use of natural resources (with charges ranging from 0.04–2.0 rbl/m^3) within standard limits, and sanctions for natural resource use which exceed the standard limits.

8.8.2 Water discharge

Charges for wastewater discharges are set out in the *Law on Natural Resource Taxes 1990*. With regard to wastewater treatment, the discharger pays fees to either the state or the owner of a private facility. The polluter, owning or operating a treatment facility, must pay the discharge fee to the state. Charges range from 20 rbl/t for non-toxic discharges to 300,000 rbl/t for "very hazardous substances".

If emissions exceed the limit specified in the permit, the charges are multiplied by a factor of three. The penalty is levied from the enterprise's disposable income after all other taxes have been paid.

8.9 Public participation

8.9.1 Public access to information

Under the *Law on Environmental Protection 1991* citizens and public organisations may request that state institutions provide information on the environmental effects of any proposed facilities or facilities under construction, and EIA statements and inquiry results.

8.9.2 Provision of information

Environmental protection institutions have a duty to regularly inform inhabitants about the condition of the environment.

The EPC issues annual reports on the state of the environment. The Hydrometeorlogical Department issues bulletins that deal with the results of monitoring. The Hydrology Department also issues a bulletin about groundwater quality which, until recently, was confidential due to fears of deliberate contamination of drinking water reservoirs.

8.9.3 Public consultation

Where an EIA is to be carried out, ie new or modified facilities, the *Law on State Environmental Impact Assessment 1990* requires the investor to discuss the project concept and its potential environmental effects with the representatives of social organisations and citizens. A detailed procedure for public consultation has not yet been introduced.

8.10 Enforcement

8.10.1 Compliance checking and monitoring

Enforcement is carried out by the regional EPCs. The company measures and records its own discharges but it is subject to two unannounced inspections by the regional and national EPC each year to verify the accuracy of the submitted figures. Records kept by the operator must be signed off by an EPC inspector.

8.10.2 Sanctions

The enterprise pays water use and discharge taxes based on its own calculations but the EPC verifies the figures submitted. The EPC has three years to demand payment of funds which have been illegally withheld. Sanctions which may be applied are administrative fines, permit withdrawal, facility shut-down or criminal sanctions.

9. Noise requirements applicable to the operation of industrial and commercial facilities

9.1 Summary

Authorities:	Regional Environmental Protection Committee.
Types of Activity:	All proposed commercial and industrial operations or modifications to existing facilities.
Permits:	Noise is included in the EIA approval. A separate permit is not needed.
Timing:	Three months.
Public Information:	Citizens and public organisations may request that state institutions publish information on the environmental effects of any proposed facilities or facilities under construction and make the EIA available.
Public Consultation:	There is no formal process of public participation. The developer has a duty to discuss the project and its environmental effects with the public.

9.2 Sources of legislation relating to environmental noise

- *Sanitary Norms for Inhabited Areas, No. 3077-84 1984;*
- *Aviation: Allowable Noise Levels for Inhabited Areas, GOST 22283-88 1988.*

9.3 Noise zones

All air fields are obliged to submit documents showing noise zones which have been co-ordinated with local government health protection services. The following must be set out:

- Equivalent noise level;
- Maximum noise level;
- Night noise level.

Noise zones do not exist for factories or streets.

9.4 Activities subject to noise regulation

All proposed commercial and industrial operations or modifications to existing facilities may be subject to noise control.

9.5 Standards

All former USSR standards have been adopted and remain in force until their repeal or replacement. Standards are set out in the legislation listed above.

There are approximately 20 standard measuring methods in force from former USSR legislation including the following:

- GOST 23337-78 Noise: methods of noise measurement in residential areas and in the rooms of residential, public, and community buildings.
- GOST 15116-79 Noise: methods of sound insulation measurement of inner enclosures of buildings.
- GOST 20444-85 Noise: traffic flows; methods of noise characterisation and measurement.

9.6 Permitting process

9.6.1 Authorities

The regional Environmental Protection Committees are responsible for noise regulation.

9.6.2 Application requirements

A permit relating specifically to noise is not required for new or modified facilities. Noise is taken into account in the EIA process as described in *Section 5*.

9.6.3 Timing

As part of the EIA process, a decision must be given within three months of application.

9.7 Public participation

9.7.1 Public access to information

Under the *Law on Environmental Protection 1991* citizens and public organisations may request that state institutions provide information on the environmental effects of any proposed facilities or facilities under construction, and EIA statements and inquiry results.

9.7.2 Provision of information

Environmental protection institutions have a duty to regularly inform inhabitants about the condition of the environment. Information on applications for building permission is not published.

9.7.3 Public consultation

Where an EIA is to be carried out, ie proposals for new or modified facilities, the *Law on State Environmental Impact Assessment 1990* requires the investor to discuss the

328

project concept and its potential environmental effects with the representatives of social organisations and citizens. A detailed procedure for public consultation has not yet been introduced.

9.8 Enforcement

9.8.1 Compliance checking and monitoring
Compliance checking and enforcement is carried out by the regional Environmental Protection Inspectorate.

9.8.2 Sanctions
Violators can be fined between 2,000 and 5,000 Latvian rubles according to the *Administrative Code*.

10. Hazardous and non-hazardous waste management

10.1 Summary

Note:	The following summary outlines proposed requirements.
Authorities:	Regional Environmental Protection Committee (EPC) and Municipality.
Types of Activity:	Any activity involving hazardous waste including, production, storage, transport, treatment and disposal.
Permits:	Permit for production, treatment, transport and disposal.
Timing:	15 days.
Public Information:	The public may request information from EPC.
Public Consultation:	There is no formal system for public participation.

10.2 Sources of legislation relating to waste management

The draft Law on Hazardous Wastes is to be submitted to the Supreme Council for approval in 1993. There is no existing legislation on hazardous or non-hazardous waste management.

10.3 Categories of waste

The draft law categorises waste as hazardous or non-hazardous. Types of hazardous waste are classified, eg oil products, heavy metals etc.

10.4 Waste storage and treatment

10.4.1 Generator permits and other requirements

According to the draft Law, a declaration to the municipal government and regional EPC is required from every person/company intending to conduct an activity involving hazardous wastes.

10.4.2 Operator permits and other requirements

According to the draft Law, a declaration to the municipal government and regional EPC is required from every person/company intending to conduct an activity involving hazardous wastes.

10.5 Waste disposal

10.5.1 Generator permits and other requirements

Activities involving hazardous wastes including production, transport, treatment and disposal will be allowed only after a declaration has been submitted to the municipal authority (acting in co-operation with the EPC) and the appropriate permit has been issued. Hazardous wastes are defined in the draft Law on Hazardous Waste as those substances which may be:

- Explosive;
- Flammable;
- Toxic;
- Corrosive;
- Chemically reactive;
- Carcinogenic and the cause of mutations.

According to the draft Law, the EPC and municipal authority will be responsible for co-ordinating and issuing permits for activities involving hazardous wastes. It will also be able to issue permits for activities involving disposal of new chemicals (those not included in the 100 substances listed in the Latvian register of allowed chemical materials) or their wastes.

The issue of permits is to be carried out as a co-ordinated effort between the regional EPCs and municipal government.

Municipal government, in co-ordination with the regional EPC, will be given authority to determine the siting of regionally significant hazardous waste treatment and disposal facilities. A decision on the granting of a licence must be made within 15 days of receipt of the application. Permits for the transportation of hazardous wastes are issued by the appropriate regional EPC within the same 15 day limit.

The Council of Ministers, in co-operation with the EPC, will determine the procedure for nationally significant hazardous waste collection facilities, treatment and utilisation facilities, disposal site selection, and also for hazardous waste treatment, utilisation, transport, and disposal. The Council of Ministers will designate nationally significant hazardous waste facilities, and disposal site requirements. It also determines the charges for activities involving hazardous wastes, with a compensation system set up according to the level of ecological risk factor.

10.5.2 Operator permits and other requirements

According to the draft Law, a declaration to the municipal government and regional EPC is required from every person/company intending to conduct an activity involving hazardous wastes.

10.6 Transport of waste

The draft Law provides for a system of notification documents for waste transport.

10.6.1 Labelling and containers

The draft law includes provisions for the labelling of hazardous waste which is to be transported.

10.6.2 Transboundary movement

Latvia has ratified the Basle convention and it is expected that legislation on transboundary movement of hazardous waste will be introduced.

10.7 Waste charges

Charges for activities involving hazardous wastes are levied by volume for waste disposal in five hazard categories (non-toxic substances, medium-hazard substances, hazardous substances, very hazardous substances, and extremely toxic substances) according to the *Law on Natural Resource Taxes 1990*.

10.8 Recycling requirements

Recycling is not required under current legislation though recycling is stated as a goal in the Latvian's 1990 EPC Report. Examples in practice include a programme to recycle mercury light bulbs (50,000 in 1991 in Liepaja).

10.9 Public participation

The draft Law on Hazardous Waste does not provide for public participation and information.

10.9.1 Public access to information

Under the *Law on Environmental Protection 1991* citizens and public organisations may request that state institutions publish information on the environmental effects of any proposed facilities or facilities under construction, and EIA statements and inquiry results.

10.9.2 Provision of information

Environmental protection institutions have a duty to regularly inform inhabitants about the condition of the environment.

10.9.3 Public consultation

Where an EIA is to be carried out, ie new or modified facilities, the *Law on State Environmental Impact Assessment 1990* requires the investor to discuss the project concept and its potential environmental effects with the representatives of social organisations and citizens. A detailed procedure for public consultation has not yet been introduced.

10.10 Enforcement

10.10.1 Compliance checking

According to the draft Law on Hazardous Wastes, municipal government institutions will be empowered to enforce compliance for the timely submission of declarations, permitting requirements, the payment of obligatory environmental charges, and compliance with waste collection and transport plans.

The EPC is to enforce compliance at both regional and national level for activities involving any type of hazardous wastes.

10.10.2 Sanctions

Breach of waste requirements can result in administrative sanctions leading to fines and facility shut down.

11. Chemicals storage, handling and emergency response

11.1 Summary

There is no specific legislation on chemicals storage, handling or emergency response. These issues may be covered in part, by the EIA system for new or modified facilities.

11.2 Legislation relating to chemicals storage, handling and emergency response

All former USSR standards have been adopted and remain in force until their repeal or replacement. A proposal for a Latvian law "On Chemical Substances", is in the drafting process.

Storage and secondary containment of chemical substances currently is primarily controlled by former USSR technical safety measures, not environmental regulations. Environmental regulations only cover the emission of pollutants.

11.2.1 Storage

There is no specific environmental protection legislation concerning chemicals storage. Current control of chemicals storage is based on legislation of the former USSR which focuses largely on occupational health and safety and is considered to be inappropriate by the Latvian authorities. It is expected that new legislation will be introduced in the future.

11.2.2 Handling

There is no specific environmental protection legislation in relation to chemicals handling.

11.2.3 Emergency response

According to the *Administrative Code*, failure to report the release of hazardous substances is an offence.

11.3 Regulatory requirements

There are no specific regulatory requirements relating to chemicals safety and the environment.

11.4 Public participation

There are no specific requirements relating to public information or participation although for facilities requiring an EIA, information relating to the EIA may be relevant (*see Section 5*).

11.5 Enforcement

11.5.1 Compliance checking

Currently, most questions connected to the storage and secondary containment of chemical substances are handled not by environmental institutions, but by the State Technical Supervision Board, which makes periodic inspection of chemical facilities. This is done in accordance with former USSR technical safety regulations.

It is expected that the EPC would become involved where a chemical spill resulted in pollution of the environment. A Chemical Inspectorate is likely to be established with the EPCs. Chemists have been recruited at every regional EPC with this task in mind.

11.5.2 Sanctions

In practice, small administrative penalties are the only sanctions available. Theoretically, facility shut down is possible but it is rarely used and in cases where facilities have been shut down the decision has been quickly reversed by higher authorities.

Annex A

List of Key Legislation

1. Environmental liability

- *LSSR Administrative Violation Code 1990;*
- *Law on Environmental Protection 1991;*
- *Resolution No. 1, on Compensation for Damaged Caused by Air Pollution from Stationary Sources Operating Without a Permit or While Exceeding State Emissions Standards of 7 May 1992.*

2. Land use planning

- *Law on Parish Municipal Govenment 1992;*
- *Law on District Minicipal Governments 1992;*
- *Council of Ministers Regulation No.73 on the procedure for the allotment of water objects for separate utilisation and withdrawal from separate utilisation 1990.*

USSR land use regulations:

- OND 1-84, with supplements No. 3 and No. 6;
- SNIP Construction Regulations and Requirements;
- Sanitary Regulations, which regulate safety requirements.

3. Environmental Impact Assessments (EIAs)

- *Law on the Environmental ProtectionCommittee of the Republic of Latvia 1990;*
- *Law on State Environmental Impact Assessments 1990;*
- *Law on Environmental Protection 1991;*
- *Regulation on the Environmental Protection Inspectorate 1990;*
- Confirmed Instruction. *"The Rational Use of Natural Resources and Protection Projects In Melioration";*
- *Council of Ministers Resolution on the State Specially Protected Cultural/Historical "Livod Rānda" 1991;*
- *Council of Ministers Resolution on the Baltic Sea and Gulf of Riga Coastal Protection Regime 1990;*
- *Law on Natural Resources Taxes 1990;*
- *Environmental Protection Committee Resolution on Water Use Permits 1991.*

4. Air emission requiremtns applicable to the operation of industrial and commercial facilities

- *Council of Ministers Resolution No. 337 of August 14 1992.*

5. Water requirements applicable to the operation of industrial and commercial facilities

- *Resolution No. 3 Water Pollution Hazard Caregories and their Maximum Allowable Concentration in Above-Ground Water Objects and Waste Water Discharge Sites 1991;*
- *Resolution on Water Use Permits of 29 November 1991.*

6. Noise requirements applicable to the operation of industrial and commercial facilities

- *Sanitary Norms for Inhabited Areas, No. 3077-84 1984;*
- *Aviation: Allowable Noise Levels for Inhabited Areas, GOST 22283-88-1988.*

7. Other sectors

There is no specific environmental legislation on the following:

- Environmental audits;
- Integrated permitting;
- Hazardous and non-hazardous waste management;
- Chemical storage, handling and emergency response.

Annex B

List of Permitting and Enforcement Authorities

Regional Environmental Protection Committees

Riga
17 L Pils Iela, Riga; Tel 212619; Chairman: Andrejs Laskovs

Madona
7 Blaumana; Tel: 23774; Chairman: Jergenijs Sabbo

Valmiere
Valmiera; Tel: 22593; Chairman: Timars Englitis

Ventspils
25 Bijusa Lenina Iela; Tel 24660; Chairman: Velga Borovikova

Daugaupils
29 Orlovska Iela, Tel: 23606; Chairman: Leopolds Zilinskis

Jelgava
6/8 Elektribas Iela; Tel: 23228; Chairman: Margarita Olande

Rezekne
5 Gorkija Iela; Tel: 23667; Chairman: Janis Karro

Leipaja
2 Jauna Ostmalos Iela; Tel: 24826; Chairman: Leonids Zelenskis

Ogre
2 Kranciema Iela; Tel: 26616

Annex C

List of Proposed Legislation

Legislation is in preparation on the following subjects:

- Hazardous waste;
- Chemical substances;
- Use of water resources;
- Explotation of underground resources;
- Soil protection;
- Air protection;
- Specially protected nature objects;
- Drinking water standards;
- Air standards;
- Methods for the calculation of damages (for water pollution);
- Protection and utilisation of animals;
- Protection and utilisation of plants;
- Use of forests;
- Fauna.

Annex D

Environmental Standards

Environmental Quality Standards for emissions to air
The following examples are taken from former USSR standards.

Substance	24 hr Maximum allowable concentration (mg/m^3)
SO_2	0.50
NO	0.085
Prticulates	0.0500
Lead	0.003
Nickel	0.001
Cadmium	0.003
Mercury	0.003
Cobalt	0.001
Copper	0.002
Tungsten	0.001
Chlorine	0.100
Flourine	0.02
Acetone	0.35

Annex E

International Conventions

Latvia is involved with the following international conventions:

- Participant in the Ronneby Conference and endorsed the Baltic Sea Environment Declaration (1990);
- Retified the Basle Convention on the Control of Transboundary Movement of Hazardous Wastes and their Disposal in December 1991;
- Signed bi-lateral co-operation agreements with Denmark, Finland, Ukraine and Sweden;
- Signed the new text of the Helsinki Convention in March 1992.

Lithuania

Prepared for the European Bank for Reconstruction and Development and the
Commission of the European Communities by
Environmental Resources Limited*

1. Overview

1.1 The Guidelines

1.1.1 Background

Investments in Lithuania are subject to many legal and economic requirements. This document focuses specifically on those compliance, operational and liability issues which arise from environmental protection measures and affect investments.

The Guidelines are intended to enable investors to familiarise themselves with the basic environmental regulatory regime relating to commercial and industrial greenfield site developments, joint venture operations or company acquisitions in Lithuania.

The Guidelines review institutional arrangements for environmental control, legislative requirements and procedures, time implications for permitting, public access to information, liability and sanctions. Because environmental policy, legislation and infrastructure in Lithuania are currently undergoing radical change the review covers both current and proposed future arrangements.

Guidelines for the following CEE countries have been prepared on behalf of the European Bank for Reconstruction and Development and the Commission of the European Communities by Environmental Resources Limited and White & Case:

- Bulgaria;[1]
- Czech Republic and Slovak Republic;[1]
- Estonia;[2]

---

[1] Guidelines prepared by White & Case.
[2] Guidelines prepared by Environmental Resources Limited.

* Environmental Resources Limited acknowledges the valuable contribution in the preparation of the *Investors' Environment Guidelines: Lithuania* of Dr David Gilbert of Environmental Resources Limited and Peter Zigalvis Esq.

- Hungary;[1]
- Latvia;[2]
- Lithuania;[2]
- Poland;[1]
- Romania[2]

These Guidelines present a description of the environmental regulatory framework as of February 1993. They provide a first step for investors in understanding environmental requirements but do not substitute for specific legal advice relating to particular sites.

Administrative and legal arrangements for environmental regulation are in a transition phase in the countries covered by these Guidelines. Requirements and implementation systems are subject to change. Investors are advised to discuss details of requirements with the authorities and check for any changes which may have taken place since February 1993.

1.1.2 Using the Guidelines

The Guidelines provide general guidance on environmental regulatory requirements applicable to foreign investment in commercial and industrial sectors of the economy. Some sections of the Guidelines, such as *Section 4* on Land Use Planning and *Section 5* on EIAs are also applicable to other sectors of the economy such as agriculture, mining, forestry and fisheries. In relation to such types of activities however, it is advisable to review other applicable requirements which are outside the scope of the Guidelines.

Section 1 provides a quick reference to environmental regulatory requirements in two case studies, and in Figure *1.1.2(a)* and *Figure 1.1.2(b)*. *Figure 1.1.2(b)* indicates how the Guidelines should be used by reference to the type of investment decision that has to be made.

The remainder of this section provides background information on the country and the following:

- Administrative structure;
- Legislative process and key items of legislation;
- Quick reference to the permitting process;
- Enforcement;
- Public participation.

Section 2 highlights the potential liabilities of investors. Liabilities potentially arising from past pollution to be taken into account at the time an investment is made and liabilities arising in the course of operating commercial and industrial facilities are presented separately. Additional details relating to specific sectors of control are provided in subsequent sections.

Section 3 identifies any environmental auditing requirements and comments on the role of voluntary audits in achieving compliance.

---

[1] Guidelines prepared by White & Case.
[2] Guidelines prepared by Environmental Resources Limited.

Figure 1.1.2(a) Using the Guidelines: report structure

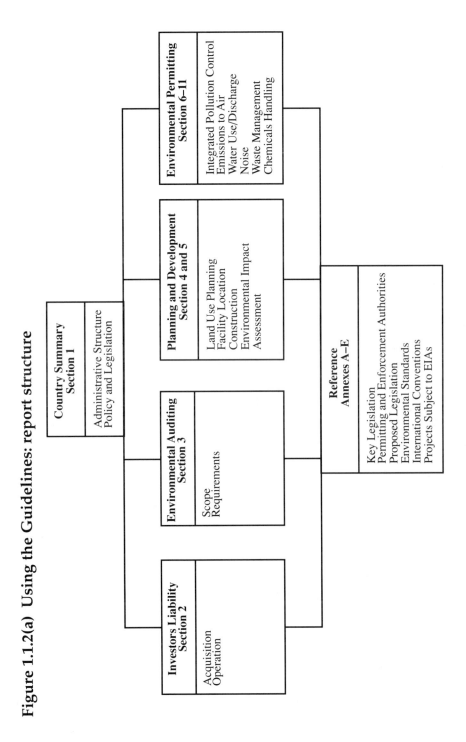

Figure 1.1.2(b) Using the Guidelines: summary by type of investment decision

Investment Decisions	Environmental Concerns	Sections in Guidelines
Choice of investment sector (eg commercial, services, manufacturing, energy)	Government and environmental bodies	1.4, 1.7, Annex B
	Existing and proposed legislation	1.5, Annex A & C
	Available forms of investment	1.2, 2.3.2
	Purchase of land	4.3
	Investments subject to EIA	5
	Activities subject to permitting	6–11
	Permitting overview and examples	1.6
Development of a "greenfield site"	Government and environmental bodies	1.4, 1.7, Annex B
	Existing and proposed legislation	1.5, Annex A & C
	Purchase of land	4.3
	EIA requirements	5
	Public participation	1.8
	Environmental standards	7, 8, Annex D
Acquisition of existing facility and privatisation	Government and environmental bodies	1.4, 1.7, Annex B
	Privatisation	1.2
	Environmental liability	2
	Cleanup of contaminated sites	2.3
	Indemnification by government	2.3
	Environmental audits	3
	Environmental standards	7, 8, Annex D
	EIA requirements (especially where modifications are made to existing facilities)	5

Investment Decisions	Environmental Concerns	Sections in Guidelines
Redevelopment and expansion of commercial and industrial facilities	Government and environmental bodies	1.4, 1.7, Annex B
	Change of land use	4
	Construction permits	4
	EIA requirements	5
	Permitting requirements	6–11
	Public participation	1.8
Operation of industrial and commercial facilities	Government and environmental bodies	1.4, 1.7, Annex B
	Environmental liability	2
	EIA requirements	5
	Public participation	1.8
	Integrated permitting	6
	Air requirements	7, Annex D
	Water requirements	8
	Noise requirements	9
	Waste management	10
	Chemical storage and handling	11
	Permitting overview and examples	1.6
	Compliance with international law	Annex E

Sections 4–11 provide guidance on permitting and related regulatory requirements for setting up and operating a commercial or industrial enterprise. Key aspects are presented at the beginning of each section for quick reference. Each section identifies the following:

- Key legislation;
- Activities covered;
- Requirements and procedures;
- Timing;
- Public participation;
- Enforcement and sanctions.

Sections 4 and 5 outline requirements and procedures relating to land use planning, facility location and construction, and environmental impact assessment. *Section 6* indicates the extent to which environmental permitting is integrated. Permitting and other regulatory requirements relating to air, water, noise, waste and chemicals are set out in *Sections 7–11*.

Annexes provide quick reference to existing and proposed legislation, contact points for the regulatory agencies, environmental standards, and ratification of international conventions.

1.2 The country

1.2.1 Background

The Republic of Lithuania has 3.7 million inhabitants and a population density of 57 inhabitants per sq. km. The country has a parliamentary democracy that held its first free elections under Lithuanian Law since the 1920s, on 25 October 1992. The currency is the Lithuanian talonas (700 Lithuanian talonas = £1 sterling as of 2 April 1993).

1.2.2 Investment

Lithuania faces economic, social and environmental problems that resulted from the integration of its economy with the Soviet Union during the period 1940 to 1990. Divisions of larger industries producing for the Soviet market were built up in Lithuania for example, producing parts in Lithuania for assembly in the Ukraine.

Foreign capital investment is now seen as essential to economic reform. Economic priorities include:

- Developing industry in a manner consistent with Lithuania's status as a sovereign nation;
- Increasing efficiency during the transition to a market economy;
- Expanding certain industries;
- Making fundamental changes to the infrastructure of certain industries;
- Providing guidelines for expansion of selected industries.

Priority will be given to the redevelopment of the following industries:

- Forestry and wood processing;
- Agricultural and food processing machinery;

- Radioelectronics and precision instruments;
- Flax farming and processing;
- Leather and fur processing;
- Pharmaceuticals;
- Tourism.

In 1991, the National Energy Conservation Programme was prepared, with major goals to reduce natural resource consumption and impacts on the environment. Lithuania does not possess any substantial energy resources and over 95% of fuel consumed is imported. The largest electricity producer in Lithuania is the Ignalia nuclear power plant, which is expected to be the primary energy producer for the next 10–15 years.

1.2.3 Environmental protection

Lithuania plans to introduce comprehensive environmental legislation with decentralised, integrated environmental management systems providing a balance between "command and control" regulatory methods and market mechanisms. The first step will be the adoption and implementation of water and air quality and emission standards based on EC legislation. It is anticipated that such standards will encourage the use of more efficient production technology.

Fiscal measures are being introduced to encourage pollution prevention. Natural resource users that successfully implement clean technologies and innovative production strategies are subsidised through tax credits, for instance they are exempt from paying taxes on profits which they reinvest in the development or utilisation of environmentally sound technologies.

1.3 Administrative structure

Lithuania is a centralised country divided into 44 Districts and 11 Towns. The roles and responsibilities of local government are set out in the *Law on the Fundamentals of Local Government 1990*. The administrative structure is currently under review and one proposal foresees 10 Counties and 84 Municipalities, while another, 16 Counties and 123 Municipalities.

Environmental protection is administered by the Environmental Protection Department (EPD), based in Vilnius, and its Inspectorate, based in eight Regional Environmental Protection Departments which each have jurisdiction over six or seven districts.

1.4 Government and environmental bodies

1.4.1 Ministries

The *Law on the Government of Lithuania 1990* sets out the powers and responsibilities of the executive branch and its ministries in environmental protection. Central government is given primary responsibility for managing natural resources in accordance with the norms and limits set by the Environmental Protection Department. Institutional arrangements are undergoing reform.

1.4.2 Environmental bodies

The *Law on the Environmental Protection Department* was passed by the Supreme Council on 13 July 1991. It established the EPD as the primary State institution regulating the environment. The EPD is part of the legislative branch and answers directly to the Supreme Council. This approach has been adopted to avoid conflicts of interest between public ownership and environmental policy, as prior to privatisation all major industry is run by the executive branch of the Council of Ministers. It is expected that the EPD will be transformed to a Ministry of the Environment and take its place in the executive branch. This change is planned for 1993.

The EPD has powers to:

- Direct environmental policy in Lithuania;
- Recommend environmental protection measures to the legislative and executive branches;
- Comment on the environmental impact of construction, relocation, or expansion of industry;
- Suspend the construction or relocation of enterprises which would violate environmental legislation;
- Suspend the activities of facilities violating or failing to implement environmental regulations.

The EPD is the principal authority issuing permits for the exploitation and use of natural resources, storage and disposal of waste, and the discharge of pollutants. The Department can request the Supreme Council to repeal Government decisions that violate Lithuanian environmental laws or regulations.

The *Law on the Fundamentals of Local Government 1990* sets out the powers of Districts and Towns and includes responsibilities in environmental protection. The most significant of these are the following:

- The issue of environmental permits;
- The right to delay or suspend the activities of facilities which violate environmental or natural resource use regulations;
- The right to set new and additional regulatory measures to deal with regional environmental issues.

1.4.3 Environmental Funds

The State Environmental Protection Fund established in 1988 finances extra-budgetary environmental protection measures. The fund is resourced from pollution and natural resources charges. Development of the procedure for the distribution of funds is the responsibility of the Supreme Council and has yet to be fully determined.

1.5 Environmental legislation

1.5.1 Legislative process

Environmental legislation in Lithuania is passed by the Supreme Council. Draft legislation may be submitted to the Supreme Council by:

- Members of the Lithuanian Saeima (Parliament);
- The Supreme Council Presidium;

- The President of the Supreme Council;
- Supreme Council standing committees;
- The government;
- The Prosecutor General;
- The Supreme Court;
- Political parties;
- Public organisations.

If the draft does not conflict with Lithuania's *Provisional Basic Law 1990* (which serves as a temporary Constitution), and the body of Lithuanian law, then it can be registered and submitted to the appropriate standing committee and the Supreme Council Presidium for review. The draft is also distributed to all standing committees, Supreme Council factions, Members of the Lithuanian Saeima (Parliament) and the government. The draft is then presented to the Supreme Council plenary session. Three readings are required for the passage of a law. Two-thirds of the Saeima Members must be in attendance and a simple majority of deputies taking part in the session is required for the passage of a law. The Supreme Council can decide to submit a draft for public approval in the form of a referendum.

1.5.2 Legislation

The foundation for Lithuania's environmental legislation is the *Law on Environmental Protection*, which was passed by the Supreme Council on 21 January 1992. The Law establishes a system for the implementation of environmental policy and sets out the following aims:

- Development of an Environmental Impact Assessment (EIA) programme;
- Review of environmental standards in force with the long-term goal of upgrading existing standards to EC recommended levels;
- The use of economic incentives to reduce pollution;
- The establishment of a system of environmental education;
- Increasing co-operation in environmental protection with international and regional organisations;
- Adherence to the "polluter pays" principle;
- Improvement in the environmental monitoring system.

The *Provisional Basic Law 1990* makes the following references to the environment:

citizens of Lithuania shall protect, preserve and contribute to the natural environment (Article 42).

the competence of local municipalities to co-ordinate and control the enterprises, institutions, and organisations in their territory in the field of environmental protection (Article 104).

Other key items of legislation relevant to the environment are listed below:

- *Law on Environmental Protection 1992*;
- *Law on the Environmental Protection Department 1990*;
- *EPD Order on the Rules of Determination of Environmental Pollution Norms and the Issue of Permits for the Exploitation of Natural Resources 1991*;
- *Interim Principal Law 1990*;

- *Law on the Government of Lithuania 1990;*
- *Law on the Fundamentals of Local Government 1990;*
- *Enterprise Law 1990;*
- *Law on Spheres of Business Activity wherein Foreign Investment is Prohibited or Limited 1991;*
- *Resolution on the Republic of Lithuania Law of Spheres of Business Activity wherein Foreign Investment is Prohibited or Limited 1991;*
- *Law on State Natural Resources 1991;*
- *Law on Taxes on Environmental Pollution 1991;*
- *Decision on Tax Rates of Natural Resources 1991.*

Laws are currently being drafted on:

- Environmental impact assessment;
- Protected areas;
- Protection and use of forests;
- Waste management;
- Protection of biological diversity;
- Protection and use of soil;
- Protection and use of coastal areas and the continental shelf;
- Water resources;
- Air quality;
- Measures to halt the pollution of the Baltic Sea.

1.6 Overview of permitting process and other regulatory requirements

1.6.1 General

Investors in Lithuania must conform to an integrated environmental permitting system. For proposed facilities or modifications to existing facilities, environmental impact assessment provides the focus for the permitting process.

Any investor of a proposed development, either at a greenfield site or at an existing facility, must firstly *register* the proposed activity with the local authority.

The Environmental Protection Department (EPD) reviews the registration document and decides whether an *environmental permit* is needed; in general, any activity which uses natural resources or discharges pollutants, requires an environmental permit.

Next, the investor makes an application for both an environmental permit and a *construction permit* simultaneously by completing a Technical Economic Calculation (TEC). The environmental section of this forms an EIA and is passed for review to the regional EPD. For proposals of national significance, the application is passed to the national EPD. The construction section is reviewed by the local authority and in cases dealt with by the national EPD, the State Construction Committee for proposed facilities, and the State Institute of Planning and Land Use for modifications to existing facilities. If the EPD approves the EIA a draft environmental permit is issued, and the local authority may then issue a construction permit.

The environmental permit includes individual sectoral permits as appropriate (eg emissions to air, water use, discharge to water etc). The permits are initially issued in draft form, with conditions based on information provided in the EIA. Separate permits for noise and chemical storage are not required, but these issues are addressed in the EIA and subsequent environmental permit. Before final permits are issued, a pre-operation check of the facility is made by the regional EPD. If there is compliance with the draft permits, final permits are issued.

The permitting process generally takes about 30 days plus up to 15 days for the pre-operation check and issue of final permits. However, for proposals which are of national significance, or affect environmentally sensitive or highly polluted areas, the process may be significantly longer.

Existing facilities with no permits which are to continue operation, or facilities which need permit renewal, require permits under the new legislation. In these cases, permit applications are made to the EPD but no EIA is needed; instead, the EPD carries out an Ecological Examination of the site which is, in effect, a mini-EIA carried out by EPD.

1.6.2 Case study 1

For a foreign investor acquiring a greenfield site for development of a new paper mill, the permitting procedure would involve the following steps.

First the investor must register the activity with the local authority. Secondly, a Technical Economic Calculation (TEC) form must be completed and submitted to the local authority. This includes both a section on construction and an EIA (if deemed necessary by EPD). The construction application is reviewed jointly by the State Construction Committee and the local authority. The EIA is reviewed by the EPD, and if approved, an environmental permit is issued, including draft sectoral permits for air, water and waste as appropriate. Issue of the environmental permit enables the local authority to issue a construction permit. This procedure would generally take about 30 days, but longer if the project is considered to be either of national significance, or to be in an environmentally sensitive or highly polluted area.

Following construction of the facility, a pre-operation check must be carried out by the regional EPD within a 15-day period. If compliance with the draft permits is found, then final permits are issued.

A summary of the permitting procedure is presented schematically in *Figure 1.6.2(a)*.

1.6.3 Case study 2

For a foreign investor forming a joint venture with an existing company, acquiring two factories, closing one and refurbishing the other to produce tyres, the permitting procedure would involve the following steps.

To close the existing factory the investor would not require any specific environmental permits, but would need to register the proposal with the Economics Ministry and comply with any regulations issued. In particular, the privatisation law places restrictions on the reduction of a workforce.

To refurbish the existing factory to produce tyres the investor would firstly need to register the proposal with the Economics Ministry and comply with any regulations issued. Following this, the investor would need to complete the TEC, detailing his pro-posals for site modification and including an EIA and applications for environmental sectoral permits. The subsequent stages, are the same as for a new facility (*see Section 1.6.2*).

A summary of the permitting procedure for closure and modification of existing facilities is presented schematically in *Figure 1.6.3(a)*.

351

Figure 1.6.2(a) Environmental permitting procedure for a proposed facility

Main Steps	*Authority*	*Timing*
Step 1. Construction Permit and Environmental Permits		
Submission of TEC, including EIA if required ↓	Local authority (or State Construction Committee)* and EPD	
Review of construction and EIA applications ↓	Local authority and EPD	
Decision on EIA and issue of draft environmental permit including draft sectoral permits ↓	EPD	
Issue of construction permit	Local authority	30 days (average)

Step 2. Construction of Facility		

Main Steps	*Authority*	*Timing*
Step 3. Pre-Operational Check		
Applications for pre-operational check ↓	EPD	
Check for compliance with draft sectoral environmental permits ↓	EPD	
Issue of final sectoral environmental permits	EPD	15 days

* For cases under review by National EPD.

Figure 1.6.3(a) Environmental permitting procedure for closure and modification of existing facilities

Main Steps	Authority	Timing
Step 1. Construction Permit and Environmental Permits		
Submission of TEC, including EIA if required ↓	Local authority and EPD (or State Institute of Land Use Planning)*	
Review of modification and EIA applications ↓	Local authority and EPD	
Decision on EIA and issue of environmental permit including draft sectoral environmental permits ↓	EPD	
Issue of permit to modify facility	Local authority	
Step 2. Modification of Facility		
Step 2. Pre-Operational Check		
Applications for pre-operational check ↓	EPD	
Check for compliance with draft sectoral environmental permits ↓	EPD	
Issue of final sectoral environmental permits	EPD	15 days

* For cases under review by National EPD.

1.7 Enforcement of environmental legislation

The EPD Inspectorate is responsible for the enforcement of environmental legislation. The *Law on Environmental Protection 1992* bases the enforcement process largely on a system of self monitoring. The EPD inspectors make periodic checks of pollution emissions to verify the accuracy of operators' reports on pollution releases.

The *Law on Taxes on Environmental Pollution 1991* includes economic sanctions for pollution. If an operator exceeds permissable pollution limits then a payment of three times the standard tax assessed for pollution discharge must be paid; if the discharger conceals or falsifies information on discharges, the charge is ten times the standard tax. The law specifies that this penalty cannot be passed on to the consumer. In the event that the EPD inspectors find that the reported discharges from the operators' self-monitoring are exceeded, the discharger will be assessed at the higher discharge rate for the entire three months reporting period.

The Lithuanian Administrative Code also specifies penalties for violations of environmental law. Violations include the following:

- Failure to report, or fraudulent reporting of ecological information or the use of natural resources;
- Releasing pollutants to the environment without a permit.

Violations may result in financial penalties and the closure of the enterprise is also possible.

The Districts and Towns also have the right to restrain or forbid economic activity or to halt the activities of specific enterprises or organisations if environmental protection requirements are being violated.

1.8 Public participation

1.8.1 Public access to information

Under the *Law on Environmental Protection 1992* citizens have the right to receive accurate and up to date information on environmental quality.

1.8.2 Provision of information

State authorities have a duty under the 1992 on *Law on Environmental Protection* to announce publicly plans for economic activities which may have a hazardous impact on the environment.

1.8.3 Public consultation

Under the 1992 *Law on Environmental Protection*, citizens have the right to take part in discussions relating to projects for establishing facilities and demand that activities which are hazardous to the environment are terminated. The public also has the right to request that sanctions are imposed on those guilty of endangering the environment, and officers who are not fulfilling their duties.

Detailed provisions relating to public participation and the role of the investor are expected in future legislation.

2. Environmental liability

2.1 Summary

Environmental Liabilities of Investors:	Although not specifically stated in law, liability is generally taken to be with the new investor.
Successor Liability:	The new owner generally adopts liability for past pollution unless contractually agreed otherwise.
Investor Clean-up of Contaminated Sites:	No standards exist which either trigger a clean-up obligation or for restoration levels.
Civil Liability:	Under the *1992 Law on Environmental Protection*, fault based liability applies. All losses must be compensated and where possible, the environment restored. There is no provision for strict liability.
Administrative Liability:	The *Administrative Code* lists environmental violations. Remedies include fines, permit revocation, or the closing of a facility.
Criminal Liability:	According to the *Criminal Code*, infringements of measures to protect the environment can result in fines, revocation of permits and imprisonment.

2.2 Sources of legislation relating to environmental liability

The new Lithuanian *Civil Code* was adopted in June 1992. It is a reformed version of the Lithuanian Soviet Socialist Republic (LSSR) Civil Code. Environmental liability provisions can also be found under the *Administrative* and *Criminal Codes*.

Further provisions relating to liability are set out in Chapter 7 of the *Law on Environmental Protection 1992* entitled "Liability for Violation of the Law of Environmental Protection and the Settlement of Disputes Concerning Issues of Environmental Protection".

2.3 Environmental liabilities for past pollution

2.3.1 Types of environmental liabilities

Past environmental liabilities

As yet, no law specifically addresses liability for on-site pollution arising from past operations, but it is expected that the purchaser will adopt all responsibility.

Reimbursement of clean-up costs

According to the *Civil Code*, Article 495, a person who has been required to pay compensation for environmental damage which resulted from the action of a former owner or other person, has the right to recover the amount from the person responsible for the damage.

If a contractual agreement were made to leave environmental liability with the vendor, it may be possible for the purchaser to sue the vendor in the Civil Court regarding remediation costs arising from the actions of the vendor. This has yet to be tested in the courts.

2.3.2 Government indemnification of environmental liabilities

There are no specific provisions regarding the indemnification by government of investor for liabilities.

It is expected that indemnification from liability will be available for an organisation that has publicly announced its liquidation and settled its accounts with all creditors, claimants etc.

2.3.3 Investor clean-up of contaminated sites

Environmental clean-up standards

Clean-up standards have not yet been established.

Escrow accounts

No requirements have been established for escrow accounts.

Environmental funds

The State Environmental Protection Fund established in 1988 finances extra-budgetary environmental protection measures. The fund is resourced from pollution and natural resources charges. Development of the procedure for the formation and distribution of funds is the responsibility of the Supreme Council and has yet to be fully determined. Resources will be used by the state for environmental improvement, but will not be made available to investors for the clean-up of land or water polluted prior to an investment.

2.3.4 Case examples

At the time of writing no examples of cases relating to investor liability resulting from site acquisition have been identified.

2.4 Environmental liabilities arising from facility operation

2.4.1 Civil liability

The new *Civil Code* was adopted in June 1992. It is a reformed version of the LSSR Civil Code.

Chapter 7 of the *Law on Environmental Protection 1992* entitled "Liability for Violation of the Law of Environmental Protection and the Settlement of Disputes Concerning Issues of Environmental Protection" is applicable.

Fault based liability

According to the *Law on Environmental Protection 1992*, a person engaged in unlawful activity who causes damage to the environment or to the life or health of a given person(s) must compensate all losses, and if possible restore the damage to the environment.

A claim for compensation may be made by persons suffering damage to health, property or interests, or by the Environmental Protection Department (EPD) with regard to damage to the interests of the state.

Strict liability

There is no provision for strict liability.

Statutes of limitation

The statute of limitations begins from either the time of the violation or when the damage becomes apparent. The statute of limitations has a one year period but may be extended if there is evidence to support the necessity of such an extension.

Remedies

Under the *Law on Environmental Protection 1992* damage to the environment resulting from unlawful activities must be restored where possible by the person responsible for the damage. Costs incurred in the eradication of a situation of ecological disaster (not defined) must be borne by the person responsible for the disaster.

Natural resource damage is calculated according to the methodologies of the former USSR and the EPD. Rates of compensation are to be established by the EPD.

Case examples

In March 1992 0.5 t of oil was spilt from a storage facility in Vilnius. The EPD calculated damages at 50,200 Lithuanian talonas. The facility was required by the civil court to pay this sum in compensation.

2.4.2 Administrative liability

Types of administrative liability

The *Administrative Code* specifies penalties for violations of environmental law. As in the other Baltic Nations, the LSSR Administrative Code has been adopted temporarily, but it is in the process of revision.

Article 7 of the *Administrative Code* includes more than 30 types of administrative liability as listed in *Table 2.4.2(a)*.

Remedies

Administrative fines may be imposed for breach of the *Administrative Code*. Fines range from 100–4000 Lithuanian talonas.

In addition to fines and taxes, the EPD and local government have the power to halt environmentally dangerous activities. The revocation of a permit is a further possible

Table 2.4.2(a)   Administrative Liability

- Non-realisation of means of environmental protection.
- Confirmation of projects in which means of environmental protection are not foreseen.
- Construction, reconstruction, expansion, or the handing over for usage of projects which breach environmental protection requirements.
- Household or industrial waste pollution.
- Pollution of the environment with poisonous and harmful substances.
- Pollution of the environment with radioactive materials.
- Pollution of the water with leakage of oil products.
- Failing to report or fraudulently reporting the use of natural resources.
- Concealment, failure to report, or fraudulent report of ecological information.
- Failure to obey the instructions of state officials who are in charge of environmental control.
- Impeding environmental protection enforcement.
- Soil damage.
- Breach of forest resource utilisation and forest renewal regulations.
- Breach of requirements for land use.
- Breach of requirements for the protection of ground, soil and mineral resources.
- Breach of requirements regarding the excavation of fossils.
- Breach of regulations for geologic exploration.
- Breach of water protection regulations.
- Breach of the water use procedures.
- Breach of regulations for the use of hydrological equipment and mechanisms.
- Breach of land reclamation regulations.
- Improper utilisation of state forests.
- Breach of the established procedure for the preparation of timber, resin, and secondary materials on timber-lots and transportation of the above materials.
- Illegal cutting of trees in forests and on plantations, damaging or destroying young trees.
- Intentional destruction of young forests.
- Breach of forest resource utilisation and forest renewal regulations.
- Intentional destruction of the forest floor.

remedy. Under the *Law on Environmental Protection 1992* the public may take steps via the courts to ensure that sanctions are taken against offenders.

There are also citizen's suit provisions under the supplement to the *Administrative Code*. Under Article 2(9), if a citizen makes a private complaint to the EPD which is not dealt with satisfactorily, the citizen has the right to appeal the case to the regional Court and then to the Supreme Court.

Case examples

In the current economic situation, almost no economic activity is being halted. Fines are being levied for administrative violations.

2.4.3 Criminal liability

Types criminal liability

According to the *Criminal Code*, infringements of measures to protect the environment can result in fines, revocation of permits and imprisonment.

Case examples

In practice, the authorities rely largely on administrative rather than criminal sanctions. There are no examples of criminal sanctions against investors.

3. Environmental audits

3.1 Sources of legislation relating to environmental audits

There are no legal requirements to undertake pre-acquisition audits. Such requirements are subject to discussion amongst environmental officials but there are no definite plans for legislation on this issue.

Modification of an existing facility however, may require that a State Ecological Examination is undertaken which would include assessment of compliance with environmental standards and other regulatory requirements, ie an audit.

The investor should consider carrying out a pre-acquisition audit to determine that the facility is in compliance and whether any liability exists and discuss potential liability issues with the authorities.

3.2 National experience with environmental audits

It is expected that projects sponsored by financial institutions such as the IFC and EBRD would include requirements for some form of environmental audit to be undertaken. There appears to be no example of auditing in practice as yet.

4. Land use planning

4.1 Summary

Authorities:	Local authorities (Districts and Towns) State Institute of Land Use Planning and State Construction Committee.
Types of Activity:	All forms of economic activity and registered enterprises. *Local Authority* — Construction permit for proposed facilities and modifications to existing facilities. *State Institute* — Construction permit, for modifications to existing facilities under national review. *State Committee* — Construction permit for proposed facilities under national review.
Permits:	Construction permit.
Timing:	30 days in general, although can be extended, depending on the EIA process (see *Section 5*).
Public Information:	State authorities have a duty to publicly announce plans for economic activities which may have a hazardous impact on the environment.
Public Consultation:	Citizens have the right to take part in discussions relating to proposals for establishing facilities and to demand that activities which are hazardous to the environment are terminated. The public also has the right to request sanctions on those endangering the environment.

4.2 Sources of relevant land use legislation

- *Law on the Fundamentals of Local Government 1990*;
- *Law on Environmental Protection 1992*;
- *Law and Resolution on Spheres of Business Activity Where Foreign Investment is Prohibited or Limited 1991*;
- *Law on Procedures and Conditions for the Restoration of Land Ownership Rights of Citizens 1992*;
- *Law on Land Taxes 1992*;
- *Law on Land Reform 1992*;
- *Land Code 1970*;
- *Civil Code 1964*;
- *Lithuanian Constitution 1992*.

The most significant regulations of the former USSR dealing with land use are the following:

- OND 1-84, with supplements No. 3 and No. 6;
- SNIP Construction Regulations and Requirements;
- Sanitary Regulations, which regulate safety requirements.

These regulations chiefly address the approval of proposed construction and remain in force until replaced by Lithuanian legislation.

4.3 Scope of activities subject to land use regulation

Land use planning legislation requires that a construction permit is obtained for proposed new facilities and facilities undergoing modification for all forms of economic activity.

Land use planning is governed primarily by the *Law on the Fundamentals of Local Government 1990* which determines the competence of the Districts and Towns (local authorities) in the field of environmental protection.

The *Law and Resolution on Spheres of Business Activity Where Foreign Investment is Prohibited or Limited 1991* prohibits foreign investment in mining where this is designated as relating to national economic security except in accordance with a special permit, and completely prohibits foreign investment in other activities, eg oil pipelines and communications.

Land deeds issued to new land owners, as part of the privatisation process, are to include a clause specifying land use requirements. The clause is to include environmental protection measures, for instance to prevent erosion.Under the Soviet system industrial zones were established by the appropriate project institute in co-ordination with the State Architecture, Construction, and Environment Committees, and the local authority. Each zone was confirmed by the State Plan which was the responsibility of the Council of Ministers.

4.4 Permitting process

4.4.1 Authorities

Economic planning and land-use planning are within the competence of local and central government (Council of Ministers).

Local authorities (Districts and Towns) and the State Institute of Land Use Planning grant permits for all economic activities and registered enterprises. The competencies of the authorities is set out in the *Law on the Fundamentals of Local Government 1990*.

Currently, local planning and construction permitting is carried out by local authorities taking into account the EIA process which is reviewed by the regional EPD for the environmental approval of the project. In the case of proposed facilities of national significance, construction permit applications must be approved by the State Construction Committee for proposed facilities and by the State Institute of Land Use Planning for modifications to existing facilities and the EIA by the national EPD. The regional EPD determines where a proposal is of national significance.

4.4.2 Application requirements

Prior to application for a construction permit, an investor must first register the company with the local government.

To obtain a construction permit, the investor must complete the "Technical/Economic Calculation" (TEC), which includes two sections; one on construction and one on EIA. The construction section is reviewed by the local government, and in some cases, either the State Construction Committee or the State Institute of Land Use Planning. The EIA must include proposals for the rational use of natural resources, avoidance of industrial accidents and compliance with environmental standards. The EIA section of the TEC is submitted to the EPD by the local government. Both the construction and environmental issues are reviewed simultaneously. Approval of the EIA by the EPD enables the local authority to issue a *construction permit.*

4.4.3 Fees

Fees are not charged for the design or construction permit.

4.4.4 Timing

The issue of a construction permit is linked to the Environmental Impact Assessment (EIA) process and depends on the time taken to approve the EIA. For projects determined at the regional level, a permit is generally issued within 30 days. For projects reviewed by the national EPD the permit may take several months to be issued.

4.4.5 Permit conditions

Permit conditions are derived from the following regulations of the former USSR:

- OND 1-84, with supplements No. 3 and No. 6;
- SNIP Construction Regulations and Requirements;
- Sanitary Regulations, which regulate safety requirements.

4.5 Public participation

4.5.1 Public access to information

Under the *Law on Environmental Protection 1992* citizens have the right to receive accurate and up to date information on environmental quality.

4.5.2 Provision of information

State authorities have a duty under the 1992 Law to announce publicly plans for economic activities which may have a hazardous impact on the environment.

4.5.3 Public consultation

Under the 1992 Law, citizens have the right to take part in discussions relating to proposals for establishing facilities and demand that activities which are hazardous to the environment are terminated. The public also has the right to request that sanctions are imposed on those guilty of endangering the environment, and on officers who are not fulfilling their duties.

Detailed provisions relating to public participation are expected in future legislation.

4.6 Enforcement

Regional EPD inspectors are responsible for enforcement but in some cases, the national EPD takes enforcement actions, eg where construction is proposed in protected areas. Construction may be halted and administrative fines imposed in the range of 100–4,000 Lithuanian talonas.

5. Environmental Impact Assessments (EIAs)

5.1 Summary

Authorities:	Regional or National Environmental Protection Department (EPD).
Types of Activity:	All economic activities which use natural resources or discharge pollutants. *Regional EPD* — Projects of only local significance *National EPD* — Projects of national significance or those involving environmentally sensitive or highly polluted areas.
Permit:	Approval of EIA.
Timing:	30 days in general, although can be significantly longer for projects reviewed at national level.
Public Information:	State authorities have a duty to publicly announce plans for economic activities which may have a hazardous impact on the environment.
Public Consultation:	Citizens have the right to take part in discussions relating to proposals for establishing facilities and to demand that activities which are hazardous to the environment are terminated. The public also has the right to request sanctions on those endangering the environment.

5.2 Sources of legislation relating to the environmental impact of industrial and commercial developments

The *Law on Environmental Protection 1992* sets out general requirements and procedures for investors to forecast the environmental impact of economic activities. A law on EIA and a series of regulations implementing it is in draft. Other relevant legislation is as follows:

- *Law on Environmental Protection 1992*;
- *Law on the Environmental Protection Department 1990*;

- *EPD Order on the Rules of Determination of Environmental Pollution Norms and the Issue of Permits for the Exploitation of Natural Resources 1991*;
- *Interim Principal Law 1990*;
- *Government Law 1990*;
- *Law on the Fundamentals of Local Government 1990*;
- *Enterprise Law 1990*;
- *Law on Spheres of Business Activity wherein Foreign Investment is Prohibited or Limited 1991*;
- *Resolution on the Republic of Lithuania Law of Spheres of Business Activity wherein Foreign Investment is Prohibited or Limited 1991*;
- *Law on State Natural Resources 1991*;
- *Law on Taxes on Environmental Pollution 1991*;
- *Decision on Tax Rates of Natural Resources 1991*.

A Law on Environmental Impact Assessment is in draft.

5.3 Scope of activities subject to EIA process

EIA is required for all proposed "economic activities" but this is not defined in the legislation. According to the *Enterprise Law* all enterprises engaged in economic activities must obtain an environmental permit from the EPD if they use natural resources or discharge pollutants to the environment. An EIA must be approved as a pre-requisite for obtaining an environmental permit for new or modified facilities. The complexity of an EIA will vary according to the project.

Existing facilities which do not have an environmental permit or are due for permit renewal must undergo an "ecological examination" which is an assessment by the EPD of compliance and of the extent of existing and possible future threats to the environment.

For the following types of project, the EPD has special responsibility for carrying out pre-feasibility and feasibility documentation rather than just confirming it:

- Construction planned for protected territories (reserves, national parks, nature parks, nature sanctuaries and territories);
- General plans for nationally significant cities;
- Major industrial projects with a significant impact on the environment (eg Ignalin Nuclear Power Plant, Mazeikai Oil Refinery, Janava "Azotas", Akmene "Cementas", Kaisiadorys Hydro-accumulative Power Plant, Kedainiai Fertilizer Factory, Elektrenai Power Plant, Klaipeda Cardboard Mill, Klaipeda "Sirijus", Panevezys "Lietkabelis", Kaunas Artificial Fibre Plant). EIAs have been carried out for all these projects under the USSR system. Any proposals for expansion or other alteration would be considered by the EPD at national level;
- Natural resource exploitation projects;
- Industrial joint ventures.

5.4 EIA process

5.4.1 Authorities

An EIA of a simple project of local significance may be handled by a regional EPD while a project of national significance or one involving an environmentally sensitive or highly polluted area, may be processed by a board of experts selected by the national EPD. The national EPD may either choose to intervene, or the regional EPD may request their input.

There are several anticipated changes to the existing EIA system which may be introduced after the creation of an independent EIA agency outside the Ministry. Tasks which the agency would carry out include:

- Acting as the central depository for all EIA studies and reports;
- Evaluating EIA reports;
- Checking EIA studies for accuracy;
- Approving EIAs.

All ministries involved in, or affected by, the activity in question would be responsible for:

- The provision of full information to the public on the projected environmental impact of activities;
- Appointing specialists to review proposals;
- The proposal of alternatives with lower environmental impacts.

Other possible changes include the following:

- The role of local government to be defined more precisely;
- The scope and level of the EIA process to be defined so that operations and activities will be grouped according to the degree of their environmental impact and the extent of that impact, from local to national to international significance;
- The establishment of procedures for conflict resolution and arbitration;
- The establishment of procedures to allow broad public discussion of proposed activities and the related EIA studies.

5.4.2 Documentation

If the planned development will have an impact on the environment, the investor must obtain approval of the EIA from the regional EPD in order tobegin construction.

To do this, the investor must complete a technical economic calculation (TEC) form for the project. The questions on the TEC chiefly centre on construction, but there is also a section on environmental protection measures planned by the investor which is the basis for the EIA.

The documentation must include information on:

- Projected releases of pollutants to the water and air;
- Projected volumes of wastes, hazardous and non-hazardous, that the proposed activity will generate.

Preparation of this documentation will be financed entirely by the investor.

The EIA process is geared towards compliance with pollution discharge standards. Other issues, however, could be included as part of the "possible impact of economic activities on environment" (*Environmental Protection Law 1992*) for example effects on sites of natural beauty, cultural impact, indirect environmental effects (eg traffic generation), or the need and alternatives for economic activity.

The EIA and the construction permit application form separate parts of the same TEC document, and after separate review by the EPD and local authority respectively, the complete application is returned to the local authority.

5.4.3 Experts and consultants

Consultants and experts undertaking EIAs do not need to be licensed by the authorities.

5.4.4 Timing

Projects reviewed at a regional level are generally completed within 30 days. EIAs of larger projects carried out by the national EPD may take several months.

5.4.5 Standard of review

EIAs of projects of only local environmental significance are reviewed by the regional EPD. Review of EIAs of major projects and projects connected with Lithuania's environmentally sensitive areas is carried out by a board of experts appointed by the national EPD. This is to be made up of "specialists from both Lithuanian and international organisations". In the future, the Environmental Protection Department plans to revise the EIA process to give more responsibility to the regional level divisions.

Evaluation of the EIA is made on the basis of compliance with pollution discharge standards in force in Lithuania. Projects are reviewed in accordance with these standards. Stricter standards will be imposed on existing industry if new industry is necessary in an area and if ambient quality standards have been reached. If pollution in an area already exceeds standards then no new permits can be issued in that area. Projects that cannot meet the standards will not receive approval.

The EPD conclusion on the EIA is final. There is no system of appeal against its decision although the EPD is accountable to the Supreme Council.

5.5 Public participation

5.5.1 Public access to information

Under the *Law on Environmental Protection 1992* citizens have the right to receive accurate and up to date information on environmental quality.

5.5.2 Provision of Information

State authorities have a duty under the *Law on Environmental Protection 1992* to announce publicly plans for economic activities which may have a hazardous impact on the environment and carry out an environmental impact assessment, or justifiably decline, at the request of the public.

5.5.3 *Public consultation*

Under the *Law on Environmental Protection 1992*, citizens have the right to take part in discussions relating to projects for establishing facilities and demand that activities which are hazardous to the environment are terminated. Details for procedures for public consultation and the role of the investor have yet to be determined. The public also has the right to request that sanctions are taken against those guilty of endangering the environment, and officers who are not fulfilling their duties.

It is expected that in future legislation the following procedures will be introduced for public participation:

- Documents submitted by the investor/developer to the EPD must describe in detail the impact that the project will have on the environment;
- Information on impacts must be provided by the EPD to the public;
- After the EPD issues its expert opinion, public input on the project will be taken into account;
- Consultation will take place with the investor/developer regarding the EPD opinion and public views.

5.6 *Enforcement*

Providing false information to the authorities may result in sanctions according to the *Administrative Code*. Administrative fines in the range 100–4,000 Lithuanian talonas may be imposed.

5.7 *National experience with EIAs*

In 1990, when the USSR imposed an economic blockade on Lithuania, a decision was taken to build an oil terminal north of Klaipeda in the north west of the country as an alternate oil supply source. The relevant ministries supported the project despite certain environmental drawbacks. An EIA was prepared by the Ministry of Energy for review by the national EPD in 1991.

An expert Review Board comprising 17 experts included two representatives of the national EPD. The Board did not approve the EIA on two counts:

- A reduction in the size of the beach at the site would be required;
- Part of the terminal would have to be constructed in the sea.

A second potential site was identified at Klaipeda but was eliminated because of pressure from local residents. Subsequently a new project was developed with two alternative sites, Butinge and Melnrage. The Review Board did not approve the EIA for the Butinge site on the following grounds:

- The assessment of potential environmental effects was inadequate;
- The seashore was found to be unsuitable for the projects;
- Any accident would be likely to cause significant damage to marine flora and fauna.

The EIA for the Melnrage site was approved by the Board. A final decision on the site has not yet been made.

6. Integrated permitting requirements applicable to the operation of industrial and commercial facilities

6.1 Summary

Authorities:	Environmental Protection Department (EPD), regional or national.
Types of Activities:	All facilities which use natural resources and discharge pollutants into the environment.
Permits:	Permit for Usage of Natural Resources.
Timing:	30 days in general, although can be extended depending on the EIA process for new or modified facilities.
Public Information:	State authorities have a duty to publicly announce plans for economic activities which may have a hazardous impact on the environment.
Public Consultation:	Citizens have the right to take part in discussions relating to proposals for establishing facilities and to demand that activities which are hazardous to the environment are terminated. The public also has the right to request sanctions on those endangering the environment.

6.2 Sources of legislation relating to intergrated permitting

- *Law on Environmental Protection 1992;*
- *Law on Taxes on Environmental Pollution 1991;*
- *Decision No. 190 on Taxes on Natural Resources 1991;*
- *Environmental Protection Department Order No. 11 Procedure for Determining Environmental Pollution Standards and for Issue of Permits for Usage of Natural Resources.*

6.3 Scope of activities subject to integrated permitting

According to the *Law on Environmental Protection 1992* all facilities which use natural resources and discharge pollutants into the environment must obtain a permit. The permit (Permit for Usage of Natural Resources) contains the following four parts:

- Part I: Water Use.
- Part II: Discharge of Pollutants with Sewage Water.

368

- Part III: Emission of Pollutants into the Atmosphere from Stationary Sources.
- Part IV: Storage of Waste, Landfills, and Waste Treatment.

Facilities using or discharging water below prescribed limits are not required to obtain Parts I and II of the permit. The types of facility requiring Part III of the permit are listed in the legislation (see *Sections 7* and *8*). Facilities which are not required to obtain a permit must comply with environmental quality standards.

6.4 Permitting process

6.4.1 Authorities
Permits are issued by regional Environmental Protection Departments (EPD). In cases where a facility is of national significance, as determined by the regional EPD, the application will be determined by the national EPD.

6.4.2 Application requirements
Application for the Permit for Usage of Natural Resources is closely linked to the EIA process. Initially, a draft permit is issued, on the basis of information provided in the EIA application. Subsequently, and prior to starting up a new or modified facility, a pre-operation review must be carried out by the regional EPD. The review is carried out to ensure that the facility complies with requirements set out in the draft permit. If the facility is found to be in compliance, a final permit can be issued.

Where it is proposed to modify an existing facility or process, it is necessary to apply for a modification permit. The following information must be provided:

- An application describing the reasons for a change in the permit;
- An information sheet on the fulfilment of the requirements contained in the current permit as well as implementation of foreseen measures;
- Data on compliance with environmental quality norms fixed for discharges and emissions as well as data on the results of control measurements.

6.4.3 Fees
There are no charges for integrated environmental permitting.

6.4.4 Timing
The initial stage of permitting leading to the draft permit, generally takes 30 days. However, for proposed facilities or modifications to existing facilities the process is closely linked to the EIA process and the overall time may be extended to several months depending upon the size and complexity of the facility. In addition, the pre-operation review and determination of the final permit is to be carried out within 15 days of application.

6.4.5 Permit conditions
The decision to issue the Permit for Usage of Natural Resources, is based on the EPD review of Maximum Permissible Emissions (MPE) or Temporary Permissible Emission (TPE) standards which are derived from environmental quality standards. For existing

facilities, waste records and data of emissions of pollutants will be taken into account. The permit is issued for a five-year term, but MPE or TPE standards for the volume of emissions into the atmosphere or surface waters are usually fixed for one year. The standards are reviewed annually and the permit may thus be modified.

The type of standard (MPE or TPE) is stated in the permit. A draft MPE standard is prepared for a period of not longer than five years. However, the duration of Part III of the permit (for the emission of pollutants into the atmosphere from stationary sources) varies as follows:

- Up to one year, in cases where the enterprise is required to implement urgent atmosphere protection measures;
- For one year, when modifications to achieve the MPE or TPE standard will have to be undertaken;
- For two to three years, when the MPE or TPE standards are met, and reconstruction, conversion, or expansion are not anticipated.

The *Law on Environmental Protection 1992* imposes a general requirement that operators of "potentially hazardous" facilities must monitor environmental pollution and its impact on the environment; ("potentially hazardous" is not defined). Operators of facilities must keep records of the use of natural resources and of the releases of pollutants to the environment.

6.5 Public participation

6.5.1 Public access to information

Operators of facilities which are "potentially hazardous" to the environment (not defined) are required by the *Law on Environmental Protection 1992* to make available to the public information on pollution from their operations. The Law also gives citizens the right to receive accurate and up to date information on environmental quality.

6.5.2 Provision of information

State authorities have a duty under the *Law on Environmental Protection 1992* to announce publicly plans for economic activities which may have a hazardous impact on the environment.

6.5.3 Public consultation

In the case of proposed developments, under the *Law on Environmental Protection 1992*, citizens have the right to take part in discussions relating to projects for establishing facilities and demand that activities which are hazardous to the environment are terminated. The public also has the right to request that sanctions are taken against those guilty of endangering the environment, and officers who are not fulfilling their duties.

Detailed provisions relating to public participation and the role of the investor have not yet been determined and are expected in future legislation.

6.6 Enforcement

6.6.1 Compliance checking and monitoring

Inspection is carried out by the regional EPD according to an inspection checklist which includes the verification and enforcement of pollution taxes and checking of the operators' monitoring data.

6.6.2 Sanctions

If facilities do not comply with requirements fines can be imposed, permits revoked, or the activity halted. Fines range between 100–4000 Lithuanian talonas.

7. Air emission requirements applicable to the operation of industrial and commercial facilities

7.1 Summary

Authorities:	Regional Environmental Protection Department (EPD).
Types of Activities:	All activities contributing to the pollution of the atmosphere and prescribed activities.
Permits:	Permit for Emission of Pollutants into the Atmosphere from Stationary Sources as part III of the Permit for Usage of Natural Resources.
Timing:	30 days in general, although can be extended, depending on the EIA process (see *Section 5*).
Public Information:	State authorities have a duty to publicly announce plans for economic activities which may have a hazardous impact on the environment.
Public Consultation:	Citizens have the right to take part in discussions relating to proposals for establishing facilities and to demand that activities which are hazardous to the environment are terminated. The public also has the right to request sanctions on those endangering the environment.

7.2 Sources of legislation relating to air emissions

- *Law on Environmental Protection 1992;*
- *Law on Taxes on Environmental Pollution 1991;*
- *Environmental Protection Department Order No. 11 Procedure for Determining Environmental Pollution Standards and for Issue of Permits for Use of Natural Resources.*

7.3 Air protection zones

Zones in which levels of environmental pollutants exceed prescribed standards are termed "non-conforming" zones. In these zones, facilities can only obtain temporary, annual permits. It is anticipated that emission limits will be stricter in each annual permit thereby reducing overall emissions until the zones conform with environmental quality standards.

7.4 Scope of activities subject to air emission regulations

Part III of the Permit for Usage of Natural Resources concerning the emission of pollutants into the atmosphere from stationary sources is required for the following:

- All enterprises contributing to the pollution of the atmosphere;
- Large power plants (regional electric power-plants, heat generating plants, regional boiler-houses);
- Boiler houses that burn annually:
- (i)   more than 1.5 million m^3 of natural gas;
- (ii   more than 500 t of fuel oil;
- (iii)   more than 200 t of coal;
- Printing-houses;
- Oil supply enterprises;
- Mobile construction units;
- Technical service stations;
- Dry-cleaners;
- Gas and oil pipelines;
- Gas distribution stations;
- Railway units.

7.5 Standards

7.5.1 Ambient quality standards

Former USSR ambient air quality standards for over 800 pollutants remain in force in Lithuania. They specify 30 minute and 24 hour averages for maximum allowable concentrations (MACs) which are based on concentrations of chemical substances or chemical combinations which do not affect respiratory reflex actions in rural locations within 20–30 minutes.

It is expected that proposed legislation, which will gradually introduce standards based on EC legislation, will be adopted in May 1993.

7.5.2 Emission limit values

A document *On the Procedure for Determining Environmental Pollution Standards and the Issue of Permits for the Use of Natural Resources*, was issued by the EPD in January

1991. This document defines two classes of emissions standards, based on former USSR maximum allowable concentrations:

- Maximum Permissible Emissions (MPE);
- Temporary Permissible Emissions (TPE).

MPE is defined as the maximum permissible quantity of pollutants that can be discharged into the atmosphere by a stationary source per time unit, which does not exceed the established near-the-surface maximum allowable concentrations (MAC).

In determining air pollution standards, the EPD has taken into account the recommendations outlined in the 1979 Geneva Convention on Long-Range Transboundary Air Pollution. Because economic realities make these levels unattainable in the short-term, the EPD has created the temporary permissible emission levels, based on the quantities currently discharged and the present level of technology.

The EPD has begun a comprehensive programme for the attainment of MPE levels, based on annual reviews of activities and emissions until MPE has been attained.

The following additional steps have been taken in Lithuania to protect air quality:

- A commitment has been made to implement the requirements of the Geneva Convention on Long-Range Transboundary Air Pollution by utilising less sulphurous (up to 2.5%) petroleum, and where possible, natural gas (lack of hard currency may hinder this commitment);
- Implementation of already established requirements for the introduction of treatment facilities in thermoelectric power plants;
- Phasing out the use of ozone depleting substances (CFCs) by 1995, replacing them with safer alternatives (eg CFC 22).

All major thermal power plants are being required to install filters for sulphur dioxides and nitrogen oxides. However, the capital required may not be available.

MPE standards for emissions into the atmosphere are determined following the recommendations given in the *Methods for Calculation of Noxious Substances — Concentrations in the Atmosphere Emitted by Industrial Enterprises — OND 86 and in Instructions for Setting the Rates of Emissions of Noxious Substances into the Atmosphere and Surface Waters*. Standards are registered in the manner prescribed in *Guidelines on the Preparation and Registration of Draft MPE Standards for Emissions into the Atmosphere*.

The specific emission limits for plants are set using simplified dispersion algorithms used in the former USSR.

7.5.3 *Technology based standards*

In cases where it is technically impossible for an enterprise to achieve MPE standards because of the absence or low capacity of air treatment equipment TPE standards are applied until techniques to achieve ways to meet MPE standards are introduced. TPE standards are based on emissions achievable with the existing technology.

7.6 Permitting process

7.6.1 Authorities
Permits are issued by regional Environmental Protection Departments.

7.6.2 Application requirements
The procedure for obtaining an environmental permit is set out in EPD *Order No. 11 — The Procedure For Establishment of Standards for Emission of Pollutants into the Environment and for Issue of Permits for Usage of Natural Resources*, which was confirmed on 31 January 1991.

Operators must calculate MPE standards for the facility which must then be agreed by the EPD. All previously approved project documentation (for reconstruction, expansion, conversion of production, technical calculations, economic calculations, and development plans for the industrial area) must be evaluated. Enterprises which are being constructed or modified must have MPE standards established at the design stage (ie they must be included in the environmental section of the TEC, construction permit application).

For existing facilities discharging a substance into the atmosphere for which MAC (or an approximate harmless level) has not been determined, the enterprise must apply to the appropriate scientific organisation to establish the value and to evaluate the overall impact of the discharge of the substance. The enterprise must then submit a copy of its application to the appropriate regional EPD.

When assessing MPE standards for harmful substances, it is necessary to take into account the background concentration created by neighbouring sources. Calculation of background values takes into account only the emissions overlapping the impact zone of the enterprise in question. The list of enterprises, parameters of sources of pollution, and the volumes of emissions needed to conduct these calculations are provided by the regional EPDs in accordance with guidelines on background concentrations.

To obtain the background concentration values or data to calculate them, an application should be submitted to the appropriate regional EPD containing the following information:

- The name and address of the organisation;
- The city for which the background information is needed;
- The enterprise to which the background value is assigned, indicating whether it is currently in operation, under construction, under reconstruction, or under expansion;
- The address of the enterprise, description of its location in the General Plan of the city. In a case where the enterprise has several production sites or the background values are needed for several enterprises, the data is presented for each of the sites/enterprises separately, together with short descriptions of site locations;
- A list of the harmful substances which are emitted by the enterprise (plant) into the atmosphere;
- The time period over which the background values are requested; the duration of construction, reconstruction, or expansion, the schedule for the beginning of production or when full production capacity will be reached.

In certain cases, the MPE standards set in a permit may be modified by the EPD, eg where there are changes in the ecological situation, plant closures, establishment of new pollution sources, conversion of technology, conversion of production, or the implementation of more effective pollution abatement techniques.

7.6.3 Fees
There are no charges for permitting.

7.6.4 Timing
The initial stage of permitting leading to the draft permit, generally takes 30 days. However, for proposed facilities or modifications to existing facilities the process is closely linked to the EIA process and the overall time may be extended to several months depending upon the size and complexity of the facility. In addition, the pre-operation review and determination of the final permit is to be carried out within 15 days of application.

7.6.5 Permit conditions
As the basis for the setting of standards, all industrial enterprises and enterprises emitting noxious substances must establish an "inventory" of sources of pollution. Inventories of pollutants are based on field measurements carried out in accordance with existing monitoring standards and the recommendations approved by the EPD.

MPE standards are written into the permit for every substance emitted and for every source of pollution on the condition that the volume of pollutants emitted in combination with the emissions from other sources in the area do not exceed the MAC standards.

When the technological aspects of production, have been evaluated the total emission standard is determined based on MPEs (or TPEs) of individual sources of pollution. The annual emissions standards are determined in accordance with the average annual emissions and depend on changes in operation, characteristics of technological processes, equipment, raw materials, fuel, etc. It is also necessary to evaluate and categorise emergency emissions in the calculation of the MPE.

If it is not possible to achieve the MPE standard, reduction of emissions can be carried out in a staged manner. For every stage of the reduction process, the TPE and the necessary steps to reduce the emissions, and the persons responsible for implementation of said steps should be determined.

The *Law on Environmental Protection 1992* imposes the general requirement that operators of "potentially hazardous" facilities must monitor environmental pollution and its impact on the environment. ("Potentially hazardous" is not defined.) Operators of facilities must keep records of the use of natural resources and on the releases of pollutants to the environment.

7.7 Charges for emissions

According to the *Law on Taxes on Environmental Pollution 1991*, charges for air emissions are to be paid according to the volume and environmental hazard level of the emission in question. Charges set out in the 1991 Law range from 1–6.3 million rubles.

375

7.8 Public participation

7.8.1 Public access to information

Operators of facilities which are "potentially hazardous to the environment" (not defined) are required under the *Law on Environmental Protection 1992* to make available to the public information on pollution from their operations. The Law also gives citizens the right to receive accurate and up to date information on environmental quality.

7.8.2 Provision of information

State authorities have a duty under the *Law on Environmental Protection 1992* to announce publicly plans for economic activities which may have a hazardous impact on the environment.

7.8.3 Public consultation

Under the 1992 Law, citizens have the right to take part in discussions relating to projects for establishing facilities and demand that activities which are hazardous to the environment are terminated. The public also has the right to request that sanctions are taken against those guilty of endangering the environment, and officers who are not fulfilling their duties.

Detailed provisions relating to public participation and the role of the investor have not yet been determined and are expected in future legislation.

7.9 Enforcement

7.9.1 Compliance checking and monitoring

Inspection is carried out by the regional EPD according to an inspection checklist which includes the verification and enforcement of pollution taxes and checking of the operators' monitoring data.

7.9.2 Sanctions

If facilities do not comply with requirements fines can be imposed, permits revoked, or their activity halted. Fines range between 100–4,000 Lithuanian talonas. If the operator conceals or falsifies nformation on discharges, a charge ten times the standard tax is imposed.

8. Water requirements applicable to the operation of industrial and commercial facilities

8.1 Summary

Authorities:	Regional Environmental Protection Department (EPD).
Types of Activities:	*Part I Permit*: Facilities taking in, consuming, or transferring more than 10 m³ of water per day.

	Part II Permit: Facilities discharging more than 5 m^3 of polluted sewage into their own sewage system and further discharging that into surface water bodies or into accumulation reservoirs for filtration or to agricultural irrigation fields.
Permits:	Part I permit for water use. Part II permit for discharge of pollutants with sewage water.
Timing:	30 days in general, although can be extended, depending on the EIA process (see *Section 5*).
Public Information:	State authorities have a duty to publicly announce plans for economic activities which may have a hazardous impact on the environment.
Public Consultation:	Citizens have the right to take part in discussions relating to proposals for establishing facilities and to demand that activities which are hazardous to the environment are terminated. The public also has the right to request sanctions on those endangering the environment.

8.2 Sources of legislation relating to water requirements

- *Law on Environmental Protection 1992;*
- *Law on Taxes on Environmental Pollution 1991;*
- *Decision No. 190 on Taxes on Natural Resources 1991;*
- *Environmental Protection Department Order No. 11 Procedure for Establishment of Standards for Determining Environmental Pollution Standards and for Issue of Permits for Usage of Natural Resources.*

8.3 Water management

8.3.1 Water quality categories

Water quality standards are defined in terms of the Maximum Allowable Concentrations (MACs) for household/service sector water use, for recreational water use, and for fishery use, groundwater, and surface water. Surface waters are further differentiated into lakes and rivers.

8.3.2 Water management bodies

The national and regional Environmental Protection Departments are responsible for water management.

8.4 *Activities subject to water use and discharge regulation*

8.4.1 *Water use*
Facilities which are required to obtain a Part I permit as part of the integrated environmental Permit for the Usage of Natural Resources relating to water use, are those "taking in, consuming, or transferring more than 10 m³ of water per day".

8.4.2 *Water discharge*
Facilities which are required to obtain a Part II Permit for the purposes of the Permit for the Usage of Natural Resources relating to discharge of pollutants with sewage water are those "discharging more than 5 m³ per day of polluted sewage per day into their own sewage system and further discharging that into surface water bodies or into accumulation reservoirs for filtration or to agricultural irrigation fields".

8.5 *Standards*

8.5.1 *Ambient quality standards*
All former USSR standards have been adopted and remain in force, to the extent that they do not conflict with Lithuanian law, until their repeal or replacement. The substances regulated are listed in *Table 8.5.1(a)*.

Table 8.5.1(a)   Regulated Water Pollutants

- suspended sol
- chloride
- sulphate
- BOD21
- COD
- nitrate, nitrite
- ammonia, phosphate
- detergents (eugenic, non-eugenic)
- iron
- Caprolactam
- fat substances
- tannin
- lignosulphanic acids
- furfurol (C₄H₃O)
- oil products
- phenol
- fluoride
- methanol
- formaldehyde
- sulphite, thiosulphate, sulphide
- active chloride
- cyanide
- acrylonitrile
- chromium III and VI
- nickel
- cadmium
- copper
- zinc
- manganese
- lead

8.5.2 Discharge limit values

Discharge limit values correspond to the water contamination standards accepted by the Helsinki Convention on the Protection of the Marine Environment of the Baltic Sea Area (1974), specifically:

- BOD5 — 15 mg/l.
- Nitrogen — 8-12 mg/l.
- Phosphorus — 1.5 mg/l.

Discharge limit values for other substances are developed case-by-case based on ambient quality standards and are written into permits.

Lithuania aims to achieve EC water quality and sewage discharge standards, however economic conditions makes the achievement of this goal difficult. The Environmental Protection Board has requested funds from the state budget for the development of standards.

8.5.3 Technology based standards

Where existing wastewater treatment technology at a facility is not adequate to meet appropriate discharge standards a temporary permit may be issued based on the capability of the existing equipment.

8.6 Water use permitting process

8.6.1 Authorities

The regional Environmental Protection Departments are responsible for issuing permits.

8.6.2 Application requirements

Application for permits for water use and sewage discharge, as part of the Permit for Usage of Natural Resources is closely linked to the EIA process. Initially, a draft permit is issued, on the basis of information provided in the EIA application. Subsequently, and prior to starting up a new or modified facility, a pre-operation review must be carried out by the regional EPD. The review is carried out to ensure that the facility complies with requirements set out in the draft permit. If the facility is found to be in compliance, a final permit is issued.

Where it is proposed to modify an existing facility or process, it is necessary to apply for a modified permit. The following information must be provided:

- An application describing the reasons for a change in the permit;
- An information sheet on the fulfilment of the requirements contained in the current permit as well as implementation of foreseen measures;
- Data on compliance with environmental quality norms fixed for discharge and emissions as well as data on the results of control measures.

8.6.3 Fees

There are no charges for permitting.

8.6.4 Timing

The initial stage of permitting leading to the draft permit, generally takes 30 days. However, the process is closely linked to the EIA process and the overall time is likely to range from a few weeks to several months depending upon the size and complexity of the facility. Additionally, the pre-operation review and determination of the final permit is to be carried out within 15 days of application.

8.6.5 Permit conditions

Conditions may be attached to permits governing quantities of water used and the source of water.

8.7 Water discharge permitting process

8.7.1 Authorities

Permits for wastewater discharge are issued by the regional EPD.

8.7.2 Application requirements

Permitting requirements are outlined in *EPD Order No. 11 The Procedure for Determining Environmental Pollution Standards and for Issue of Permits for Usage of Natural Resources*, which was confirmed on 31 January 1991.

Operators whose economic or other activities have a negative effect on the environment must prepare a calculation of the maximum discharge which does not exceed the receiving water quality standards established in The *Rules for Protection of Surface Waters from Sewage Pollution* (USSR). The maximum discharge must be agreed by the EPD.

In cases where the enterprise is discharging a substance into the water for which a maximum allowable concentration MAC has not been determined, the enterprise must apply to the appropriate scientific organisation to establish these values and to evaluate the overall impact of the discharge of the substance. The enterprise must then submit a copy of its application to the appropriate regional EPD. The maximum permissible emission (MPE) standard is then determined based on the existing situation.

In cases where it is not technically possible for an enterprise to achieve MPE standards because of the absence, or low capacity of, wastewater treatment equipment Temporary Permissible Emission (TPE) standards are applied until techniques to meet MPE standards are introduced.

The MPE standards may be revised by the EPD for example where there are changes in the ecological situation, plant closures, establishment of new pollution sources, conversion of technology, conversion of production, or the implementation of more effective pollution abatement techniques.

As the basis for the setting of standards, all industrial enterprises and enterprises discharging emitting noxious substances must establish an `inventory' of sources of pollution.

The decision to issue the Permit for Usage of Natural Resources is based on the review by the EPD of submitted MPE or TPE standards, and in some cases on data of actual discharges of pollutants. The permit is issued for a five year term, but MPE or TPE standards for the volume of emissions to surface waters are usually fixed for one year. The standards are subsequently reviewed annually.

Application for the Permit for Usage of Natural Resources is closely linked to the Environmental Impact Assessment process and application. Information produced in the EIA application will form the basis for integrated permitting process.

In applying for a modified permit for an existing facility, eg where it is proposed to alter the facility or processes, it is necessary to provide the following:

- An application describing the reasons for a change in the permit;
- An information sheet on the fulfilment of the requirements contained in the current permit as well as implementation of foreseen measures;
- Data on compliance with environmental quality norms fixed for discharges and emissions as well as data on the results of control measurements.

Prior to starting up a new or modified facility, a pre-operation review must be carried out by the regional EPD. The review is carried out to ensure that the facility complies with requirements set out in the draft permit. If the facility is found to be in compliance, the final permit is issued.

8.7.3 Fees
There are no charges for permitting.

8.7.4 Timing
The initial stage of permitting leading to the draft permit, generally takes 30 days. However, the process is closely linked to the EIA process and the overall time is likely to range from a few weeks to several months depending upon the size and complexity of the facility. Additionally, the pre-operation review and determination of the final permit is to be carried out within 15 days of application.

8.7.5 Permit conditions
As the basis for the setting of standards, all industrial enterprises and enterprises emitting noxious substances must establish an "inventory" of sources of pollution for existing facilities. Inventories of pollutants are based on field measurements following the existing monitoring standards and the recommendations approved by the EPD.

MPE standards are fixed for every substance discharged and for every source of pollution on the condition that the volume of pollutants discharged in combination with the discharges from other sources in the area do not exceed the MAC standards.

If it is not possible to achieve the MPE standard, reduction of discharges can be carried out in a staged manner. For every stage of the reduction process, the TPE and the necessary steps to reduce the emissions, and the persons responsible for implementation of said steps should be determined.

When the technological aspects of production have been evaluated the total discharges standard is determined based on MPEs (or TPEs) of individual sources of pollution. The annual discharges standards are determined in accordance with the average annual discharges and depend on changes in operation, characteristics of technological processes, equipment, raw materials, fuel, etc. It is also necessary to evaluate and categorise emergency discharges in the calculation of the MPE.

The *Law on Environmental Protection 1992* imposes the general requirement that operators of "potentially hazardous" facilities must monitor environmental pollution and its impact on the environment. ("Potentially hazardous" is not defined.) Operators of facilities must keep records of the use of natural resources and on the releases of pollutants to the environment.

8.8 Water charges

8.8.1 Water use
Taxes for ground and surface water use are imposed by *Decision No. 190 on Taxes on Natural Resources 1991* and range from 0.01–0.1 ruble/m^3.

8.8.2 Water discharge
Wastewater discharge taxes are set out in the *Law on Taxes on Environmental Pollution 1991*. Taxes, range from 1–92.8 million rubles.

8.9 Public participation

8.9.1 Public access to information
Operators of facilities which are "potentially hazardous to the environment" (not defined) are required under the *Law on Environmental Protection 1992* to make available to the public information on pollution from their operations. The Law also gives citizens the right to receive accurate and up-to-date information on environmental quality.

8.9.2 Provision of information
State authorities have a duty under the *Law on Environmental Protection 1992* to announce publicly plans for economic activities which may have a hazardous impact on the environment.

8.9.3 Public consultation
Under the *Law on Environmental Protection 1992*, citizens have the right to take part in discussions relating to projects for establishing facilities and demand that activities which are hazardous to the environment are terminated. The public also has the right to request that sanctions are taken against those guilty of endangering the environment, and officers who are not fulfilling their duties.

Detailed provisions relating to public participation and the role of the investor have not yet been produced but are expected in future legislation.

8.10 Enforcement

8.10.1 Compliance checking and monitoring
Enforcement is carried out by the regional EPDs. Water use and discharges must be monitored by the operator and records kept under the *Law on Environmental Protection 1992*.

8.10.2 Sanctions

Sanctions available are administrative fines, permit withdrawal, and facility shutdown. Fines range between 100–4,000 Lithuanian talonas.

If the operator conceals or falsifies information on discharges, a charge ten times the standard tax is imposed.

9. Noise requirements applicable to the operation of industrial and commercial facilities

9.1 Summary

Authorities:	Environmental Protection Department.
Types of Activities:	All commercial and industrial activities.
Permits:	A separate permit for noise is not required. Noise is included in the EIA.
Timing:	30 days in general, although can be extended, depending on the EIA process (see *Section 5*).
Public Information:	State authorities have a duty to publicly announce plans for economic activities which may have a hazardous impact on the environment.
Public Consultation:	Citizens have the right to take part in discussions relating to proposals for establishing facilities and to demand that activities which are hazardous to the environment are terminated. The public also has the right to request sanctions on those endangering the environment.

9.2 Sources of legislation relating to environmental noise

- *Sanitary Norms for Inhabited Areas, No. 3077-84 1984;*
- *Aviation: Allowable Noise Levels for Inhabited Areas, GOST 22283-88 1988.*

9.3 Noise zones

All air fields must submit documents showing noise zones which have been co-ordinated with local government health protection services.

The following must be set out:

- Equivalent noise level;
- Maximum noise level;
- Night noise level.

Noise zones do not exist for industrial plants or streets.

9.4 Activities subject to noise regulation

All commercial and industrial activities subject to EIA must address noise issues.

9.5 Standards

All former USSR standards have been adopted and remain in force until their repeal or replacement. The following legislation applies:

- *Sanitary Norms for Inhabited Areas, No. 3077–84*, passed on 3 August 1984;
- *Aviation: Allowable Noise Levels for Inhabited Areas, GOST 22283-88.*

There are approximately 20 standards and methods in force from former USSR legislation including the following:

- GOST 23337-78 Noise: methods of noise measurement in residential areas and in the rooms of residential, public, and community buildings.
- GOST 15116-79 Noise: methods of sound insulation measurement of inner enclosures of buildings.
- GOST 20444-85 Noise: traffic flows; methods of noise characterisation and measurement.

9.6 Permitting process

9.6.1 Authorities
The regional EPD is responsible for noise regulation.

9.6.2 Application requirements
A permit relating specifically to noise is not required. Noise is taken into account in the EIA process as set out in *Section 5*.

9.6.2 Timing
Noise is taken into account in the EIA process. Approval of the EIA generally takes 30 days but it may take several months for developments reviewed at national level.

9.7 Public participation

9.7.1 Public access to information
Operators of facilities which are potentially hazardous to the environment (not defined) are required under the *Law on Environmental Protection 1992* to make available to the public information on pollution from their operations. The Law also gives citizens the right to receive accurate and up-to-date information on environmental quality.

9.7.2 *Provision of information*

State authorities have a duty under the *Law on Environmental Protection 1992* to announce publicly plans for economic activities which may have a hazardous impact on the environment.

9.7.3 *Public consultation*

Under the *Law on Environmental Protection 1992*, citizens have the right to take part in discussions relating to projects for establishing facilities and demand that activities which are hazardous to the environment are terminated. The public also has the right to request that sanctions are taken against those guilty of endangering the environment, and officers who are not fulfilling their duties.

Detailed provisions relating to public participation and the role of the investor have not yet been introduced but are expected in future legislation.

9.8 *Enforcement*

9.8.1 *Compliance checking and monitoring*

Enforcement is undertaken by the regional EPDs.

9.8.2 *Sanctions*

Violation of any noise standards result in fines according to the *Administrative Code*.

10. Hazardous and non-hazardous waste management

10.1 *Summary*

Authorities:	Environmental Protection Department.
Types of Activities:	All enterprises that are involved with waste management.
Permits:	Declaration of hazardous waste production and a Part IV permit for waste management.
Timing:	30 days in general, although can be extended, depending on the EIA process (see *Section 5*).
Public Information:	State authorities have a duty to publicly announce plans for economic activities which may have a hazardous impact on the environment.
Public Consultation:	Citizens have the right to take part in discussions relating to proposals for establishing facilities and to demand that activities which are hazardous to the environment are terminated. The public also has the right to request sanctions on those endangering the environment.

10.2 Sources of legislation relating to waste management

- *Law on Environmental Protection 1992;*
- *Order No. 16-1950 on Waste Standards 1989.*

Legislation on waste management, which will cover waste production, processing and disposal ("cradle to grave"), is being drafted. The draft law, supplemented by rules and regulations, will control:

- Accounting;
- Collection;
- Sorting;
- Transport;
- Recycling;
- Treatment;
- Disposal of waste.

10.3 Categories of waste

Waste is categorised in the *Law on Environmental Protection 1992* as follows:

- Toxic and injurious;
- Radioactive;
- Other waste.

Detailed categories of waste are not defined in the legislation.

10.4 Waste storage and treatment

10.4.1 Generator permits and other requirements

Under the *Law on Environmental Protection 1992*, "users of natural resources must keep records of waste and must comply with regulations concerning the identification, utilisation, storage, dumping, and treatment of waste."

The EPD has a system of declarations that requires the completion and submission of an annual return regarding hazardous wastes. Each waste is assigned a code and activities involving hazardous wastes must be recorded on a daily basis.

10.4.2 Operator permits and other requirements

The *Law on Environmental Protection 1992* states that "sites for the containment, storage, dumping, and treatment of toxic and radioactive waste shall be allotted by the Government of the Republic of Lithuania in the established manner."

The only hazardous waste known to be currently treated in Lithuania is the sludge produced by the plating industry. All other hazardous waste is being stored at the site of production. Plans for a waste treatment and disposal facility are being developed in co-operation with the Government of Denmark.

Part IV of the Permit for the Usage of Natural Resources relates to the storage of waste, landfills, and waste treatment. A Part IV permit is necessary for all enterprises which are involved in waste storage landfilling or treatment. Application for the permit is closely linked to the Environmental Impact Assessment process. Initially, a draft permit is issued, on the basis of information provided in the EIA application. Subsequently, and prior to starting up a new or modified facility, a pre-operation review must be carried out by the regional EPD. The review is carried out to ensure that the facility complies with requirements set out in the draft permit. If the facility is found to be in compliance, the final permit is issued.

For an existing facility where it is proposed to alter the facility or processes, it is necessary to apply for a modified permit. The following information must be provided:

- An application describing the reasons for a change in the permit;
- An information sheet on the fulfilment of the requirements contained in the current permit as well as implementation of foreseen measures;
- Data on compliance with environmental quality norms fixed for discharges and emissions as well as data on the results of control measurements.

Operators of waste management facilities must prepare draft standards on household, hazardous, and other types of waste in accordance with *Governmental Order No. 16-1950*, which was adopted on 9 February 1989. Draft waste standards should contain records of raw materials consumed in the production process, and waste generated. Departmental accountability, the control system, and technical solutions for storage and treatment issues should be listed, including sites and implementation procedures.

Since the methods for establishing waste standards, the evaluation of different technologies and types of production have not yet been prepared and the MPE standards for household, hazardous and other types of waste have not yet been fixed, actual waste volume should be regarded as a TPE standard.

A new system of permitting is proposed in the draft Law on Waste Management.

10.4.3 Fees
There are no charges for permitting.

10.4.4 Timing
The initial stage of permitting leading to the draft permit, generally takes 30 days. However, for new or modified facilities, the process is closely linked to the EIA process and the overall time is likely to range from a few weeks to several months depending upon the size and complexity of the facility. Additionally, the pre-operation review and determination of the final permit is to be carried out within 15 days of application.

10.5 Waste disposal

10.5.1 Generator permits and other requirements
Under the *Law on Environmental Protection 1992*, "users of natural resources must keep records of waste and must comply with regulations concerning the identification, utilisation, storage, dumping, and treatment of waste."

387

The EPD has a system of declarations that requires the completion and submission of an annual return regarding hazardous wastes. Each waste is assigned a code and activities involving hazardous wastes must be recorded on a daily basis.

10.5.2 Operator permits and other requirements

Operator requirements are as described in *Section 10.5.1*.

10.5.3 Fees

There are no charges for permitting.

10.5.4 Timing

The initial stage of permitting leading to the draft permit, generally takes 30 days. However, for proposed facilities or modifications to existing facilities the process is closely linked to the EIA process and the overall time is likely to range from a few weeks to several months depending upon the size and complexity of the facility. Additionally, the pre-operation review and determination of the final permit is to be carried out within 15 days of application.

10.6 Transport of waste

10.6.1 Labelling and containers

Requirements relating to waste labelling and containers are to be introduced by the draft Law on Waste Management.

10.6.2 Transboundary movement

The *Law on Environmental Protection 1992* prohibits the import of waste for purposes of storage, treatment or dumping. Controls over the transport of toxic and radioactive waste across Lithuanian borders are to be established on the basis of international treaties. Lithuania has indicated its accession to the Basle Convention on the Control of Transboundary Movements of Hazardous Wastes and their Disposal 1989.

10.7 Waste charges

Taxes for waste discharge range from 150–15,000 rubles per tonne depending on toxicity.

10.8 Recycling requirements

National environmental policy aims to promote recycling, but there are currently no facilities to carry out recycling on a large scale. The draft law on waste includes provisions for recycling.

The *Law on Environmental Protection 1992* states that "legal and natural persons shall be liable for toxic, injurious, and radioactive waste which is the result of production until it is recycled or treated in the established manner."

The *Law on Profit Taxes* provides an economic incentive for recycling by taxing recycling enterprises at a 15% rate instead of at the 30% rate customary for profits. The draft Law on Waste Management includes provision for state financial assistance for development and implementation of waste free technologies, recycling programmes and scientific research.

10.9 Public participation

10.9.1 Public access to information

Operators of facilities which are potentially hazardous to the environment (not defined) are required under the *Law on Environmental Protection 1992* to make available to the public information on pollution from their operations. The Law also gives citizens the right to receive accurate and up to date information on environmental quality.

10.9.2 Provision of information

State authorities have a duty under the *Law on Environmental Protection 1992* to announce publicly plans for economic activities which may have a hazardous impact on the environment.

10.9.3 Public consultation

Under the *Law on Environmental Protection 1992*, citizens have the right to take part in discussions relating to projects for establishing facilities and demand that activities which are hazardous to the environment are terminated. The public also has the right to request that sanctions are taken against those guilty of endangering the environment, and officers who are not fulfilling their duties.

Detailed provisions relating to public participation are expected in future legislation.

10.10 Enforcement

10.10.1 Compliance checking

The competent authority for waste regulation is the Environmental Protection Department.

10.10.2 Sanctions

Breach of requirements relating to waste management can result in administrative and criminal sanctions including fines and facility shut down. Administrative fines for illegal disposal of waste are set according to the class of hazard of the waste ranging from 45,000 Lithuanian talonas for "extremely hazardous" waste to 450 talonas for municipal waste. The draft waste management law is to establish a system of fines for non-approved or improperly stored waste.

11. Chemicals storage, handling and emergency response

11.1 Summary

Regulations on chemical handling storage and emergency response are currently being drafted. Regulations from the former USSR focus largely on occupational health and safety.

11.2 Legislation relating to chemicals storage, handling and emergency response

- *Law on Environmental Protection 1992.*

11.2.1 Storage and handling

The *Law on Environmental Protection 1992* imposes a general requirement that persons using toxic and injurious chemicals must comply with State regulations for the use, storage, transport or dumping of the materials. State regulations have yet to be introduced. Regulations of the former USSR on chemical safety are still in force but these focus largely on occupational health and safety.

The 1992 Law provides for lists of toxic and injurious materials to be drawn up and approved by the Ministry of Health and the Environmental Protection Department (EPD). Lists have yet to be produced. Legislation relating to ozone depleting chemicals is to be prepared by the EPD.

11.2.2 Emergency response

Article 24 of the *Law on Environmental Protection 1992* deals with emergency situations, which are defined as "a hazardous environmental state which, as the result of nature, accidents, economic activity, or other events, exceeds standards of environmental quality".

According to the Law, an area where an emergency situation has occurred can be declared a zone of ecological danger or ecological disaster (not defined) and the Law requires operators to:

eradicate both the cause and the consequences and inform the public, the local governments, the Ministry of Health, the Government, and the Department of Environmental Protection, and fulfil other requirements established by the administration.

The 1992 Law requires that the activities of facilities situated in zones of ecological danger or disaster are suspended, restricted or prohibited. Local authorities are responsible for emergency response in zones of ecological danger and the central government and its EPD are responsible for zones of ecological disaster.

11.3 Public participation

Under the *Law on Environmental Protection 1992* facility operators are required to inform the public in the event of an emergency situation.

11.4 Enforcement

11.4.1 Compliance checking
Enforcement related to the transportation or spill of chemical substances is carried out by the EPD.

11.4.2 Sanctions
Facilities may be subject to fines and shut down.

Annex A

List of Key Legislation

1. Environmental liabilities

- *Lithuanian Civil Code 1992;*
- *LSSR Administrative Violation Code 1990;*
- *Criminal Code;*
- *Law on Environmental Protection 1992.*

2. Land use planning

- *Law on the Fundamentals of Local Government 1990;*
- *Law on Environmental Protection 1992;*
- *Law and Resolution on Spheres of Business Activity where Foreign Investment is Prohibited or Limited 1991;*
- *Law on Procedures and Conditions for the Restoration of Land Ownership Rights of Citizens 1992;*
- *Law on Land Taxes 1992;*
- *Law on Land Reform 1992;*
- *Land Code 1970;*
- *Civil Code 1964;*
- *Lithuanian Construction 1992.*

USSR land use regulations

- OND 1-84, with supplements No. 3 and No. 6;
- SNIP Construction Regulations and Requirements;
- Sanitary Regulations, which regulate safety requirements.

3. Environmental Impact Assessments (EIAs)

- *Law on Environmental Protection 1992;*
- *Law on the Environmental Protection Department 1990;*
- *EPD Order on the Rules Determination of Environmental Pollution Norms and the Issue of Permits for the Exploitation of Natural Resources 1991;*
- *Interim Principal Law 1990;*

- *Government Law 1990;*
- *Law on the Fundamentals of Local Government 1990;*
- *Enterprise Law 1990;*
- *Law on Sheres of Business Activity wherein Foreign Investment is Prohibited or Limited 1991;*
- *Resolution on the Republic of Lithuania Law of Spheres of Business Activity wherein Foreign Investment is Prohibited or Limited 1991;*
- *Law on State Natural Resources 1991;*
- *Law on Taxes on Environmental Pollution 1991;*
- *Decision on Tax Rates of Natural Resources 1991.*

4. Integrated permitting requirements applicable to the operation of industrial and commercial facilities

- *Law on Environmental Protection 1992;*
- *Law on Taxes on Environmental Pollution 1991;*
- *Decision No. 190 on Taxes on Natural Resources 1991;*
- *Environmental Protection Department Order No. 11 Procedure for Determining Environmental Pollution Standards and for Issue of Permits for Usage of Natural Resources.*

5. Air emission requirements applicable to the operation of industrial and commercial facilities

- *Law on Environmental Protection 1992;*
- *Law on Taxes on Environmental Pollution 1991;*
- *Environmental Protection Department Order No. 11 Procedure for Determining Environmental Pollution Standards and for Issue of Permits for Usage of Natural Resources.*

6. Water requirements applicable to the operation of industrial and commercial facilities

- *Law on Environmental Protection 1992;*
- *Law on Taxes on Environmental Pollution 1991;*
- *Decision No. 190 on Taxes on Natural Resources 1991;*
- *Environmental Protection Department Order No. 11 Procedure for Establishment of Standards for Determining Environmental Pollution Standards and for Issue of Permits for Usage of Natural Resources.*

7. Noise requirements applicable to the operation of industrial and commercial facilities

- *Sanitary Norms for Inhabited Areas, No. 3077-84 1984;*
- *Aviation: Allowable Noise Levels for Inhabited Areas, GOST 22283-88 1988*

8. Hazardous and non-hazardous waste management

- *Law on Environmental Protection 1992;*
- *Order No. 16-1959 on Waste Standards 1989.*

9. Chemical storage, handling and emergency response

- *Law on Environmental Protection 1992.*

10. Other sectors

There is no specific legislation on the following:
- *Environmental audits.*

Annex B

List of Permitting and Enforcement Authorities

Regional Environmental Protection Departments

	Telephone
Vilnius	35 8086
Kauno	20 4381
Klaipedos	5 5059
Siauliu	2 9414
Panevezio	3 5409
Alytaus	5 2667
Marijampoles	5 0454
Utenos	5 8606

Annex C

List of Proposed Legislation

Laws are currently being drafted on the following:

- Protection areas;
- Protection and use of forests;
- Waste management;
- Protection of biological diversity;
- Protection and use of soil;
- Protection and use of coastal areas and the continental shelf;
- Water resources;
- Air quality;
- Measures to halt the pollution of the Baltic Sea.

Annex D

Environmental Standards

Environmental Quality Standards for emissions to air

The following examples are taken from former USSR standards.

Substance	*24 h Maximum allowable concentration (mg/m^3)*
SO_2	0.50
NO	0.085
Paticulates	0.05
Lead	0.003
Nickel	0.001
Cadmium	0.003
Mercury	0.003
Cobalt	0.001
Copper	0.002
Tungsten	0.001
Chlorine	0.100
Flourine	0.02
Acetone	0.35

Annex E

International Conventions

National legislation is to be introduced to implement the following international agreements which Lithuania has signed:

- Convention on the Protection of the Marine Environment of the Baltic Sea Area (Helsinki, 1974);
- Convention on Fishing and Conservation of the Fishing Resources in the Baltic Sea and Belts (Gdansk, 1973), and Supplementary Protocol (Warsaw, 1982);
- Basle Convention on the Control of Transboundary Movements of Hazardous Wastes and their Disposal (Basle, 1989);
- Convention on the Conservation of European Wildlife and Natural Habitats (Bern, 1979);
- Convention on the Conservation of Migratory Species of Wild Animals (Bonn, 1979);
- Convention on Long-range Transboundary Air Pollution (Geneva, 1979) and its related protocols;
- Vienna Convention for the Protection of the Ozone Layer (Vienna, 1985) and the Montreal Protocol (1987), as amended;
- IAEA Convention on Early Notification of Nuclear Accidents (Vienna, 1986) and the related convention on assistance.

Poland

Prepared for the European Bank for Reconstruction and Development and the
Commission of the European Communities by
White & Case*

1. Overview

1.1 The Guidelines

1.1.1 Background

Investments in Poland are subject to many legal and economic requirements. This document focuses specifically on those compliance, operational and liability issues which arise from environmental protection measures and affect investments.

The Guidelines are intended to enable investors to familiarise themselves with the basic environmental regulatory regime relating to commercial and industrial greenfield site developments, joint venture operations or company acquisitions in Poland.

The Guidelines review institutional arrangements for environmental control, legislative requirements and procedures, time implications for permitting, public access to information, liability and sanctions. Because environmental policy, legislation and infrastructure in Poland are currently undergoing radical changes the review covers both current and proposed future arrangements.

Guidelines for the following CEE countries have been prepared on behalf of the European Bank for Reconstruction and Development and the Commission of the European Communities by Environmental Resources Limited and White & Case:

- Bulgaria;[1]
- Czech Republic and Slovak Republic;[1]

[1]   Guidelines prepared by White & Case.

*   White & Case acknowledges the valuable contribution in the preparation of the *Investors' Environmental Guidelines: Poland* of Richard A. Horsch, Esq., Sophia Drewnowski, Esq., Joanna Gomula, Esq. and Andrzej Blach, Esq. of White & Case.
    White & Case would like to thank Dr. Stanislaw Wajda and Professor Wojchiech Radecki who acted as consultants to White & Case in its preparation of these Guidelines.

- Estonia;[2]
- Hungary;[1]
- Latvia;[2]
- Lithuania;[2]
- Poland;[1]
- Romania.[2]

These Guidelines present a description of the environmental regulatory framework as of February 1993. They provide a first step for investors in understanding environmental requirements but do not substitute for specific legal advice relating to particular sites.

Administrative and legal arrangements for environmental regulation are in a transition phase in the countries covered by these Guidelines. Requirements and implementation systems are subject to change. Investors are advised to discuss details of requirements with the authorities and check for any changes which may have taken place since February 1993.

1.1.2 Using the Guidelines

The Guidelines provide general guidance on environmental regulatory requirements applicable to foreign investment in commercial and industrial sectors of the economy. Some sections of the Guidelines, such as *Section 4* on Land Use Planning and *Section 5* on EIA are also applicable to other sectors of the economy such as agriculture, mining, forestry and fisheries. In relation to such types of activities however, it is advisable to review other applicable requirements which are outside the scope of the Guidelines.

Section 1 provides a quick reference to environmental regulatory requirements in two case studies, and in *Figure 1.1.2(a)* and *Figure 1.1.2(b)*. *Figure 1.1.2(b)* indicates how the Guidelines should be used by reference to the type of investment decision that has to be made.

The remainder of this section provides background information on the country and the following:

- Administrative structure
- Legislative process and key items of legislation
- Quick reference to the permitting process
- Enforcement
- Public participation.

Section 2 highlights the potential liabilities of investors. Liabilities potentially arising from past pollution to be taken into account at the time an investment is made and liabilities arising in the course of operating commercial and industrial facilities are presented separately. Additional details relating to specific sectors of control are provided in subsequent sections.

Section 3 identifies environmental auditing requirements and comments on the role of voluntary audits in achieving compliance.

---

[1] Guidelines prepared by White & Case.
[2] Guidelines prepared by Environmental Resources Limited.

Figure 1.1.2(a) Using the Guidelines: report structure

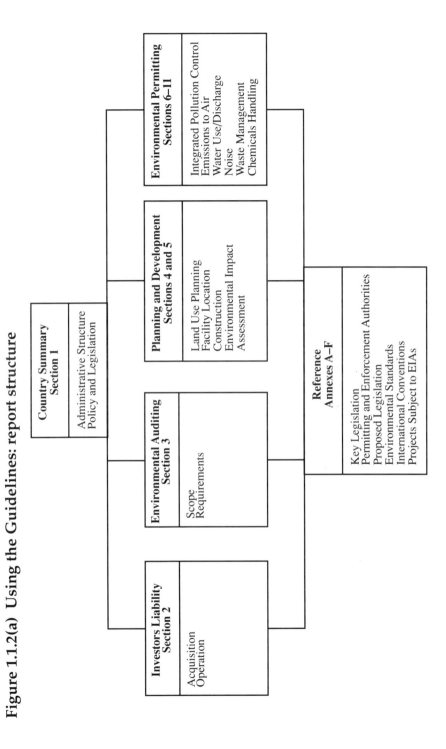

Figure 1.1.2(b) Using the Guidelines: summary by type of investment decision

Investment Decisions	*Environmental Concerns*	*Sections in Guidelines*
Choice of investment sector (eg commercial, services, manufacturing, energy)	Government and environmental bodies	1.4, 1.7, Annex B
	Existing and proposed legislation	1.5, Annex A & C
	Available forms of investment	1.2, 2.3.2
	Purchase of land	4.3
	Investments subject to EIA	5, Annex F
	Activities subject to permitting	6–11
	Permitting overview and examples	1.6
Development of a "greenfield site"	Government and environmental bodies	1.4, 1.7, Annex B
	Existing and proposed legislation	1.5, Annex A & C
	Purchase of land	4.3
	EIA requirements	5, Annex F
	Public participation	1.8
	Environmental standards	7, 8, 9, Annex D
Acquisition of existing facility and privatisation	Government and environmental bodies	1.4, 1.7
	Privatisation	1.2, 2.3.2
	Environmental liability	2
	Cleanup of contaminated sites	2.3
	Indemnification by government	2.3
	Environmental audits	3
	Environmental standards	7, 8, 9, Annex D
	EIA requirements (especially where modifications are made to existing facilities)	5, Annex F

Investment Decisions	Environmental Concerns	Sections in Guidelines
Redevelopment and expansion of commercial and industrial facilities	Government and environmental bodies	1.4, 1.7, Annex B
	Change of land use	4
	Construction permits	4
	EIA requirements	5, Annex F
	Permitting requirements	6–11
	Public participation	1.8
Operation of industrial and commercial facilities	Government and environmental bodies	1.4, 1.7, Annex B
	Environmental liability	2
	EIA requirements	5, Annex F
	Public participation	1.8
	Integrated permitting	6
	Air requirements	7, Annex D
	Water requirements	8, Annex D
	Noise requirements	9, Annex D
	Waste management	10
	Chemical storage and handling	11
	Permitting overview and examples	1.6
	Compliance with international law	Annex E

Sections 4–11 provide guidance on permitting and related regulatory requirements for setting up and operating a commercial or industrial enterprise. Key aspects are presented at the beginning of each section for quick reference. Each section identifies the following:

- Key legislation
- Activities covered
- Requirements and procedures
- Timing
- Public participation
- Enforcement and sanctions.

Sections 4 and 5 outline requirements and procedures relating to land use planning, facility location and construction, and environmental impact assessment ("EIAs"). *Section 6* indicates the extent to which environmental permitting is integrated. Permitting and other regulatory requirements relating to air, water, noise, waste and chemicals are set out in *Sections 7–11*.

Annexes provide quick reference to existing and proposed legislation, contact points for the regulatory agencies, environmental standards, ratification of multilateral international conventions and investment projects subject to EIAs which are specifically identified in legislation.

1.2 The country

The Republic of Poland has a population of 38 million and covers a territory of 323,250 sq. km. In 1991, following the first free parliamentary elections after World War II, Poland became a parliamentary democracy.

The country embarked on a programme of privatisation and reforms to restructure its economy. Central to this programme was the passage in July 1990 of the *Law on the Privatisation of State-Owned Enterprises* ("*Privatisation Law*") and the establishment in September 1990 of the Ministry of Ownership Changes ("Privatisation Ministry"). The government has adopted a multi-track approach to privatisation, including the sale of large companies through public offerings and trade sales to domestic and foreign investors, sectoral privatisation within individual industry sectors, liquidation of assets of non-viable companies and mass privatisation through the distribution of vouchers.

The economic policy of the former communist regime favoured the development of heavy industry without regard for environmental consequences. However, Poland's National Environmental Policy, published in November 1990 by the Ministry of Environmental Protection, Natural Resources and Forestry ("Environment Ministry") and adopted by the Polish Parliament in May 1991, set a new agenda based on the "polluter pays" and "user pays" principles, the universal right of access to information about the state of the environment and the concept of sustainable development.

Poland is pursuing political and economic integration with Western Europe. In 1991 Poland signed an Association Agreement with the European Community ("EC") which will establish free trade in goods, services, capital and labor between Poland and the EC. Consequently, environmental regulations and policies are likely to be harmonised with the EC.

1.3 Administrative structure

The Republic of Poland is a centralised country consisting of 49 Districts further divided into 2,459 self-governing Communes.

Most legislative and executive powers are concentrated at central government level and lie with the Sejm and the Senate — Poland's Parliament — and the Council of Ministers.

The 49 Districts have a total of 267 Regional Offices, headed by regional directors. The work of the Districts is supervised and co-ordinated by the Council of Ministers. Districts perform general executive functions which correspond to the tasks of central government. They also issue environmental and land use permits and play an important role in the enforcement of environmental regulations. Their planning authorities have responsibilities in the land use area. Regional Offices through their planning authorities carry out administrative functions in relation to construction permits.

Communes may exercise administrative powers pertaining to local matters which are not within the exclusive authority or jurisdiction of other governmental bodies. Communes through their planning authorities carry out functions on the local level with regard to land use matters. They also have responsibilities in the environmental area. Local ordinances are adopted by Commune councils.

Poland's administrative structure is undergoing a process of reform. It is proposed that 12 Districts will replace the existing 49 Districts. Each of the Districts will be divided into Counties. Communes will continue to exist but as self-governing authorities.

1.4 Government and environmental bodies

1.4.1 Ministries

Environmental decision-making is carried out principally by the central government. The most significant government institution in the environmental area is the Environment Ministry. The functions of the Environment Ministry are as follows:

- Protection of the environment;
- Management of natural resources;
- Management of waters and protection against floods;
- Protection and management of forests;
- Meteorology;
- Hydrology;
- Geology.

The Environment Ministry is empowered to:

- Determine the principles of state policy with respect to environmental protection, natural resources and forestry;
- Participate in social, economic and financial planning;
- Create economic, financial, organisational and technical conditions for environmental protection and the management of natural resources and forestry;
- Create conditions for economic, scientific and technical co-operation with other countries;

405

- Prepare opinions on scientific projects in its area of responsibility;
- Determine the principles of environmental protection and of rational management of waters, forests and mining;
- Determine the principles for the introduction of new technology.

The Environment Ministry supervises seven Water Management Boards in Gdansk, Katowice, Krakow, Poznan, Szczecin, Warsaw and Wroclaw. Their responsibilities include:

- Management of water resources;
- Construction and operation of water plants;
- Maintenance of water banks.

The Environment Ministry also supervises the following research institutions:

- Institute of Environmental Protection;
- Institute of Meteorology and Water Management;
- National Institute of Geology;
- National Institute of Forestry;
- Research and Development Center for Geological Expertise.

The Ministry of Environment also supervises the State Forest Boards which administer Poland's forests.

The Privatisation Ministry is primarily responsible for the supervision and co-ordination of the process of ownership changes in Poland including:

- Determination of fundamental policy principles for the privatisation of state enterprises;
- Execution of tasks specified in various laws regulating privatisation in Poland;
- Co-operation with trade unions, associations and state authorities in the establishment and development of Poland's private sector.

Pursuant to the *Privatisation Law*, the Privatisation Minister plays a major role in the privatisation of state-owned enterprises through their transformation into joint stock companies and their subsequent sale.

The Ministry of Health establishes and enforces health standards. It supervises the State Sanitary Inspectorate.

The Ministry of the Interior issues permits allowing foreign entities to purchase land in Poland.

1.4.2 Environmental bodies

The Environment Ministry enforces environmental laws in Poland through the State Inspectorate of Environmental Protection. This agency was created by the 1991 *Law on the State Inspectorate of Environmental Protection*. It exercises its functions through the Chief Inspector of Environmental Protection and District Environmental Inspectors.

The Chief Inspector is responsible for co-ordinating the State Environmental Monitoring System. Its purpose is to collect, analyse and make available data concerning the environment. Relevant executive acts have not yet been passed. Administrative authorities, Communes, universities and businesses will participate in the implementation of the Monitoring System.

The Environment Ministry is advised by a number of State Councils. The State Council of Environmental Protection is an advisory body to the Environment Ministry in matters of environmental protection. It is composed of 70 members who are appointed by the Environment Minister and issues opinions on environmental programmes and legislative proposals.

The State Council of Nature Protection is an advisory body to the Environment Ministry in matters of nature protection. It is composed of 30 prominent scientists, academics and environmentalists who are appointed by the Environment Minister.

The State Geological Service, under the supervision of the Environment Ministry, is responsible for the management of mining resources and their protection.

There is a proposal to establish a State Water Council which would be analogous to the State Council of Environmental Protection.

The Ministry of Health enforces health standards through the State Sanitary Inspectorate.

The Inter-Ministerial Committee on Ecological Matters and the Facilitation of Privatisation, established on 19 May 1992 by a joint decision of the Environment Minister and the Privatisation Minister, has the task of setting environmental standards in the privatisation process. One of its tasks is to propose principles for the apportionment of environmental liability, particularly for past pollution, between the State Treasury and other economic entities. The aim of the Committee is to establish an Inter-Ministerial Coordinating Unit at the Privatisation Ministry to provide solutions to specific environmental problems which may arise during the privatisation process.

The Commission on Environmental Impact Assessments created by a *Decree of the Minister of Environmental Protection dated December 29, 1989*, reviews Environmental Impact Assessments ("EIAs") of investments deemed to be of national importance or those considered exceptionally harmful to the environment. The Commission is composed of 75 experts nominated for a period of four years.

1.4.3 *Environmental Funds*

The National Fund for Environmental Protection and Management of Water Resources is an independent legal entity, supervised by the Environment Ministry. It provides financial resources for investments in the field of environmental protection. Poland also has 49 District Funds. The income of these Funds is derived from charges imposed on companies for use of the environment and fines for violation of environmental regulations. It is apportioned in the following way:

- 40% to the National Fund;
- 60% to the District Fund.

The National Environmental Fund assists the Environment Ministry in the following activities:

- Development of industries producing technical and monitoring equipment serving the purposes of environmental protection and water management;
- Development of potential expert resources for the implementation of investments in the field of environmental protection and water management;
- Development of a network of monitoring stations, laboratories and data processing centres dealing with the quality of the environment;

- Implementation of complex scientific, development and promotional programmes, as well as programmes of ecological education;
- Exercise of other tasks connected with environmental protection and water management, as determined in the plan of activity of the National Environmental Fund.

The income of the National Fund for Environmental Protection may also be used for the following purposes:

- Grants of interest-bearing loans;
- Grants of subsidies, especially in the case of projects involving more than one District;
- Investment in companies, including companies with foreign participation;
- Provision of pollution control equipment to newly established enterprises and new departments or divisions in existing enterprises;
- Grants of awards for activities connected with environmental protection and water management.

The National Fund for Environmental Protection recently created the Bank of Environmental Protection which makes loans to finance environmental projects. Some of the income of the National Fund is paid to the Bank.

The income of District Funds may be used for:

- Investments serving the needs of environmental protection and water management;
- Execution of tasks relating to the storage and recycling of waste;
- Construction and promotion of model monitoring and pollution control equipment;
- Development and promotion of new techniques and technologies, in particular concerning the treatment of sewage and waste;
- Protection against floods and other threats to the environment;
- Development and dissemination of technical information concerning environmental protection and water management;
- Verification of pollution monitoring data and preparation of data required for the calculation of environmental fees and fines.

Recent proposals include the creation of additional environmental funds at Commune level.

1.5 Environmental legislation

1.5.1 Legislative process

The supreme legislative body in Poland is the Parliament which is divided into two chambers: the Sejm — the supreme legislative body, and the Senate. All basic social, economic and political questions are regulated by Laws. Other sources of legislation can be found in Ordinances, Decrees and Resolutions.

The process of passing a Law is commenced at the initiative of either one of the following:

- Members of the Sejm;
- Members of the Senate;
- President;
- Council of Ministers.

A Law is prepared in a draft form within a Ministry and then presented to the Council of Ministers which decides whether to submit it to the Parliament. After two readings in the Sejm, the draft Law must receive a simple majority of votes before passing to the Senate for review. If the Senate introduces amendments or objects to certain provisions of the Law, such amendments or objections may be rejected by an absolute majority. The draft Law is enacted once it is signed by the President of the Republic of Poland and after its publication in Poland's official law journal, *Dziennik Ustaw*. The President has a power of veto over legislation. His veto power may be overridden by an absolute majority of the Sejm.

A Law may provide for the issuance of executive acts by the Council of Ministers or by individual Ministers. Executive acts, which are subordinate to Laws enacted by the Parliament, may take either the form of Ordinances or Decrees.

Ordinances are issued by the Council of Ministers or individual Ministers and are published in *Dziennik Ustaw*.

Decrees are issued by individual Ministers and are published in *Monitor Polski* or in a journal published by the issuing Minister.

Pursuant to the so-called Small Constitution — *The Law on Mutual Relations between the Legislative and Executive Authorities in the Republic of Poland and on the Territorial Self-Government of October 17, 1992*, the Council of Ministers may be authorised by the Parliament to issue Decrees with the force of law.

In case of a conflict, Laws prevail over Ordinances and Decrees, and Ordinances prevail over Decrees.

The Parliament and the Council of Ministers may also pass Resolutions. Parliamentary Resolutions usually address policy matters. Resolutions are published in *Monitor Polski*.

1.5.2 Legislation

The *Law on the Protection and Shaping of the Environment of January 31, 1980* ("*1980 Environmental Law*") is still the principal environmental framework statute in Poland and provides the legal basis for the regulation of air pollution, waste and noise. The main statute in the water area is the *Water Law of October 24, 1974* ("*1974 Water Law*"). Land use planning and permitting of waste storage, treatment and disposal sites are governed by the *Law of July 12, 1984, on Land Use Planning*. Several recent Decrees and Ordinances of special environmental importance are listed below:

- *Ordinance of the Environment Minister of February 12, 1990, on the Protection of the Air against Pollution*;
- *Ordinance of the Environment Minister of November 5, 1991, on the Classification of Waters and the Required Conditions for Waste Disposal into Waters or the Soil*;
- *Ordinance of the Council of Ministers of December 21, 1991, on Charges for Economic Use of the Environment and Making Changes Therein*, as amended by the *Ordinance of the Council of Ministers of October 14, 1992* and the *Ordinance of the Council of Ministers of January 26, 1993*.

New laws are currently being drafted on the following:

- Water;
- Land use planning;

- Protection of forests and agricultural lands;
- Emergency response;
- Waste management;
- Noise.

Several amendments to the *1980 Environmental Law* are currently under consideration. The concept of a new framework environmental statute which was initially prepared in a draft form has been shelved at present.

1.6 Overview of permitting process and other regulatory requirements

1.6.1 General

The principal permits and approvals required by an investor intending to build and operate a commercial or industrial facility in Poland fall into three categories: (i) land use and construction permits; (ii) EIAs; and (iii) operational requirements.

Land use and construction permits are discussed in detail in *Section 4* below. EIAs, which must be performed for certain projects, are discussed in detail in *Section 5* below. Operational requirements with respect to water, air, noise, waste, and chemical storage and handling are discussed in *Sections 6–10* below.

EIAs are required with respect to investments which are exceptionally harmful to the environment and human health, as well as to those investments which could result in a deterioration of the environment. EIAs may also be required at the discretion of the District.

As regards operational requirements, permits are required for air emissions, water use, wastewater discharge, and the operation of waste storage, treatment or disposal sites. There is no integrated permitting system in Poland. Investors need not apply for noise permits. However, Districts at their discretion may set noise levels for individual facilities if ambient noise levels are being exceeded.

Steps of the permitting process

- Where a facility is to be built on a "greenfield site", a location directive and a location decision must be obtained from the Central Planning Office, the District or the Commune planning authorities.
- If the "greenfield" investment involves the purchase of land by a foreign investor, a permit to allow the land purchase must be obtained from the Ministry of Interior. The same applies where the investor obtains the right of perpetual usufruct from the land owner.
- If an EIA is required, initial and detailed EIAs, where necessary, must be submitted with the application for a location directive and in some cases with the application for a location decision.
- Permits from the District for water use and wastewater discharge and air emissions must be obtained. Permits for the operation of a storage, treatment or disposal site, if necessary, must be obtained from the Regional Office planning authority.

- The investment implementation plan must be approved and a construction permit obtained from the Regional Office planning authority.
- Once the facility is completed, approval by the Regional Office planning authority is required before commencement of operations.
- Once the facility is completed, the District Environmental Inspector must be notified of the commencement of operations. If environmental requirements have not been satisfied, the District Environmental Inspector may halt the operations of the facility.

At present, the law does not require that permits be obtained in any special sequence, except that location directives, location decisions and approval of EIAs must precede construction permits. Usually, operational permits will be required before approval of the commencement of operations.

The principal steps of the permitting and approval process are summarised in *Figure 1.6.1*. The practical application of the permitting and approval process is illustrated in the two case studies discussed below.

1.6.2 Case study 1

For a foreign investor acquiring a greenfield site for development of a new paper mill, the permitting procedure would involve the following steps.

Land use

The purchase of land by a foreign entity requires a permit which may be obtained from the Minister of Interior. A company will be regarded as a "foreign entity" if at least 50% of its initial capital is owned by a natural person who is not a Polish citizen or a legal person having its seat abroad.

Since the construction of a paper mill would be treated as a "construction investment", the company must apply for a location directive, and a location decision. If the paper mill qualifies as an investment of national importance (e.g., employing over 500 persons) the location directive will be issued by the Central Planning Office, and the location decision by the District planning authority.

Environmental Impact Assessments (EIAs)

Because the investment is of a kind that could be classified as potentially harmful to the environment or could result in a deterioration of the environment, the application for a location directive should be accompanied by an initial EIA. A final EIA will have to accompany the application for a location decision if it is determined that the investment is exceptionally harmful to the environment.

Operating permits

Operating permits will be required before the Regional Planning Office Authority allows the facility to commence operations.

The following operating permits which are issued by Districts must be obtained:

- Water use;
- Wastewater discharge;
- Air emissions.

411

Figure 1.6.1 Environmental permitting procedure

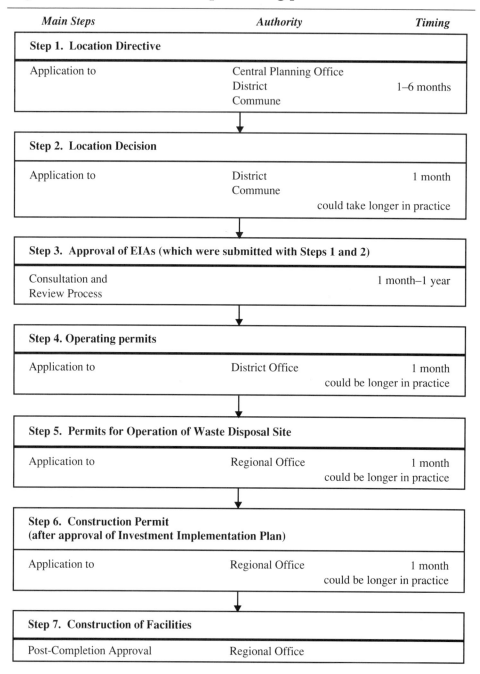

Main Steps	Authority	Timing
Step 1. Location Directive		
Application to	Central Planning Office District Commune	1–6 months
Step 2. Location Decision		
Application to	District Commune	1 month could take longer in practice
Step 3. Approval of EIAs (which were submitted with Steps 1 and 2)		
Consultation and Review Process		1 month–1 year
Step 4. Operating permits		
Application to	District Office	1 month could be longer in practice
Step 5. Permits for Operation of Waste Disposal Site		
Application to	Regional Office	1 month could be longer in practice
Step 6. Construction Permit (after approval of Investment Implementation Plan)		
Application to	Regional Office	1 month could be longer in practice
Step 7. Construction of Facilities		
Post-Completion Approval	Regional Office	

The manner of waste disposal, if such waste is deemed to be exceptionally harmful to the environment, will require consultation with the District and the District Sanitary Inspector. If an investor intends to operate a storage, treatment or waste disposal facility, a permit must be obtained from the Regional Office.

Construction permit

After obtaining a location decision, an approval of the investment implementation plan and a permit for the purchase of the land, the company must obtain a construction permit from the Regional Office planning authority. Once construction of the facility is completed, the Regional Office planning authority approves the commencement of the facility's operations. The company must notify the District Environmental Inspector of the commencement of the facility operations.

1.6.3 Case study 2

Foreign investor forming a joint venture with an existing company, with the joint venture acquiring two industrial plants and wishing to close one and refurbish the other to produce tyres.

Land use

The joint venture may require a permit of the Minister of Interior for the purchase of the two industrial plants. Such a permit will be required if the joint venture is "controlled" by the foreign investor, that is, if the foreign investor holds at least 50% of its initial capital. Depending on the scope of the refurbishment, a location directive and a location decision may have to be obtained.

Environmental Impact Assessment (EIAs)

Depending on the scope of the refurbishment of the second plant and initial EIA, a detailed EIA may have to be submitted with the application for a location directive and a location decision. In addition, the District, in its discretion may request an EIA of the investment whether or not a location directive or decision is required.

Operating permits

Operating permits must be obtained from the District before the Regional Office planning authority issues an approval to set the facility into operation.

The following operating permits which are issued by the District must be obtained:

• Water use;
• Wastewater discharge;
• Air emissions.

The manner of waste disposal, if such waste is exceptionally harmful to the environment, will also require consultation with the District and the District Sanitary Inspector. If an investor intends to operate a storage, treatment or waste disposal facility, a permit must be obtained from the Regional Office.

413

Construction permits

As regards the first plant, the Regional Office planning authority must be notified if buildings are to be removed. The Regional Office may decide that a separate permit to destroy the existing buildings is necessary.

As regards the second plant, if the refurbishment entails modifications to the buildings, a construction permit will be necessary. Even if no additional construction work is intended, the Regional Office planning authority might still have to issue a permit if in its opinion the change of the use of the site would adversely affect the conditions of the environment or the safety of humans or property.

Once the construction is completed, approval of the Regional Office planning authority is required before commencement of operations. The company must notify the District Environmental Inspector about the commencement of facility operations.

1.7 Enforcement of environmental legislation

The State Inspectorate of Environmental Protection acting through its District Environmental Inspectors is responsible for the enforcement of environmental regulations. It has the power to inspect industrial facilities and to issue decisions concerning their operation. In particular, District Environmental Inspectors may issue post-inspection orders which specify the nature of a violation and mandate corrective action. They may also issue orders to a polluting entity to halt all activities which are in violation of environmental regulations. The orders may take effect immediately if the activity in question directly threatens human life or health, or if there is a direct risk of substantial harm to the environment.

District Environmental Inspectors can prevent a company's use of any equipment which could cause harm to the environment. The prohibition may be lifted by the District Environmental Inspectors after the facility or equipment complies with the requirements of environmental protection. District Environmental Inspectors may also prohibit the production, import or introduction into the market of raw materials, fuels, machinery and other equipment which do not comply with the applicable requirements of environmental protection.

The State Inspectorate of Environmental Protection may initiate proceedings against persons responsible for violations of environmental rules. Cases involving violations of civil or criminal law are adjudicated by the courts.

In exercising its functions, the State Inspectorate of Environmental Protection must cooperate with other central government institutions and agencies such as the State Sanitary Inspectorate and the Communes.

The decision of District Environmental Inspectors can be appealed to the Chief Inspector of Environmental Protection. The Chief Inspector's decision can in turn be appealed to the Supreme Administrative Court.

1.8 Public participation

1.8.1 Public access to information

Under current environmental laws the community as a whole does not have a right of access to environmental information about specific polluters. The "right to know" as regards specific environmental matters is limited to citizens who have legal standing in administrative proceedings. Court proceedings are public, but most court decisions are not officially published.

1.8.2 Provision of information

Information on environmental protection is published annually for the whole country and selected regions by the Central Bureau of Statistics in the Yearbook of Statistics. Pursuant to the *Law of February 26, 1982 on State Statistics* (Dz.U. 1989, No. 40, item 221) all economic entities have an annual duty to make available information concerning environmental pollution to the Central Bureau of Statistics. According to a Decree of the President of the Central Bureau of Statistics published on 7 December, 1989 this information includes reports on air emissions, the condition of pollution control equipment, water management, wastewater, water pollution and industrial waste. Selected entities must submit reports on forest protection, water use in agriculture, forestry and fishery, communal wastewater treatment plants, nature and landscape protection and the protection of agricultural land.

Detailed information concerning environmental protection for all Districts can be found in the *Report on Environmental Protection* which has been published annually by the Central Bureau of Statistics since 1990.

1.8.3 Public consultation

Public consultation is required by law in a limited number of instances.

The process of drafting national, regional, and local land use plans requires the government to consult with the public. With respect to the National Land Use Plan, the Central Planning Office is required to consult with parliamentary committees and with state agencies, as well as with civic, professional and scientific associations.

No consultation with the public is required when the District issues environmental permits to a facility.

2. Environmental liability

2.1 Summary

Liability of Investors for Past Pollution:	Foreign investors assume liability for pollution when buying stock in privatised state-owned enterprises or when purchasing substantial assets of an enterprise. In principle the purchaser is jointly and severally liable with the seller; but when the State Treasury is the seller, the State Treasury's liability is less certain.
Government Indemnification:	The State Treasury may assume all or part of the debt of a company offered for sale to foreign investors. Indemnifications can be granted to investors in individual cases.

Investor Clean-up of Contaminated Sites:	No standards exist which specifically trigger a clean-up obligation. For ambient water standards *See Annex D.*
Civil Liability:	Fault-based liability as well as strict liability of owners and operators of industrial facilities.
Administrative Liability:	Fines and injunctions in cases of violation of the environmental laws.
Criminal Liability:	Various violations of environmental rules qualify as petty offenses and are punishable by fines and/or imprisonment for up to three months. Certain aggravated violations are crimes punishable with up to ten years of imprisonment.

2.2 Sources of legislation relating to environmental liability

- *Civil Code of 1964* (Dz.U. 1964, No. 16 item 93, as amended);
- *Commercial Code of 1934* (Dz.U. 1934, No. 57 item 502, as amended);
- *Petty Offences Code of May 20, 1971* (Dz.U. 1971, No. 12, item 114);
- *Criminal Code of April 19, 1969* (Dz.U. 1969, No. 13, item 98, as amended);
- *Water Law of October 24, 1974* (Dz.U. 1974, No. 38, item 240, as amended);
- *Law on the Protection and Shaping of the Environment of January 31, 1980* (Dz.U. 1980, No. 3, item 6, as amended);
- *Law of July 13, 1990 on the Privatisation of State-Owned Enterprises* (Dz.U. 1990, No. 51, item 298, as amended);
- *Law of June 14, 1991 on Companies with Foreign Capital Participation* (Dz.U. 1991, No. 60, item 253, as amended);
- *Ordinance of the Council of Ministers of January 23, 1987 on the Detailed Principles Governing the Protection of Topsoil* (Dz.U. 1987, No. 4, item 23);
- *Ordinance of the Council of Ministers of December 23, 1987, on the Amounts, Principles and Procedure of Imposing Fines for Violation of Environmental Protection Rules* (Dz.U. 1991, No. 89, item 404);
- *Ordinance of the Environment Minister of December 21, 1991, on Fines for Violation of Requirements Applicable to Waste Discharged into the Water or the Ground* (Dz.U. 1991, No. 125, item 557);
- *Ordinance of Minister of Health and Social Security of May 31, 1977, on the Requirements which should be Fulfilled by Potable Water and Water Used for Economic Purposes* (Dz.U. 1977, No. 18, item 72), as amended by *Ordinance of Minister of Health and Social Security of May 4, 1990* (Dz. U. 1990, No. 35 item 205).

2.3 Environmental liabilities for past pollution

2.3.1 Environmental liabilities and investment

An investor must be aware of two types of potential environmental liabilities when making an investment in Poland:

- Liabilities arising from past environmental pollution caused by the former operation of Polish state enterprises. These liabilities can encompass pollution at the site of the enterprise, contamination migrating from off-site landfills used by the enterprise, and damage claims of employees and nearby residents.
- Liabilities associated with the current operations of a facility by the investor. These liabilities can encompass violations of law relating to permitting and other issues and liability for environmental damage under civil and criminal statutes.

An investor's exposure to environmental liabilities arising from past pollution is discussed herein in *Section 2.3*. Liabilities associated with the current operations of a facility are discussed below in *Section 2.4*.

The exact extent of an investor's liability for past pollution will depend on a variety of factors including the form of the investment transaction and commercial laws governing that transaction, various environmental liability provisions and any indemnification provided to investors by the government. Should the investor become responsible for the remediation of past pollution, any applicable environmental cleanup standards will have a bearing on the cost of such remediation.

2.3.2 Types of environmental liabilities

Investments in Poland may take a variety of forms. The *Foreign Investment Law* provides for Polish joint ventures with foreign partners, or the establishment of companies wholly owned by foreign investors. Such enterprises may take either the form of joint stock companies or limited liability companies, incorporated under Polish law. Foreign investors may also acquire stock in existing companies. In particular the *Privatisation Law* provides for the possibility of acquiring stock in former state-owned companies which have been transformed into joint stock companies wholly owned by the State Treasury. The *Privatisation Law* also allows for "privatisation through liquidation" i.e., termination of the existence of an enterprise as a separate legal entity and the disposal of all its assets.

Stock transactions

Under general Polish commercial law principles, in the event of a merger of two corporations or an acquisition of one corporation by another, as a result of which shareholders of the acquired company receive stock in the surviving company, the surviving company assumes all rights and liabilities of the company being liquidated (Articles 285.3 and 465.3 of the *Commercial Code*). The liability of the surviving corporation does not depend either on knowledge or notice as to the existence of prior liabilities; it is unlimited i.e., it may exceed the actual value of the acquired company. While the *Commercial Code* does not specifically mention environmental liabilities, a reasonable interpretation thereof would include the company's environmental liabilities.

A foreign investor may choose to acquire stock in one of the new wholly Treasury-owned companies which were created through the transformation of state-owned enterprises. Pursuant to the *Privatisation Law* such corporations will acquire all rights and liabilities of their predecessors, unless the state chooses to assume all or some of the pre-existing liabilities in individual cases. As a general rule therefore, the new company is the only entity liable for past pollution and the investor may be exposed to such a liability to the full extent of his equity stake in the company.

Assets transactions

An investor may acquire the assets of a former state enterprise. The *Privatisation Law* provides for "privatisation through liquidation" i.e., termination of the existence of an enterprise as a separate legal entity and the disposal of all its assets. The *Privatisation Law* does not specifically determine the consequences of such sale with respect to environmental liabilities.

Article 526 of the *Civil Code* provides that the acquirer of an enterprise or a farm is jointly and severally liable with the seller for obligations stemming from the operation of the enterprise or the farm. In this context the term "enterprise" is used to describe the pool of assets. Thus, the buyer cannot invoke as a defence the fact that the liability arose before the transfer of ownership. The buyer is exempted from liability if he was not aware of the obligations despite the exercise of due diligence. The liability is limited to the value of the enterprise as of the time of purchase. It may also be limited or excluded with the consent of creditors.

The applicability of Article 526 to the sale of assets of liquidated state-owned enterprises involving State Treasury has never been tested in the courts. However, if one were to apply the liability principles of Article 526 to state-owned enterprises which have been liquidated pursuant to the *Privatisation Law*, one might conclude that the liability for past pollution lies with the State Treasury and is limited to the net value of the liquidated enterprise. Once the assets of the enterprise are sold by the State Treasury to a foreign investor, both the Treasury and the foreign investor might be jointly and severally liable for past pollution attributable to the assets in question.

In a recent legislative proposal, the government is seeking to clarify the responsibilities of the State Treasury in the sale of assets of former state-owned enterprises because of a possible conflict between the application of Article 526 to the sale of assets of liquidated state-owned enterprises and Article 40.1 of the *Civil Code*, which expressly provides that the State Treasury shall bear no liability for the obligations of state-owned enterprises.

Pending a clarification of the applicable law in this area, under general rules of law, the environmental liabilities associated with the assets of former state-owned enterprises can always be apportioned between the State Treasury and the foreign investor by drafting the appropriate contractual provisions in the asset purchase agreement.

2.3.3 *Governmental indemnification of environmental liabilities*

The *Privatisation Law* provides that prior to the offering of shares of an enterprise wholly-owned by the State Treasury to third parties, the Privatisation Minister, with the consent of the Finance Minister can assume all or part of the company's debt. The provision is applicable also to environmental liability. As a practical matter, the government is reluctant to grant indemnification for environmental liability to foreign investors. Nevertheless, a number of foreign investors have negotiated environmental indemnities for environmental liabilities arising from past pollution which are subject to financial caps and limited in time.

2.3.4 *Investor clean-up of contaminated sites*

Environmental clean-up standards

At present there are no legally binding clean-up standards pertaining to the remediation of groundwater pollution at the site of former state-owned enterprises. Ambient water standards are set out in the *Ordinance of the Minister of Health and Social Security on the Requirements which Should Be Fulfilled by Potable Water and Water Used for Economic Purposes* as amended by *Ordinance of May 4, 1990*. The *Ordinance* specifies ambient concentration level for a large number of substances in water.

The *Ordinance of the Council of Ministers of January 23, 1987, on the Detailed Principles for the Protection of Topsoil* states generally that land may be used only in accordance with the applicable land use plans and in compliance with the environmental rules and regulations pertaining to the protection of arable lands and forests. The *Ordinance* prohibits activities which may cause pollution and physical destruction or damage caused, for example, by discharge of wastewater and inappropriate storage of waste, use of chemicals, construction of buildings in a manner adversely affecting the topsoil, or running an industrial facility in a manner affecting the shape of the land and the topsoil. A company which carries out prohibited activities and causes damage to the environment may be required by District Environmental Inspectors to remediate the land to its "proper state". Section 2.4 of the *Ordinance* may require the restoration of the natural and commercial value of the damaged land, of the landscape etc. The *Ordinance* does not expressly require the return of the land to its original state nor does it set standards for the permissible concentrations of pollutants in soil.

No guidelines are in existence which interpret this provision nor does this provision appear to have been relied on to date. As a practical matter a number of investors, in their negotiations with the Polish government regarding the level of required remediation, have proposed to apply clean-up standards borrowed from various Western European countries such as the Netherlands, Denmark or Germany. It is to be expected that the Environment Ministry will impose uniform standards in the near future.

Escrow accounts

The Privatisation Ministry recently adopted a policy of setting aside part of the purchase price paid by investors for privatised companies into individual escrow accounts. The purpose of the escrow account is to provide funds for the remediation of past contamination which has been identified at the site of the privatised companies. Remediation activity must usually commence within one year of the sale, otherwise, the escrowed funds are turned over to the State Treasury. Usually, the escrow agreements are effective for three or four years from the date of sale. The establishment of escrow accounts requires the approval of the Minister of Finance. Use of the funds is supervised by the Privatisation Minister.

Environmental Funds

The Polish government has not specifically designated part of the income of its National and District Environmental Funds to finance the remediation of environmental pollution at the sites of former state-owned enterprises.

2.3.5 Case examples

- International Paper purchased a paper mill in 1992. It obtained an indemnification from the Polish government for any environmental liabilities arising from off-site pollution which may have been caused by the operations of the paper mill prior to purchase.
- In the sale of the Polam Pila Company to Phillips Lighting, B.V., the purchaser assumed the responsibility for site remediation in consideration for an increased number of shares of the company.

2.4 Environmental liabilities arising from facility operation

2.4.1 Civil liability

Fault-based liability

Article 415 of the *Civil Code* provides that any person who through his own fault causes damage to another person has an obligation to redress the damage. For damages resulting from a wrong, three elements have to be shown:(i) damage;(ii) fault; and (iii) a causal link between the damage and the wrong or omission. Fault is assessed pursuant to a two-part test: a violation of law must be established as well as wrongful intent or recklessness. The courts construe recklessness using a fairly objective standard of required diligence, corresponding to the standard of "a reasonable person acting under similar circumstances".

Unlike criminal liability, civil liability can be attributed to a legal person. Article 416 of the *Civil Code* provides that a legal person is obliged to compensate damage caused by its actions, such as the actions of a statutory body of a corporation. If the damage is caused by an officer of a state-owned enterprise the liability is borne by the enterprise in question (Article 420). For the purpose of such a liability courts define an officer of the state enterprise as any employee of that enterprise. Although in theory the plaintiff bears the burden of proving the wilful conduct or recklessness of a particular employee, the Supreme Court has held that it is sufficient for the plaintiff to establish that damage was caused by a wrong or omission of one of the members of a team of officers. The person at fault need not be identified. In effect, the state-owned enterprise is vicariously liable for the wrongful acts of its employees, possibly subject to a defence of lack of fault on the part of an employee, if such employee who caused damage to the plaintiff can be identified.

The State Treasury is liable for damage caused by a state official in the performance of his functions. Article 417 of the *Civil Code* defines state officials as employees of state authorities, administration or national economy, as well as persons acting on behalf of these authorities, elected personnel, judges and public prosecutors and members of the armed forces.

Strict liability

Strict liability, referred to in Polish law as the risk based liability, is imposed by Article 435 of the *Civil Code* on the operator of an enterprise set into motion by "forces of nature" such as steam, gas, electricity and liquid fuel. This provision has been interpreted to apply to any industrial facility.

The plaintiff has to prove the damage and a causal link between the damage and the operation of the enterprise. The operator may be absolved from liability in two situations:

- The damage was a result of a *force majeure* (extraordinary circumstances beyond its control, external to the operation of the enterprise);
- The damage was due exclusively to the fault of the injured party or a third person for whom the operator of the enterprise was not responsible.

Nuisance

Under Article 144 of the *Civil Code* owners of real property have a duty to refrain from activities which may cause nuisance to adjacent plots. Courts have established that air and water pollution and noise fall within the definition of nuisance. Under the *1980 Environmental Law*, not only owners of real estate, but also lessees have standing to bring this type of action.

Remedies

Polish law provides for monetary damages or specific performance.

- Pecuniary compensation:
  The scope of pecuniary compensation is limited to the "ordinary" consequences of the action or omission from which the damage resulted. An injured party may demand compensation for direct loss to his or her assets and for loss of expected profits. Non-pecuniary damage, such as emotional distress, in most cases cannot be compensated.
- Restitution to former state:
  Pursuant to Article 222 of the *Civil Code*, an owner of property whose rights have been or are being violated is entitled to demand the restoration of the property to its former state and an order of injunction against further violations. Proof of actual damage is not required. The injured party may usually choose between pecuniary compensation and the so-called "restoration to the former state". Should the restoration be impossible or entail excessive hardship to the defendant, the injured party is entitled only to monetary damages.
- Special remedies are available in order to prevent the damage from occurring. Under Article 439 of the *Civil Code*, if there is direct danger caused by lack of adequate supervision of the operation of an enterprise or the condition of a building or equipment, the person exposed to the risk may demand that the owner or possessor take the measures necessary to eliminate the danger or, should the need arise, that adequate security be provided.

Statutes of limitation

The general statute of limitations is three years with respect to claims concerning periodic performance or claims arising from economic activity, and ten years for all other claims. The *Civil Code* contains numerous special provisions which take precedence over the general rule. Claims based on liability in tort are time barred after three years from the moment the injured person learned of the damage and of the identity of the responsible person, or, in any case, after ten years from the date the wrong occurred. Wrongs constituting felonies or misdemeanours are subject to a longer, ten years statute of limitation.

Case Examples

• A Supreme Court opinion of 6 October, 1976 concerning strict liability, stated that even if an enterprise does not violate administrative standards of pollution, it is not released from civil liability for damage. Thus, compliance with pollution standards is not a defense in environmental damage cases. Furthermore, the causal link between the illness of the plaintiff and the operation of an enterprise emitting harmful substances should be presumed when a plaintiff is exposed to harmful substances and when the plaintiff's illness potentially could be caused by the pollution. The burden of proof shifts from the plaintiff to the defendant, who may escape liability only if the plaintiff's illness could not have possibly been caused by the pollution. The Court also held that in the case of several pollution sources (cumulative pollution), it is sufficient to demonstrate that any one of the sources could have caused the illness.

• A Supreme Court opinion of 29 November, 1982 involved the contamination of a well located on a farmer's land by the operation of a neighbouring enterprise. Although the enterprise was willing to pay pecuniary damages, the owners insisted on the construction of a new well. The Supreme Court decided in favor of the farmer and issued an order of specific performance requiring a "restoration to the former state".

2.4.2 Administrative liability

Types of administrative liability

Administrative liability arises in the event of violations of environmental permits or statutes, regulations and other legal requirements. The liability of a party under administrative laws does not preclude a civil law suit.

There are two types of administrative remedies: fines and administrative orders.

Fines

Fines may be imposed without proof of damage or establishment of fault by District Environmental Inspectors. They may be imposed for:

• Exceeding permitted emissions levels;
• Exceeding permitted noise or vibration levels;
• Storage or disposal of waste in places not intended for that purpose or in violation of a permit;
• Discharge of waste in violation of specified conditions or without a permit;
• Use of water in quantities in excess of permit limits.

In all cases, with the exception of water use, fines are obligatory in the event of a violation. The decision of a District Environmental Inspector may be appealed to the Chief Inspector. A final decision of the Chief Inspector may be appealed to the Supreme Administrative Court if it has been issued in violation of law.

Fines may be imposed by Communes for:

- Damage to green areas, trees and bushes;
- Removal of trees and bushes without a permit.

Fines must be paid within 14 days. In case of default, penalty interest will accrue. At the request of the fined party, the payment of a fine may be postponed or the fine may be paid in installments if the party agrees to eliminate the source of the pollution within five years. Decisions regarding the terms of payment of a fine are made by the agency authorised to impose the fine.

Administrative orders

In the event of permit violations, District Environmental Inspectors may at their discretion order the cessation of facility operations. Under the *1980 Environmental Law* however, District Environmental Inspectors must halt facility operations if they are a cause of deterioration of the environment and if there is threat to human life or health. Orders to halt facility operations may be lifted if adequate pollution control equipment is installed and the facility comes into compliance with the law.

Under the *1980 Environmental Law* a Commune may issue orders requiring the operators of machines or equipment to take adequate measures to limit its negative impact on the environment.

Under the *Water Law*, in cases of water management resulting in discharges in excess of permit levels, inadequate maintenance of water equipment and noncompliance with any other obligation regarding water, Districts may issue orders requiring compliance with environmental regulations within a specified period of time. In case of persistent noncompliance, Districts may halt the operations of an entire facility or parts thereof.

Under the *Building Law*, the authorities shall order a termination of construction work if it is carried out in a manner threatening to the environment.

Case examples
- During the first nine months of 1992 the State Inspectorate of Environmental Protection performed almost 12,000 inspections, as a result of which it suspended the operation of 15 enterprises; issued 13 decisions prohibiting the commencement of facility operations, and imposed 860 fines for non-compliance with environmental rules and standards which amounted to 146.1 million zlotys. Fines for the exceeding of permitted levels of pollution amounted to approximately 614 billion zlotys.
- In a ruling of 3 April, 1989 the Supreme Administrative Court upheld an order to terminate the operation of a chemical plant which for many years had been violating air emission standards. The plant appealed the order arguing that the cessation of its activities would be tantamount to its liquidation and would be in conflict with the *Law on State Enterprises*. On appeal the Court stated the order was based on a provision of the *1980 Environmental Law* which, in that case, has priority with respect to environmental matters.

2.4.3 Criminal liability

Under Polish law only natural persons may be criminally liable. There are two types of criminal offences in Polish law: petty offences and crimes.

Petty offences

Petty offenses are criminal offences punishable by up to three months of imprisonment or restricted liberty, a fine of 5 million zlotys, or a reprimand, imposed by special administrative boards ("Petty Offences Boards"). Petty offenses relating to environmental protection are envisaged in the *1980 Environmental Law*, the *1971 Petty Offences Code*, the *Law on Nature Protection*, the *Water Law* and the *Building Law*. A decision of the petty offences administrative board may be appealed to a court.

Under the *1980 Environmental Law* the following acts are classified as petty offences:

- Failure to perform required measurements by air polluting entities;
- Failure to take the necessary environmental measures when building constructions which may affect water resources or failure to observe the conditions for proceeding with constructions;
- Failure to comply with orders to reduce or stop air emissions or prohibitions related to protected areas;
- Destruction of plants or animals beneficial to the environment; use of chemical substances or technical equipment resulting in the destruction of trees;
- Failure to comply with regulations governing waste disposal;
- Failure to comply with regulations governing treatment of radioactive materials.

Under the *Petty Offences Code* the following acts are classified as petty offences:

- Water pollution;
- Failure to clean one's property;
- Destruction of trees or green areas;
- Causing damage to fields, forests or gardens.

Crimes

Crimes are criminal offences punishable by imprisonment or restricted liberty exceeding three months and/or a fine greater than 5 million zlotys. Felonies are punishable by imprisonment of three to 15 years. Decisions of criminal courts may be appealed to an Appellate Court. Article 140 of the *Criminal Code*, provides that it is a crime to intentionally create a grave public danger to human life, health or property resulting from the pollution of water, air or soil.

Pursuant to the *1980 Environmental Law* the following acts are crimes:

- Creating danger to human life or health through pollution of the water, air or soil;
- Neglecting to maintain proper pollution control equipment or failure to use it;
- Violation of duties connected with the protection of agricultural or forest land;
- Importation of waste from abroad.

Pursuant to an amendment to the *1980 Environmental Law*, which is not yet in force, importation of non-hazardous waste will be permitted.

3. Environmental audits

3.1 Summary

Sources of Legislation:	Audits are not expressly required by law but the policy of the Privatisation Ministry has been to require them as part of the privatisation process.
Scope of Activities:	Mostly performed in connection with privatisation of state-owned enterprises.
Approval Requirements:	No specific requirements as to the qualifications of consultants or as to the scope of an audit. No binding clean-up standards.

3.2 Sources of legislation relating to environmental audits

- *Law of July 13, 1990 on the Privatisation of State-Owned Enterprises* (Dz.U. 1990, No. 51, item 298, as amended);
- *Ordinance of the Council of Ministers of December 23, 1987, on the Amounts, Principles and Procedure of Imposing Fines for Violation of Environmental Protection Rules* (Dz.U. 1991, No. 89, item 404);
- *Ordinance of Minister of Health and Social Security of May 31, 1977, on the Requirements which should be Fulfilled by Potable Water and Water Used for Economic Purposes* (Dz.U. 1977, No. 18, item 72), as amended by *Ordinance of Minister of Health and Social Security of May 4, 1990* (Dz.U. 1990, No. 35, item 205).

3.3 Scope of activities subject to environmental audits and audit process

Polish law does not expressly require the performance of environmental audits as part of the process of privatisation of state-owned enterprises.

The policy of the Privatisation Ministry has been to interpret the *Privatisation Law* to require environmental audits. Article 20, paragraph 1 of that Law provides that: "an economic and financial study be prepared for the purpose of asset valuation as well as establishing whether the implementation of organisational, economic or technical changes is required." In practice, as part of the asset valuation of enterprises slated for privatisation, evaluations of the environmental liabilities of such enterprises have been submitted to the Privatisation Ministry.

The costs of environmental audits performed within the Ministry's sectoral privatisation programme are usually borne by the Ministry or the audited enterprise.

As a practical matter, environmental audits have been mostly performed in connection with the privatisation of state enterprises. The Privatisation Ministry, which has responsibility for the country's privatisation programme, has indicated that environmental audits are usually prepared in two phases. During phase one the company production history, compliance status, records of chemical releases, and environmental management practices are reviewed. Depending upon the results of the phase one audit, a phase two audit involving on-site testing of soil and groundwater may be performed. For the most part the Environment Ministry has not been involved in the supervision of the audits, and has had little influence on the scope of such audits. In 1991, the Ministry prepared a draft "instruction" on the performance of environmental audits during the privatisation process which has not been adopted to date. The creation on 19 May, 1992 of an Inter-Ministerial Committee on Environmental Matters and the Facilitation of Privatisation by a joint decision of the Environment Minister and the Privatisation Minister is expected to increase the influence of the Environment Ministry in the setting of environmental audit guidelines during the privatisation process.

3.4 Requirements relevant to environmental audits

Approved consultants

Environmental audits are usually performed by foreign consulting firms hired following a competitive bidding process, working together with Polish consultants.

Neither the *Privatisation Law* nor any guidelines or regulations establish the precise requirements or scope of environmental audits.

Applicable clean-up standards

At present there are no legally binding clean-up standards pertaining to the remediation of groundwater pollution at the site of former state-owned enterprises. Ambient water standards are set out in the *Ordinance of the Minister of Health and Social Security on the Requirements which Should Be Fulfilled by Potable Water and Water Used for Economic Purposes*, as amended by *Ordinance of May 4, 1990*. The *Ordinance* specifies ambient concentration level for a large number of substances in water.

The *Ordinance of the Council of Ministers of January 23, 1987 on the Detailed Principles for the Protection of Topsoil* states generally that land may be used only in accordance with the applicable land use plans and in compliance with the environmental rules and regulations pertaining to the protection of arable lands and forests. The *Ordinance* prohibits activities which may cause pollution and physical destruction or damage caused by for example, discharge of wastewater and inappropriate storage of waste, use of chemicals, construction of buildings in a manner adversely affecting the topsoil or running an industrial facility in a manner adversely affecting the shape of the land and the topsoil. A company which carries out prohibited activities and causes damage to the environment may be required to the remediate the land to its "proper state". Section 2.4 of the *Ordinance* may require the restoration of the natural and commercial value of the damaged land, the landscape etc. The *Ordinance* does not expressly require the return of the land to its original state nor does it set standards for the permissible concentrations of pollutants in soil.

No guidelines are in existence which interpret this provision nor does it appear to have been relied on to date. As a practical matter a number of investors, in their negotiations with the Polish government regarding the level of required remediation, have proposed to apply clean-up standards borrowed from various Western European countries such as the

Netherlands, Denmark or Germany. It is to be expected that the Environment Ministry will impose uniform standards in the near future.

Preparation and approval of remediation plans

In sectoral privatisations, such as the privatisation of Poland's heavy chemical and cement sectors, the Privatisation Ministry and its consultants have determined the scope and methodology of environmental audits of each company and the scope of remediation required. It is expected that in cases where investors will draw on funds set aside in escrow accounts to finance the clean-up at the sites of former state enterprises, the Privatisation and Environment Ministries will play an active role in the approval of remediation plans.

3.5 National experience with environmental audits

According to the Privatisation Ministry approximately 40 environmental audits have been performed, mostly at the investors' initiative in connection with the privatisation of Poland's former state enterprises.

The government's involvement in environmental audits of 20 large enterprises, which have been the subject of "trade sales" to investors, has been relatively limited. The investors have been primarily responsible for setting the scope of the audit and for the hiring of appropriate consultants.

4. Land use planning

4.1 Summary

Land Use Planning Authorities:	Plans, determining permissible use of land are prepared on the national level by the Central Planning Office and on the regional and local level by Districts and Communes. Location directives are issued either by the Central Planning Office, the District or Commune planning authorities. Location decisions are issued either by the District or Commune planning authorities. Investment implementation plans are approved and construction permits are issued by Regional Offices.
Required Permits:	A location directive, a location decision approval of an investment implementation plan and a construction permit.
Timing:	One month which may be extended. In practice, administrative procedures take longer.
Public Participation:	Drafting of land use plans involves consultation with the public.

4.2 Sources of legislation relating to land use

- *Law of March 24, 1920 on Purchasing Real Property by Foreigners* (Dz.U. 1933, No. 24, item 202, as amended);
- *Building Law of October 24, 1974* (Dz.U. 1974, No. 38, item 229, as amended);
- *Law on the Protection and Shaping of the Environment of January 31, 1980* (Dz.U. 1980, No. 3, item 6, as amended);
- *Law on the Protection of Agricultural and Forest Land of March 26, 1982* (Dz.U. 1982, No. 11, item 79);
- *Law of July 12, 1984, on Land Use Planning* (Dz.U. 1989, No. 17, item 99, as amended);
- *Ordinance of the Environment Minister of February 20, 1975, on Urban Construction Supervision* (Dz.U. 1975, No. 8, item 48, as amended);
- *Ordinance of the Minister of Administration* (now: Minister of Land Use and Construction) *of July 3, 1980, on Technical Requirements to be Fulfilled by Buildings* (Dz.U. 1980, No. 17, item 62, as amended);
- *Ordinance of the Council of Ministers of June 27, 1985, on the Classification of Investments and the Scope, Principles and Procedure of their Location* (Dz.U. 1990, No. 11, item 75).

4.3 Scope of activities subject to land use regulation

Investors planning to build new facilities on "greenfield sites" or to expand or redevelop existing facilities will have to comply with Polish land use and building regulations.

Land use plans which determine the permissible use of land in different parts of the country are prepared at:

- National level by the Central Planning Office;
- District level by Districts;
- Local level by Communes.

Land is classified by land use plans into three categories:

- Arable land;
- Forest land;
- Development land.

Acquisition of real property in Poland by foreign individuals and companies is regulated by the *Law of March 20, 1920 on Purchasing Real Property by Foreigners.* A foreign person wishing to purchase land or acquire a right of perpetual usufruct of land must obtain a permit from the Minister of Interior who issues the permit after consultation with the Minister of National Defence. No restrictions apply as to the specific type of land (agricultural, industrial etc) which may be purchased; however, a consultation with a relevant ministry, such as the Ministry of Agriculture, may be required. The rules apply to individuals who are not Polish citizens, to foreign companies and to Polish companies which are controlled directly or indirectly by foreign individuals or entities.

In particular a permit must be obtained by joint ventures incorporated as Polish commercial companies, if at least 50% of their founding capital is held directly or indirectly by foreigners.

Foreign investors and joint ventures with foreign capital participation do not need a permit to acquire other limited property rights including limited rights to occupy, use or build on land.

The siting of a development project in Poland takes place in two stages. An investor must obtain a location directive regarding his desired location of a development project or possible alternative sites. The investor chooses a preferred site from among those indicated in the location directive and applies for a detailed consent called a location decision which approves the details of the development project.

Both location directives and location decisions must conform with the relevant land use plans for that part of the country. Non-conforming location directives or decisions are void by operation of law.

Thus investment projects on "greenfield sites" and the expansion or redevelopment of existing facilities require a location directive, a location decision and a construction permit. Approval of the investment implementation plan must be obtained before a construction permit is issued.

In addition, investors may have to perform initial and final EIAs as discussed in *Section 5* below and obtain certain environmental permits which are discussed in *Sections 6–10* below. The environmental provisions of the *1980 Environmental Law* require developers to use materials and construction method which will not have an adverse impact on the environment.

4.4 Permitting process

4.4.1 Authorities

Location directives

Depending on the type of investment, as determined in the *Ordinance of the Council of Ministers of June 27, 1985 on the Classification of Investments and the Scope, Principles and Procedures of their Location*, different bodies have the authority to consider an investor's request for a location directive, as described below:

- The Central Planning Office issues location directives for 18 different types of investments deemed to be of national importance such as:
  (i)   Highways;
  (ii) Airports;
  (iii) Marine ports;
- District planning authorities issue location directives for 16 different types of investments deemed to be of importance at District level. These types of investments include construction investments and usually affect only one District;
- Commune planning authorities issue location directives for all other investments which are treated as local investments.

429

As regards investments considered to be exceptionally harmful to the environment, consultation must take place between the issuing authority and the Environment Ministry the District Sanitary Inspector in case of investments of national and District importance or with the District in case of local investments.

Location decisions

Depending on the type of investment, different bodies have the authority to consider an investor's request for a location decision.

- For investments of national importance, investments of importance to Districts concerning roads, and investments directly connected with national defence, location decisions are issued by District planning authorities;
- In all other cases, location decisions are issued by Commune planning authorities.

Construction permits

Regional Office planning authorities issue construction permits for the construction, assembly, refurbishment or destruction of a building or any part thereof or any of the above as regards advertising signs, works of art and other devices which affect the outside appearance of a building.

4.4.2 Application requirements

Change of use of arable land

Change of use of land may be done only through the amendment of land use plans. If the change concerns land which has been classified as agricultural or forest land, prior consent has to be obtained from the Minister of Agriculture or the Environment Minister at the request of the District, in cases specified in the *Law on the Protection of Agricultural and Forest Land of March 26, 1982*. In other cases, such consent is obtained from the district at the request of the Commune.

Location directives

The application for a location directive should include:

- General description of the project;
- Location of the proposed development;
- Anticipated level of employment;
- Anticipated volume of production and services;
- Description of the main buildings to be constructed;
- Expected requirements as to communication services, energy and water supply, sewage and waste disposal;
- Other necessary information and documents relevant to the specific project;
- Necessary environmental permits, such as air emission and wastewater discharge permits;
- Initial EIA.

If the development project is of national or district importance and could be considered exceptionally harmful to the environment or human health, location directives may be issued only after consultation with the Environment Minister and the Chief Sanitary Inspector. If the development project is of local importance only a consultation takes place on environmental issues with the District.

Location decisions

An application for a location decision should include:

- Land use and site plan indicating the proposed use of land, the basic architectural design of the buildings and other information which may be deemed necessary;
- Two copies of maps of the location;
- Extract from a land register;
- Certified copies of other documents required by law (e.g., mining licences);
- A final EIA if the project is of the kind that could be exceptionally harmful to the environment and human health, or which could cause the state of the environment to deteriorate.

With respect to investments which could be harmful to the environment, the investor must obtain consent of the District as to the specific environmental solutions to be adopted by the investor. Such solutions are evaluated by experts indicated by the District.

Construction permits

A construction permit gives its holder the right to undertake construction work. The definition of "building activities" includes the construction of new buildings and the re-development of existing ones.

Before a construction permit can be issued by the Regional Office planning authority, an investor must obtain approval of:

- Investment implementation plan which is required both in case of investments on "greenfield sites" and expansion or redevelopment at existing facilities;
- Any EIAs which may be required.

An application for a construction permit should include:

- Approval of the investment implementation plan by the Regional Office planning authority;
- A document confirming the investor's right to construct on the land (either title deeds or permission from the land owner);
- Environmental permits for the eventual operation of the facility;
- Other documents, as required in the decision affirming the investment implementation plan.

Stamp duty is payable with all applications for permits and upon receipt of the requested permit. The stamp duty ranges from 15,000 zlotys for the filing of an application to 30,000,000 zlotys for the issuance of a requested permit.

4.4.3 Timing

In most cases there is no special timing requirement with respect to the issuance of government permits or approvals and directives. According to the *Code of Administrative Pro-*

cedure which governs the location procedure, the issuing body must render a decision within one month of the date of application. This period may be extended which, in practice happens quite often.

Location directives

In practice most location directives for the construction of industrial facilities are issued within one to two months.

Location directives for projects involving the construction of residential buildings should be issued by District or Commune planning authorities within six months from the filing of the application.

Location decisions

The investor should file an application for a location decision within six months of obtaining the location directive. If the delay is justified, this period may be extended by the District or Commune planning authorities. The location decision expires if the investor does not obtain rights of ownership or usufruct with respect to the land which is to be the site of the investment, or if the investor does not apply for a construction permit within three years of the issuance of the decision.

Construction permits

The approval of the investment implementation plan expires if the investor does not apply for a construction permit within one year of its issuance.

If construction has not been commenced within two years of issuance of a construction permit or has been suspended for a period longer than two years the construction permit will expire.

4.4.4 *Permit conditions*

- *Location directives* contain information from land use plans concerning the site where the investment may be implemented and the conditions under which such implementation may take place.
- *Location decisions* address, among other things, changes in use of land, creation of protective zones, permitted levels of air emissions, terms of water supply and waste water disposal, terms of waste storage; other conditions relating to the implementation of the project.
- *Construction permits* specify the conditions of construction activities with special emphasis on human safety, property protection and environmental protection. Additionally, the Regional Office planning authorities may condition the construction of buildings on the implementation of measures to ensure the safety of humans and property.

4.5 Public participation

Land use plans

The drafting of national, regional, and local land use plans by the government must be done after consultation with various administrative authorities professional and scientific associations and non-governmental organisations.

The commencement of drafting of regional plans is announced in the local press. The land use plans should also be published in the District official journal.

The Districts responsible for preparing the plans establish advisory committees which should include representatives of civic, professional and economic associations, scientific institutions and experts. During the drafting process, Districts are obliged to consult with enterprises, civic and professional organisations and scientific institutions.

With respect to local plans, the commencement of drafting of such plans should be announced in the local press or in another customarily accepted way. Local self-governments and non-governmental organisations should be notified in writing. Interested persons also may submit their comments and conclusions to the Commune planning authorities. The publication of the plan should be announced in the local press at least seven days in advance. It should be made public for a period of at least 21 days. Interested persons may submit their comments to the plan. If such comments are not taken into consideration when adopting the plan, a written justification must be submitted to such persons.

Location decisions

The location of an investment which may have a serious effect on the environment involves consultation between the District or Commune planning authorities and non-government organisations which may submit their comments and reservations within 30 days of the notification. The state authority is obliged to consider such comments and inform such organisations of the outcome, although in practice this does not happen very often.

4.6 Enforcement

Construction permits

Supervision of compliance with construction laws is exercised by Regional Office planning authorities. During the construction of a facility, the Regional Office planning authorities which issue construction permits must suspend construction if no permit has been issued. If construction is conducted in violation of law or of conditions set forth in the permit or if it is conducted in a manner which could constitute a threat to persons, property or the environment, the Regional Office planning authorities may order that construction be halted.

As soon as the construction work has been completed, the District Environmental Inspector must be notified of the commencement of operations of the facility. The District Environmental Inspector may suspend facility operations if environmental requirements have not been satisfied.

5. Environmental Impact Assessments (EIAs)

5.1 Summary

Scope of Activities:	Mandatory EIAs are required for potentially harmful and exceptionally harmful proposed investments. EIAs are required for existing facilities at the discretion of the Districts.
Procedure:	Initial EIAs are submitted with applications for a location directive. Final EIAs are submitted with applications for a location decision.
Experts:	Consultants who perform EIAs are indicated by Districts from a list of experts designated by the Environment Ministry.
Timing:	For investments of national importance which are exceptionally harmful to the environment, the EIA Commission conducts an EIA review within an unofficial time frame of three months. Reviews can take longer. Other EIAs are reviewed by Districts.
Public Participation:	There are no formal guarantees of public participation in the EIA process. Nevertheless, non-governmental bodies can be invited to hear the discussions conducted by the EIA Commission and by Districts.

5.2 Sources of legislation relating to the environmental impact of industrial and commercial developments

- *Law of January 31, 1980 on the Protection and Shaping of the Environment* (Articles 68–70) (Dz.U. 1980, No. 3, item 6, as amended);
- *Law of July 12, 1984 on Land Use Planning* (Article 39) (Dz.U. 1989, No. 17, item 99, as amended);
- *Decree of the Environment Minister of April 23, 1990 on Investments Exceptionally Harmful to the Environment and Human Health and the Conditions of Environmental Impact Assessments Prepared by Experts for Investments and Buildings* (M.P. 1990, No. 16, item 126);
- *Decree No. 22 of the Environment Minister of December 29, 1989*, which created a EIA Commission to review EIAs of projects of national importance and exceptionally harmful to the environment.

5.3 Scope of activities subject to EIA process

EIAs of investment projects and facilities are either discretionary or mandatory depending on the nature of the projects and facilities in question. They are required in the following situations:

- *Existing facilities*:
  At the discretion of Districts existing facilities may be required to perform EIAs to evaluate the past and future impact of such facilities on the environment.
- *Potentially harmful investments*:
  They are mandatory. The investor must present an initial EIA with the application for a location directive. A final EIA need not be prepared if it is determined that the investment is not exceptionally harmful to the environment.
- *Exceptionally harmful investments*:
  They are mandatory. The investor must present an initial EIA with the application for a location directive as well as a final EIA with the application for a location decision.
- *Other investments*:
  At the discretion of Districts an EIA may be required with respect to any investment. The criteria for determining whether an investment project is exceptionally harmful are set out in the *Decree of April 23, 1990* (see *Annex F*).

5.4 EIA process

5.4.1 Authorities

- *Existing facilities*:
  At the request of Districts owners of existing facilities may have to perform EIAs.
- *Potentially harmful investments*:
  The investor submits an initial EIA with his application for a location directive either to the Central Planning Office, the District or the Commune (*see Section 4* above). At the District level, the procedure is as follows:
  The investor submits an initial EIA to the District with his application for a location directive. Consultation takes place between the District planning authority and the District environmental authority. The EIA is then reviewed at a meeting convened by the District planning authority with the participation of the investor, the project engineer and the EIA consultant. A decision is made as to whether the investment is likely to cause a deterioration of the environment. If an investment is unlikely to have an adverse environmental impact there will be no need for a final EIA.
- *Exceptionally harmful investments*:
  The investor submits an initial EIA with his application for a location directive either to the Central Planning Office, the District Planning Authority or the Commune Planning Authority. EIAs concerning investments considered exceptionally harmful to the environment are reviewed by the Commission on EIAs which is composed of 75 experts nominated for a period of four years. A final EIA is submitted with an application for a location decision (*see Section 4* above).

435

5.4.2 Documentation

Basic requirements

The *Decree of April 23, 1990* provides for the basic requirements of an EIA, leaving the details on the scope and methodology of an EIA to the EIA consultant. An EIA must include a review of the following:

- Construction and operation stages of the investment;
- Quantitative data relating to the condition of the environment;
- Proposed technical and technological solutions;
- Required energy and water consumption, and types and quantities of expected waste and pollution;
- Measures to mitigate environmental harm, including the necessary equipment, assessing its efficiency;
- Estimate of the probable impact of the investment on the environment;
- Applied technical solution with technologies currently used in Poland and elsewhere.

Where the investor proposes alternative sites for the development project, his application for a location directive must be accompanied by an EIA for each such alternative site.

Final EIAs

A final EIA submitted with an application for a location decision should, in addition to the above matters, also include a review of:

- Land adjacent to the development site identifying elements on which the project will have a considerable impact;
- Permissible impact and burden of the project on the environment;
- Expected direct, indirect and long-term impact on each environmental medium and human health;
- Data necessary to determine permitted levels of emissions and discharges;
- Conditions of use of the environment.

Existing facilities

An EIA of an existing facility should include a review of:

- Former and future operation and, if necessary, the liquidation of the facility;
- Data on environmental pollution covering the period preceding commencement of the operations;
- Quantitative data concerning use of water, wastewater discharge and air emission during the period of operation of the facility;
- Estimate of existing and expected impact on each element of the environment, human health and landscape.

5.4.3 Experts and consultants

EIAs are prepared at the cost of the investor by consultants indicated by the District from a list of Polish experts and institutions designated by the Environment Ministry.

436

5.4.4 Timing

No specific time limit is set for a decision on the initial and final EIAs. The Polish *Code of Administrative Procedure* provisions allow for one month which is acknowledged to be insufficient time. As regards investments of national importance or considered exceptionally harmful to the environment, the EIA Commission unofficially attempts to review EIAs within a three-month period. Sometimes the Commission's review can exceed one year, since it may require the EIA to be amended or supplemented.

5.4.5 Standard of review

Conditions for granting EIA approval depend on whether an EIA is required in connection with an application for a location directive or a location decision, and depending on the nature of the investment.

5.5 Public participation

Since there is no formal EIA process there is no formal guarantee of public participation in the EIA procedure.

As part of the formal review of EIAs accompanying location directives, the District planning authority may arrange a meeting with the developer, the project engineer and the EIA consultant where representatives of the public, such as non-government organisations may be invited to attend.

As regards investments of national importance or considered exceptionally harmful to the environment, the internal regulations of the EIA Commission provide for representatives of non-government organisations, local press, District Offices, and Communes to be present at the EIA Commission meetings. These groups can take part in the discussions relating to the impact of the environmental development project but do not have the right to approve or reject the EIA.

5.6 Enforcement

Since EIAs must be submitted with an application for a location directive or a location decision, these steps cannot be completed unless the investor performs the required EIA. The issuance of a location directive and a location decision is necessary to obtain a construction permit.

5.7 National experience with EIAs

Since its creation, the EIA Commission has considered 14 investments of national importance or exceptionally harmful to the environment. In six cases it has given a negative opinion regarding the impact of such investments on the environment.

The EIA Commission has required 80 industrial facilities, which have been identified as having an extremely negative impact on the environment, to prepare EIAs. By 1995 these facilities must introduce new technologies, install adequate pollution control equipment, and prepare analyses as to their future impact on the environment.

Three EIA commissions have been established at District level.

6. Integrated permitting requirements applicable to the operation of industrial and commercial facilities

6.1 Extent of integrated permitting

There is no integrated permitting system in Poland. Individual permits must be applied for. For further information *see Sections 7–11*.

7. Air emission requirements applicable to the operation of industrial and commercial facilities

7.1 Summary

Air Requirements:	Permits are issued by Districts and are of a limited duration. Charges are payable for air emissions.
Timing:	Permits are issued within one month of the date of application. The one-month period may be extended.
Public Participation:	The public has a right of access to general information on the state of the environment. There is no public participation in the permitting process.
Enforcement:	The District imposes fines for violations of air standards and can order facilities to halt their operation until adequate air pollution control equipment is installed.

7.2 Sources of legislation relating to air emissions

- *Law of January 31, 1980, on the Protection and Shaping of the Environment*, Articles 25–32 (Dz.U. 1980, No. 3, item 6, as amended);
- *Ordinance of the Environment Minister of April 17, 1987, on the Types and Amounts of Admissible Combustion Engine-Generated Pollutants* (Dz.U. 1987, No. 14, item 87);
- *Ordinance of the Council of Ministers of December 23, 1987, on the Amounts, Principles and Procedure of Imposing Fines for Violation of Environmental Protection Rules* (Dz.U. 1991, No. 89, item 404);
- *Ordinance of the Environment Minister of February 12, 1990, on the Protection of the Air against Pollution* (Dz.U. 1990, No. 15, item 92);
- *Ordinance of the Council of Ministers of December 21, 1991, on Charges for Economic Use of the Environment and Making Changes Therein* (Dz.U. 1991, No. 125, item 558, as amended).

438

7.3 Air protection zones

Pursuant to the *1980 Environmental Law*, enterprises have a duty to employ technical measures to protect the air against pollution and, if necessary, to apply for the creation of protective zones.

Permitted levels of air emissions depend on whether a facility is located in, or affects a specially protected area such as a national park, a nature reserve or a health resort, or affects any other area.

7.4 Scope of activities subject to air emission regulation

Polish regulations govern the level of pollutants in ambient air. In addition, authorities set permissible levels of air emissions for specific facilities.

Polish law distinguishes two types of air pollution sources: stationary sources and mobile sources generated by combustion engines.

Emission of lead compounds will be prohibited after the year 2000 in accordance with Poland's desire to harmonise its environmental laws with those of the EC.

7.5 Standards

7.5.1 Ambient quality standards

The *Ordinance of February 12, 1990, on the Protection of the Air against Pollution* regulates the permissible levels of a large number of pollutants in ambient air. Permissible concentration levels of these pollutants are regulated over periods of 30 minutes, one day or as an annual average. Different concentration levels apply in specially protected areas and in other areas. The permissible levels of air emissions set in individual facility air permits must not result in concentrations of pollutants in ambient air in excess of ambient air standards set forth in Annex No. 1 to the *Ordinance*.

7.5.2 Emission limit values

The *Ordinance of February 12, 1990, on the Protection of Air against Pollution* also sets forth in its Annex No. 2 the permissible emissions of sulphur dioxide, nitrogen dioxide and dust for combustion processes. Such emission levels have been specified for pit coal, brown coal, coke, heating oil, natural gas and wood, and are dependent on the type of furnace. Three levels of emission (Level A, B and C) have been determined by reference to the relative age of the facilities:

- *Facilities in existence on 28 March 1990*:
    - (i)   Emissions at Level A will be binding until December 31, 1997;
    - (ii) Emissions at Level B will be binding after December 31, 1997.
- *Facilities which will commence operation after 31 December, 1994, or whose construction began after 28 March, 1990*
    - (i)   These facilities must comply with Emissions at Level C.

7.5.3 Technology based standards

Technology based air emission standards have been set for power plants. They will be applicable to power plants which will commence operation after 31 December, 1994 or whose construction began after 28 March, 1990.

7.6 Permitting process

7.6.1 Authorities

Air emission permits are issued by Districts. The decision of the District not to issue a permit may be appealed to the Environment Minister whose decision is final. Final decisions may be appealed to the Supreme Administrative Court only if they have been issued in violation of the law.

7.6.2 Application requirements

An application for an air emission permit should be accompanied by a description of:

- Technology to be used;
- Each emission source;
- Estimated time during which each emitting facility is in operation over an annual period;
- Types and volumes of emitted dust and gases, specified in tons per annum, in kilograms per hour (average value), in grams per second (maximum value), and in kilograms per one unit of production for each source of emission;
- Pollution control equipment and its effectiveness;
- Conditions of air emission;
- Existing air pollution and expected pollution caused by the operation of the facility;
- Time and scope of maximum concentrations and volumes of polluting substances;
- Conditions of diffusion of pollutants into ambient air;
- Planned measures to reduce air pollution levels caused by the operation of the facility.

7.6.3 Timing

Pursuant to the *Code of Administrative Procedure*, an administrative decision should be issued within one month. In practice the District has the power to extend this period. Consequently, it may take longer than one month from the date of application to obtain an air emission permit.

7.6.4 Permit conditions

Charges are imposed by Districts for the emission of any one of the polluting substances listed in the *Ordinance of December 21, 1991*, as amended by the *Ordinance of October 27, 1992* and of *January 26, 1993* and, in addition, for pollution of the air caused by refueling operations.

Air emission permits are issued for a limited period of time. The permit specifies the type and level of permitted pollution for each source of air emission and for each emitting facility as a whole, and also imposes certain conditions relating to pollution control. Such obligations may also be imposed by the District at a later time in a separate decision.

7.6.5 Charges for emissions

Business concerns and industrial facilities are required to submit to the District by 31 January of each year a list indicating the amounts of air pollutants emitted in the previous year in respect of which charges must be paid. The District may request that such information be presented at the end of each quarter. If the requested information is not presented or is unsatisfactory, the District imposes emission charges according to its own calculations.

The *Ordinance of December 21, 1991* was amended on *October 27, 1992*. Charges for air emissions are now calculated by multiplying the original charges by the following ratios: for pollutants in Group I — 0.1 (with the exception of benzopyrene, tin and zinc); for pollutants in Group II and III — 0.7 (with the exception of mineral acids and anhydrides and organic derivatives of sulphur compounds). The 27 October, 1992 amendment also abolished higher charges in the Districts of Krakow and Katowice which were originally introduced because of the heavy pollution in those areas. Pursuant to a new amendment by the *Ordinance of January 26, 1993* which comes into force on 1 April, 1993 charges for air emissions will be higher once again across the entire country.

7.6.6 Public participation

No consultation with the public is required when the District issues environmental permits to a facility. *See Section 1.8* above.

7.7 Enforcement

7.7.1 Compliance checking and monitoring

Business concerns and industrial facilities are obliged to monitor air emission levels, in accordance with terms specified in the permits issued by the District. The methodology used by the industrial facilities is regulated by the District which has the ability to perform its own monitoring operations. Other governmental agencies authorised to monitor air emissions are the State Inspectorate of Environmental Protection acting through the District Environmental Inspection and the State Sanitary Inspectorate acting through Sanitary Inspectors. The monitoring results obtained by government bodies and agencies must be sent to the operator of the facility within 21 days.

Air emissions of sulphur dioxide in excess of 1,200 kilograms per hour or dust in excess of 800 kilograms per hour require constant monitoring. Where an industrial facility could potentially discharge more than 100 kilograms of dust or sulphur dioxide per hour, testing must be conducted twice a year according to a schedule agreed with the District. Additionally, facilities are required to prepare an evaluation of the effectiveness of existing pollution control equipment at least once every two years.

7.7.2 Penalties and sanctions

The State Inspectorate of Environmental Protection enforces environmental regulations regarding air pollution.

Fines are imposed by District Environmental Inspectors for violations of the terms of an air pollution permit, that is for emission of substances other than those permitted or in excess of permitted levels. Fines are calculated on an hourly basis, by multiplying by a factor of ten the emission fees for one unit of the air pollutant. If a facility has not obtained an air pollution permit, emission charges are increased by 100% until an application for a permit is submitted to the District. The District may waive the fee if it would not exceed 5 million zlotys.

8. Water requirements applicable to the operation of industrial and commercial facilities

8.1 Summary

Water Requirements:	Permits for water use, wastewater discharge and construction of water treatment facilities are obtained from Districts. Charges for water use are imposed by Districts depending on the type of water and its intended use. Wastewater discharge charges are imposed by Districts depending on the amount, type and average composition of wastewater discharged and the level of concentration of pollutants.
Timing:	Permits should be issued within one month of the date of application. The one-month period may be extended.
Public Participation:	The public has a right of access to general information on the state of the environment. There is no public participation in the permitting process.
Enforcement:	District Environmental Inspectors impose fines for violations of water standards and can order facilities to halt their operations.

8.2 Sources of legislation relating to water requirements

- *Water Law of October 24, 1974* (Dz.U. 1974, No. 38, item 230, as amended);
- *Ordinance of the Council of Ministers of June 3, 1977, on Supervision and Control of Water Management* (Dz.U. 1977, No. 19, item 78);
- *Ordinance of Minister of Health and Social Security of May 31, 1977, on the Requirements which Should Be Fulfilled by Potable Water and Water Used for Economic Purposes* (Dz.U. 1977, No. 18, item 72), as amended by *Ordinance of Minister of Health and Social Security of May 4, 1990* (Dz.U. 1990, No. 35, item 205);
- *Ordinance of Council of Ministers of March 11, 1985, on Types of Special Use of Waters and the Construction and Exploitation of Water Equipment not Requiring a Water Permit* (Dz.U. 1985, No. 13, item 55);

- *Ordinance of the Council of Ministers of November 11, 1985, on the Principles and Methods of Determining Fines for Extraction of Water in Amounts Greater than Those in a Water Permit* (Dz.U. 1985, No. 52, item 271);
- *Ordinance of Environment Minister of November 5, 1991, on the Classification of Waters and the Required Conditions for Waste Water Discharge into Waters or Soil* (Dz.U. 1991, No. 116, item 503);
- *Ordinance of Council of Ministers of December 21, 1991, on Fees for Special Use of Water and Water Equipment* (Dz.U. 1991, No. 125, item 556);
- *Ordinance of Environment Minister of December 21, 1991, on Fines for Violation of Requirements Applicable to Waste Discharged into the Water or the Ground* (Dz.U. 1991, No. 125, item 557);
- *Decree of Minister of Agriculture of January 26, 1976, on the Requirements to be Fulfilled by a Water Operation Permit* (M.P. 1976, No. 6, item 32).

8.3 Water management

8.3.1 Water management bodies
Administration of water resources is exercised by seven Water Management Boards. Supervision and control of water management is exercised by the Environment Ministry.

8.3.2 Water quality categories
Pursuant to the *Ordinance of November 5, 1991* water is classified into four types:

- Class I: potable water;
- Class II: water suitable for swimming and recreation;
- Class III: water suitable for industrial purposes;
- Water below established quality standards.

8.3.3 Activities subject to regulation
The specific activities subject to regulation as a general matter include:

- Water use;
- Discharge of wastewater;
- Construction of wastewater treatment facilities and new sources of ground water intake.

8.4 Standards

8.4.1 Ambient quality standards
Ambient water quality standards are set out in the *Ordinance of the Minister of Health and Social Security of May 31, 1977, on the Requirements which Should Be Fulfilled by Potable Water and Water Used for Economic Purposes* as amended by the *Ordinance of May 4, 1990* (Dz.U. 1990, No. 35, item 205). The *Ordinance* specifies ambient concentration levels for a large number of polluting substances in water. Recently the *Ordinance*

was amended and the standards have become stricter. It was not published as of the time of writing.

8.4.2 Discharge limit values

The *Ordinance of November 5, 1991 of the Environment Minister, on the Classification of Waters and the Required Conditions for Wastewater Discharge into Waters or Soil* sets discharge limit values for wastewater. Paragraph 11.1 of the *Ordinance* states that it is forbidden to dilute wastewater by cooling water or other water in order to reach the specified discharge limits. Paragraph 12 of the *Ordinance* states that if the wastewater effluent of a facility contains substances other than those listed in Attachment 1 of the *Ordinance*, the Districts can set specific discharge limit values for those substances in the facility's water permit. Individual Districts had no obligation to co-ordinate their efforts in setting discharge limits when one river flows through several Districts. The new administration of water resources by seven Water Management Boards organised into watersheds is designed to rationalise the control of water pollution. The change in administration will be fully operational when the draft water law is enacted.

8.4.3 Technology based standards

There are no technology based standards in the water area.

8.5 Water use permitting process

8.5.1 Authorities

Districts issue water use permits for:

- Use of surface waters in amounts exceeding 500,000 m^3 per year or less, but exceeding 10% of the average annual water flow, and abstraction of waters for enterprises of a water power exceeding 100 kV;
- Use of ground waters if the source is located below 150 m or the abstraction exceeds 50 m^3/hour.

Permits for construction of water treatment and the other facilities are issued by Districts for navigable waters and by Communes for other waters.

8.5.2 Application requirements

A water permit is issued on the basis of a set of documents called "operat". The required documentation is described in detail in the *1974 Water Law*.

If it is not possible to determine the degree of harm to the environment caused by the anticipated water use, the applicant may be required to submit an analysis prepared by an expert designated by the permit issuing authority. The costs of the analysis are borne by the applicant.

8.5.3 Timing

Pursuant to the *Code of Administrative Procedure*, all administrative procedures should take one month. In practice the District has the power to extend this period. Consequently, it may take longer than one month from the date of application to obtain a water use permit.

8.5.4 *Permit conditions*

If the water use or construction of water equipment could be harmful to the environment, the user has a duty to install and maintain pollution control equipment. Such a duty may also be imposed on the user in a separate District decision.

A water permit may be revoked for several reasons specified in the *1974 Water Law*:

- If the permit is no longer necessary for the operation of a facility;
- If the water equipment is maintained in a way that constitutes a threat to the safety of humans or animals;
- For any reason justified by the interest of residents or environmental protection.

8.5.5 *Charges for water use*

Charges are imposed for the use of state-owned waters and are calculated according to whether the water is surface or groundwater and its intended use. A user is obliged to measure the amount of water used. The amount of charges is determined by the District on the basis of information which an enterprise should make available by 31 January of each year. The District may request that such information be presented by the last day of each quarter.

If the user does not furnish the above information in time, the fee is determined by the District on the basis of available data.

Charges for groundwater use for industrial purposes depend on the level of available supply of water in a particular District as well as on the intended use of water. A substantial discount is provided for some uses involving the production of food and pharmaceuticals.

A considerably lower charge is levied on the use of surface or groundwater if the water is used for the purposes of the community, for supply of water to humans, the maintenance of green areas, the cleaning of towns and cities, agricultural production, livestock breeding, or for the improvement of farm land and forests.

Charges are not levied on the use of water for the supply of fire companies, for fishing purposes, for mining, or the use of groundwater for the operation of turbines and other water equipment, the heating of dwellings or office space, or purposes connected with the generation of electricity or heat.

The District may abstain from collecting charges for water use if they would not exceed 2 million zlotys.

Charges should be paid within two weeks from the date of the final decision. In case of delay, penalty interest is calculated.

8.6 *Water discharge permitting process*

8.6.1 *Authorities*

Districts issue wastewater discharge permits for discharge into surface and groundwaters.

8.6.2 Application requirements

Under the *1974 Water Law* wastewater discharge into surface waters and the ground requires a water permit. If the wastewater is discharged through communal sewage systems, a contract should be executed with the sewage treatment works.

8.6.3 Timing

Pursuant to the *Code of Administrative Procedure*, all administrative procedures should take one month. In practice the District has the power to extend this period. Consequently, it may take longer than one month from the date of application to obtain a water discharge permit.

8.6.4 Permit conditions

A wastewater discharge permit is issued for a limited period of time and may be conditioned on the use of monitoring equipment to measure discharges into water. The permit specifies the amount, nature and composition of the permitted wastewater discharge. It may also provide for other obligations with respect to environmental protection. The District is authorised to set out more stringent wastewater discharge standards or decline to issue the permit if:

- Wastewater is to be discharged into waters in national parks, nature reserves, scenic parks, within health or tourist resorts, or within town or city boundaries;
- The average amount of wastewater discharged per day exceeds 10% of the average flow of the water;
- At a stretch of 10 kilometers of a river or stream where the average low flow is lower than 1.5 m^3/second, the total daily amount of waste is greater than 10% of the average flow.

8.6.5 Charges for water discharge

The amount of charges paid for wastewater discharges is determined by the District on the basis of information as to the amount, type and average composition of wastewater discharged and the level of concentration of pollutants. The information should be made available by 31 January of each year. The District may request that such information be furnished by the last day of each quarter of the year. If the enterprise does not furnish the above information in a timely manner, the fee is determined by the District on the basis of available data.

The level of charges will also depend on the types of activity. Different types of facilities are categorised in descending order according to the level of wastewater charges to be imposed:

- Plants operating in the chemical, fuel and energy, metallurgical, electrical machinery, and light industry;
- Plants operating in the wood and paper industry;
- Plants operating in the food industry;
- Water-supply and sewage equipment in cities;

446

- Water-supply and sewage equipment in villages and hospitals and social welfare institutions;
- Other facilities.

The District may abstain from collecting the fee if it would not exceed 1 million zlotys and the waste would not cause a harmful pollution of surface and ground waters or agricultural food products.

Fees should be paid within 14 days from the date of the final decision. In case of default, a penalty interest will accrue.

8.6.6 Public participation

No consultation with the public is required when the District issues environmental permits to a facility. *See Section 1.8* above.

8.7 Enforcement

8.7.1 Compliance checking and monitoring

The State Sanitary Inspectorate is responsible for monitoring the quality of potable water and water used for industrial purposes. Enterprises which are aware of facts or circumstances which could affect water quality are obliged to inform District Sanitary Inspectors in a timely manner. If the quality of water falls below the specified requirements and its use would pose a threat to human health, the Sanitary Inspector may issue an order prohibiting wastewater discharges or the operation of water treatment plants.

Under the *1974 Water Law* a Commune may request that an owner of land install the necessary water treatment equipment and may prohibit wastewater discharges.

8.7.2 Penalties and sanctions

Fines for waste discharge into waters or the ground in violation of water permits are imposed by District Environmental Inspectors. A facility which does not hold a water permit establishing the permissible levels of discharge will be held liable for the total volume of the discharged pollutants.

The level of the fine depends on the amount, state and composition of wastewater discharged into waters or the ground and is based on measurements of the composition of the waste discharged by the facility, performed by the District Environmental Inspector three times within an hour. The District Environmental Inspector is obliged to make available to the operator of the facility the results of such measurements within 21 days of their performance, if they indicate that pollution standards have been violated. The District Environmental Inspector may abstain from imposing the fine if it would not exceed 1 million zlotys.

A District Environmental Inspector can request that an enterprise cease the discharge of wastewater if its volume and composition potentially causes harm to the environment. If the enterprise fails to comply within a given time, the District Environmental Inspector may order the entire facility or part of it to cease operations.

9. Noise requirements applicable to the operation of industrial and commercial facilities

9.1 Summary

Noise Requirements:	No noise or vibration permits are required. Districts determine ambient noise levels in a given locality. If the noise concentrations exceed permitted ambient levels, Districts issue decisions setting permitted levels of noise and vibration for specific facilities.
Public Participation:	The public has a right of access to general information on the state of the environment.
Enforcement:	Fines are imposed by District Environmental Inspectors for violations of permissible noise and vibration levels. They may also halt the operations of a facility for exceeding specific noise and vibration levels set in decisions.

9.2 Sources of legislation relating to environmental noise

- *Law on the Protection and Shaping of the Environment of January 31, 1980*, Articles 49–52, (Dz.U. 1980, No. 3, item 6, as amended);
- *Ordinance of the Council of Ministers of September 30, 1980, on the Protection of the Environment against Noise and Vibration* (Dz.U. 1980, No. 24, item 90);
- *Ordinance of the Council of Ministers of December 23, 1987, on the Amounts, Principles and Procedure of Imposing Fines for Violation of Environmental Protection Rules* (Dz.U. 1991, No. 89, item 404).

9.3 Noise zones

Protective zones should be established by enterprises in order to protect the environment from sources of noise and vibration. In addition, zones of "limited noise" may be established, where the level of noise concentration should be lower than as required by the *Ordinance of September 30, 1980*. There are five noise zones with different noise level requirements from health resort areas to inner cities.

9.4 Activities subject to noise regulation

Regulations prohibit activities which result in noise in excess of permitted levels and concentrations. Businesses which operate machines which emit noise and vibrations are obliged to employ adequate technical measures to reduce or eliminate such noise or vibrations. Pursuant to Article 52 of the *1980 Environmental Law*, the Commune may impose limitations as to the time of equipment or vehicle use. Article 76 of the *1980 Environmental Law* provides that the Commune may request that the user of equipment implement adequate measures in order to limit the level of noise.

Existing legislation relating to noise and vibrations will soon be harmonised with EC legal requirements.

9.5 Standards

Ambient noise standards are measured in decibels and depend on the area affected and the time of day. Noise levels are also indicated for maximum levels for short-term noise. For example the following standards apply in inner cities and health resorts:

Zones	Day Standard	Night Standard	Maximum Short-Term Standard
Inner Cities	60 db	50 db	85 db
Resorts, historic areas	40 db	30 db	65 db

The Districts may determine permitted noise concentration levels in areas not covered by the law.

9.6 Permitting process

9.6.1 Authorities

According to the provisions of the *1980 Environment Law* if environmental noise and vibrations exceed permissible levels, Districts may set specific noise and vibration levels for individual enterprises. Government control of noise is most effectively exercised through the EIA process. An investment project will not be allowed to proceed if it is determined from the information provided in the EIA that it would violate applicable noise standards.

9.6.2 Application requirements

The District determines the permissible ambient noise concentrations in a region not falling within one of the five groups specified in the *Ordinance of September 30, 1980*. In all cases, if the noise concentrations exceed permissible levels the District may issue decisions determining permitted levels of noise and vibration for specific facilities. The decision may be vacated or amended if circumstances so require.

There are no formal application requirements since decisions on permitted levels of noise are issued not at the request of the enterprise, but *ex officio* by the District. The District may request information from the economic entity necessary to issue a decision.

449

9.6.3 Timing

The general rules of the *Code of Administrative Procedure* set a one-month period for all administrative procedures.

9.6.4 Permit conditions

The District may in its decision regarding a specific facility set levels of noise during certain hours.

9.6.5 Public participation

Public participation in determining ambient noise levels or noise levels emanating from individual facilities is not provided for. Nevertheless, the review of an investment project by the EIA commission, which includes a review of the environmental impact of noise generated by the project, in practice does involve consultation with non-government organisations.

9.7 Enforcement

9.7.1 Compliance checking and monitoring

Commune may impose restrictions as to the time of use of noise-generating equipment or vehicles. Communes may also designate zones of limited noise where noise levels should be lower than those provided in the *Ordinance of September 30, 1980*. The State Sanitary Inspectorate is charged with the task of monitoring noise levels. Districts and Communes have enforcement powers of their own.

9.7.2 Penalties and sanctions

Fines for exceeding the permitted level of noise are imposed by the District Inspector. They are calculated per day and range from 40,000 zlotys for exceeding the permitted level by one decibel to 162,000 zlotys for 16 decibels or more. If the violation continues for three subsequent years, the fines after that period are increased by 100%.

If a facility exceeds permitted levels of noise or vibration specified in an individual permit, the District Inspector may impose a duty to eliminate the violation within the specified time. If the violation persists, the operation of the facility may be halted. At the discretion of the Inspector the operation may be halted by the District Inspector immediately, without extending an additional grace period to the facility.

10. Hazardous and non-hazardous waste management

10.1 Summary

Categories of Waste:	Waste classification under Polish law is being revised to conform to EC laws.

Permits:	Waste storage treatment and disposal facilities are established pursuant to land use regulations (*Section 4*). Facilities which generate waste exceptionally harmful to the environment must consult with the Districts and Sanitary Inspectors regarding the manner of such disposal.
Charges:	Charges are imposed by Districts for waste disposal relative to 152 substances.
Enforcement:	Fines are imposed by District Environmental Inspectors for storage or disposal of waste in locations not intended for that purpose.

10.2 Sources of legislation relating to waste management

- *Law of January 31, 1980, on the Protection and Shaping of the Environment* (Articles 53–58) (Dz.U. 1980, No. 3, item 6, as amended);
- *Building Law of October 24, 1974* (Dz.U. No. 38, item 229, as amended);
- *Ordinances of the Minister of Health on Toxins and Hazardous Substances* (Dz.U. 1964, No. 2, item 9; Dz.U. 1965, No. 40, item 252; Dz.U. 1983, No. 13, item 67);
- *Ordinance of the Council of Ministers of September 30, 1980, on the Protection of the Environment against Waste and Other Pollution and the Maintenance of a Clean Environment and Order in Towns and Villages* (Dz.U. 1980, No. 24, item 91);
- *Law on Road Traffic of February 1, 1983* (Dz.U. 1983, No. 6, item 35);
- *Ordinance of the Council of Ministers of December 23, 1987, on the Amounts, Principles and Procedure of Imposing Fines for Violation of Environmental Protection Rules* (Dz.U. 1991, No. 89, item 404);
- *Ordinance of the Council of Ministers of December 21, 1991, on Charges for Economic Use of the Environment and Making Changes Therein* (Dz.U. 1991, No. 125, item 558, as amended), as amended by *Ordinance of the Council of Ministers of January 26, 1993* (Dz.U. 1993, No. 5, item 44).

10.3 Categories of waste

The *Ordinance on the Protection of the Environment against Waste and Other Pollution and the Maintenance of a Clean Environment* distinguishes three special categories of waste:

- Hazardous waste which contains one or more of 65 regulated toxic substances or one or more of 187 regulated hazardous substances;
- Infectious waste containing pathogenic micro-organisms;
- Radioactive waste.

Work is underway to establish a new classification of wastes which is compatible with EC standards. Draft laws on waste management have been prepared.

10.4 Waste storage and treatment

10.4.1 Generator requirements

Chapter 8 of the *1980 Environmental Law* sets out the general obligations of waste generators as regards waste disposal. Article 54 provides that waste which cannot be used for commercial purposes must be destroyed, neutralised, stored or disposed of at sites designated for that purpose in land use plans in such a way as to ensure protection of the environment.

The manner of storage and treatment of hazardous, infectious and radioactive waste should be determined by waste generators after consultation with the District Authority and Sanitary Inspectors.

By some accounts, 60% of waste generated by industry in Poland is recycled or reused for economic purposes — primarily for land levelling, construction and road building works. In the event generators of industrial waste which would be harmful to the environment when discarded wish to recycle or reuse that waste, they must notify the District Authority of the method of such reuse or recycling.

No specific recordkeeping requirements are imposed on generators of waste. By 31 January of each year however, the District must be provided with information as to the amount and type of waste generated in the previous year, and its storage location. The District may request that such information be submitted by the enterprise on a quarterly basis. If the requested information is not presented or is unsatisfactory, the District calculates the charges on the basis of its own calculations.

10.4.2 Operator requirements

Waste storage and treatment sites have to be included in land use plans. Owners and operators of waste storage and treatment facilities must obtain the necessary permits. Permits are issued by Regional Offices pursuant to the *Building Law* and should indicate:

- Any obligation to create and maintain protective zones;
- Any technical requirements with respect to the waste storage site;
- A description of site use, including limitations on types of substances stored, selective storage of waste, ways to isolate the waste, permitted levels of storage;
- Any requirement to provide an expert analysis;
- Any duty to prepare instructions with respect to the use of the site;
- Any duty to perform continuous or periodical analyses of the impact of the site on the environment.

The above conditions may also be imposed after the permit has been issued by means of a separate decision.

Operators of waste storage and treatment facilities are required to:

- Keep a record of the amounts and types of waste accepted for storage;
- Maintain and operate the site in a way which will ensure compliance with sanitary and environmental standards;
- Refuse to accept waste of unknown composition;
- Inform the permit issuing authority if the operation of the site has been terminated.

A permit to maintain a site shall be refused if the waste is suitable for reuse.

Hazardous and radioactive waste should be stored in sealed containers and precautions should be taken to prevent further chemical reactions. The storage site should be protected against access by unauthorised persons. Infectious waste, much of which is generated in a health care setting, must be detoxified and destroyed on the premises of the health care facility through incineration.

10.5 Waste disposal

10.5.1 Generator requirements

Chapter 8 of the *1980 Environmental Law* sets out the general obligations of waste generators as regards waste disposal. Article 54 provides that waste which cannot be used for commercial purposes must be destroyed, neutralised, stored or disposed of at sites designated for that purpose in land use plans in such a way as to ensure the protection of the environment.

The manner of waste disposal for hazardous, radioactive and infectious waste should be determined after consultation with the District and the District Sanitary Inspector regarding the required manner for treatment and disposal.

10.5.2 Operator requirements

Waste disposal sites must be included in land use plans. Owners and operators of waste disposal sites must obtain the necessary permits. Permits are issued by Regional Offices. The application process and conditions of permits are the same as described in *Section 4* (location directives, location decisions, construction permits).

10.5.3 Charges

Waste disposal charges are imposed by Districts. They depend on the amount of the waste and the extent to which it is harmful to the environment. The law classifies 152 substances into four categories which differ with respect to the level of possible harm to the environment. The District may abstain from collecting charges for storage or disposal of waste if the charges would not exceed 5 million zlotys.

As of 1 April, 1993, charges will be increased.

10.6 Transport of waste

10.6.1 Labelling and containers

Vehicles transporting hazardous substances must be adequately marked, pursuant to the *Law on Road Traffic of February 1, 1983*.

They should be stored in a way to prevent pollution and spills, in labelled containers indicating the name of the substance, a warning about the hazard, information about the special effects caused by the substance, and a reminder of the need to take special protective measures.

10.6.2 Transboundary movement

Under an amendment of 27 April, 1989 to the *1980 Environmental Law* it is prohibited to import waste into Poland. Violation of this law is a crime which is punishable by imprisonment of up to three years and a fine. Pursuant to a draft amendment, recently introduced in Parliament, the importation of non-toxic waste for economic reasons may be permissible in near future.

10.7 Recycling requirements

A permit to maintain a waste storage site shall be refused if the waste is suitable for recycling.

Under the *1980 Environmental Law* businesses which produce packaging materials and other goods which, when discarded, could pose a threat to the environment, are required to determine the ways in which the materials will be reused or eliminated so as to ensure protection of the environment.

10.8 Enforcement

10.8.1 Compliance checking and monitoring

Fines are imposed by District Environmental Inspectors for storage or disposal of waste in places not intended for that purpose or in violation of the decision as to the location of a waste storage site.

10.8.2 Penalties and sanctions

The methods of calculation and level of fines are regulated in the *Ordinance on the Amounts, Principles and Procedure of Imposing Fines.*

Fines are increased by 100% if:

- The waste is discharged into surface waters, or territorial sea waters;
- The waste is stored or discharged near water tanks, especially in protective water zones;
- The waste is stored or discharged in forests, health resorts, or places intended for tourism and recreation.

The fine is calculated on a daily basis from the date the violation was ascertained. Repeated violations result in fine increases of 100%.

11. Chemicals storage, handling and emergency response

11.1 Summary

Permits:	The manufacture, import and sale of toxic substances requires a permit from the District Sanitary Inspector. In the case of toxins to be used for the purposes of disinfection, de-infestation or extermination of rats, a permit must be issued by the Minister of Health.
Timing:	Permits are issued within one-month of the date of application. The one month period may be extended.
Enforcement:	Sanitary Inspectors may impose fines for violations of law. They may also prevent the sale of toxic substances and seize toxic substances.

11.2 Sources of legislation relating to chemicals storage, handling and emergency response

11.2.1 Storage
See Section 11.2.2 below.

11.2.2 Handling

- *Law of May 21, 1963, on Harmful Substances* (Dz.U. 1963, No. 22, item 116, as amended);
- *Ordinance of the Minister of Health of December 28, 1963, on the Labelling of Harmful Substances* (Dz.U. 1963, No. 2, item 8, as amended);
- *Ordinance of the Minister of Health of December 28, 1963, on the List of Toxic and Harmful Substances* (Dz.U. 1963, No. 2, item 9; Dz.U. 1965, No. 40, item 252; Dz.U. 1983, No. 13, item 67);
- *Ordinance of the Minister of Health of October 2, 1964, on Permits for the Production of and Trade in Toxins, Register of Toxins and Principles of Action of Bodies Controlling Harmful Substances* (Dz.U. 1964, No. 7, item 45).

11.2.3 Emergency response
Decree of the Minister of Chemical and Light Industry of June 30, 1986, on the Principles of Warning the Public about Contamination by Harmful Industrial Substances (M.P. 1986, No. 27, item 191).

11.3 *Regulatory requirements*

11.3.1 *Storage and handling*

The manufacture, import and sale of harmful substances requires a permit issued by the District Sanitary Inspector. In the case of toxins to be used for the purposes of disinfection, de-infestation or extermination of rats, a permit must be issued by the Minister of Health.

Harmful substances and hazardous chemicals should be stored in a way to prevent pollution and spills, in labelled containers indicating the name of the substance, a warning about the hazard, information about the special effects caused by the substance, and reminder of the need to take special protective measures. Vehicles transporting hazardous substances must be adequately marked, pursuant to the *Law on Road Traffic of February 1, 1983* (Dz.U. 1983, No. 6, item 35).

11.3.2 *Emergency response*

As regards spills or emissions of harmful industrial substances, the facility responsible for such contamination must warn the residents of the area by a warning siren.

11.4 *Public participation*

There are no legal provisions giving the public access to detailed information about the storage and handling of chemical substances or about spills or emissions of harmful substances. See also *Section 1.8* above.

11.5 *Enforcement*

The State Sanitary Inspectorate is charged with the enforcement of legislation relating to toxic substances.

11.5.1 *Compliance checking and monitoring*

The State Sanitary Inspectorate has the power of control over the implementation of rules concerning hazardous or toxic substances.

11.5.2 *Penalties and sanctions*

Sanitary Inspectors may:

- Issue a temporary prohibition on trade in harmful substances or mixtures containing such substances;
- Temporarily seize the harmful substances, as well as related books and documents.

In case of threat of harm or harm to the environment, general environmental rules apply. Underground storage tanks are regulated by the *Building Law*.

If an underground storage tank may have a detrimental effect on the environment, the establishment of a protective zone will be necessary. Protective zones are regulated by the

Ordinance of the Council of Ministers of September 30, 1980, on the Establishment and Management of Protective Zones (Dz.U. 1980, No. 24, item 92) and the *Decree of Minister of Administration of November 9, 1982, on Detailed Principles of Determining the Boundaries and Area of Protective Zones and Principles according to which their Width is Determined* (M.P. 1982, No. 27, item 241).

Annex A

List of Key Legislation

1. Overview

- *Law on the Protection and Shaping of the Environment of January 31, 1980* (Dz.U. 1980, No. 3, item 6, as amended);
- *Water Law of October 24, 1974* (Dz.U. 1974, No. 38, item 240, as amended);
- *Law of July 12, 1984, on Land Use Planning* (Dz.U. 1989, No. 17, item 99, as amended);
- *Ordinance of the Environment Minister of February 12, 1990, on the Protection of the Air against Pollution* (Dz.U. 1990, No. 15, item 92);
- *Ordinance of Environment Minister of November 5, 1991, on the Classification of Waters and the Required Conditions for Waste Disposal into Waters or the Soil* (Dz.U. 1991, No. 116, item 503);
- *Ordinance of the Council of Ministers of December 21, 1991, on Charges for Economic Use of the Environment and Making Changes Therein* (Dz.U. 1991, No. 125, item 558, as amended).

2. Environmental liability

- *Civil Code of 1964* (Dz.U. 1964, No. 16, item 93, as amended);
- *Commercial Code of 1934* (Dz.U. 1934, No. 57, item 502, as amended);
- *Petty Offences Code of May 20, 1971* (Dz.U. 1971, No. 12, item 114);
- *Criminal Code of April 19, 1969* (Dz.U. 1969, No. 13, item 98, as amended);
- *Water Law of October 24, 1974* (Dz.U. 1974, No. 38, item 240, as amended);
- *Law on the Protection and Shaping of the Environment of January 31, 1980* (Dz.U. 1980, No. 3, item 6, as amended);
- *Law of July 13, 1990, on the Privatisation of State-Owned Enterprises* (Dz.U. 1990, No. 51, item 298, as amended);
- *Law of June 14, 1991, on Companies with Foreign Capital Participation* (Dz.U. 1991, No. 60, item 253, as amended);
- *Ordinance of the Council of Ministers of January 23, on the Detailed Principles Governing the Protection of Topsoil* (Dz.U. 1987, No. 4, item 23);
- *Ordinance of the Council of Ministers of December 23, 1987, on the Amounts, Principles and Procedure of Imposing Fines for Violation of Environmental Protection Rules* (Dz.U. 1991, No. 89, item 404);

- *Ordinance of the Environment Minister of December 21, 1991, on Fines for Violation of Requirements Applicable to Waste Discharged into the Water or the Ground* (Dz.U. 1991, No. 125, item 557);
- *Ordinance of Minister of Health and Social Security of May 31, 1977, on the Requirements which should be Fulfilled by Potable Water and Water Used for Economic Purposes* (Dz.U. 1977, No. 18, item 72), as amended by *Ordinance of Minister of Health and Social Security of May 4, 1990* (Dz.U. 1990, No. 35, item 205).

3. Environmental audits

- *Law of July 13, 1990, on the Privatisation of State-Owned Enterprises* (Dz.U. 1990, No. 51, item 298, as amended);
- *Ordinance of the Council of Ministers of December 23, 1987, on the Amounts, Principles and Procedure of Imposing Fines for Violation of Environmental Protection Rules* (Dz.U. 1991, No. 89, item 404);
- *Ordinance of Minister of Health and Social Security of May 31, 1977, on the Requirements which should be Fulfilled by Potable Water and Water Used for Economic Purposes* (Dz.U. 1977, No. 18, item 72), as amended by *Ordinance of Minister of Health and Social Security of May 4, 1990* (Dz.U. 1990, No. 35, item 205).

4. Land use planning

- *Law of March 24, 1920, on Purchasing Real Property by Foreigners* (Dz.U. 1933, No. 24, item 202, as amended);
- *Building Law of October 24, 1974* (Dz.U. 1974, No. 38, item 229, as amended);
- *Law on the Protection and Shaping of the Environment of January 31, 1980* (Dz.U. 1980, No. 3, item 6, as amended);
- *Law on the Protection of Agricultural and Forest Land of March 26, 1982* (Dz.U. 1982, No. 11, item 79);
- *Law of July 12, 1984, on Land Use Planning* (Dz.U. 1989, No. 17, item 99, as amended);
- *Ordinance of the Environment Minister of February 20, 1975, on Urban Construction Supervision* (Dz.U. 1975, No. 8, item 48, as amended);
- *Ordinance of the Minister of Administration* (now: Minister of Land Use and Construction) *of July 3, 1980, on Technical Requirements to be Fulfilled by Buildings* (Dz.U. 1980, No. 17, item 62, as amended);
- *Ordinance of the Council of Ministers of June 27, 1985, on the Classification of Investments and the Scope, Principles and Procedure of their Location* (Dz.U. 1990, No. 11, item 75).

5. Environmental Impact Assessments (EIAs)

- *Law on the Protection and Shaping of the Environment of January 31, 1980* (Dz.U. 1980, No. 3, item 6, as amended) (Articles 68–70);
- *Law of July 12, 1984, on Land Use Planning* (Article 39) (Dz.U. 1989, No. 17, item 99, as amended);
- *Decree of the Environment Minister of April 23, 1990, on Investments Especially Harmful to the Environment and Human Health and the Conditions of Environmental Impact Assessments for Investments and Buildings, Prepared by Experts* (M.P. 1990, No. 16, item 126);
- *Decree No 22 of the Environment Minister of December 29, 1989.*

6. Air emission requirements applicable to the operation of industrial and commercial facilities

- *Law on the Protection and Shaping of the Environment of January 31, 1980* (Articles 25–32) (Dz.U. 1980, No. 3, item 6, as amended);
- *Ordinance of the Environment Minister of April 17, 1987, on the Types and Amounts of Admissible Combustion Engine-Generated Pollutants* (Dz.U. 1987, No. 14, item 87);
- *Ordinance of the Council of Ministers of December 23, 1987, on the Amounts, Principles and Procedure of Imposing Fines for Violation of Environmental Protection Rules* (Dz.U. 1991, No. 89, item 404);
- *Ordinance of the Environment Minister of February 12, 1990, on the Protection of the Air against Pollution* (Dz.U. 1990, No. 15, item 92);
- *Ordinance of the Council of Ministers of December 21, 1991, on Charges for Economic Use of the Environment and Making Changes Therein* (Dz.U. 1991, No. 125, item 558, as amended).

7. Water requirements applicable to the operation of industrial and commercial facilities

- *Water Law of October 24, 1974* (Dz.U. 1974, No. 38, item 230, as amended);
- *Ordinance of the Council of Ministers of June 3, 1977, on Supervision and Control of Water Management* (Dz.U. 1977, No. 19, item 78);
- *Ordinance of Minister of Health and Social Security of May 31, 1977, on the Requirements which Should Be Fulfilled by Potable Water and Water Used for Economic Purposes* (Dz.U. 1977, No. 18, item 72), as amended by *Ordinance of Minister of Health and Social Security of May 4, 1990* (Dz.U. 1990, No. 35, item 205);

- *Ordinance of Council of Ministers of March 11, 1985, on Types of Special Use of Waters and the Construction and Exploitation of Water Equipment not Requiring a Water Permit* (Dz.U. 1985, No. 13, item 55);
- *Ordinance of the Council of Ministers of November 11, 1985, on the Principles and Methods of Determining Fines for Extraction of Water in Amounts greater than those in a Water Permit* (Dz.U. 1985, No. 52, item 271);
- *Ordinance of Environment Minister of November 5, 1991, on the Classification of Waters and the Required Conditions for Waste Disposal into Waters or the Soil* (Dz.U. 1991, No. 116, item 503);
- *Ordinance of Council of Ministers of December 21, 1991, on Fees for Special Use of Water and Water Equipment* (Dz.U. 1991, No. 125, item 556);
- *Ordinance of Environment Minister of December 21, 1991, on Fines for Violation of Requirements Applicable to Waste Discharged into the Water or the Ground* (Dz.U. 1991, No. 125, item 557);
- *Decree of Minister of Agriculture of January 26, 1976, on the Requirements to be Fulfilled by a Water Operation Permit* (M.P. 1976, No. 6, item 32).

8. Noise requirements applicable to the operation of industrial and commercial facilities

- *Law on the Protection and Shaping of the Environment of January 31, 1980* (Articles 49–52) (Dz.U. 1980, No. 3, item 6, as amended);
- *Ordinance of the Council of Ministers of September 30, 1980, on the Protection of the Environment against Noise and Vibration* (Dz.U. 1980, No. 24, item 90);
- *Ordinance of the Council of Ministers of December 23, 1987, on the Amounts, Principles and Procedure of Imposing Fines for Violation of Environmental Protection Rules* (Dz.U. 1991, No. 89, item 404).

9. Hazardous and non-hazardous waste management

- *Law on the Protection and Shaping of the Environment of January 31, 1980* (Articles 53-58) (Dz.U. 1980, No. 3, item 6, as amended);
- *Building Law of October 24, 1974* (Dz.U. 1979, No. 38, item 229, as amended);
- *Ordinances of the Minister of Health on Toxins and Hazardous Substances* (Dz.U. 1964, No. 2, item 9; Dz.U. 1965, No. 40, item 252; Dz.U. 1983, No. 13, item 67);
- *Ordinance of the Council of Ministers of September 30, 1980, on the Protection of the Environment against Waste and Other Pollution and the Maintenance of a Clean Environment and Order in Towns and Villages* (Dz.U. 1980, No. 24, item 91);
- *Ordinance of the Council of Ministers of December 23, 1987, on the Amounts, Principles and Procedure of Imposing Fines for Violation of Environmental Protection Rules* (Dz.U. 1991, No. 89, item 404);

- *Law on Road Traffic of February 1, 1983* (Dz.U. 1983, No. 5, item 35);
- *Ordinance of the Council of Ministers of December 21, 1991, on Charges for Economic Use of the Environment and Making Changes Therein* (Dz.U. 1991, No. 125, item 558, as amended).

10. Chemicals storage, handling and emergency response

- *Law of May 21, 1963, on Harmful Substances* (Dz.U. 1963, No. 22, item 116, as amended);
- *Ordinance of the Minister of Health of December 28, 1963, on the Labelling of Toxic Substances* (Dz.U. 1963, No. 2, item 8, as amended);
- *Ordinance of the Minister of Health of December 28, 1963, on the List of Toxic and Harmful Substances* (Dz.U. 1963, No. 2, item 9; Dz.U. 1965, No. 40, item 252; Dz.U. 1983, No. 13, item 67);
- *Ordinance of the Minister of Health of October 2, 1964, on Permits for the Production of and Trade in Toxins, Register of Toxins and Principles of Action of Bodies Controlling Harmful Substances* (Dz.U. 1964, No. 7, item 45);
- *Law on Road Traffic of February 1, 1983* (Dz.U. 1983, No. 5, item 35);
- *Decree of the Minister of Chemical and Light Industry of June 30, 1986, on the Principles of Warning the Public about Contamination by Harmful Industrial Substances* (M.P. 1986, No. 27, item 191).

Annex B

List of Permitting and Enforcement Authorities

Ministry of Environmental Protection, Natural Resources and Forestry
ul. Wawelska 52/54, 00-922 Warsaw
tel.: (48-22) 25-00-01 or 25-40-01
fax: (48-22) 25-33-53 or 25-39-72

Ministry of Health and Social Welfare
ul. Miodowa 15, 00-246 Warsaw
tel.: (48-22) 31-34-41 or 26-06-76

Ministry of Interior
ul. Rakowiecka 2b, 02-514 Warsaw
tel.: (48-22) 21-02-51 or (48-2) 601-18-69
fax: (48-2) 603-44-93

Central Planning Office
Plac Trzech Krzyzy 5, 00-507 Warsaw
tel.: (48-2) 693-50-00
fax: (48-2) 628-57-44

State Inspectorate of Environmental Protection
ul. Wawelska 52/54, 00-922 Warsaw
tel.: (48-22) 25-00-01 or 25-40-01
fax: (48-22) 25-04-65

State Sanitary Inspectorate
ul. Miodowa 1, 00-00923 Warsaw
tel.: (48-22) 26-40-41 or 31-34-61
fax: (48-22) 26-09-66

Commission on EIAs (Environment Ministry)
ul. Wawelska 52/54, 00-922 Warsaw
tel.: (48-22) 25-00-01 or 25-40-01
fax: (48-22) 25-33-53

Annex C

List of Proposed Legislation

- *Water Law* — The draft has been presented for inter-ministerial comments three times; it has received an opinion from the Legislative Council of the Government and should be submitted to the Council of Ministers and later to the Parliament in 1993.
- *Geology and Mining Law* — The draft has been the subject of discussion in a special parliamentary sub-commission.
- *Law on Waste* — The draft has twice been presented for inter-ministerial consultations; an inter-ministerial committee has been established to revise it. It is expected that the draft will be submitted to Parliament in the second half of 1993.
- *Law on Extraordinary Hazards to the Environment* — The draft was prepared by the State Inspectorate of Environmental Protection, in cooperation with the Ministry of Defense and the Ministry of Interior. There have been five inter-ministerial meetings concerning the draft.
- *Law on Air Protection* — Work has begun at the Environment Ministry; so far there have been no inter-ministerial consultations.
- *Amendments to the 1980 Environmental Law* — Amendments of provisions on charges, waste and the National Fund should be enacted in 1993.
- *Law on Noise Abatement* — Work has begun at the State Environmental Inspectorate.

Annex D

Environmental Standards

- *Ordinance of Minister of Health and Social Security of May 31, 1977, on the Requirements which Should Be Fulfilled by Potable Water and Water Used for Household Purposes* (Dz.U. 1977, No. 18, item 72);
- *Ordinance of Minister of Health and Social Security of May 4, 1990,* amending the *Ordinance on the Requirements which Should Be Fulfilled by Potable Water and Water Used for Household Purposes* (Dz.U. 1990, No. 35, item 205);
- *Ordinance of the Council of Ministers of September 30, 1980, on the Protection of the Environment against Noise and Vibration* (Dz.U. 1980, No. 24, item 90);
- *Ordinance of the Environment Minister of February 12, 1990, on the Protection of the Air against Pollution* (Dz.U. 1990, No. 15, item 92);
- *Ordinance of Environment Minister of November 5, 1991, on the Classification of Waters and the Required Conditions for Waste Disposal into Waters or the Soil* (Dz.U. 1991, No. 116, item 503);
- *Ordinance of Environment Minister of December 21, 1991, on Fines for Violation of Requirements Applicable to Waste Discharged into the Water or the Ground* (Dz.U. 1991, No. 125, item 557);
- *Ordinance of the Council of Ministers of December 21, 1991, on Charges for Economic Use of the Environment and Making Changes Therein* (Dz.U. 1991, No. 125 item 558);
- *Ordinance of the Council of Ministers of October 14, 1992,* amending the *Ordinance on Charges for Economic Use of the Environment and Making Changes Therein* (Dz.U. 1992, No. 79, item 400);
- *Ordinance of the Council of Ministers of January 26, 1993,* amending the *Ordinance on Charges for Economic Use of the Environment and Making Changes Therein* (Dz.U. 1993, No. 9, item 44).

Annex E

International Conventions

- *Protocol of 1978 Relating to the International Convention for the Prevention of Pollution from Ships, 17 February 1978,* 17 I.L.M. 546 (entered into force 2 October, 1983).
- *International Convention for Civil Liability for Oil Pollution Damage,* 29 November 1969, 973 U.N.T.S. 3.
- *International Convention Relating to Intervention on the High Seas in Cases of Oil Pollution Casualties,* 29 November, 1969, 970 U.N.T.S. 211 (entered into force 6 May 1975).
- *Convention on the Prevention of Marine Pollution by Dumping of Wastes and Other Matter,* 29 December 1972, 1046 U.N.T.S. 120 (entered into force 30 August 1975).
- *Convention Concerning Protection of the World Cultural and Natural Heritage,* 16 November 1972, 1037 U.N.T.S. 151 (entered into force 17 December 1975).
- *Protocol Relating to Intervention on the High Seas in Cases of Marine Pollution by Substances Other Than Oil,* 2 November 1973, 13 I.L.M. 605 (entered into force 30 March 1983).
- *Convention on the Protection of the Marine Environment of the Baltic Sea Area,* 22 March 1974, 13 I.L.M. 544.
- *Convention on Long-Range Transboundary Air Pollution,* 13 November 1979, 18 I.L.M. 1442 (entered into force 16 March 1983).
- *Protocol on Long-Term Financing of the Co-operative Program for Monitoring and Evaluation of the Long-Range Transmission of Air Pollutants in Europe,* 28 Septmber 1984, 24 I.L.M. 484 (entered into force 28 January 1988).
- *Convention for the Protection of the Ozone Layer,* 22 March 1985, 26 I.L.M. 1529 (entered into force 22 September 1988).
- *Convention on Early Notification of a Nuclear Accident,* 26 September 1986, 25 I.L.M. 1370 (entered into force 27 October 1986).
- *Montreal Protocol on Substances that Deplete the Ozone Layer,* 16 September 1987, 26 I.L.M. 1550 (entered into force 1 January 1989).
- *Convention on the Control of Transboundary Movements of Hazardous Wastes and Their Disposal,* 22 March 1989, 28 I.L.M. 649 (entered into force May 1992).

Annex F

Investment Projects
Subject to EIAs

The criteria for determining whether an investment project is exceptionally harmful and therefore subject to a mandatory Environmental Impact Assessment are set out in the *Decree of April 23, 1990*. They include projects which generate or result in:

- Emissions of pollutants to the air in excess of 20,000 tons per annum (5,000 tons per annum in protected areas);
- Discharges of sewage:
  - (i)   Directly into border waters;
  - (ii)   To running waters in highly polluted areas or specially protected areas;
  - (iii) Into the Baltic Sea, lakes, artificial reservoirs and the ground in quantities greater than 100 m³/day;
  - (iv)   To running water in quantities greater than 5,000 m³/day;
- Deterioration of water resources in specially protected areas and areas of special social and economic value;
- Generation or storage of hazardous waste;
- Contamination of the surface of the ground or soil or a change in the structure of agricultural land or forests over an area greater than: 50 hectares in highly polluted areas and specially protected areas, and over an area greater than 100 hectares in other areas;
- Use of water:
  - (i)   From border waters;
  - (ii)   From groundwater in quantities greater than 5,000 m³/day (2,000 m³/day in highly polluted or specially protected areas);
  - (iii) From surface waters in amounts greater than 40,000 m³/day, (20,000 m³/day in highly polluted areas or specially protected areas);
- Production of an electromagnetic fields of 0.1–300,000 Mhz;
- Noise levels in excess of legal limits.

Additionally, EIAs must be performed in the following cases:

- Electromagnetic lines and equipment of 400 kV or more;
- Airports;
- Highways and main roads;
- Railway junctions and railway lines of national importance;
- Power generating plants, thermal-electric plants and thermal nuclear plants, radioactive waste storage sites and nuclear reactors located within administrative boundaries of a town or city;
- Gas and fuel pipelines of national or international importance.

Romania

Prepared for the European Bank for Reconstruction and Development and the
Commission of the European Communities by
Environmental Resources Limited*

1. Overview

1.1 *The Guidelines*

1.1.1 *Background*

Investments in Romania are subject to many legal and economic requirements. This document focuses specifically on those compliance, operational and liability issues which arise from environmental protection measures and affect investments.

The Guidelines are intended to enable investors to familiarise themselves with the basic environmental regulatory regime relating to commercial and industrial greenfield site developments, joint venture operations or company acquisitions in Romania.

The Guidelines review institutional arrangements for environmental control, legislative requirements and procedures, time implications for permitting, public access to information, liability and sanctions. Because environmental policy, legislation and infrastructure in Romania are currently undergoing radical change, the review covers both current and proposed future arrangements.

Guidelines for the following CEE countries have been prepared on behalf of the European Bank for Reconstruction and Development and the Commission of the European Communities by Environmental Resources Limited and White & Case:

- Bulgaria;[1]
- Czech and Slovak Republics;[1]

---

[1] Guidelines prepared by White & Case.

---

* Environmental Resources Limited acknowledges the valuable contribution in the preparation of the *Investors' Environmental Guidelines: Romania* of Dr David Gilbert of Environmental Resources Limited.
  Environmental Resources Limited would also like to thank Dr Dumitra Popescu, of the Institute for Legal Research of the Romanian Academy, for her advisory role in the preparation of these Guidelines.

- Estonia;[2]
- Hungary;[1]
- Latvia;[2]
- Lithuania;[2]
- Poland;[1]
- Romania.[2]

These Guidelines present a description of the environmental regulatory framework as of February 1993. They provide a first step for investors in understanding environmental requirements but do not substitute for specific legal advice relating to particular sites.

Administrative and legal arrangements for environmental regulation are in a transition phase in the countries covered by these Guidelines. Requirements and implementation systems are subject to change. Investors are advised to discuss details of requirements with the authorities and check for any changes which may have taken place since February 1993.

1.1.2 Using the Guidelines

The Guidelines provide general guidance on environmental regulatory requirements applicable to foreign investment in commercial and industrial sectors of the economy. Some sections of the Guidelines, such as *Section 4* on Land Use Planning and *Section 5* on EIA are also applicable to other sectors of the economy such as agriculture, mining, forestry and fisheries. In relation to such types of activities however, it is advisable to review other applicable requirements which are outside the scope of the Guidelines.

Section 1 provides a quick reference to environmental regulatory requirements in two case studies, and in *Figure 1.1.2(a) and Figure 1.1.2(b)*. *Figure 1.1.2(b)* indicates how the Guidelines should be used by reference to the type of investment decision that has to be made.

The remainder of this section provides background information on the country and the following.

- Administrative structure;
- Legislative process and key items of legislation;
- Quick reference to the permitting process;
- Enforcement;
- Public participation.

Section 2 highlights the potential liabilities of investors. Liabilities potentially arising from past pollution to be taken into account at the time an investment is made and liabilities arising in the course of operating commercial and industrial facilities are presented separately. Additional details relating to specific sectors of control are provided in subsequent sections.

Section 3 identifies any environmental auditing requirements and comments on the role of voluntary audits in achieving compliance.

---

[1]   Guidelines prepared by White & Case.
[2]   Guidelines prepared by Environmental Resources Limited.

470

Figure 1.1.2(a) Using the Guidelines: report structure

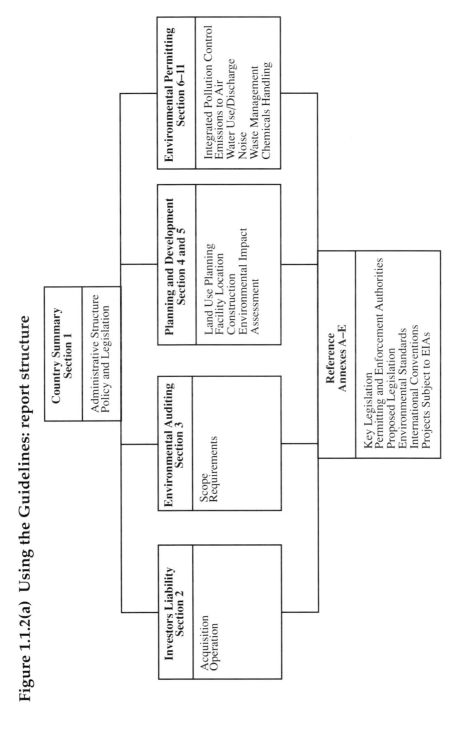

Figure 1.1.2(b) Using the Guidelines: summary by type of investment decision

Investment Decisions	Environmental Concerns	Sections in Guidelines
Choice of investment sector (eg commercial, services, manufacturing, energy)	Government and environmental bodies	1.4, 1.7, Annex B
	Existing and proposed legislation	1.5, Annex A & C
	Available forms of investment	1.2, 2.3.2
	Purchase of land	4.3
	Investments subject to EIA	5
	Activities subject to permitting	6–11
	Permitting overview and examples	1.6
Development of a "greenfield site"	Government and environmental bodies	1.4, 1.7, Annex B
	Existing and proposed legislation	1.5, Annex A & C
	Purchase of land	4.3
	EIA requirements	5
	Public participation	1.8
	Environmental standards	7, 8, Annex D
Acquisition of existing facility and privatisation	Government and environmental bodies	1.4, 1.7, Annex B
	Privatisation	1.2
	Environmental liability	2
	Cleanup of contaminated sites	2.3
	Indemnification by government	2.3
	Environmental audits	3
	Environmental standards	7, 8, Annex D
	EIA requirements (especially where modifications are made to existing facilities)	5

Investment Decisions	*Environmental Concerns*	*Sections in Guidelines*
Redevelopment and expansion of commercial and industrial facilities	Government and environmental bodies	1.4, 1.7, Annex B
	Change of land use	4
	Construction permits	4
	EIA requirements	5
	Permitting requirements	6–11
	Public participation	1.8
Operation of industrial and commercial facilities	Government and environmental bodies	1.4, 1.7, Annex B
	Environmental liability	2
	EIA requirements	5
	Public participation	1.8
	Integrated permitting	6
	Air requirements	7, Annex D
	Water requirements	8, Annex D
	Noise requirements	9
	Waste management	10
	Chemical storage and handling	11
	Permitting overview and examples	1.6
	Compliance with international law	Annex E

Sections 4–11 provide guidance on permitting and related regulatory requirements for setting up and operating a commercial or industrial enterprise. Key aspects are presented at the beginning of each section for quick reference. Each section identifies the following:

- Key legislation;
- Activities covered;
- Requirements and procedures;
- Timing;
- Public participation;
- Enforcement and sanctions.

Sections 4 and 5 outline requirements and procedures relating to land use planning, facility location and construction, and environmental impact assessment EIA. *Section 6* indicates the extent to which environmental permitting is integrated. Permitting and other regulatory requirements relating to air, water, noise, waste and chemicals are set out in *Sections 7–11*.

Annexes provide quick reference to existing and proposed legislation, contact points for the regulatory agencies, environmental standards, and ratification of international conventions.

1.2 The country

1.2.1 Background

Romania's population in 1991 was 23 million, with over 50% living in urban areas and a population density of 98 per km^2. Romania's economy combines strong industrial and agricultural sectors. The Romania unit of currency is Lei, with a present exchange rate of Lei 980 = £1 sterling (as of 2 April 1993).

1.2.2 Investment

Romania's national government is a parliamentary democracy. The first democratic national elections were held in May 1990. Romania is moving to a market economy from a centrally planned and controlled political regime in which there was intensive energy use and little attention paid to practical aspects of environmental protection. The radical transformation of the Romanian economic system, which aims to promote privatisation and a market economy, has short-term goals of ensuring economic stability, reducing inflation, restoring market equilibrium and stimulating economic growth through market mechanisms.

In 1990–91 a package of legal reforms was introduced to state ownership, to create and develop the private sector. More than 100,000 private enterprises, mostly small businesses, have already been established, representing an estimated 10% of GNP. Legislation to encourage foreign investment by permitting full foreign ownership of enterprises was introduced in 1991. Since 1990 approximately 16,000 foreign investment projects have been initiated. Economic reform is likely to result in a shift away from heavy industry towards lighter industries and services. Major industrial sectors include:

- Mining;
- Machine building;

- Aerospace;
- Chemicals;
- Electrical equipment.

The consumer goods sectors are growing and the gross national product (GNP) per capita in 1990 was US$ 1,700. The priority sectors for foreign investment include:

- Energy;
- Agriculture;
- Transport and telecommunications;
- Tourism;
- Banking and insurance;
- Textiles;
- Paper and board;
- Construction materials;
- Other industries such as chemicals, engineering, and electronics.

Historically, Romania has followed the environmental quality approach to environmental standard setting, ie imposing limits on levels of pollutants in the environment (environmental quality or ambient standards) rather than limits on releases to the environment (emission standards). Currently there are ambient standards in place for air and water discharge standards for certain substances discharged to water. Emission standards for air are in preparation.

It is intended that there will be a move towards the approaches of other jurisdictions in standard setting, eg US, European Community and its Member States. New standards will initially be applied to new facilities and introduced gradually for existing operations. There are no standards for hazardous waste management although the import of hazardous waste is controlled by legislation. Proposed legislation is being developed for waste management activities.

1.3 Administrative structure

Romania has a centralised administrative system with certain tasks delegated to the 41 Branch Agencies of the national Ministries situated in each of the prefectures and one in Bucharest. Environmental protection responsibilities lie largely with the Ministry of Waters, Forests and Environmental Protection and its Branch Agencies. The Ministry was established by *Government Decision No. 264, 1990* and Branch Agencies by *Government Decision No. 983/1991* which has been replaced by Government Decision No. 792/1992. The function of the Branch Agencies is set out in the *Regulations for the Organisation and Function of Branch Agencies, No. 3775 1991*.

Local government, ie prefectures and town authorities, is responsible for land use planning and public services including water supply, wastewater treatment and municipal waste collection and disposal. *Law No. 69 on Local Public Administration 1991* provides for the appointment of a Prefect in each prefecture to represent the national government, and to co-ordinate and supervise public services of Ministries and other central authorities. The Prefect is appointed by central government.

Administrative structures are well established and it is expected that they will be strengthened as further environmental legislation is introduced. The draft Law on Environmental Protection will re-enact the administrative arrangements relating to the Ministry of Waters, Forestry and Environmental Protection and Branch Agencies. The draft provides for a fund to be established which will draw resources from several sources including permit charges and fines. The fund will be used for environmental remediation and protection, inspection activities and environmental education.

1.4 Government and environmental bodies

1.4.1 Ministries

The current institutional arrangements for environmental management were established in 1990 with the formation of the Ministry of Environment which became the Ministry of Waters, Forestry and Environmental Protection in December 1992. The Ministry provides an integrated setting for a range of activities which were previously carried out by sectoral organisations, eg National Water Council, National Council for Environmental Protection and Commission for Protection of National Monuments.

The Ministry of Waters, Forestry and Environmental Protection is the principal Ministry for the administration, compliance checking and enforcement of legislation relating to environmental protection, water, waste and forestry as set out in *Governmental Decision No. 792 on the Organisation and Function of the Ministry of Waters, Forestry and Environmental Protection 1992*. The Ministry comprises three Departments, Waters, Forestry and Environmental Protection. Water and forestry management also involves two autonomous state companies, Apele Romane, Water Authority and ROMSILVA, the States forestry company which are attached to the relevant Secretaries of State of the Ministry.

Department of Environmental Protection

The Department has four Directorates with the following roles:

- Environmental strategies, drafting laws, issuing administrative regulations, and Environmental Impact Assessment (EIAs);
- Environmental monitoring and management of protected areas;
- Environmental inspection;
- International and public relations.

Department of Water

The Department of Water comprises a two Directorates and an Inspectorate. The first Directorate is responsible for strategic planning, drafting laws and issuing administrative regulations, and for water quality and inter-ministerial coordination. Standard setting and permitting are under the overall control of this Directorate and permits are issued by local water authorities. Day to day management of water resources (quality and quantity) of the 13 regional river basins is the responsibility of the autonomous state company, Apele

Romane. The second Directorate co-ordinates water management and is responsible for hydrological and meteorological assessment and flood control.

Department of Forests

A quarter of Romania's surface area is forested, almost all of which is state-owned. The Directorate and its State Inspectorate of Forests are responsible for the promotion of productivity and protection against over-exploitation. Day-to-day management is undertaken by ROMSILVA.

National Commission for Nuclear Activities Monitoring

The National Commission is within the Ministry and controls safety and environmental protection at nuclear facilities including facility location, construction, commissioning and operation.

1.4.2 Environmental bodies

Branch Agencies, in each of the 40 prefectures and one in Bucharest, represent central government and are under the direct control of a Secretary of State in the central Ministry of Waters, Forestry and Environmental Protection. *Regulation No. 3775 for the Organisation and Function of Branch Agencies 1991* sets out the structure, roles and responsibilities of the Agencies.

The Agencies are headed by the Prefect who is responsible for public services and other central Ministry functions. The Agencies play a central role in the practical implementation of environmental policy and legislation including permitting, monitoring, compliance checking and instigating legal action for non-compliance. Responsibilities of the Agencies include pollution control, conservation and ecological restoration. Agencies are financed by the central Ministry and they typically employ 70 staff.

The Prefect has a judicial role and is not involved in practical, day-to-day aspects of the Agencies functions. Agencies are managed by the Director, a Direction Committee and an Administrative Council. Key environmental protection functions are the responsibilities of the Section for Regulations, which issues environmental permits and collects data and information, and the Section for Inspection. Other Sections deal with laboratory services and monitoring.

1.4.3 Environmental Funds

Charges for the use of water and wastewater discharge are paid into the Water Fund which is managed by the Water Directorate within the Ministry. The fund is to be used to provide economic assistance for investment in wastewater treatment, discharge control and other water-related investment.

The draft Law on Environmental Protection provides for a fund to be established which will draw resources from several sources including permit charges and fines. The fund will be used for environmental remediation and protection, activities, and environmental training and education.

1.5 Environmental legislation

1.5.1 Legislative process

The new legal system in Romania is based on the *Constitution of 1991*. Powers are divided as follows:

- The Parliament is responsible for enacting primary legislation;
- The Government has executive powers;
- The Courts hold the judicial authority.

Statutory control is provided by legislation comprising laws (primary legislation) and delegated or secondary legislation in the form of governmental decisions and ministerial orders, regulations, instructions, standards and decisions which are all legally binding instruments. Powers to make secondary legislation is provided for by the laws.

Arrangements for the development and introduction of legislation are established by the Constitution. Draft laws are prepared by a lead Ministry with advice from other relevant Ministries, including the Ministry of Justice, and the Constitutional Court. The amended draft goes to Cabinet and if agreed is passed to Parliamentary review bodies of the two houses of Parliament, and finally to the Chamber of Deputies and the Senate. If both houses of Parliament agree, the law is adopted by Parliament and signed by the President. Legislation introduced prior to the constitutional reform remains in force until it is revoked by new legislation.

The government is empowered by the *Constitution* to adopt Decisions and Orders. The function of a government Decision is to provide for the organisational arrangements for the implementation or execution of laws whilst an Order is issued under an enabling law to implement specific provisions as prescribed by the law. Decisions are initiated by a Minister, developed in consultation with technical, judicial and administrative experts by an Inter-Ministerial Committee. The Ministers involved and the Cabinet must agree the draft which may then be adopted by signature of the Prime Minister. Ministerial Orders can be initiated by a Directorate or division of a Ministry and are adopted by signature of the Minister. The development of Orders can involve consultation with other relevant Ministries.

Ministers are empowered to adopt regulations and instructions. Standards are adopted by a Minister and the national Standards Institute, and decisions are issued by an Under-secretary or Secretary of State. In the previous administrative system there were a number of other types of legal instruments which in some cases are still in force, eg Decisions of the State Council, the President or the Council of Ministers, and the Guidelines.

1.5.2 Legislation

Legislation in Romania concerning the control of the operation of industrial and commercial facilities is undergoing radical change. The system of control comprises both legislation in force prior to the political reform and legislation introduced during since 1990. Key items of legislation are as follows:

- *Law No. 9 on Environmental Protection 1973*;
- *Law No. 8 on Water 1974*;

- *Ministerial Order No. 91 on Forms, Applications and Permitting Procedure;*
- *Order No. 623 of Health Ministry Establishing Sanitary Rules on Environmental Protection of Human Settlements;*
- *Ministerial Order No. 170 on the Issuing of Permits 1990;*
- *Ministerial Order No. 113 on Documentation Required for Permit Applications 1990;*
- *Ministerial Order No. 715 concerning approvals for administration of water 1991;*
- *Ministerial Order No. 435 concerning authorisations for administration of water 1991;*
- *Law No. 5 on the Rational Management, Protection and Assurance of the Quality of Waters 1989;*
- *Governmental Decision No. 1001 on the Establishment of a Unitary System of Payments for Products and Services of Water Husbandry 1990* (as amended 1991 and 1992);
- *Decree Establishing Permissible Limits of the Main Polluting Substances Prior to Discharge 1979;*
- *Ministerial Order No. 437 on Certificates 1991;*
- *Decree No. 465 on Waste Collection, Minimisation and Re-use 1979;*
- *Decision No. 340 on Waste Imports and Residues 1992* (as amended 1992).

A draft Law on Environmental Protection has also been prepared.

The focus for the development of environmental protection and improvement policy is the draft framework Law on Environmental Protection which will replace the *Law on Environmental Protection, 1973*. The draft Law has entered the parliamentary process and is expected to be enacted in 1993.

The draft, which includes general requirements for waste recovery and recycling, environmental impact assessment and facility permitting, indicates that environmental protection, at least in the short term, will rely on a "command and control" approach. The draft states that environmental protection is a prerequisite for sustainable development, imposes a general duty on facilities for environmental protection, ie the "polluter pays principle" and requires production processes and technologies to be as clean as possible ie using "best available technology". The draft also requires facilities carrying out high risk activities to be insured against damage caused to the environment.

Further items of legislation in preparation includes draft Laws on air, waste management, water, pesticides and forests. Legislation is also being developed to introduce new environmental standards.

It is anticipated that detailed requirements will be established in subordinate legislation, eg Decisions, Orders etc to implement the general provisions of the draft framework law although in the case of permitting, a system has already been established by *Ministerial Order No. 170 on the Issuing of Permits 1990 and Ministerial Order No. 437 on Certification 1991*.

The draft Law on Environmental Protection sets out a number of general provisions including the following:

- Right of access to information on environmental quality;
- Right to information and of consultation regarding facility location;
- Right to indemnity for harm suffered as a result of environmental damage.

The draft states that environmental protection is a general duty imposed on business and citizens. Commercial and industrial activities must be carried out so as to provide for a sustainable environment, and production processes and technology must be as clean as possible. Operators must ensure that equipment for pollution control is properly maintained, staff responsible for environmental protection are trained, and releases to the environment are monitored and recorded. Other general requirements relate to the following:

- Carrying out environmental impact assessments (EIA), the results of which are to be made publicly available;
- Waste recovery, recycling and energy recovery;
- Prompt action and reporting when accidental pollution occurs;
- Provision of monitoring data to the authorities;
- Administrative fines and environmental restoration in the case of releases of pollutants in excess of prescribed limits;
- Keeping a fund of 10% of any investment to be used for the removal of sources of pollution;
- Insurance against environmental damage for high risks activities.

More detailed requirements of the draft law are set out under the structure:

- Permitting and EIA;
- Toxic products and hazardous waste;
- Fertiliser and pesticide marketing and use;
- Natural resources (including protection of water, air and soil, protected areas, land use planning and nuclear safety);
- Administrative arrangements;
- Sanctions.

It is anticipated that provisions relating to environmental permitting and EIA to be introduced by the new legislation will be along very similar lines to existing requirements introduced by Ministerial Order in 1990.

1.6 Overview of permitting process and other regulatory requirements

1.6.1 General

An integrated permitting system was introduced in 1991. An environmental permit is required for new and modified facilities. Conditions relating to air, water and soil which reflect existing standards or more stringent standards may be attached to the permit. A further requirement is an environmental certificate which confirms that the facility is operating in accordance with relevant standards and/or the environmental permit. Facilities in operation prior to 1991 can continue to operate without an environmental permit except where modification has taken place or is planned in which case a permit is required. Pre-1991 facilities must however obtain an environmental certificate.

The development of a new facility or modification of an existing facility requires a town development certificate, a construction permit and approval of an environmental impact assessment. Sectoral permits must then be obtained ie water use, wastewater discharge, emissions to the atmosphere. When all the sectoral permits been obtained, application is made for the environmental permit and certificate. Existing facilities (pre-1991) must have an environmental certificate which demonstrated compliance with relevant environmental standards. Local authorities are largely responsible for permitting in relation to land use and construction, and the Ministry of Waters, Forests and Environmental Protection deal with sectoral environmental permits and the integrated environmental permit and certificate.

1.6.2 Case study 1

For a foreign investor acquiring a greenfield site for development of a new paper mill, the permitting procedure would involve the following steps.

First the investor must apply for a town development certificate and a construction permit from the Prefectural or town authority which takes 30 days to process. Charges are imposed for both the certificate and permit calculated on the basis of the land area of the development. Thirty days prior to starting construction the investor must inform the regional branch of the State Construction Inspectorate of the proposed starting date.

Following this an Environmental Impact Assessment (EIA) must be undertaken either by the Institute for Environment within the Ministry of Waters, Forests and Environmental Protection or by an officially authorised company. There is no prescribed time frame for the EIA.

The next stage is to obtain permits for air, water use and wastewater discharge. The Ministry of Waters, Forests and Environmental Protectionand its regional Branch Agencies are responsible for air emissions permitting. In general, permitting is undertaken by the Branch Agencies but if a facility may have a major impact on the environment, the application is passed to the national Ministry. The water permits are dealt with by the Ministry and the regional Water authorities. In each case the time for determination of the permit is 20 days.When the sectoral permits have been obtained an application is made for the environmental permit from the Ministry of Waters, Forests and Environmental Protection or Branch Agency. Once a facility is in operation, the Ministry or Agency check that operations are in compliance with conditions and standards set out in the permit. Where the facility is in compliance, an environmental certificate is issued. Permits are not currently required in regard to noise, waste and chemicals handling and storage. A summary of the process is presented in *Figure 1.6.2(a)*.

1.6.3 Case study 2

A foreign investor forming a joint venture with an existing company, acquiring two factories, closing one and refurbishing the other to produce tyres, the permitting procedure would involve the following steps.

There are no specific environmental requirements to close a factory unless this involves demolition. In order to demolish a factory, a demolition permit would be required from the Prefecture. The purpose of the demolition permit is to ensure that damage is not caused to other buildings or underground structures. In cases where historical monuments may be affected a further demolition permit would be required from the National Commission for Historical Monuments.

Figure 1.6.2(a) Environmental permitting procedure for a proposed facility

Main Steps	Authority	Timing
Step 1. Construction and Development Permits		
Application for town development certificate ↓	Prefecture or town authority	30 days
Application for construction permit ↓	Prefecture or town authority	30 days
Step 2. Environmental Impact Assessment (EIA) and Environmental Permits		
Preparation of EIA by State Institute for Environment or authorised company ↓		No fixed time
Application for permits for air, water use, discharge ↓	Ministry of Waters, Forestry and Environmental Protection ↓	20 days
Application for integrated environmental permit	Ministry of Waters, Forestry and Environmental Protection	20 days
Step 3. Construction and Environmental Certificate		
Notification of construction 30 days in advance ↓	Regional branch of State Construction Inspectorate	
Construction ↓		
Application for environmental certificate	Ministry of Waters, Forestry and Environmental Protection	20 days

Permitting and other regulatory requirements for refurbishing the facility are the same as those for the establishment of a new facility on a greenfield site as outlined in *Section 1.6.2* and *Figure 1.6.2(a)*.

1.7 Enforcement of environmental legislation

Enforcement of environmental legislation relating to commercial and industrial operations is the responsibility of the State Inspectorates for Environment and for Water and the Romanian Water Authority, Apele Romane. The State Inspectorates and the Water Authority undertake some of the inspections and have a supervisory role over inspection by the Branch Agencies. Branch Agencies are required to prepare annual plans including *inter alia* the predicted number of inspection visits and permits to be issued, which are then submitted to the Ministry for approval. Agencies must then report quarterly on their performance in meeting targets set in the annual plan. Reports from the agencies are not made publicly available.

The Agencies have responsibility for enforcement in industrial facilities, agricultural units and public works. The State Inspectorate co-operates with other Ministries, eg Health, Industry, Agriculture, and with local authorities and the police in the enforcement process.

Both Ministry and Branch Agency Inspectors may inspect facilities. Each Ministry Inspector is responsible for supervising the enforcement activities of three to four Agencies and accompanies Agency inspectors on facility visits according to an inspection programme. A report is then made to the Chief Inspector. Agency Inspectors both check compliance and advise operators on how to meet standards and permit conditions.

A facility which is not in compliance with the relevant standards or permit is first given a warning by the Inspector. If the facility does not take the necessary steps, an administrative fine may be imposed by the Inspector. The size of fines is prescribed in the legislation. Administrative fines may be imposed continually. Finally, non-compliance may result in court action. Details of sanctions are set out in *Section 2*.

1.8 Public participation

1.8.1 Public access to information

The Romanian *Constitution* provides for public access to information of public interest and Government is obliged to ensure that such information is provided to the public. The *Law on Environmental Protection 1973* includes a public right to information on environmental issues but this does not give access to decisions on permit applications. The draft Law on Environmental Protection constrains general provisions which will allow public access to information on the environment.

1.8.2 Provision of information

There are no general requirements for the authorities to provide information to the public. A list of permits and certificates for construction and town planning is published.

1.8.3 Public consultation

There are no provisions in the legislation for public consultation in permitting decisions except for construction permits where the authority has the power to require that public consultation takes place for proposals of national interest. The draft Law on Environmental Protection contains provisions which will allow public participation in decisions relating to the environment. It is expected that new legislation on Environmental Impact Assessments (EIAs) will include the right for public participation in the EIA process.

2. Environmental liability

2.1 Summary

Note:	Liability law is currently being revised in the draft Law on Environmental Protection. This summary includes proposed legislation.
Environmental Liabilities of Investors:	The draft law requires companies carrying out high risk activities to take out insurance against damage to the environment.
Successor Liability:	There is no liability provision relating to past pollution.
Investor Clean-up of Contaminated Sites:	No standards exist which either trigger a clean-up obligation or for restoration levels.
Civil Liability:	Under the *Civil Code*, civil liability currently operates on the basis of fault based liability. The draft law introduces the concept of strict liability.
Administrative Liability:	Violations of the *Civil Code* may result in fines and facility shut down.
Criminal Liability:	Criminal liability is defined under the *Penal Code*. Sanctions including fines and imprisonment, are set out in the *1973 Law on Environmental Protection*. Criminal liability is extended in the draft law.

2.2 Sources of legislation relating to environmental liability

- *Penal Code*;
- *Civil Code*;
- *Law on Environmental Protection 1973*;
- *Law on Water 1974*;
- Draft Law on Environmental Protection.

2.3 Environmental liabilities for past pollution

2.3.1 Types of environmental liability

There are no liability provisions relating to past environmental liabilities. The law is being developed in this area.

2.3.2 Government indemnification of environmental liabilities

There are no provisions for government to indemnify investors against environmental liability for past pollution.

The draft Law on Environmental Protection requires companies carrying out high risk activities (not defined) to take out insurance against damage to the environment.

2.3.3 Investor clean-up of contaminated sites

Environmental clean-up standards

There are no environmental clean-up standards.

Escrow accounts

The draft Law on Environmental Protection sets a requirement for facilities which cause pollution to establish a fund of 10% of the total investment which will be dedicated to removing pollution sources.

Environmental Funds

Charges for the use of water and wastewater discharge are paid into the Water Fund which is managed by the Water Directorate within the Ministry of Waters, Forestry and Environmental Protection. The fund is to be used to provide economic assistance for investment in wastewater treatment, discharge control and other water related investment. Recent fund expenditure has include remediation of water management works following flood damage and the development of a system for water monitoring.

The draft Law on Environmental Protection provides for a fund to be established which will draw resources from several sources including permit charges and fines. The fund will be used for environmental remediation and protection, activities, and environmental training and education.

2.4 Environmental liabilities arising from facility operation

2.4.1 Civil liability

Fault based liability

Under Article 998 of the *Civil Code* any person causing damage to another must repair the damage. Article 1,000 make persons liable for damage caused by persons for which they are responsible and Article 1,008 provides for joint liability.

Strict liability

Strict liability for damage caused to the environment will be imposed on enactment of the draft Law on Environmental Protection (Article 7(1)).

Statutes of limitation

There are no provisions for the limitation of liability. The law is being developed in this area.

Remedies

Compensation may be awarded in cases brought under Article 998 of the *Civil Code*.

Case examples

At the time of writing, there are no examples of civil liability relevant to the environment.

2.4.2 *Administrative liability*

Types of administrative liability

Administrative fines for infringement of the requirements set out in the draft Law on Environmental Protection may be imposed by persons authorised by the Ministry of Waters, Forestry and Environmental Protection, and in their fields of competence, other Ministries, police officers, and local authorities.

Remedies

Violations of the *Civil Code* may result in fines and facility shut down. Examples of administrative fines are given in *Table 2.4.2(a)*.

Case examples

Fines have been imposed by the State Inspectorate for Environment for breaches of environmental legislation, eg violating standards for releases to air and water, by both privae and state companies. The most polluting part of a textiles facility in Succava has been shut down.

2.4.3 *Criminal liability*

Types of criminal liability

The *Penal Code* (Articles 248–249) creates liability for "abuse of duty against the general interests" and for "negligence of that duty".

Remedies

Sanctions set out in the *Law on Environmental Protection, 1973* include the following:

- Release to air of damaging substances or causing noise above legal limits, which endanger human health: three months – two years' imprisonment or a fine (unspecified);

Table 2.4.2(a)   Administrative Fines

- *Fine of 25,000–150,000 lei for*:
  - pollution releases from installations, equipment, and combustion engines above prescribed limits;
  - non-compliance with noise insulation requirements resulting in standards being exceeded;
  - non-compliance with requirements for training of staff with special environmental protection responsibilities.
- *Fine of 50,000–300,000 lei for*:
  - absence of, or inadequate operation of, suitable pollution control equipment, and operation without such equipment;
  - failing to take proper measures or ensuring conditions for waste management;
  - failing to observe measures regarding subsoil and natural resources;
  - carrying out EIAs without authorisation by Ministry of Waters, Forestry and Environmental Protection.
- *Fine of 75,000–350,000 lei for*:
  - failing to keep a fund of 10% of the investment for pollution clean-up;
  - preventing access of the authority to facilities and failing to provide requested data;
  - operating a facility without and environmental permit and/or certificate and failure to comply with their requirements;
  - failing to analyse environmental impacts and measures to prevent environmental damage;
  - failing to supervise construction and facility operation in order to avoid damage and accidental pollution;
  - failure to keep records relating to toxic products and dangerous waste;
  - discharge of untreated wastewaters, oil products and other pollutants to surface or irrigation water, or drainage canals;
  - disposal of waste to surface water or storing waste on river beds or banks;
  - injection of waste underground without authorisation;
  - refusal to provide data requested by environmental authorities.

- Storage or disposal of domestic or industrial residues in breach of requirements so as to endanger human health: one month–one year imprisonment or a fine (unspecified);
- Operation of new facilities or development of existing facilities without suitable air and water pollution control equipment.

The *Law on Waters 1974* makes it an offence to discharge wastewater or dispose of waste materials in waters in quantities or concentrations so as to cause harm to health, animal life, industrial production, agriculture or fish. The penalty is three months–two years' imprisonment or a fine of 3,000–10,000 lei.

It is also an offence to operate new facilities, develop existing ones, or use modified production technology without a permit, with a penalty of six months–three of years imprisonment or a fine of 5,000–15,000 lei.

Where offences are committed without intention less severe penalties are prescribed. The Law also provides for more severe penalties in certain circumstances.

Proposals

Under the draft Law on Environmental Protection prescribed actions which endanger people, animal health, or terrestrial or aquatic ecosystems may result in imprisonment or a fine as set out in *Table 2.4.3(a)*. Prosecution may be initiated by the criminal prosecuting bodies or the Ministry of Waters, Forestry and Environmental Protection.

Case examples

At the time of writing there have been no cases under the Criminal Code against foreign investors in relation to the environment.

Table 2.4.3(a)   Draft criminal sanctions

- *Imprisonment for 1–6 months, or a fine of 10,000–60,000 lei for*:
  - pollution caused by premeditated release to water, air, soil or wastewater of gas powders, residues, toxic waste, or any other kind of noxious chemical or biological agent which may give rise to high toxicological, pathological or ecological risk;
  - failing to monitor the operation and behaviour of technological and treatment equipment, installation and construction in order to prevent damage and accidental pollution.
- *Imprisonment for 6 months–2 years or a fine of 15,000–75,000 lei for*:
  - failing to respond quickly, removing causes and limiting harmful effects of accidental pollution and not informing the authorities, and companies and the population that might be affected.
- *Imprisonment for 2–5 years or a fine of 50,000–150,000 lei for*:
  - failing to comply with legal requirements relating to the production, transport, storing, trading, using or removing dangerous toxic substances including pesticides;
  - failing to respond to the suspension of a permit;
  - injection for storage underground of liquid, gaseous or chemical waste without consent of the authorities;
  - giving false conclusions or information in ecological impact studies and analyses.

---

3. Environmental audits

3.1 Sources of legislation relating to environmental audits

There are no legal requirements to undertake pre-acquisition audits. Such requirements are subject to discussion amongst environmental officials but there are no definite plans for legislation on this issue.

Existing facilities however, require an Environmental Certificate from the Ministry of the Environment or a Branch Agency, which includes assessment of compliance with environmental standards and other regulatory requirements, ie an audit.

The investor should consider carrying out a pre-acquisition audit to determine that the facility is in compliance and whether any liability exists and discuss potential liability issues with the authorities.

3.2 National experience with environmental audits

It is expected that projects sponsored by financial institutions such as the IFC and EBRD would include requirements for some form of environmental audit to be undertaken. There appears to be no example of auditing in practice as yet.

4. Land use planning

4.1 Summary

Authorities:	Prefectural and town authorities.
Types of Activity:	Prefectures: major developments and other specified industrial, commercial and public works.
Permits:	*Town authorities*: activities not dealt with by the prefectures. *Town Development Certificate*: detailing the legal, economic and technical status of the site. *Construction/demolition permit*: for the construction, reconstruction, modification, extension or closure of any facility.
Timing:	30 days.
Public Information:	All documents submitted by the investor, permits and certificates are made available to the public.

Public Consultation:	Certificates and permits are made available for public consultation. For developments of national significance the authority dealing with the application for a town development certificate may arrange for a public consultation process.

4.2 Sources of relevant land use legislation

Land use planning and construction are controlled by the following legislation:

- *Law No. 50 on Authorisation of Construction and Measures for House Building, 1991 (Law on Construction)*;
- *Ministerial Order No. 91 on Forms, Applications and Permitting Procedure under the Law on Construction of 25 October 1991*;
- *Law No. 18 on Land Fund 1991*;
- *Law No. 9 on Environmental Protection 1973*;
- *Law No. 8 on Water 1974*;
- *Order No. 623 of Health Ministry Establishing Sanitary Rules on Environmental Protection of Human Settlements*;
- Draft Law on Environmental Protection.

4.3 Scope of activities subject to land use regulation

The *Law on Environmental Protection 1973* and the *Law on Water 1974* impose general requirements that facilities must be located so as to minimise the environmental impacts of technical failure which may result in pollution.

A construction permit is required for the construction of any type of facility, and for reconstruction, modification, extension or closure under the *Law on Construction 1991*. The Law also sets out requirements for the approval of town development and territorial plans.

4.4 Permitting process

4.4.1 Authorities

Construction/demolition permits and town development certificates are obtained from the prefectural or town authorities. Prefectures are responsible for dealing with construction applications for activities including the following:

- Government approved projects (ie developments with a 500 m lei budget or more financed by the state);
- Public works;
- Industrial facilities;
- Commercial establishments;
- Shops;
- Religious establishments;

- Social-cultural establishments;
- Other activities outside town boundaries.

Town authorities are responsible for construction permitting for activities other than those dealt with by the prefectures.

4.4.2 Application requirements

Prior to acceptance of an application for a construction permit, a town development certificate must be obtained which includes details of the legal, economic and technical status of the site and building, including evidence of ownership.

Specific requirements for construction are set out in the *Ministerial Order No. 91 on Forms, Applications and Permitting Procedure under the Law on Construction 1991*.

Thirty days prior to starting construction the investor must announce to the regional branch of the State Inspectorate of Construction, Public Works, and Town Planning the proposed date of starting construction or facility modification according to *Government Decision No. 25 on the Quality of Construction 1992*.

The *Law on Land Fund 1991*, which provides for the redistribution of land and private ownership, also includes environmental protection requirements. The 1991 Law states that technical, economic and environmental documentation relating to the various sectors, eg agriculture, forestry, water management, transport, and housing development must be prepared by the developer. All construction must take place within town boundaries except for facilities which, by their nature, may cause environmental pollution. For these facilities, the law requires that an environmental impact assessment is submitted.

Construction of any kind (unless exempted) is forbidden outside town boundaries on agricultural land (grade 1 and 2) and on vine or orchard land, national parks, and conservation areas. Agricultural, military, railway and pipeline construction is exempted from this prohibition.

In protected areas, the developer must obtain advice from the National Commission for the Protection of National Monuments and in the case of development in national parks, from the Ministry of Waters, Forestry and Environmental Protection. Further locational restriction are imposed by *Order No. 623 of the Health Ministry Establishing Sanitary Rules on Environmental Protection of Human Settlements*, which sets minimum distances between pollution sources including waste facilities, and human settlements.

Proposals

The draft Law on Environmental Protection specifies that the location, development and operation of waste storage facilities must take account of the protection of adjacent land, water, the atmosphere, residential areas, and areas of landscape and tourist interest.

A general responsibility is imposed on companies by the draft Law such that the location of industrial facilities does not impair sanitation, the environment, leisure and recreation, and public health and comfort.

4.4.3 Fees

Fees for obtaining an Town Development Certificate are set according to the area of land in question. In urban areas, the fee is 500 lei up to $150m^2$, 1,500 lei for 500–1000 m^2 and 1,500 lei plus 1 lei per m^2 over 1,500 m^2. In rural areas fees are 50% lower.

For a construction permit, a fee of 2% of the construction value is charged and for a demolition permit, 1% of the value of the work is payable.

4.4.4 Timing

A construction permit and Town Development Certificate must be issued within 30 days of application.

4.4.5 Permit conditions

The authorities are required to set a fixed time period of between three and 24 months during which certificates remain valid. If construction has not commenced at the end of the period, the certificate is invalid. Construction permits are valid for 12 months. Extensions of up to 12 months may be available for both certificates and permits.

4.5 Public participation

4.5.1 Public access to information

Construction permits and Town Development Certificates are made available for public information and consultation. All documents provided by the developer during the application process are also made available to the public.

4.5.2 Provision of information

When Town Development Certificates and construction permits have been issued they are registered in the Registry of Construction and Demolition and a list of certificates and permits is published by the authority.

4.5.3 Public consultation

In the case of development of national significance the authority dealing with the Town Development Certificate application has the power to require that public consultation takes place regarding siting, aesthetic factors and operation of the activity. The authority is responsible for organising the consultation process.

Proposals

The draft Law on Environmental Protection includes a general provision for freedom of access to environmental information and public consultations.

4.6 Enforcement

4.6.1 Authority

Enforcement of land use planning requirements is the responsibility of the prefectures and town authorities.

4.6.2 Sanctions

Administrative fines may be imposed and construction or demolition halted by prefectures or town authorities in cases where any works are undertaken in breach of conditions of the permit. Fines range from 10,000 to 40,000 lei and may be imposed by the permitting authority ie prefecture or town authority or the State Inspectorate for Environment. In cases of continued non-compliance court action may be taken.

5. Environmental Impact Assessments (EIAs)

5.1 Summary

Authorities:	Ministry of Waters, Forestry and Environmental Protection and its Branch Agencies.
Types of Activity:	Activities requiring an EIA are prescribed in Ministerial Order No. 113, and include activities of the Chemical, Food, Textiles, Rubber, Energy, and Infrastructure industries. Further requirements for EIA are specified in the draft Law on Environmental Protection. Ministerial Order No. 170 prescribes which types of development fall within the remit of the Ministry and which, its Branch Agencies. In general, the Ministry deals with EIAs of major, potentially more harmful facilities.
Permits:	Environmental permit.
Timing:	No prescribed time limit.
Public Information:	There is no formal mechanism for provision of information to the public. EIA reports are not made available to the public. The draft law includes a general provision for freedom of access to information on environmental quality and the location of new developents.
Public Consultation:	There is no formal mechanism for public consultation on EIAs. The draft law provides for public consultation on the location of new developments.

5.2 Sources of legislation relating to the environmental impact of industrial and commercial developments

There is no specific legislation on environmental impact assessment (EIA). EIA requirements are included however in legislation setting out procedures for environmental permitting, *Ministerial Order No. 170 on the Issuing of Permits 1990* and *Ministerial Order No. 113 on Documentation Required for Permit Applications 1990*. EIA requirements are also set out in the draft Law on Environmental Protection.

5.3 Scope of activities subject to EIA process

Applications for an environmental permit must include an EIA, carried out by the investor, for the list of activities set out in *Table 5.3(a)* as prescribed in Annex 2 of *Ministerial Order No. 113 on Documentation Required for Permit Applications 1990*.

Proposals

Requirements for EIAs to be carried out are also set out in the draft Law on Environmental Protection. The draft specifies that an EIA will be required by the authorities (Ministry of Waters, Forestry and Environmental Protection and the Branch Agencies) prior to obtaining an environmental permit for urban and territorial development plans, new activities, development projects, and changes to existing facilities which may damage the environment at local, regional or global levels.

5.4 EIA process

5.4.1 Authority

EIAs are approved by the Ministry of Waters, Forestry and Environmental Protection and its Branch Agencies. *Ministerial Order No. 170 on the issuing of Permits 1990* prescribes generically which types of development must be approved by the central Ministry and those which fall under the remit of Branch Agencies. In general, the central Ministry is responsible for the major, potentially more harmful, facilities. With regard to air emissions, the central Ministry is the competent authorities for facilities releasing emissions into the atmosphere in towns of more that 100,000 population and the Branch Agencies for facilities releasing emissions in towns of less than 100,000 population.

5.4.2 Documentation

Under *Decision No. 113 on Documentation Required for Permit Applications 1990*, EIAs must be prepared either by the Institute for Environment with the Ministry of Waters, Forestry and Environmental Protection or an officially authorised company at the cost of the investor. The investor must provide all the relevant information. Specific procedures for EIA have not been prescribed although the level of detail required for assessments for smaller facilities is less than for larger operations.

Under the draft Law on Environmental Protection, EIAs are to be drawn up by the dedicated units of the Ministry, or by Romanian or foreign organisations authorised by the Ministry. The experts engaged in carrying out the EIAs must be registered or officially acknowledged by the competent authority. The cost of the assessment is the responsibility of the investor. The impact study must be presented with the application for the environmental permit. The draft states that rules approved by the Ministry setting out procedures and minimum requirements for EIAs will be produced within 30 days of the Law coming into force.

In situations of uncertainty regarding the EIA, especially those involving major ecological risk, the environmental authority can require that a separate independent survey is undertaken. It will be an offence to submit a 'false' report.

Table 5.3(a)   Activities subject to EIA

- *Chemical Industry*
    - the treatment of intermediary products and manufacture of chemical products;
    - manufacture of pesticides; pharmaceutical products, colouring and glazing products, elastomers and peroxides;
    - oil storage, petrochemical and chemical products installations;
    - raw oil distillery, gasification and liquefaction larger than 500 tons of coal per day;
    - integrated chemical installations.
- *Food Products Industry*
    - vegetable oil and animal fats industry;
    - food preservation;
    - manufacture of dairy products, beer, malt, sugar products and sugar, flour, fish flour and oil;
    - slaughter houses.
- *Textile and Leather Industry, Wood Industry and Paper*
    - manufacture of textiles of paper past of paper, cardboard and cellulose;
    - activities of washing, degreasing, whitening, dye houses of fibres;
    - tanning.
- *Rubber Industry*
    - manufacture and treatment of products on the bases of elastomers.
- *Extractive Industry*
    - extraction of peat, minerals, pitcoal, lignite, oil, natural gas, metalliferous minerals, installations for extraction of asbestos;
    - installation for manufacture of cement, coking plant, processing of asbestos;
    - geometrical drilling for water supply, storage of nuclear wastes.
- *Energy Industry*
    - industrial installations for producing electricity, steam, hot water;
    - installations for transportation and storage of energy steam and hot water;
    - installations for stocking or elimination of nuclear wastes;
    - installation for product enriching and re-treatment of nuclear fuel.
- *Industry of processing metals*
    - smelting, forging, rolling;
    - surface treatments and rolled metals, cutting;
    - naval works, construction of railway material, installations of calcination, metallic construction for communication ways.
- *Transport*
    - transport infrastructure, highways, navigable ways, airports.
- *Agriculture–Forest (Silviculture)*
    - Rural and agricultural development, reafforestations, deforestation;
    - salmonides, fisheries; land recovery.
- *Glass Industry*
    - manufacture of glass.
- *Infrastructure Projects*
    - works of urban development of industrial zones, hydrotechnical, pipelines of gas and liquid transport, recreation establishment;
    - installations for toxic wastes disposal, wastewater purification stations, processing and storage of residual mud, engines test stands, turbines, reactors, manufacture and manipulation of explosives, slaughter houses for stray dogs.

5.4.3 Experts and consultants

Experts and consultants undertaking EIAs on behalf of developers must be authorised by the Ministry of Waters, Forestry and Environmental Protection.

5.4.4 Timing

There is no prescribed time period for EIA approval.

5.4.5 Standard of review

There are no specific provisions for the review and approval of EIAs or for post-study monitoring.

5.5 Public participation

5.5.1 Public access to information

The Romanian *Constitution* (Article 31) gives the right to citizens to access to any information of public interest.

Proposals

The draft Law on Environmental Protection includes a general provision for freedom of access to information on environmental quality, and the right to information and consultation regarding decisions on territorial and local development, and on the location of facilities which might be detrimental to the environment.

5.5.2 Provision of information

There are no formal mechanisms for the provision of information to the public on EIAs. Public announcements are not made regarding applications, public hearings, appeals, and decisions on applications, and EIA reports are not made available to the public.

5.5.3 Public consultation

There are no formal mechanisms for public consultation on EIAs.

5.6 Enforcement

5.6.1 Authorities

Enforcement is the responsibility of the Ministry of Waters, Forestry and the Environmental Protection and its Branch Agencies.

5.6.2 Sanctions

The draft Law on Environmental Protection includes sanctions relating to EIA requirements. Failure to undertake an EIA required by the authority may result in a fine of 75,000–350,000 lei. Providing false conclusions or information may result in two to five years imprisonment or a fine of 50,000–150,000 lei.

5.7 National Experience with EIA's

EIAs have been conducted for several projects including Brown coal extraction in Judet Gorj, the Resita oil platform, Crisu dam, water use and wastewater treatment at the Phoenix-S.A. Baia Mare and Sometraes-S.A. Copsa Mica, the Bucharest-Fundulea and Fetesti-Cernavoda sections of the trans-European highway, and the nuclear power plant at Cernavoda.

6. Integrated permitting requirements applicable to the operation of industrial and commercial facilities

6.1 Summary

Authorities:	Ministry of Waters, Forestry and Environmental Protection and the Branch Agency Section for Regulations.
Types of Activity:	Activities requiring an environmental permit are pre-scribed in *Ministerial Order No. 113* and those requiring an *environmental certificate*, in *Ministerial Order No. 437*. The majority of industrial commercial activities are included.
	The national Ministry deals only with applications for activities which may have a major impact on the environment whilst the Branch Agency deals with the remaining majority.
Permits:	*Environmental permit*: required for proposed facilities and modifications to existing facilities.
	Environmental certificate: required for all facilities to confirm that operation is in compliance with standards.
Timing:	20 days.
Public Information:	There is no formal mechanism for provision of information to the public. The draft *Law on Environmental Protection* includes a general provision for freedom of access to information on environmental quality and data relating to compliance with legal requirements.
Public Consultation:	There is currently no formal mechanism for public consultation on environmental permits and certificates. The draft Law provides for public consultation on the location of new developments.

6.2 Sources of legislation relating to integrated permitting

The *Law on Environmental Protection 1973* provides the framework for environmental aspects of commercial and industrial facilities. Requirements for the environmental permit are set out in *Ministerial Order No. 170 on Permitting 1990 and Ministerial Order No. 113 on Documentation Required for Permit Applications 1990*. Requirements for environmental certificates are set out in *Ministerial Order No. 437 on Certificates 1991*.

6.3 Scope of activities subject to integrated permitting

Activities requiring an environmental permit as prescribed by *Ministerial Order No. 113 on Document Required for Permit Applications 1990* are set out in *Section 5.2*. The permit is required for new facilities and those undergoing modification. The list of activities requiring an environmental *certificate* as prescribed by Annex 1 of *Ministerial Order No. 437 on Certification* are set out in *Annex F*.

Proposals

The draft Law on Environmental Protection will re-enact provisions of *Ministerial Order No. 437 on Certification 1991, Ministerial Order 170 on Permitting 1990 and Ministerial Order No. 113 on Documentation Required for Permit Applications 1990*. The draft lists types of new activity which will require permits, or in the case of existing facilities, certificates, as set out in *Table 6.3(a)*. It also includes the "catch all" clause, ie "any other activity that can damage the environment".

Where a permit or permit renewal is required for an *existing* facility, ie a facility in operation on the date when the law comes into force, the competent authority (central Ministry of Waters, Forestry and Environmental Protection and/or Branch Agency) *may* also require an EIA to be carried out.

Where an operator considers that standards set in a permit issued by a Branch Agency are too stringent an appeal can be made to the Ministry of Waters, Forestry and Environmental Protection. Appeal is not available in relation to a permit issued by the Ministry. Branch Agencies are not able to appeal against a permitting decision made by the central Ministry in relation to a facility in the jurisdiction of the agency.

6.4 Standards

6.4.1 Ambient quality standards

Historically, Romania has followed the environmental quality approach to environmental standard setting ie imposing limits on levels of pollutants in the environment (environmental quality or ambient standards) rather than limits on releases to the environment (emission standards). Currently there are ambient standards in place for air and water. Applicable standards ambient quality are:

- Air — STAS 12574-8;
- Water — STAS 4706-88;

Table 6.3(a) Activities subject to Integrated Permitting under Draft Legislation

- Construction and operation of social and economic activities impacting on the environment.
- Town and territorial development plans.
- Transport infrastructure, hydrotechnical works, land reclamation and improvement of surface water courses.
- Underground exploration, prospecting and exploitation.
- Exploitation of mineral and biological resources of public interest and fishing waters.
- Exploitation of forests of public interest, forestry plantations and hunting.
- Management of coastal zones and exploitation of their natural resources.
- Fruit plantations within water quality protection zones.
- Activities within ecological protection zones.
- Production, marketing and use of toxic products.
- Use of plant protection products within special zones.
- Import and export of indigenous flora and fauna.
- Import, export and transport of toxic products and wastes.
- Location and construction of facilities for toxic residue and waste storage, treatment, neutralisation and disposal.
- Any other activities that can damage the environment.

- Discharge to sewer — STAS 1846-75;
- Environmental noise — STAS 10009-88.

Sections 7 and *8*, provide details of relevant environmental quality standards.

It is intended that there will be a move towards the approaches of other jurisdictions in standard setting, eg US, European Community and its Member States. New standards will initially be applied to new facilities and introduced gradually for existing operations. There are no standards for hazardous waste management although the import of hazardous waste is controlled by legislation. Proposed legislation is being developed for waste management activities.

6.4.2 Emission standards

Limits for ten substances/parameters have been set for water prior to discharge, emission standards for air and water are currently being developed.

Emission standards for individual permits are calculated on the basis of ambient quality standards and take account of environmental factors such as the dilution factors, volume and category of water to which a discharge is made, other activities in the locality, and climatic factors.

6.4.3 *Technology based standards*

There are no technology based standards. The draft Law on Environmental Protection includes general provisions which will require that production processes and technology are as clean as possible.

6.5 *Permitting process*

6.5.1 *Authorities*

The environmental permit generally issued by the Ministry of Waters, Forestry and Environmental Protection Branch Agency Section for Regulations although permitting of facilities which may have a major impact on the environment is carried out by the central Ministry.

Ministerial Order No. 170 on Permitting 1990 gives certain criteria to determine the authority which is responsible for permitting and enforcement (either the central Ministry of Waters, Forestry and Environmental Protection or the Branch Agency). In general, the central Ministry is responsible for the major, potentially more harmful, facilities. With regard to air emissions, the central Ministry is the competent authority for facilities releasing emissions into the atmosphere in towns of more than 100,000 population and the Branch Agencies for facilities releasing emissions in towns of less than 100,000 population.

Prior to issue, all permits and certificates issued by Branch Agencies must be submitted to the central Ministry which can override decisions of the Agency.

The environmental permit comprises information supplied in the application, the authorities' evaluation of the application, a statement of acceptance of the application and any attached conditions.

6.5.2 *Application requirements*

A system of integrated permitting has been in operation in Romania since 1991. The integrated environmental *permit* represents the final stage of the permitting process and it is only issued when other relevant permits have been obtained eg construction permit, town development certificate, and permits for water abstraction, wastewater discharge and air emissions, and where required, an EIA has been undertaken. The permit is required under *Ministerial Order No. 170 on Permitting 1990* for new and modified facilities. Conditions relating to air, water and soil which reflect existing standards or more stringent standards may be attached to the permit.

A further requirement, under *Ministerial Order No. 437 on Certificates 1991*, is an environmental *certificate* which confirms that the facility is operating in accordance with all the relevant standards and/or the environmental permit. Facilities in operation prior to the introduction of integrated permitting system can continue to operate without an environmental permit except where modification has taken place or is planned in which case a permit is required but they are required to obtain an environmental certificate.

The environmental permit comprises information supplied in the application, the evaluation by the authority, a statement of approval of the application and any attached conditions.

The permit must be obtained at an early stage in the planning of a new facility or modification of an existing facility and in particular, prior to construction. When the activity is ready to commence, an environmental certificate must be obtained. The certificate demonstrates that the authority is satisfied that requirements of the permit have been met.

For existing facilities (ie pre–1991) a permit is not required (except if the facility is modified) but an environmental certificate must be obtained. In this case, the certificate demonstrates that the facility is in compliance with relevant standards. Application for a certificate must include a description of the operation regarding environmental and economic aspects.

The technical documentation to be included in the application for the permit, as prescribed in Annex 1 to the *Ministerial Order No. 113 on Documentation Required for Permit Applications 1990,* is given in *Table 6.5.2(a).*

Additional documentation and information requirements are imposed on certain categories of works in relation to specific resources, ie water, air soil, subsoil, forest, nature conservation, human settlements. These requirements apply to works included in the list of activities for which an environmental permit is required as prescribed in *Ministerial Order No. 113 on Documentation Required for Permit Applications 1990 (see Section 5.2).* Information requirements are as set out in *Table 6.5.2(b).*

Documentation requirements for environmental certificates, as set out in *Ministerial Order No. 437 on Certificates 1991,* are similar to those outlined above for environmental permits.

6.5.3 Fees

Fees are not charged for the environmental permit or certificate but charges are payable for the construction permit (*see Section 4*).

Proposals

The draft Law on Environmental Protection provides for fees to be charged for permitting and certification. The level of the charge is to be determined by subordinate legislation.

6.5.4 Timing

The time period for issuing permits is 20 days from receipt of the documentation by the permitting authority.

6.5.5 Permit conditions

All new and existing facilities are required to comply with standards set out in the permit which are relevant to the operations. Conditions relating to air, water and soil which reflect existing standards or set more stringent standards may be attached to the permit. Emission standards are not set in the legislation but are derived from statutory ambient quality standards.

Permits include conditions for self-monitoring of releases to the environment and the reporting of monitoring data. The *Ministerial Order No. 170 on Permitting 1990* provides for the revision of an environmental permit if new information arises on detrimental environmental effects which were not known at the time of issuing the permit.

Table 6.5.2(a) Technical Information Required in Integrated Environmental Permit Application

- Details of applicant, location (including identification of the water basin and watercourses).
- A statement of the necessity and opportunity of the investment and the relationship of the investment to the environment.
- Copies of previous permits, environmental studies on the potential sources of pollution, and studies on health, agriculture, forestry, hydrology, sanitation and town development.
- Presentation of permits which have been obtained from the following authorities.
- Water authority.
- Forestry Inspectorate.
- Department of Mines and Geology.
- Ministry of Industry.
- National Commission for the Protection of Historic Monuments.
- Ministry of Public Works and Land Planning—General Directorate of town planning and land planning.
- State Inspectorate on Construction, Public Works and Land Planning.
- Ministry of Health, Sanitary Police Inspectorate.
- Prefecture and municipality.
- Any other relevant authorities (as advised by Ministry of Waters, Forestry and Environmental Protection or the Branch Agency.
- Short presentation of the nature of the project including operational and technological aspects, production capacity, rates of consumption of raw materials and production of wastes, and arrangements for the collection, transport, treatment and storage of waste.

Table 6.5.2(b) Additional Requirements for Permit Application

- Requirements for works on, or in relation to water:
  Quantity of water to be used in m^3/day and l/s; mud, residues and waste management, purification and wastewater discharge, conservation of ecological balance, protection of environment, soil erosion, floods and all other measures for environmental protection.
- Environmental requirements concerning air:
  Dispersion of pollutants; volume and concentration of pollutants; collection and purification of residual gas; volume and concentrations of entering and exiting the purification plant; provisions of pollutant dispersion study; provisions of the law; and the system of monitoring.
- Environmental requirements concerning soil and subsoil relate to measures as for water but with emphasis on groundwater protection and soil erosion and degradation.
- Environmental requirements concerning forests and nature conservation:
  Maintaining ecological balance, and the protection of nature reservations (ie parks and other protected zones).
- Environmental requirements regarding human settlements:
  Identification of water categories, physico-chemical properties, storage and safety; underground water protection; provisions on the collection, separation, transport, neutralisation, reuse and minimisation of wastes; the system of environmental monitoring; noise and vibration control measures; and any other measures for environmental management and national heritage protection.

Proposals

The draft Law on Environmental Protection provides for the revision or withdrawal of permits in cases where new environmental issues come to light which were not know at the time of permitting. Permits may also be revised where new environmental standards are introduced. The new standards must be made public or notified to the operator 30 days before permit revision.

The draft Law also includes a general requirement for facility operators to have measuring systems for treatment processes and discharges, to have qualified staff and to keep records. In the case of accidental pollution, the draft Law imposes a general requirement for operators to act promptly to eliminate the cause, limit damage, and immediately inform the environmental authorities, and any companies and the population which might suffer damage.

6.6 Public participation

6.6.1 Public access to information

There are no formal mechanisms for the provision of information to the public or public participation regarding environmental permits and certificates. Public announcements are not made regarding applications, public hearings, appeals, and decisions on applications, and EIA reports are not made available to the public. However the Romanian *Constitution* (Article 31) bestows the right on the individual to access to any information of public interest.

Proposals

The draft Law on Environmental Protection includes a general provision for freedom of access to information on environmental quality.

6.6.2 Provision of information

In the case of accidental pollution, the draft Law on Environmental Protection imposes a general requirement for operators to act promptly to eliminate the cause, limit damage, and immediately inform members of the public who might suffer damage. A further general provision will require commercial and industrial operators to provide on request, any information or data relating to compliance with legal requirements.

6.6.3 Public consultation

There are no provisions providing rights to public consultation in relation to applications for environmental permits and certificates.

Proposals

The draft Law on Environmental Protection includes a general provision for the right to information and consultation regarding decisions on territorial and local development, and on the location of facilities which might be detrimental to the environment. Detailed requirements have not been introduced in the legislation.

6.7 Enforcement

6.7.1 Compliance checking and monitoring

The Ministry of Waters, Forestry and Environmental Protection and Branch Agency Inspectors may inspect facilities. Inspection may involve cooperation with local authorities and the Ministry of Health's Sanitary Police. Each Ministry Inspector is responsible for supervising the enforcement activities of three to four Agencies and accompanies Agency Inspectors on facility visits according to an inspection programme. A report is then made to the Chief Inspector. Agency Inspectors both check compliance and advise on how to meet standards or permit conditions.

A facility which is not in compliance with the relevant standards or permit is first given a warning by the Inspector. If the facility does not take the necessary steps, an administrative fine may be issued by the Inspector. The size of fines is prescribed in the legislation. Administrative fines may be imposed continually. Finally, non-compliance may result in court action.

It is understood that many existing facilities do not meet the relevant standards. In theory, facilities must upgrade operations to comply with standard or face facility shut down. In practice this does not happen and enforcement relies on fines. Where existing facilities do not meet relevant standards, it is an aim of the enforcement authorities to introduce gradual upgrading schedules.

Proposals

The draft Law on Environmental Protection empowers the authorities to shut down facilities which are not in compliance with conditions of the environmental certificate until the necessary steps are taken to meet the conditions.

The draft also provides for the authority to issue a warning and then suspend a permit in cases of non-compliance with permit conditions. The suspension remains in effect until the necessary steps to ensure compliance are taken. Under special circumstances a facility may be permanently closed down by the government at the request of the Ministry of Waters, Forestry and Environmental Protection. The circumstances in which facility shut down may take place are not defined but it is understood that this would apply to facilities which are of national interest. For example this may include facilities with a particularly large workforce or the sole manufacturer of an important product.

6.7.2 Sanctions

Breach of permitting and certification requirements may give rise to administrative or criminal sanctions.

Proposals

The draft Law on Environmental Protection prescribes sanctions for a range of infringements. Relevant examples are set out in *Section 2* above.

7. Air emission requirements applicable to the operation of industrial and commercial facilities

7.1 Summary

Authorities:	Ministry of Waters, Forestry and Environmental Protection or the Branch Agency.
Types of Activity:	A permit for emissions to atmosphere is a component of an environmental permit for which activities are prescribed in *Ministerial Order No. 113*.
Permits:	Permit for emissions to atmosphere, as a component of an environmental permit.
Timing:	20 days.
Public Information:	There is no formal mechanism for provision of information to the public. The draft Law on Environmental Protection includes a general provision for freedom of access to information on environmental quality and data relating to compliance with legal requirements.
Public Consultation:	There is currently no formal mechanism for public consultation. The draft law provides for public consultation on the location of new developments.

7.2 Sources of legislation relating to air emissions

- *Order No. 623 of the Health Ministry Establishing Sanitary Rules on Environmental Protection of Human Settlements*;
- Draft Law on Environmental Protection.

7.3 Air protection zones

The legislation does not provide for air protection zones.

7.4 Scope of activities subject to air emission regulations

A permit for emissions to the atmosphere is a component of an environmental permit as outlined in the previous section.

7.5 Standards

7.5.1 Ambient quality standards
Maximum Admissible Concentrations for 29 substances in the atmosphere are pre-scribed in the standards STAS 12574-8, 1987.

The standards are derived from maximum concentrations set out in the *Order of the Health Ministry Establishing Sanitary Rules for Environmental Protection of Human Settlements*.

7.5.2 Emission limit values
Emission limits for individual permits are calculated on the basis of ambient quality standards and take account of environmental factors such as the dilution factors, volume and category of water to which a discharge is made, other activities in the locality, and climatic factors. Standards for emissions are currently being developed.

7.5.2 Technology based standards
There are no technology based standards. The draft Law on Environmental Protection includes general provisions which will require that production processes and technology are as clean as possible.

7.6 Permitting process

Permitting requirements for air emissions are incorporated into the integrated permit-ting system described in the previous section.

Proposals
The draft Law on Environmental Protection sets out a number of general requirements relating to the protection of the atmosphere including the following:

- Use of pollution control monitoring equipment to ensure that emissions and the environmental quality around the plant do not exceed permissible limits;
- Use of raw materials and fuels with a reduced content of noxious material;
- Improve technical performance and energy efficiency so as to reduce pollution;
- To use sound insulation to ensure maximum limits are not exceeded;
- To prevent atmospheric pollution from waste management activities;
- To incinerate wastes or other toxic residues only at approved facilities and in accord-ance with any conditions established by the environment and health authorities;
- To maintain and extend the area of trees and bushes, "green spots", parks etc, in order to improve air quality and reduce noise exposure.

7.6.1 Authorities
The permitting authority is the Ministry of Waters, Forestry and Environmental Protec-tion or Branch Agency.

7.6.2 Application requirements

Permit applications must include details of volumes and concentrations of pollutants, dispersion characteristics and systems for monitoring.

7.6.3 Fees

There are no fees for permitting.

7.6.4 Timing

The time period for issuing permits is 20 days from receipt of the documentation by the permitting authority.

7.6.5 Permit conditions

Permit conditions include facility specific emission limits and requirements for emissions monitoring and recording.

7.7 Charges for emissions

There are no charges for emissions to the atmosphere.

7.8 Enforcement

7.8.1 Compliance checking and monitoring

The Ministry of Waters, Forestry and Environmental Protection and Branch Agency Inspectors may inspect facilities. Inspection may involve co-operation with local authorities and the Ministry of Health's Sanitary Police. Each Ministry Inspector is responsible for supervising the enforcement activities of three to four Agencies and accompanies Agency Inspectors on facility visits according to an inspection programme. A report is then made to the Chief Inspector. Agency Inspectors both check compliance and advise on how to meet standards or permit conditions.

A facility which is not in compliance with the relevant standards or permit is first given a warning by the Inspector. If the facility does not take the necessary steps, an administrative fine may be issued by the Inspector. The size of fines is prescribed in the legislation. Administrative fines may be imposed continually. Finally, non-compliance may result in court action.

It is understood that many existing facilities do not meet the relevant standards. In theory, facilities must upgrade operations to comply with standard or face facility shut down. In practice this does not happen and enforcement relies on fines. Where existing facilities do not meet relevant standards, it is an aim of the enforcement authorities to introduce gradual upgrading schedules.

Proposals

The draft Law on Environmental Protection empowers the authorities to shut down facilities which are not in compliance with conditions of the environmental certificate until the necessary steps are taken to meet the conditions.

The draft also provides for the authority to issue a warning and then suspend a permit in cases of non-compliance with permit condition. The suspension remains in effect until the necessary steps to ensure compliance are taken. Under special circumstances a facility may be permanently closed down by the government at the request of the Ministry of Waters, Forestry and Environmental Protection. The circumstances in which facility shut down may take place are not defined but it is understood that this would apply to facilities having environmental effects which are of national interest. For example, this may include facilities with a particularly large workforce or the sole manufacturer of an important product.

7.8.2 Sanctions

Breach of permitting and certification requirements may give rise to administrative or criminal sanctions. The *Law on Environmental Protection, 1973* prohibits the release of pollutants to the air above statutory environmental quality limits and the introduction of new facilities or the development of existing ones unless suitable equipment is fitted to reduce air pollution.

Proposals

The draft Law on Environmental Protection prescribes sanctions for a range of infringements. Relevant examples are set out in *Section 2* above. The draft also provides that where meteorological conditions are unfavourable and emissions may result, or have resulted, in pollutants rising above environmental quality standards the public health or environmental authorities are empowered to temporarily shut down the facility or require measures to be taken to abate emissions.

7.9 Public participation

7.9.1 Public access to information

There are no formal mechanisms for the provision of information to the public or public participation regarding environmental permits and certificates. Public announcements are not made regarding applications, public hearings, appeals, and decisions on applications, and EIA reports are not made available to the public. However the Romanian *Constitution* (Article 31) bestows the right on the individual to access to any information of public interest.

Proposals

The draft Law on Environmental Protection includes a general provision for freedom of access to information on environmental quality.

7.9.2 Provision of information

In the case of accidental pollution, the draft Law on Environmental Protection imposes a general requirement for operators to act promptly to eliminate the cause, limit damage, and immediately inform members of the public who might suffer damage. A further general provision will require commercial and industrial operators to provide on request, any information or data relating to compliance with legal requirements.

7.9.3 Public consultation

There are no provisions providing rights to public consultation in relation to applications for environmental permits and certificates.

8. Water requirements applicable to the operation of industrial and commercial facilities

8.1 Summary

Authorities:	Regional branches or national office, of the state water company Apele Romane.
Types of Activity:	Activities requiring a certificates for water use or a permit for wastewater discharge are specified in *Ministerial Order No. 435.* *National office* deals with permits where works cross the state border or are situated in more than one water basin. *Regional branches* deal with all other applications.
Permits:	Water use certificate. Wastewater discharge permit.
Timing:	20 days.
Public Information:	There is no formal mechanism for provision of information to the public. The draft Law on Environmental Protection includes a general provision for freedom of access to information on environmental quality and data relating to compliance with legal requirements.
Public Consultation:	There is currently no formal mechanism for public consultation. The draft law provides for public consultation on the location of new developments.

8.2 Sources of legislation relating to water requirements

Key items of legislation include the following:

- *Environmental Protection Act 1973;*
- *Law on Waters 1974;*
- *Ministerial Order No. 715 Concerning Approvals for Administration of Water 1991;*

509

- *Ministerial Order No. 435 Concerning Authorisations for Administration of Water 1991;*
- *HMC No. 2496 Concerning the Establishment of and Sanctions for Violations Relating to Water 1969;*
- *Normative C-90 Concerning the Disposal of Wastewater in Public Sewerage Networks 1983;*
- *Law No. 5 on the Rational Management, Protection and Assurance of the Quality of Waters 1989;*
- *Governmental Decision No. 1001 on the Establishment of a Unitary System of Payments for Products and Services of Water Husbandry 1990* (as amended 1991 and 1992);
- *Decree Establishing Permissible Limits of the Main Polluting Substances Prior to Discharge 1979;*
- Draft Law on Environmental Protection.

8.3 Water management

8.3.1 Water management bodies
The Romanian Water Authority, Apele Romane and the 13 regional Water Authorities are responsible for water management.

8.3.2 Water quality categories
The scope of the *Law on Waters 1974* and the draft Law on Environmental Protection includes:

- Surface water;
- Inland sea waters and the territorial sea;
- Underground waters.

STAS 4706-88 establishes three water quality categories. Category I includes drinking water supply, water for the food industry, water for animal rearing, vegetable growing, fish rearing, and waters for bathing and water contact sports. Category II includes water for industrial and recreational use. Irrigation, hydroelectric power, and cooling water are included in Category III.

8.4 Activities subject to water use and discharge regulation

8.4.1 Water use
The use of water and works on or in connection with water require a certificate according to *Ministerial Order No. 435 Concerning Authorisations for Administration of Water 1991.*

8.4.2 Water discharge
A permit is required under *Ministerial Order No. 715 Concerning Approvals for Administration of Water 1991* for any works on waters or in connection with waters including

groundwater, the shore of the Black Sea and the territorial sea bed. *Ministerial Order No. 715* lists categories of works for which a permit is required include supplies of water sewerage purification, and discharges of wastewaters and other water. A full list is set out in *Annex F*.

The *Law on Environmental Protection 1973* prohibits the discharge or disposal of wastewater, waste or other substances which might pollute water so as to injure public health or damage flora and fauna. Discharges are permitted where they are in accordance with conditions set by the authority. The setting up of new facilities or development of existing ones which may cause water pollution is prohibited except where properly functioning water purification equipment is fitted which will ensure that water quality conditions are met. The *Law on Waters 1974* prohibits the pollution of waters, which is defined as alteration of the physical, chemical or biological properties of waters directly or indirectly caused by man's activities, which renders water unfit for the normal utilisation for which it was fit prior to the pollution.

8.5 Standards

8.5.1 Ambient quality standards

Standards for water pollutants are based on discharge limits. The standards are set out in STAS 4706-88 and for discharge to sewer, STAS 1846-75.

8.5.2 Discharge limit values

Normative C-90 concerning the disposal of wastewater in public sewerage networks, 1983 sets out conditions to ensure that wastewater does not degrade sewage networks or purification facilities, and does not harm public health, cause pollution or interfere with sewage purification.

Rates of water consumption per unit production and wastewater purification requirements are integrated by *Law No. 5 on the Rational Management, Protection and Assurance of the Quality of Waters 1989*. A water use permit is issued on the basis of a technical evaluation of the use and discharge of water. The permit is issued for a limited period of time but this may be extended by the issuing authority following a further assessment.

The *Decree Establishing Permissible Limits of the Main Polluting Substances Prior to Discharge 1979* prescribes limits for the following list of pollutants and measurements:

- Suspended solids;
- BOD_5;
- Sulphides;
- Cyanides;
- Iron;
- Mercury;
- Cadmium;
- Lead;
- Zinc;
- Anionic biodegradable surfactants;
- Phenols;
- pH.

The limits are given in *Annex D*.
The discharge of the following groups of compounds is prohibited:

- Persistent organohalogens, organosilcates, and organophosphorus pesticides;
- Mercury and its organic compounds (except where in compliance with specific measures to meet discharge limits, eg relating to production technology and purification systems);
- Carcinogens;
- Radioactive wastes which concentrate in the environment or aquatic organisms.

8.5.3 Technology based standards

There are no technology based standards. The draft Law on Environmental Protection includes general provisions which will require that production processes and technology are as clean as possible.

8.6 Water use permitting process

8.6.1 Authorities

Certificates for water use are issued by the regional branches of the autonomous state water company, Apele Romane. Where works cross the state border or are situated in more than one water basin, certificates are issued by the national office of Apele Romane.

8.6.2 Application requirements

A water use certificate is issued on the basis of a technical evaluation of the use and discharge of water. The certificate is issued for a limited period of time but this may be extended following a further assessment.

8.6.3 Fees

There are no fees for issuing certificates although it is expected that fees will be introduced under the Draft Law on Environmental Protection.

8.6.4 Timing

The time period for issuing certificates is 20 days from receipt of the documentation by the permitting authority.

8.6.5 Permit conditions

Conditions may be attached to certificates for water use eg volume of water taken, under the *Law on Waters 1974*.

8.7 Water discharge permitting process

According to the *Law on Waters 1974*, discharge of wastewater containing pollutants in excess of limits is forbidden. Discharge, injection or disposal of wastewater on waste materials is permitted only where it does not cause pollution of ground or surface water and it is in accordance with the conditions of a permit issued by local water authority. Injection into deep mines also requires a permit from the Ministry of Industry.

The Law prohibits bringing into service new facilities, or developing existing ones, or to use modified production technologies in existing facilities except where purification equipment is in place or other measures are taken to ensure purification of the discharged wastewater in accordance with a permit issued by the local water authority.

8.7.1 Authorities

Permits for wastewater discharge are issued by the Ministry of Waters, Forestry and Environmental Protection and the regional branches of the autonomous state water company, Apele Romane. Where works cross the state border or are situated in two or more water basins, permits are issued by the national office of Apele Romane.

8.7.2 Application requirements

Applications for wastewater discharge must demonstrate that ambient quality and emission standards will not be exceeded and include details of water purification systems.

8.7.3 Fees

There are no fees for permitting although it is expected that fees will be introduced under the Draft Law on Environmental Protection.

8.7.4 Timing

The time period for issuing permits is 20 days from receipt of the documentation by the permitting authority.

8.7.5 Permit conditions

Permit conditions include facility specific emission limits and requirements for emissions monitoring and recording.

Proposals

The draft Law on Environmental Protection includes a general provision for freedom of access to information on environmental quality, and the right to information and consultation regarding decisions on territorial and local development, and on the location of facilities which might be detrimental to the environment.

8.8 Water charges

8.8.1 Water use

Standard charges for water use are set out in *Decision No. 1001 on the Establishment of a Unitary System of Payments for Productions and Services of Water Husbandry 1990.* Annex 1 of the Decision deals with "tariffs for water supply and utilisation from rivers and underground waters". Charges are revised every four months to account for inflation. Examples of charges for abstraction by industrial facilities from various sources are as follows:

- Rivers — 2,593 lei/1,000 m^3;
- Danube — 315 lei/1,000 m^3 for the same users;

- Danube — 15 lei/m^3 for irrigation and fisheries;
- Underground waters — 3,194 lei/1,000 m^3.

Where abstraction exceeds permit conditions penalties are imposed according to Annex 4 of the *1990 Decision*.

8.8.2 Water discharge

Taxes for wastewater discharge are set out in *Decision No. 1001 on the Establishment of a Unitary System of Payments for Products and Services of Water Husbandry 1990*. Annex 2 on tariffs for wastewater services, ie receiving wastewater within permissible limits. Where pollutants in wastewater exceed limits, penalties are imposed according to Annex 4 of the *1990 Decision*. The pollutants that are regulated are listed in *Table 8.8.2(a)*.

Table 8.8.2(a)　　Regulated Water Pollutants

• Total suspended solids	• total phosphorus
• compounds of chlorides, sulphates, magnesium	• manganese
	• nickel
• sodium, calcium	• oil products
• nitrates, organic substances	• molybdenum
• BOD$_5$	• lead
• ammonium, nitrates, cobalt	• copper
• chromium III, VI	• hydrogen sulphide
• fluorine	• silver, selenium, cyanides
• detergents	• residual free chlorine
• active anions	• cadmium
• total iron	• intro compounds
• ammonium	• phenols.

8.9 Public participation

8.9.1 Public access to information

There are no formal mechanisms for the provision of information to the public or public participation regarding environmental permits and certificates. Public announcements are not made regarding applications, public hearings, appeals, and decisions on applications, and EIA reports are not made available to the public. However the Romanian *Constitution* (Article 31) bestows the right on the individual to access to any information of public interest.

514

Proposals

The draft Law on Environmental Protection includes a general provision for freedom of access to information on environmental quality.

8.9.2 Provision of information

In the case of accidental pollution, the draft Law on Environmental Protection imposes a general requirement for operators to act promptly to eliminate the cause, limit damage, and immediately inform members of the public who might suffer damage. A further general provision will require commercial and industrial operators to provide on request, any information or data relating to compliance with legal requirements.

8.9.3 Public consultation

There are no provisions providing rights to public consultation in relation to applications for environmental permits and certificates.

8.10 Enforcement

8.10.1 Compliance checking and monitoring

The Ministry of Waters, Forestry and Environmental Protection and the regional branches of Apele Romane are responsible for enforcement of requirements set out in the legislation and permits.

8.10.2 Sanctions

Non-compliance with requirements set out in legislation and permits can result in administrative or criminal sanctions. Water use certificates may be suspended or revoked where the operator is in breach of permit conditions. Under the *Law on Waters 1974* the Ministry of Waters, Forestry and Environmental Protection may shut down an installation in cases where water pollution is a threat to public health until the cause of pollution has been removed.

9. Noise requirements applicable to the operation of industrial and commercial facilities

9.1 Summary

Authorities:	Ministry of Waters, Forestry and Environmental Protection and its Branch Agencies.
Types of Activity:	Noise control is a component of an environmental permit for which activities are prescribed in *Ministerial Order No. 113*.

Permits:	Noise control is included in the integrated environmental permit; a separate noise permit is not required.
Timing:	20 days.
Public Information:	There is no formal mechanism for provision of information to the public. The draft Law on Environmental Protection includes a general provision for freedom of access to information on environmental quality and data relating to compliance with legal requirements.
Public Consultation:	There is currently no formal mechanism for public consultation. The draft law provides for public consultation on the location of new developments.

9.2 Sources of legislation relating to environmental noise

- *Law on Environmental Protection 1973;*
- *Ministerial Order No. 170 on Permitting 1990;*
- *Ministerial Order No. 113 on Documentation Required for Permit Applications 1990;*
- *Ministerial Order No. 437 on Certificates 1991;*
- *Order No. 623 Establishing Sanitary Rules on Environmental Protection for Human Settlements 1973.*

9.3 Noise zones

Noise zones have been established for residential areas in which noise limits must not be exceeded. There are no zones for industrial areas.

9.4 Activities subject to noise regulation

Noise control is included in the integrated environmental permitting system outlined in *Section 6*. A separate noise permit is not required for the operation of commercial and industrial facilities but the operations must be carried out within noise limits in order to meet requirements of the environmental permit and certificate.

9.5 Standards

Noise emission limits are set out in standard STAS 10009-88 and in the *Order No. 623 Establishing Sanitary Rules on Environmental Protection for Human Settlements 1973.*

9.6 Permitting process

9.6.1 Authorities
The authorities responsible for the regulation of noise are the Ministry of Waters, Forestry and Environmental Protection and its Branch Agencies.

9.6.2 Application requirements
There are no specific requirements relating to noise in the permitting process. Prediction or demonstration of compliance with noise standards is required in order to obtain an environmental permit and certificate.

9.6.3 Timing
The time period for issuing permits is 20 days from receipt of the documentation by the permitting authority.

9.7 Public participation

9.7.1 Public access to information
There are no formal mechanisms for the provision of information to the public or public participation regarding environmental permits and certificates. Public announcements are not made regarding applications, public hearings, appeals, and decisions on applications, and EIA reports are not made available to the public. However the Romanian *Constitution* (Article 31) bestows the right on the individual to access to any information of public interest.

Proposals
The draft Law on Environmental Protection includes a general provision for freedom of access to information on environmental quality.

9.7.2 Provision of information
In the case of accidental pollution, the draft Law on Environmental Protection imposes a general requirement for operators to act promptly to eliminate the cause, limit damage, and immediately inform members of the public who might suffer damage. A further general provision will require commercial and industrial operators to provide on request, any information or data relating to compliance with legal requirements.

9.7.3 Public consultation
There are no provisions providing rights to public consultation in relation to applications for environmental permits and certificates.

Proposals
The draft Law on Environmental Protection includes a general provision for the right to information and consultation regarding decisions on territorial and local development, and

on the location of facilities which might be detrimental to the environment. Detailed requirements have not been introduced in the legislation.

9.8 Enforcement

9.8.1 Compliance checking and monitoring
Enforcement is the responsibility of the Ministry of Waters, Forestry and Environmental Protection and its Branch Agencies.

9.8.2 Sanctions
Breach of noise standards may result in fines under the *Law on Environmental Protection 1973*.

10. Hazardous and non-hazardous waste management

10.1 Summary

Note:	The following summary outlines proposed requirements.
Authorities:	Ministry of Waters, Forestry and Environmental Protection.
Types of Activity:	Hazardous waste storage or disposal.
Permits:	Permits for storage, transport or disposal of hazardous waste.
Timing:	Not specified.
Public Information:	There is no formal mechanism for provision of information to the public. The draft Law on Environmental Protection includes a general provision for freedom of access to information on environmental quality and data relating to compliance with legal requirements.
Public Consultation:	There is currently no formal mechanism for public consultation. The draft law provides for public consultation on the location of new developments.

10.2 Sources of legislation relating to waste management

- *Law on Environmental Protection 1973;*
- *Decree No. 465 on Waste Collection, Minimisation and Re-use 1979;*

- *Law No. 10 on Waste Collection, Hygiene and Maintenance of the Exterior of Grounds and Buildings Alongside Facilities 1982;*
- *Order of the Minister of Health No. 266 Stabilising Measures for Collecting, Depositing and Disposing of Waste and Reusable Materials from Health Units 1985;*
- *Order No. 623 of the Health Ministry Establishing Sanitary Rules on Environmental Protection of Human Settlements 1973;*
- *Decision No. 340 on Waste Imports and Residues 1992* (as amended 1992);
- Draft Law on Environmental Protection;
- Draft Law on Waste.

10.3 Categories of waste

Waste is categorised as hazardous and non-hazardous.

10.4 Waste storage and treatment

10.4.1 Generator permits and other requirements

The *Order of the Health Ministry Establishing Sanitary Rules on Environmental Protection of Human Settlements 1973* establishes minimum distances between human settlements and facilities which treat waste. *Law No. 10 on Waste Collection, Hygiene and Maintenance of the Exterior of Grounds and Buildings Alongside Facilities 1982* sets general sets requirements for facility operators to ensure that their premises are kept clean and that any waste material is disposed of at waste disposal facilities.

Proposals

The draft Law on Environmental Protection includes a general provision requiring that hazardous waste storage is undertaken only where a permit has been obtained from the Ministry of Waters, Forestry and Environmental Protection.

The draft Law sets out requirements for operators involved in the production and/or management of hazardous waste who will be required to set up a register recording the nature, origin, quantity, physical and chemical characteristics, and location of hazardous waste within 90 days of the Law coming into force. The registers must be supplied to the environmental and health authorities on request. A draft Law on Waste is in preparation.

10.4.2 Operator permits and other requirements

The draft Law on Environmental Protection sets out requirements for operators involved in the production and/or management of hazardous waste who will be required to set up a register recording the nature, origin, quantity, physical and chemical characteristics, and location of hazardous waste within 90 days of the Law coming into force. The registers must be supplied to the environmental and health authorities on request. A draft Law on Waste is in preparation.

10.5 Waste disposal

10.5.1 Generator permits and other requirements

The draft Law on Environmental Protection sets out requirements for operators involved in the production and/or management of hazardous waste who will be required to set up a register recording the nature, origin, quantity, physical and chemical characteristics, and location of hazardous waste within 90 days of the Law coming into force. The registers must be supplied to the environmental and health authorities on request. A draft Law on Waste is in preparation.

10.5.2 Operator permits and other requirements

The *Order of the Health Ministry Establishing Sanitary Rules on Environmental Protection of Human Settlements* 1973 establishes minimum distances between human settlements and facilities which treat waste. *Law No. 10 on Waste Collection, Hygiene and Maintenance of the Exterior of Grounds and Buildings alongside facilities 1982* sets general sets requirements for facility operators to ensure that their premises are kept clean and that any waste material is disposed of at waste disposal facilities.

Specific requirements for waste collection are set out in the *Order of the Minister of Health No. 266 Establishing Measures for Collecting, Depositing and Disposing of Waste and Reusable Materials from Health Units 1985*. The transport of certain clinical wastes must be accompanied by a certificate of disinfection. It is forbidden to collect certain wastes from hospitals, eg dressings.

The *Law on Environmental Protection 1973* prohibits the disposal of waste whether solid, liquid or gas from industrial and other activities which may cause soil pollution except in zones located for this purpose.

Proposals

Waste of any kind, (domestic, industrial etc) may be deposited only at sites designated by the Ministry of Health and the Ministry of Waters, Forestry and Environmental Protection, and with the consent of the landowner. The location, development and operation of waste storage facilities must take account of the protection of adjacent land, water, the atmosphere, residential areas, and areas of landscape and tourist interest.

The draft Law on Environmental Protection sets out requirements for operators involved in the production and/or management of hazardous waste who will be required to set up a register recording the nature, origin, quantity, physical and chemical characteristics, and location of hazardous waste within 90 days of the Law coming into force. The registers must be supplied to the environmental and health authorities on request.

The draft Law on Environmental protection includes a general provision requiring that hazardous waste disposal is undertaken only where a permit has been obtained from the Ministry of Waters, Forestry and Environmental Protection.

10.6 Transport of waste

10.6.1 Labelling and containers

Proposals
The draft Law on Environmental Protection includes a general requirement that the transport of hazardous waste must be carried out in accordance with any conditions specified by the Ministry of Waters, Forestry and Environmental Protection or the Ministry of Health, and that waste is transported only by authorised means.

10.6.2 Transboundary movement
A general provision of *Decision No. 340 on Waste Imports and Residues 1992* prohibits the import of any kind of waste into Romania with certain exceptions. Wastes which may be imported are listed in the Decision. The Decision requires that importers of waste obtain a permit from the Ministry of Waters, Forestry and Environmental Protection and that imports are documented.

The implementation and enforcement of *Decision No. 340 on Waste Imports and Residues 1992* are the responsibility of the following:

• Ministry of Waters, Forestry and Environmental Protection;
• Ministry of Health;
• Ministry of Industry;
• Ministry of Agriculture and Food;
• Ministry of Trade and Tourism;
• Ministry of Economics and Finance, Customs Authorities;
• National Commission for Standards, Meteorology.

Proposals
The draft Law on Environmental Protection includes a ban on the import of waste either in transit, or for storage or disposal in Romania. Operators involved in the transport of hazardous waste will be required to observe any conditions imposed by the Ministry of Waters, Forestry and Environmental Protection and the Ministry of Health. Only authorised carriers and means of transport may be used.

10.7 Waste charges

No charges are imposed for the deposit of waste in landfills or other waste disposal sites.

10.8 Recycling requirements

Decree No. 465 on Waste Collection, Minimisation and Re-use 1979 obliges waste producers to recover and rescue certain prescribed types of waste. The Decree imposes a general requirement for producers to collect, separate manage and treat waste to ensure, as far as possible, that the wastes are reused. Producers arc required to identify their waste and keep an inventory of those components which can be recovered.

10.9 Public participation

10.9.1 Public access to information

There are no formal mechanisms for the provision of information to the public or public participation regarding environmental permits and certificates. Public announcements are not made regarding applications, public hearings, appeals, and decisions on applications, and EIA reports are not made available to the public. However the Romanian *Constitution* (Article 31) bestows the right on the individual to access to any information of public interest.

Proposals

The draft Law on Environmental Protection includes a general provision for freedom of access to information on environmental quality.

10.9.2 Provision of information

In the case of accidental pollution, the draft Law on Environmental Protection imposes a general requirement for operators to act promptly to eliminate the cause, limit damage, and immediately inform members of the public who might suffer damage. A further general provision will require commercial and industrial operators to provide on request, any information or data relating to compliance with legal requirements.

10.9.3 Public consultation

There are no provisions providing rights to public consultation in relation to applications for environmental permits and certificates.

Proposals

The draft Law on Environmental Protection includes a general provision for the right to information and consultation regarding decisions on territorial and local development, and on the location of facilities which might be detrimental to the environment. Detailed requirements have not beenintroduced in the legislation.

10.10 Enforcement

10.10.1 Compliance checking

Compliance checking and enforcement of provisions relating to the import and transport of hazardous waste are the Ministry of Waters, Forestry and Environmental Protection, its Branch Agencies, Customs officials, and local authorities.

10.10.2 Sanctions

Breach of requirements relating to waste management may result in fines and imprisonment under the *Law on Environmental Protection 1973*.

11. Chemicals storage, handling and emergency response

11.1 Summary

Authorities:	The following summary outlines proposed requirements.
Types of Activity:	Ministry of Waters, Forestry and Environmental Protection. Manufacture, storage and use of toxic substances.
Permits:	Permits for the manufacture, storage and use of toxic substances.
Timing:	Not specified.
Public Information:	There is no formal mechanism for provision of information to the public. The draft Law on Environmental Protection includes a general provision for freedom of access to information on environmental quality and data relating to compliance with legal requirement.
Public Consultation:	There is currently no formal mechanism for public consultation. The draft law provides for public consultation on the location of new developments.

11.2 Legislation relating to chemicals storage, handling and emergency response

- *Decree No. 466 Concerning Toxic Products and Substances 1979;*
- Draft Law on Environmental Protection.

11.2.1 Storage and handling

Facilities in which activities involving toxic products and substances are carried out must be permitted and registered under *Decree No. 466 Concerning Toxic Products and Substances 1979*. Other requirements are as follows:

- Keeping an inventory of toxic products and substances entering;
- Ensuring that necessary equipment is in place to prevent pollution;
- Handle substances and products only in designated buildings;
- Ensure safety during handling and transport;
- Manage and neutralise wastes;
- Transport substances and products only with the direction of the management of the facility which includes details of the name of products and substances, quantity,

destination, means of transport, names of persons accompanying transport, and the period of transport.

Requirements are set out relating to the keeping of registers and documentation, and rules for the manufacture, depositing, packing, transporting, handling. Technical norms set out requirements for neutralisation and elimination of substances.

Proposals

The draft Law on Environmental Protection includes a general provision requiring that the manufacture, storage and use of toxic substances and products is undertaken only where a permit has been obtained from the Ministry of Waters, Forestry and Environmental Protection.

The draft Law on Environmental Protection sets out requirements for operators involved in the manufacture, storage and use of toxic substances and products will be required to set up a register recording the nature, origin, quantity, physical and chemical characteristics, and location of hazardous waste within 90 days of the Law coming into force. The registers must be supplied to the environmental and health authorities on request.

A general requirement is set out in the draft law that the transport of toxic substances and products must be carried out in accordance with any conditions specified by the Ministry of Waters, Forestry and Environmental Protection or the Ministry of Health, and that waste is transported only by authorised means.

11.2.2 Emergency response

Proposals

In the case of accidental pollution, the draft Law on Environmental Protection sets a general requirement for operators to act promptly to eliminate the cause, limit damage, and immediately inform members of the public who might suffer damage.

11.3 Regulatory requirements

There are no specific regulatory requirements relating to chemicals safety and the environment.

11.4 Public participation

The draft Law on Environmental Protection includes a general provision for freedom of access to information on environmental quality, and the right to information and consultation regarding decisions on territorial and local development, and on the location of facilities which might be detrimental to the environment.

In the case of accidental pollution, the draft Law imposes a general requirement for operators to immediately inform members of the public who might suffer damage.

11.5 Enforcement

11.5.1 Compliance checking

The authorities responsible for chemical safety are Ministries of Waters, Forestry and Environmental Protection; Interior; Health; and Labour.

11.5.2 Sanctions

Non-compliance in relation to pollution requirements can result in administrative or criminal sanctions including fines and imprisonment.

Annex A

List of Key Legislation

1. Environmental Liability

- *Penal Code;*
- *Civil Code;*
- *Law on Environment Protection 1973;*
- *Law on Water 1974.*

2. Land use planning

- *Law No. 50 on Authorisation of Construction andMeasures for House Building 1991 (Law on Construction);*
- *Ministerial Order No. 91 on Forms, Applications and Permitting Procedure;*
- *Law No. 18 on Land Fund 1991;*
- *Law No. 9 on Environmental Protection 1973;*
- *Law No. 8 on Water 1974;*
- *Order No. 623 of Health Ministry Establishing Sanitary Rules on Environmental Protection of Human Settlements.*

3. Environmental Impact Assessments (EIAs)

- *Ministerial Order No. 170 on the Issuing of Permits 1990;*
- *Ministerial Order No. 113 on Documentation Required for Permit Applications 1990.*

4. Integrated permitting requirements applicable to the operation of industrial and commercial facilities

- *Law on Environmental Protection 1973;*
- *Ministerial Order No. 170 on Permitting 1990;*
- *Minsterial Order No. 113 on Documentation Required for Permit Applications 1990;*
- *Minsterial Order No. 437 on Certificates 1991.*

5. Air emission requirements applicable to the operation of industrial and commercial facilities

- *Order No. 623 of the Health Ministry Establishing Sanitary Rules on Environmental Protection of Human Settlements 1993.*

6. Water requirements applicable to the operation of industrial and commercial facilities

- *Environment Protection Act 1973;*
- *Law on Waters 1974;*
- *Minsterial Order No. 715 Concerning Approvals for Administration of Water 1991;*
- *Ministerial Order No. 435 Concerning Authorisations for Administration of Water 1991;*
- *HMC No. 2496 Concerning the Establishment of and Sanctions for Violations Relating to Water 1969;*
- *Normative C-90 Concerning the Disposal of Wastewater in Public Sewarage networks 1983;*
- *Law No. 5 on the Rational Management, Protection and Assurance of the Quality of Waters 1989;*
- *Governmental Decision No. 1001 on the Establishment of a Unitary System of Payments for Products and Services of Water Husbandry 1990 (as amended 1991 and 1992);*
- *Decree Establishing Permissible Limits of the Main Polluting Substances Prior to Discharge 1979.*

7. Noise requirements applicable to the operation of industrial and commercial facilities

- *Law on Environmental Protection 1973;*
- *Ministerial Order No. 170 on Permitting 1990;*
- *Ministerial Order No. 113 on Documentation Required for Permit Applications 1990;*
- *Ministerial Order No. 437 on Certificates 1991;*
- *Order No. 623 Establishing Sanitary Reules on Environemntal Protection for Human Settlements 1973.*

8. Hazardous and non-hazardous waste management

- *Law on Environmental Protection 1973;*
- *Decree No. 465 on Waste Collection, Minimisation and Re-use 1979;*
- *Law No. 10 on Waste Collection, Hygiene and Maintenance of the Exterior of Grounds and Buildings Alongside Facilities 1982;*
- *Order of the Minister of Health No. 266 Stabilising Measures for Collecting, Depositing an Disposing of Waste and Reusable Materials from Health Units 1985;*
- *Order No. 623 of the Health Ministry Establishing Sanitary Rules on Environmental Protection of Human Settlements 1973;*
- *Decision No. 340 on Waste Imports and Residues 1992* (as amended 1992).

9. Chemicals storage, handling and emergency response

- *Decree No. 466 Concerning Toxic Products and substances 1979.*

Annex B

List of Permitting and Enforcement Authorities

Central Government Ministries
Ministry of Waters, Forestry and
Environemntal Protection
B-due Libertati Nr. 12
Tronson 5-6
Tel: 40.0.31.61.04
Fax: 40.0.31.64.86

Ministry of Industry
Calea Victoriei Nr. 152
Tel: 40.0.50.31.68
Fax: 40.0.50.30.29

Alba
18, Street Tudor Vladimirescu,
Alba,
jud. Alba Iulia
Tel: 968/13248
Fax: 968/13248

Arad
16, Bd. Dragalina,
Arad,
jud. Arad
Tel: 966/12343/16853
Fax: 966/18987

Arges
8, Street Calea Cimpulung,
Pitest,
jud. Arges
Tel: 97 /634145
Fax: 97/636491

Bacau
23, Street Oituz,
Bacau,

jud. Bacau
Tel: 93 /124691
Fax: 93/112004

Bihor
35, Street Ion Bogdan,
Oradea,
jud. Bihor
Tel: 99/144590
Fax: 99/163751

Bistrita
9, Street Avram Iancu,
Bistrita,
jud. Bistrita Nasaud
Tel: 990/16628
Fax: 990/17991

Botosani
23, Street Nicolae Iorga,
Botosani,
jud. Botosani
Tel: 985/18031
Fax: 985/31593

Brasov
3, Street Eroilor,
Brasov,
jud. Brasov
TeL: 92/119013
Fax: 92/151410

Braila
39, Street Marasesti
Braila,
jud. Braila
Tel: 946/22646
Fax: 946/22222

Buzau
18, Bd. Garii,
Buzau,
jud. Buzau
Tel: 974/27100
Fax: 974/13117

Caras-Severin
9, Street Caminelor,
Resita,
jud.Caras-Severin
Tel: 96/434857
Fax: 96/434762

Calarasi
9, Sos. Chiciului,
Calarasi,
jud. Calarasi
Tel: 911/15035
Fax: 911/11926

Cluj
64, Street Motilor,
Cluj,
jud. Cluj
Tel: 95/118993
Fax: 95/112306

Constanta
Bd. Mamaia,
Constanta,
jud. Constanta
Tel: 91/646696
Fax: 91/646696

Covasna
7, Street Lunca Oltului,
Sf. Gheorghe,
jud. Covasna
Tel: 923/23701
Fax: 923/23701

Dimbovita
1, Street Canalului,
Tirgoviste,
jud. Dimbovita
Tel: 926/15960
Fax: 926/11639

Dolj
3, Street Brestei,
Craiova,
jud. Dolj
Tel: 94/112020
Fax: 94/112020

Galati
56, Street Domneasca,
Galati,
jud. Galati
Tel: 93/437100
Fax: 93/457751

Giurgiu
14, Street Dan Barbilian,
Giurgiu,
jud. Giurgiu
Tel: 912/14760
Fax: 912/11410

Gorj
76, Street Unirii,
Tirgu Jiu,
jud. Gorg
Tel: 929/15384
Fax: 929/17126

Harghita
16, Street Progresului,
Miercurea Ciuc,
jud. Harghita
Tel: 958/12766
Fax: 958/12766

Hunedoara
25, Street Aurel Vlaicu,
Deva,
jud. Hunedoara
Tel: 956/12914
Fax: 956/12252

Ialomita
1, Street Mihai Viteazul,
Slobozia,
jud. Ialomita
Tel: 910/16220
Fax: 910/15949

Iasi
10, Street Vascauteanu,
Iasi,
jud. Iasi
Tel: 981/41709

Baia Mare
46, Street gh. Sincai,
Baia Mare,
jud. Baia Mare
Tel: 99/416306
Fax: 99/416402

Mehedinti
Street Prefecturii,
Turnu Severin,
jud. Mehedinti
Tel: 978/26438
Fax: 978/20396

Mures
10, Street Podeni,
Tirgu Mures,
jud. Mures
Tel: 954/14948
Fax: 954/14475

Neamt
21, Street Maiakovski,
Piatra Neamt,
jud. Neamt
Tel: 93/618954
Fax: 93/619690

Olt
2, Street Lupeni,
Slantina,
jud. Olt
Tel: 94/422240
Fax: 94/422703

Prahova
306, Street 23 August,
Ploiesti,
jud Prahova
Tel: 97/156068
Fax: 97/155810

Satu Mare
3-5, Street Careiului,
Satu Mare,
jud. Satu Mare
Tel: 997/41009
Fax: 997/46175

Salaj
92, Street Rpublicii,
Salau,
jud. Salaj
Tel: 99/614120
Fax: 99/613370

Sibiu
48, Street Somesului,
Sibiu,
jud. Sibiu
Tel: 924/22310
Fax: 924/44145

Suceava
48, Street Universitatii,
Suceava,
jud. Suceava
Tel: 987/23391
Fax: 987/26939

Teleorman
124, Street 1 Mai,
Alexandria,
jud. Teleorman
Tel: 91/322582
Fax: 91/323177

Timis
32, Street Mihai Viteazul,
Timisoara,
jud. Timis
Tel: 96/118196
Fax: 96/114380

Tulcea
5, Street 14 Noiembrie,
Tulcea,
jud. Tulcea
Tel: 915/17322
Fax: 915/146008

Vaslui
109, Street Stefan cel Mare,
Vaslui,
jud. Vaslui
Tel: 983/12602
Fax: 983/16269

Vilcea
7, Street Oituz,
Rimnicul Vilcea,
jud. Vilcea
Tel: 94/715859
Fax: 94/715859

Vrancea
2, Street Dinicu Golescu,
Focsani,
jud. Vrancea
Tel: 939/16812

Bucuresti
Bd. M. Kogalniceanu,
Bucuresti
Tel: 90/135535

Annex C

List of Proposed Legislation

The following legislation is in preparation:

- Law of water;
- Law on air protection;
- Forest code;
- Law on protected areas;
- Law on waste;
- Law on cultivated plants and pesticides;
- Law on game and hunting;
- Ministerial order on permitting;
- Ministerial order on EIAs;
- Ministerial order on standards.

Annex D

Environmental Standards

Air pollution standards

Pollutant	Maximum Admissible Concentration (mg/m³)			
	For 30 min	Daily	Monthly	Yearly
Nitric Acid	0.4	–	–	–
Hydrochloric Acid	0.3	0.1	–	–
Acrolein	0.03	0.1	–	–
Aldehydes	0.035	0.012	–	–
Ammonia	0.3	0.1	–	–
Phosphorus anhydride	0.3	0.1	–	–
Arsenic	–	0.003	–	–
Benzene	1.5	0.8	–	–
Cadmium	–	0.00002	–	–
Chlorine	0.1	0.03	–	–
Chromium	–	0.0015	–	–
Nitrogen dioxide	0.3	0.1	–	0.04
Sulphur dioxide	0.75	0.25	–	0.06
Phenol	0.1	0.03	–	–
Flourine (gas and light aerosols)	0.015	0.005	0.0012	–
Flourine (compunds and heavy aerosols	–	0.03	–	–
Soot	0.15	0.05	–	–
Furaldehyde	0.15	0.05	–	–
Hydrogen sulphide	0.015	0.008	–	–
Manganese	–	0.01	–	–
Methanol	1.0	0.5	–	–
Methyl mecaptan	–	0.00001	–	–
Carbon menoxide	6.	2.	–	–
Ozone	0.1	0.03	–	–
Lead	–	0.0007	–	–
suspended sulphates	0.03	0.012	–	–
Carbon disulphide	0.03	0.005	–	–
Trichlorethylene	4.	1.0	–	–
suspended particles	0.5	0.15	–	0.075

Wastewater Discharge limits (mg/l)

	Dilution Factor		
	25	*100*	*100*
Suspended Solids	15	60	100
BOD5	1	50	100
Cynides	0.1	1	2
Iron	2	5	3
Mercury	0.01	0.01	0.01
Cadmium	0.1	0.1	0.1
Lead	0.2	0.2	0.2
Zinc	0.1	0.5	1
Anionic Biodegradable Surfactants	0.5	15	30
Phenols	0.02	0.3	0.6
pH	6.5–8.5	6.5–8.5	6.5–8.5

Annex E

International Conventions

Romania has participated in the following international agreements:

- Basle Convention on the Control of Transboundary Movements of Hazardous Wastes and their Disposal (Basle 1989);
- Convention on Long-range Transboundary Air Pollution (Geneva, 1979);
- Convention on Environmental Protection of the Black Sea, 1992;
- Declaration for Danube, 1985;
- IAEA Convention on early notification of Nuclear Accidents 1986;
- Ramsar Convention;
- Bilateral Agreements with Bulgaria and Germany.

Annex F

Activities Requiring Environmental Permits

Table 1   Activities requiring an environmental certificate

- *Industrial units, including small industry.*
- *Power plants, including those inside units.*
- *Units of substantial construction investment*
- *Transport:*
  - Units of road transport;
  - ways of land transport;
  - units of railway transport (train stations, roundhouse, etc) including for metro and trams;
  - railways, including for metro and trams;
  - units of air transport, including units of checking and reparation;
  - units of naval transport, including repair and construction units;
  - navigation channels;
  - units of maintaining ways and bridges;
  - bus terminals;
  - petrol stations and launderettes;
  - cable transport (cable railway, etc);
  - garages;
  - parking
- *Agriculture:*
  - agricultural farms, agricultural centres of research, testing and production;
  - small units of agriculture products preparation;
  - units of mechanising of agricultural works;
  - service units for agricultural machineries;
  - activities of fighting against pests;
  - activities of land reclamation;
  - units of treatment and cleaning of seeds and cereal plants.
- *Animal husbandry:*
  - farms, centres of research, testing and production;
  - small units of animal products preparation;
  - large units for raising and fattening animals;
  - veterinary units and laboratories;
  - centres of animal selection and reproduction;
  - collection and incineration of dead animals.
- *Silviculture (forest):*
  - forest planning;
  - pest management;
  - exploitation and transportation of woods;

- forest nurseries;
- deforestation;
- reclamation of fish breeding within forests;
- grazing into forests;
- activities for protection of wild animals and hunting;
- collection, processing and delivery of forest products;
- forest chalet.
- *Nuclear plants:*
  - geological prospecting;
  - Explotation of mineral resources;
  - Storage of products, materials and substances;
  - Pipelines for the transport of substances;
  - Transporting of dangerous materials and substances;
  - Electrical and thermal power networks;
  - Analytical laboratories;
  - Research and testing installations;
  - Activities of import-export of materials and substances;
  - The treatment and storage of radioactive wastes;
  - Deep underground injections;
  - Printing and copying installations including the storage of necessary materials and substances;
  - Testing tracks;
  - Launch platform (facilities);
  - Stations and transformers;
  - Health and treatment units;
  - Workshops;
  - Reclamation and hydrotechnical works, including activities of water management.
- *Reclamation for water use:*
  - water supplies, sewerage, purification and discharging of wastewaters from human settlements, industry, including underground water injection;
  - irrigation bed reclamation;
  - fisheries reclamation;
  - reed reclamation;
  - hydroelectrical and hydromechanical uses;
  - reclamation for navigation, rafting, etc;
  - tourism and recreation reclamations;
  - reclamations and constructions against destructive actions of water;
  - Draining and diking;
  - reclamation and consolidation of river banks and heads;
  - repair and reshaping of river banks;
  - action against soil erosion.
- *Works and constructions relating to water quality:*
  - stations and installations for water purification.
- *Works and construction modifying the regime of flowing water:*
  - dams for water storage;
  - diversion of water flow;
  - bridges and crossings;
  - arrangements for exploitation of materials from river banks and beds;
  - forestry plantations and deforestation;
  - plantations against erosion.

- *Works and construction on the seashore, the bed of territorial waters and sea, the continental shelf or for protecting the sea coast.*
- *Works of water drilling, hydrometrical installations, other study works on water.*
- *Trade-tourism:*
  - commercial activity;
  - hotels and restaurants;
  - tourist chalet;
  - camping;
  - fairs.
- *Eduction, culturem religion:*
  - units of schooling;
  - houses of culture;
  - religious establishments;
  - similar activities.
- *Sport:*
  - stadiums;
  - sport infrastructure;
  - skating rink;
  - skiing tracks (runways);
  - racecources;
  - runways for autoraces.
- *National defence and custom activity:*
  - Military units and border defence;
  - custom units;
  - military airports.
- *Activity of sport hunting and fishing.*
- *Activity of demolition.*
- Activity of storage.
- *Activity of collection, storage and reuse of wastes.*
- *Activity of salubrity of localities.*
- *Dry cleaners.*
- *Activity of slaughter houses for stray dogs.*
- *Platforms for burning wastes and toxic substances at sea.*
- *Storage, processing, incineration of human settlement wastes.*
- *Establishment of incineration of wastes and residual mud.*
- *Human cemeteries and incinerators.*
- *Other activities and objectives having impact on environment.*

Table 2   Categories of works requiring a water certificate or permit

- Supplies of water, sewerage purification, and discharge of waste waters and other water.
- Storage lakes, dams,hydroelectric plant.
- Works on water courses.
- Water course diversion and hindrance of water flow.
- Flood protection measures.
- Land reclamation, irrigation, drainage.
- Fish farming.
- Works to protect against soil erosion and flooding.
- Excavation of sand, gravel and other building materials from river beds, banks, lakes or the territorial sea.
- Industrial waste depots.
- Railways, road, and water and gas pipelines which are crossed by surface water courses.
- Power lines and transformer stations.
- Boreholes for testing or using groundwaters.
- Hydropower plants with generating capacity < 5,000 kWh.